DIAGNOSIS
OF LEARNING
DIFFICULTIES

DIAGNOSIS OF LEARNING DIFFICULTIES

Edited by
JOHN A. R. WILSON
Professor of Education
University of California, Santa Barbara

McGRAW-HILL BOOK COMPANY
New York   San Francisco   St. Louis   Düsseldorf   Johannesburg
Kuala Lumpur   London   Mexico   Montreal   New Delhi   Panama
Rio de Janeiro   Singapore   Sydney   Toronto

*This book was set in Linotype Electra by Monotype
Composition Company, and printed on permanent
paper and bound by The Maple Press Company.
The designer was Janet Bollow; the drawings were
prepared by John Foster; June Rios drew the
illustrations for Chapter 1. The editors were William
J. Willey and Michael A. Ungersma. Charles A.
Goehring supervised production.*

**DIAGNOSIS
OF LEARNING
DIFFICULTIES**

Printed in the United States of America.

Library of Congress catalog card number: 76-144771

1 2 3 4 5 6 7 8 9 0 MAMM 7 9 8 7 6 5 4 3 2 1

07-070840-1

1/31/75 Barbert Tyler 1050

CONTRIBUTORS

JOHN A. R. WILSON
Professor of Education, University of California, Santa Barbara

NORMAN W. VAN DONGE, M.D.
Ophthalmologist, Santa Barbara

THEODORE D. HANLEY
Professor of Speech, University of California, Santa Barbara

JOHN C. SNIDECOR
Professor of Speech, University of California, Santa Barbara

SANFORD E. GERBER
Associate Professor of Speech, University of California, Santa Barbara

WAYLAND A. STEPHENSON, M.D.
Neurologist, Sansom Medical Clinic, Santa Barbara

CAROLYN HEDLEY
Assistant Professor of Education, Fordham University, New York

MILDRED C. ROBECK
Professor of Education, University of Oregon, Eugene, Oregon

W. VAN SPANCKEREN
Clinical Psychologist, Devereux Ranch Schools, Santa Barbara

WILLIAM J. ELLIOTT
School Psychologist, Goleta Elementary School District

RAYMOND BAUER
Coordinator of Special Education, Goleta Elementary School District

ROBERT E. BARRY
Director of Pupil Personnel Services, Santa Barbara Schools

THOMAS J. MURPHY
Director of Special Education, Santa Barbara Schools

PREFACE

The diagnosis of learning difficulties is a most important skill for all teachers. If children did not have learning difficulties, teaching would be much simpler and less demanding; however, there seems to be little likelihood that in the near future any teachers will become bored because of the simplicity of their jobs. If teachers are to remedy accumulated defects shown by children, they need to have some basis on which to analyze what the defects are. It is difficult to get the answer when the question is unknown.

The topics in this book were selected for inclusion because special classes or special schools are provided for children and youth with the kinds of difficulties named. Teachers are quick to point out that for every young person who is in a special class or a special school there are a dozen, equally disadvantaged, who are in regular classes. This book was written for the teachers who have to work with those children in regular classes.

Each of the areas listed in the book is a specialty in its own right, requiring years of work for mastery. Properly, diagnosis should be performed by the specialists, but the generalist needs to know enough to refer the young person intelligently. In addition, many teachers do not have all of the specialists available to them and have to carry on as best they can.

This book evolved in response to the needs of a graduate class in the diagnosis of learning difficulties. It was obvious that a multiple approach to the different topics would be more successful than would a single authority, no matter how qualified. It was also obvious that it might be possible to call on a specialist once or twice, but that this would rapidly become a serious imposition. The natural solution was to have the specialists come and talk to the class, tape the things they said, and have them transcribed and put into book form so that other classes could use the same information.

As you go through the different chapters it will be apparent that the format is much more conversational *than is true in most texts. Questions and answers are inserted as they occurred in the class situation. The class members are an able group who occupy positions of authority and specialty, and they were able to ask questions that you would have liked to ask.*

One of the authors pointed out that you use different words to communicate when you are speaking than when you are writing and that he found it a strain to prepare a speech that was also going to be a chapter. Some of the chapters have been more extensively edited into a written format than have others, but all of them are more informal, and perhaps more informative, than they would have been if they had started as written papers.

I want to thank my coauthors for sharing their expertise with the original class and for having cooperated in the editing process. I also want to thank the students who participated actively in making this book what it is. They were particularly aware that not all of the experts were saying the same things on the same topics, and their questions contributed materially to the book.

Each of the chapters is introduced by a biographical sketch delineating the background of the author and his right to be heard as an authority. I hope you will find the contributions as interesting as I did.

John A. R. Wilson

CONTENTS

AN INTRODUCTION
AND
A THEORY

John A. R. Wilson

1

Dr. John A. R. Wilson is professor of education at the University of California, Santa Barbara, where he has been since 1951. From 1953 to 1963 he was director of teacher education and had close personal touch with the teachers and administrators of the public school districts. Before coming to the University of California, he taught rural elementary, junior high, and senior high school classes in British Columbia. He established the first counseling programs in New Westminster, B.C.

Dr. Wilson's research includes work with gifted nonachievers, a particularly disadvantaged group of young people. Out of this work grew an interest in the learning of young children so that some of the difficulties could be prevented rather than diagnosed later on. The thrust of his present research effort is toward an understanding of the physiological correlates of learning so that problems can be more sharply defined and remedial efforts evaluated more precisely.

Some sixty-five publications and research reports have been contributed to the literature by Dr. Wilson, including, with Mildred C. Robeck, The Kindergarten Evaluation of Learning Potential *(McGraw-Hill, New York, 1967) and, with Dr. Robeck and William B. Michael,* Psychological Foundations of Learning and Teaching *(McGraw-Hill, New York, 1969).*

This book is about people who have difficulty learning, how you can sort them out, what you can do to help them, and something about the long-term prospects or what the future holds for them. It is a book for teachers, written by experts in particular fields who are still or who have been teachers.

We have always had students in school who could not or would not learn what we, as teachers, were trying to have them learn. Sometimes they learned other things we hadn't intended, but that is a different story. Recently we have had the phenomenon of students overtly objecting to what we were trying to teach them. They have staged riots, gone on strike, and presented nonnegotiable demands for change. This unrest is causing a rethinking of our goals and of suitable methods for reaching these goals.

Independent of this turmoil there has developed a much greater willingness on the part of school authorities to work in the schools with young people who have problems. Classes have been set up for the trainable mentally retarded, who only a few years ago spent their lives in hospitals. Classes are being established for the educationally handicapped, who are defined as not mentally retarded and not physically handicapped but who still cannot learn in the regular classes. Blind students are being incorporated into the regular classroom. Children who cannot speak English are finding a place, usually in special classes, but often at least part time in regular classes. Children from disadvantaged backgrounds are suddenly aware that the good jobs go to those with educations, and the schools are responding with special teachers and classes to remove as much weakness from their backgrounds as possible. This process of increased teaching is taking place all the way from the Headstart program, which takes in 4-year-olds, to special tutoring for students admitted to a university without the necessary grade points but with a strong indication that they have the necessary potential to succeed.

Most of us do not realize what a recent phenomenon this willingness to work with the reluctant learner is. When I started teaching, fewer than 5 percent of the college-age youth went to college, and a smaller proportion of the rural population went to high school than now go to college. It is true that this was in British Columbia and that it is getting to be a long time ago, but conditions were similar or worse in most of the states of the Union. In those days many children did not get into grade eight, because at the end of grade eight there was an examination set in the capital, and teachers were judged by the percentage of their students who passed the examination. If only those who were going to be successful in the examination were allowed into grade eight, the teacher's record was improved. The attrition in high school was very high, even among those who had managed to enter that august body.

In the schools of that time and place, any help that was given to atypical students was given by the teacher. The only special schools were those for the blind, the deaf, and the severely mentally retarded. It is true that there were usually job opportunities for anyone who was willing to work and could follow orders. Lumber had to be piled by hand, ditches were dug by hand, boats were loaded by hand (of course this is still true in most ports), and there were not many managerial or professional jobs available. Many of the Canadian college graduates migrated to the United States.

Many older teachers grew up in schools where conditions similar to those outlined prevailed. Many of them became skilled in understanding the problems that plagued the children with whom they were working. Many of them find the special classes and special provisions for atypical students a form of coddling kids who should have to stand on their own feet, both for their own good and for the good of the community. All of them would agree without hesitation that a blind student should have special consideration and special teaching. They are not so sure about the emotionally disturbed child. Does not the special treatment reinforce him for his emotionally undesirable behavior? How is such a youngster going to be a contributor to the social good after he leaves school if he has never learned to put the good of others before his own temper tantrums? You who are reading this book probably have similar questions and similar fears. We hope that understanding the nature and the symptoms, as well as the prognosis and cure, of the difficulties will make it possible for you to work more comfortably with children who have learning difficulties.

ORGANIZATION OF THE BOOK

As I said at the beginning of this chapter, this book was written for teachers by experts in various fields, all of whom are or have been teachers themselves in their area of specialty. Each of the chapters represents a medical specialty or an educational specialty that requires from three to fifteen years of graduate study. It would be pure charlatanism to claim that reading what we have here would make you competent to diagnose amblyopia, dyslexia, or mental retardation, but we hope that reading the book will enable you to work more intelligently with children who suffer from these disasters. Unfortunately, as teachers, sooner or later you will have contact with all of the aberrations mentioned in these various talks. They were selected for inclusion in this volume because they are prevalent enough to require special classes, special schools, or special teachers for each of the problems.

A learning-motivation theory

This chapter outlines a learning-motivation theory that I have found useful in planning learning situations for both typical and atypical students. Probably the model is more important when consideration is being given to teaching the reluctant learners than when planning for those who are ready to learn in spite of our mistakes in teaching. This model gets at the basic nature of how and why learning takes place, with considerable emphasis placed on the higher kinds of learning, the processes of conceptualization and of creative self-directed learning. Many of the young people suffering from learning disabilities, especially those with emotional loadings, employ their creative self-direction to develop ways of avoiding learning that the teacher is trying to have them master. The model has helped me to circumvent their machinations when I have been able to analyze the mechanisms they were employing.

Often there is a great deal of threat involved in working with the children who do not learn. We are supposed to be teaching them, and when they do not learn, we are failing in our appointed task. Under some kinds of administrative supervision, this failure is ego shattering. Even when there is no pressure from administrators, personal knowledge of failure can be very disturbing. The opportunity to stand outside the system and to see how it is working, particularly how and why it is not working, gives you an opportunity to detach yourself emotionally and become more professional as you work with these children who desperately need the help you can give them. I think a theoretical framework is highly important to you. The model I have presented is not used by most of the other authors of the book, each of whom has operated from his own orientation in presenting his material.

Vision, speech, and hearing disorders

Chapters 2 through 5 deal with vision, speech, and hearing difficulties. Special schools and special classes have been available for many years for children who suffered from extreme forms of these handicaps. Often these were boarding schools where children from many communities were gathered for special instruction. The present trend, at least in California and other densely populated states, is to try to keep the child in the home and to provide the necessary special instruction in a regular school setting.

The chapter on the visually handicapped was written by Norman W. Van Donge, an opthalmologist with many years of training and specialization in the functioning of the eye. He has taught at Stanford University, as well as having extensive experience in private practice. Most young people with whom you come into contact who suffer from visual defects will be far from totally blind. Even the legally blind usually have some vision that can be used to advantage. Visual problems sometimes appear rather suddenly and may be quite severe. Often there are emotional problems that center around wearing glasses, usually the result of teasing, such as being called "four eyes" or other unhappy denigrations. A large proportion of school information comes through the eyes. Inability to see the blackboard or to see the words on the printed page can be a disastrous experience. It often is the more disastrous because the youngster has no way of knowing that other children are seeing things differently than the way they appear to him. It will enable you to help many of these children if you can learn to spot the telltale signs that indicate further checking is both necessary and desirable.

Two chapters constitute the speech section. Theodore D. Hanley of the University of California at Santa Barbara, speech department, deals with the kinds of speech problems you are likely to encounter as you work with children or young adults. The problems involved in stuttering are treated by John C. Snidecor of the same department. Stuttering is an extremely inhibiting speech problem that often causes the persons who suffer from it to be so concerned with themselves and their problems that they are unable to handle what you are trying to teach them. As a teacher you can help the stutterer overcome many of his problems, at least while he is in your classroom.

The chapter "Auditory Processes and Problems," by Sanford E. Gerber, draws attention to the symptoms to which you should become sensitive if your young people are to be referred to audiologists when they may need help. In school, almost all of the input that does not come through the eyes comes in through the ears. Often what is received is garbled, fragmentary, or nonexistent. Many of the instructions you give to the class will be missed by a few of your students who do not hear what you are saying. There will be others who do not hear because they are not attending, but at the moment we are concerned with the fact that physical impairment may restrict the ability of some students to follow instructions.

Again, they have no real way of knowing that the other children are hearing things that they are missing. There are ways in which you can minimize their disadvantage once you become aware that it exists. There are informal checkpoints that you can observe to decide whether a more formal examination seems necessary. Certain diseases are particularly likely to be disastrous to the hearing. When one of your students has been absent from school because of such an illness, you may want to make sure that he is routinely checked for hearing when he returns.

Neurological disorders

More and more often teachers are running into descriptions of causes of emotional or learning problems as being due to minimal brain damage. Quite often this term is used to mean that there is not enough damage to show up on an EEG recording or to be apparent in any other definitive way but that there must be something out of kilter in the brain to cause this kind of problem. In the chapter "Neurological Dysfunctions," Wayland Stephenson, a senior partner and the senior neurologist in the Sansum Medical Clinic of Santa Barbara discusses some of the more overt neurological problems, such as epilepsy and dysphasia. Gradually epilepsy is losing its terror for teachers and for the general populace. There is still a great deal of prejudice that diminishes life for people who suffer from this malady. As you understand what causes seizures, the different types of seizures, and the ways in which medication controls them, you will be able to support any of your students who suffer in this way.

The mechanisms that lead to dysphasia have significance for all teachers but probably especially for those who are particularly concerned with the teaching of reading. Dr. Stephenson discusses many of the nuances that are only now beginning to be understood. The brain is a complex organ, and many things are not yet known about the way in which it functions. The more you know, the more surely you can work with your students.

Reading problems

The importance of reading in the disability of learning is attested by the fact that nearly all of the authors who wrote chapters for this volume gave some attention to the difficulties of the child who does not learn to read easily and well. Two of the authors deal specifically with this problem. Carolyn Hedley of Temple University, New York, covers a wide range of difficulties that produce problem readers and ways in which these students can be helped to overcome their difficulties. Mildred Robeck of the University of Oregon gives you an insight into some of the similarities and differences in the mental function of young people who have reading problems. She reviews her own original research that shows how similar are the mental strengths and weaknesses of children and young people who have reading difficulties of different kinds. Since nearly all of you have or will have students with reading problems of some considerable intensity, the insights in this research will be most helpful. It has implications for changing the emphasis of the instructional program for those who develop difficulties. It seems safe to say that not all children are going to learn to read in the same way and that you should cultivate different techniques and some ability to distinguish which children are likely to profit from which reading approaches.

Cultural disadvantage

A massive effort has been mounted to remedy the disadvantages of the young people born into homes where the parents are unable to provide them with the educational opportunities available in the middle-class home. No pat formula has emerged that can be used with assurance in providing remediation of the deficits these children suffer. A whole series of new educational careers are emerging. These include tutoring for the children who are not doing well, adult aid programs to assist the professional teacher, special teaching for small groups with the intent that their instruction can be individualized. It may turn out that the most beneficial outcome of these federally supported programs will be an increased desire on the part of the parents of such disadvantaged children to see that their youngsters get an education better than the one they found inadequate to their own needs.

No matter at what level you teach, you will have children who have been through special programs for the disadvantaged. You can help solidify the effects of special instruction as you understand the approaches used and build on the emerging strengths. In the last few years, much of the value of special programs has been lost because teachers were not aware of the beginnings that had been made and failed to capitalize on the new but somewhat unstable learning.

Emotional maladjustment

For the last fifteen years Warner Van Spanckeren has been the clinical psychologist for the Santa Barbara branch of the Devereau Ranch Schools. He has been responsible for evaluating young people who are candidates for admission, as well as for following the progress they make as they become part of this special community where they spend twenty-four hours a day trying to create a life that is more satisfactory to themselves and to the community from which they have come. The increasing population density, the changing social mores, the more loosely knit family patterns have all joined to create increasing stress on our young people. As a result there seems to be a much higher level of emotional maladjustment than was true only a few years ago, even though each age has had its own tension-producing mechanisms and people who were incapable of coping with the tension.

You will find many children and young adults in your classes who need help with emotional problems. Most of them will not require hospitalization or even special classes, but they will be better people if you can help them to reach out successfully and share their problems. Most of us can think back to a few teachers who steadied us and helped us open doors we may not have known existed. Different teachers reach different pupils in this way. Some find it easier to function at this level than do others, but all of us can be more effective as we understand some of the dynamics that increase or diminish emotional strain.

Educational handicaps

A relatively new term has emerged that some authorities claim should be used with regard to about one-quarter of the school population. At present (1971) special financial support for this group in California is limited to 2 percent of the school population. The educationally handicapped include those who are not mentally retarded, not physically incapacitated, but who nonetheless cannot learn in the school as it has been constituted. Most of these young people are suffering from emotional maladjustments at one level or another. Many of them are suffering from damage to their motivational systems, which, of course, contain emotional loadings. William J. Elliott, a school psychologist, and Raymond Bauer, the director of the educationally handicapped program for the Goleta, California, schools, have been able to let us understand this new school specialty. We can all find ways of using the opportunities they describe to give special help to some of our atypical youngsters, who may go to special classes for part of the day or may stay with us as part of our regular class.

Social maladjustment

In our society we have jails, prisons, penitentiaries, boys' camps, schools for girls, borstal homes, juvenile halls, and other places for those of our citizens who are sufficiently maladjusted socially to warrant withdrawing them for a time from circulation in the general society. In all of these institutions the theoretic aim is to restore the individual so that he will become a valuable member of society. This aim is confused and confounded by an older punishment theory that is epitomized by the phrase "An eye for an eye."

In school, we have often been torn between the same divergent stresses as we sought to rehabilitate socially obnoxious students. We cannot quite make up our minds whether we should punish them for the damage they have done to our persons or our egos or whether we should structure learning situations that will make them less hostile and more socially desirable. I fear that in school, as in the larger community, we do neither one very successfully.

There are varying degrees of social maladjustment. Probably some of it is necessary to provide discontent leading to change, but maladjustment quickly gets out of control. One thing all of us need to keep in mind is that the social deviates usually go from the school to a rehabilitation center, and after they have "paid their debt to society," they return to school. We live in a crisis period when respect for the police and for the courts is rapidly declining, especially at the college and high school level. As the director of pupil personnel services for the Santa Barbara schools, Robert E. Barry has spent many hours in courts, in counseling students who have just been arrested, and in counseling students who have just returned from confinement of one kind or another. Most social maladjustment is not serious enough to involve the police or the courts, but many of the patterns of behavior are similar in the serious and not-quite-so-serious cases. You will have to help solve these problems if they are going to be solved.

Mental retardation

On the whole, additional schooling has made possible an advanced technological society in the United States. Only a couple of generations ago a prognosticator would have been justified in saying that the populace would be unable to perform at the level of sophistication at which our society operates routinely today. Then, as now, there were those in the society who could not function in the school situation. They learned the things taught in school very slowly, if at all. As the importance of a school education has increased, with more and more intense demands being made upon youngsters to perform satisfactorily, the proportion who cannot keep up has increased. Many of these people are not distinguishable from the mass of workers once they leave school, but as the real demands for increased intellectual functioning become more insistent, there is a danger that the deficiencies that are now apparent in school will also become apparent in industry and that an increasing segment of the population will be unable to find meaningful employment.

As director of special education for the Santa Barbara schools, Thomas J. Murphy deals with these problems on a day-to-day basis. He has been imaginative in providing transitions from the school to the world of work, so that many of the young people are able to find a comfortable and worthwhile place in society because of the programs he has organized. It may be that you will have to devise new kinds of school opportunities for students who do not learn easily. This phase of education is one that can be both challenging and frustrating. I hope you will be able to rise to the challenges without being crushed by the frustrations.

LEARNING-MOTIVATION MODEL

An understanding of learning difficulties requires a framework that can best be supplied by a theory about how learning and motivation come about. The Wilson-Robeck Learning-Motivation Theory has been useful in understanding the etiology and the remediation of many of the difficulties faced by atypical children. A review of the model and the basic research findings on which it is based should be a useful introduction to those of you who are seriously interested in understanding why and how certain habits of responding have developed in students with whom you have to work. More importantly, this model provides ideas about how the teacher or counselor can structure learning situations that will lead to changed habit patterns, changes that will make the behavior of the student more acceptable to himself, to his associates, and to the adults with whom he comes into contact.

The learning-motivation theory began as an insight about the way in which stimulus-response (S-R) theories, gestalt theories, and purposivist theories could be integrated into an interlocking, unified, hierarchical structure. The theory has evolved as neurological support for aspects of it has become apparent, as the practical application of the theory in the Kindergarten Evaluation of Learning Potential (KELP) (Wilson and Robeck, 1967) has required rethinking of details that proved awkward, and as students have questioned the logic of certain relationships. In brief outline, the theory claims that much learning of both cognitive and affective types is learned by association. On this level, learning takes place because two things occur together in time.

A child touches a hot stove and is burned. He associates hot stoves and pain. A boy follows through as his bat hits the ball, and the ball sails over the fence. The boy associates follow-through with long drives. A child smiles at his mother, and the mother smiles back. The child associates smiling with good feeling. A child sees the word *cat* and the teacher says "cat." The child learns to associate "cat" with the word *cat*. Hundreds of instances of this kind of learning take place every day. Some of them relate bits of factual knowledge, some relate actions and feelings, some relate or associate bits of knowledge with feelings of pleasure or frustration. This association level of learning is fundamental to all learning and probably accounts for the vast majority of learning that most people do.

Under favorable circumstances a person can come to conceptualize relationships within areas of factual knowledge. A child inserts different-shaped pieces into a series of openings in a plastic ball. After a certain amount of trial and error you can see him start to search for the right opening. He has conceptualized that there is a relationship between the shape of the opening and the shape of the plastic piece that fits the opening. Children lie on the floor and scream, and the parents let them have their own way. Pretty soon the child comes to say, "If you don't let me do it, I'll scream!" He has already conceptualized the efficiency of controlling his parents in this way. A wife falls ill, and her husband makes a big fuss over her. If this series of events happens regularly, the wife may conceptualize illness as a way of obtaining desired attention. In all these varied cases, there are series of events that go together and are learned by association, but over and beyond this kind of learning, there is an abstraction and generalization that comes from the events happening in a similar fashion on several occasions. The first work the child does with the plastic shapes is random, but eventually it becomes systematic and meaningful. The child screams and gets her own way, but eventually she sees the relationship between screaming and getting her own way. It takes several instances, but eventually the relationship is seen by the child. The wife is sick and gets the attention. It is only after the sequence has happened several times that the relationship between being sick and gaining attention is grasped. Even then, this relationship may be distorted or camouflaged to avoid some other learnings that make using sickness to gain attention an unacceptable way of behaving.

Some of the conceptualizations mentioned previously dealt with factual learnings, some of them dealt with emotional feelings. In many kinds of learning situations, conceptualizations take place about relationships within the content to be learned. At the same time, conceptualizations are likely to be taking place about the emotional loadings or the feelings that accompany this particular kind of learning. When a conceptualization about the relationships in the material is accompanied by a conceptualization of oneself as being able to function with pleasure and success in this area, the person is likely to be motivated to work in the area. He will undertake work on his own initiative, which means he'll be self-directing; furthermore he'll vary the rules as he repeats operations and thus become creative. As you think of the areas in which you are creative, I am sure they are situations in which you feel comfortable and sure enough of the outcomes to try variations with assurance. Some women cook in this spirit. They substitute ingredients with the idea that the substitution will improve a recipe they have used before. Some men create new designs for fences or arbors, but usually this variation is after they have tried following a set of rules and found they could do so without undue difficulty. These are mundane operations in which ordinary people like you and me operate at a creative self-directing level. There is nothing mysterious about it. No one is pushing you to perform this way, but because you got satisfaction out of working at a simpler level, you are free to go on and try new variations on your own. What is more important, you want to make these innovations. The interaction of the levels and the cognitives and affective areas are shown in Figure 1-1.

Obviously this statement is far too abstract to be swallowed in one gulp. After a look at some research findings that explain why some things are repeated and some things are avoided, a detailed and illustrated elaboration of the theory will be presented.

One of the important breakthroughs concerning the nature of learning occurred during explorations pertaining to the functions of the different parts of the brain. The brain, as you know, is composed of some ten billion neurons, which have potential for many many different kinds of patterns

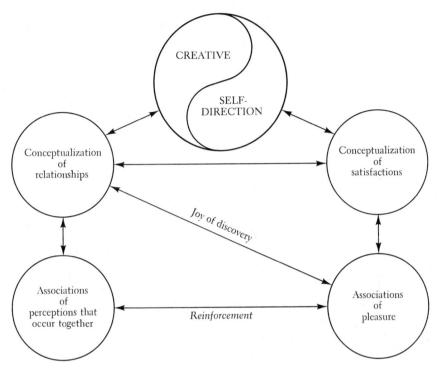

FIGURE 1-1 *The learning-motivation model (From Mildred C. Robeck and J. A. R. Wilson, KELP Resource Guide, McGraw-Hill, New York, 1969. By permission of the publisher.)*

of organization. Many of the neurons are very small, with short dendrites and short axons, and they connect only with other neurons that are close at hand, but many of the neurons have long axons that make possible connections with neurons at a great distance. Incidentally, the white layer of the brain is composed almost entirely of axons, which connect different regions of the brain.

As learning takes place, patterns of neurons are joined together, although as consolidation of the learning takes place, the original circuitry seems to be replaced by changes in the structure of RNA molecules. Much of the knowledge about the functioning of the brain has come as researchers, particularly neurologists, have explored the brain with microelectrodes preparatory to surgery to remove tumors, to repair the damage of head injuries, or to remove tissue that is involved in complex epilepsy cases. Wilder Penfield, of the Montreal Neurological Institute, used microelectrodes to make sure he was not going to remove a critical area in an operation (Penfield and Roberts, 1959).

The brain has no pain centers of its own, and it is possible to probe into it while the patient is conscious. Part of the skull is removed, and exploration is carried on by means of probes. A probe to a motor area may cause a hand to rise involuntarily, a toe to curl, or a lip to twitch. A probe to a visual area may cause a person to see stars, pinwheels, or other visual phenomena. Before cutting away an infected part of the brain, it is necessary to make sure that it is not going to prove to be vital. Sometimes it is better to live with the disease rather than live without a function controlled by the diseased part of the brain.

During one exploratory period, Penfield stimulated a section of the brain that caused the patient to relive, in video-tape reality, part of her life that had taken place twenty years before. The experience was quite different from remembering. It was a reliving of a chunk of life. Other neurologists have had patients who responded in similar ways. One of my students told about an aunt of hers who had experienced this reliving experience in Penfield's clinic. While none of the episodes were long in time—an hour is exceptionally long—it seems as though everything a person attends to is stored and could be relived.

The reliving is not contaminated in the way normal memory is by the addition of information from other experiences at other times in life. It includes trivial bits of experience such as the way the clothes are blowing on the clothesline, the way a dog is barking in the street, or what a neighbor is saying across a fence. It seems to be a true storage of living experience to which one has attended.

Positive and negative reinforcement

J. Olds (1956), while he was a graduate student, used an electrode to explore the brains of rats. In one episode he did not get the electrode into just the part of the brain he thought he was reaching. He found that the rat was repeating whatever was being done just prior to the electrode being turned on and displaying all the symptoms of being pleased about the happening. In order to test his hunch that he had stumbled onto the *pleasure centers*, he organized his apparatus so that the rat could display its desire for this particular kind of stimulation. He arranged a bar that could be pressed by the rat and that, when pressed, would activate the current in the electrode in the pleasure center. He put the rat into the box with the current disconnected in order to find a level, or reference base, for the bar pressing. The rat pressed the bar from twenty to twenty-five times an hour. When the current was turned on, the bar pressing went up to between two thousand and five thousand times an hour. This increase in rate is significant beyond the level of chance. The experiment was repeated with other rats and by other experimenters, leading to the conviction that there were centers in the brain that were pleasure producing. In one experiment with cats, a very hungry cat would choose to operate the stimulus apparatus rather than to go and eat fish of which it was particularly fond. Similar experiments have been done with other kinds of animals, including humans who report that the stimulation is pleasure producing. One psychomotor epileptic pushed a button that stimulated the centromedian region of the brain at a rate of up to eleven hundred times an hour. This stimulation induced irritability, but it brought up a memory to the tantalizing stage where it could almost be grasped. The same patient found stimulation of the septal region more pleasure producing, a fact borne out by motion pictures that indicated a transition from disorganization, rage, and persecution to happiness and mild euphoria when, unknown to him, his septal electrode was stimulated (Heath, 1963; Heath, John, and Fontana, 1968).

In other experiments *punishment centers* have been located that cause avoidance of whatever activity is happening when the stimulus is turned on. Rats used in these experiments have their hair stand on end as though in fear; they react so strongly to avoid the stimulus that they break their own teeth out. If they are put in a situation where they must keep pressing a bar in order to continually turn off the current, they become extremely irritable, and they develop symptoms of neuroticism or even paranoia. If the situation is continued for three or four hours, many of the animals will die. Rats do not like to have these centers stimulated and they will avoid whatever comes to be associated with this stimulation.

The effects of long-term damage through punishment stimulation are difficult to cure in the normal processes of remediation. The neuroticism or illness of the rat becomes a way of life that is undesirable from almost any viewpoint. There is one exception to this long remediation process. If a nearby pleasure center is stimulated, the animal that otherwise would be an emotional invalid recovers rapidly and regains his old buoyancy. This finding has great significance when the electrode stimulation is changed to

PENGUIN

FIGURE 1-2 *Association of word and figure*

internal neural connections and when the subjects become school students rather than rats. Punishing situations should be followed by success and pleasure in the same context if permanent damage is to be avoided.

Pleasure-related learning

Successful learning that leads to highly motivated, self-directing creative activity can be seen in the way in which some young children learn vocabulary, come to perceive the fact that groups of words start with similar sounds, and then go on to add new words to those already in the group or to develop new groupings of words with the same beginning sound. The material in the next two sections is adapted from the auditory perception items of the KELP (Wilson and Robeck, 1967).

When you are teaching vocabulary with the primary purpose of having the child learn a system for decoding initial beginning sounds, ordinarily you select words that are interesting, that some but not all of the children already know, and that exemplify the sound pattern that is being taught. In the KELP materials a further requirement was that a model of the noun could be obtained that would fit into a container that went into the kit.

One of the sounds that is well developed by kindergarten age is the bilabial sound of p, which is one of the earliest vocalizations children learn to make. In actually teaching this consonant as a beginning sound part, it would be put in contrast to the sounds of f and n, which not only have different beginning sounds, but for which different vocalization procedures

FIGURE 1-3 *Reinforcing action by teacher for association*

are needed for production. These vocalization procedures are not brought into the forefront of the attention of the kindergarten child during teaching, but the fact that they are different from each other provides muscular associations to the sounds that are being emphasized.

As a KELP teacher, you would hold up a model of a penguin and ask if anyone knows what it is. Someone in the group is sure to say it is a bird, although someone else is equally sure to say it is a penguin. If the bird answer comes first, it can be followed by a question such as, "Does anyone know what kind of a bird it is?" At this point, in spite of the fact that you are teaching beginning sounds, probably there should be discussion of the fact that penguins live down in Antartica where it is cold, that they waddle when they walk, that they eat fish that they catch by diving into the water, and that some of the class may have seen penguins in the zoo. You are trying to build associations to go with the word *penguin*. In all of the discussion, the word *penguin* is repeated as part of the start of questions and of repetition of answers. At this time, probably you will want to say, "What is the name of this bird?" and an individual will answer "Penguin." To picture the formation of this association, we could show Figure 1-2 where the word and figure are shown together to stress that it is the connection between the two that is being built.

When the youngster says "Penguin," you naturally will smile your approval at her for saying it so well. You may give her a squeeze or in other ways show that you think she is wonderful to have learned so well. This activity is shown in Figure 1-3.

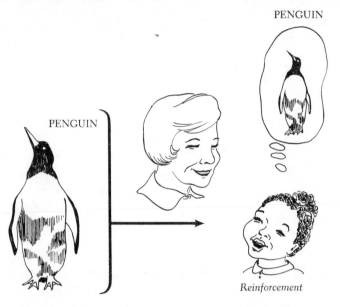

FIGURE 1-4 *Connection of association of word and figure to a pleasure center stimulated by teacher's reinforcing action*

The success in saying the word, coupled with the approval of the teacher, reinforces the youngster. Apparently there is a connection to the pleasure centers of the already-joined visual image and speech image of the word *penguin*. It seems probable that this connection to the pleasure center constitutes the reinforcement. One effect of this reinforcement is a tendency of the child to visualize the penguin and say the word over to herself. Notice the parts to this system. First, there is the association of the object with the verbalization of the word. This is followed by rewarding activity by the teacher, which stimulates a reinforcing connection within the child. The reinforcement is within the child. It is stimulated by the teacher, but the teacher is not the reinforcement; on suitable occasions, the teacher is not needed for reinforcement. The reinforcement causes the child to repeat and stabilize the association of the object with the word that represents it (Figure 1-4).

In order to get to the conceptualization of similar beginning sounds, a number of other vocabulary words should be added. A new object is held up—for instance, a parrot—and the children are asked to tell what kind of bird it is. The bright colors of the plumage and the hooked beak

penguin

PARROT

FIGURE 1-5   *Association*
of new word
and figure

make the parrot distinctive enough so that some of the children will know what it is. The others are helped to enunciate the word *parrot* in a group response, and then individual children are asked to say the word. The association of the word *parrot* with the toy parrot is shown in Figure 1-5. Note the already-stored penguin shown in smaller size in the picture.

Again, as the teacher, you smile and in other ways reward the youngster for his success in learning to say the word you have been teaching him. The connection is again made within the youngster to his pleasure center, and again he is reinforced for learning this new word. He is likely to visualize the object and repeat the word to himself as a result of the reinforcement he gets from the learning situation. Note that you are getting reinforcement from the child as well. His success stimulates reinforcement mechanisms within you and encourages you to go on with this kind of teaching. The reinforcement is shown in Figure 1-6.

The process is continued, adding other words such as *porcupine, prism, pineapple, pig.* The addition of these words to the associations in the mind of the child are shown in Figure 1-7. As a teacher you will have reinforced all of these associations.

penguin

PARROT

PARROT

Reinforcement

FIGURE 1-6 *Connection of a new association of word and figure to a pleasure center stimulated by teacher's reinforcement*

These words have all started with *p*. A part of your purpose has been to build up a situation wherein the individual children will be able to "discover" or conceptualize that this group of words all start with the same sound. This is part of a larger conceptualization that words can be grouped by the beginning sounds. In order to bring out the first of these conceptualizations, you will probably hold up each of the objects in turn and have the children name them. After this, the process will be repeated, having individual children say the words. After the words have been repeated several times, you may ask, "Can anyone tell me anything about these words?" Someone will probably say that they rhyme or that they sound the same. This lead should be followed up by asking a question such as, "What part of them sounds the same?" Some of the children will say, "At the beginning." With a little help, several of the children will have the light dawn that these words all have the same beginning sound. This is shown in Figure 1-8. Note that if the children are to make this conceptualization the group of words has to be kept free from contamination with other beginning sounds. In KELP, two other groups of beginning sounds, one set beginning with *f* and another set beginning

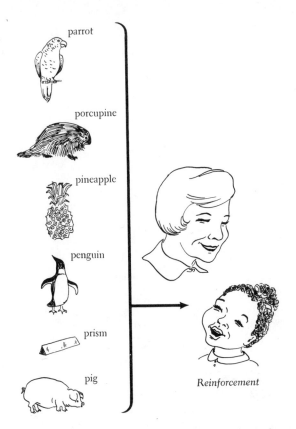

parrot

porcupine

pineapple

penguin

prism

pig

Reinforcement

FIGURE 1-7 *Pleasure connections for a number of new words and figures that have been associated*

with *n*, would be taught as contrast to the sound of *p*. These are grouped separately and provide an opportunity for additional children to pick up the idea that words can be grouped by beginning sounds. It also opens the possibility of the children making the conceptualization that words can be grouped by their beginning sounds, an exercise that takes more than one group of words for the conceptualization to emerge.

The children will enjoy this work with words if you do it properly. They are reinforced as they take each step. You want to have them conceptualize their feelings of pleasure in this particular task. Questioning such as, "Do you like working with words?" may help some of the children to come to this conceptualization. Again a light dawns (Figure 1-9).

At this point, some of the children will be exploring the beginning

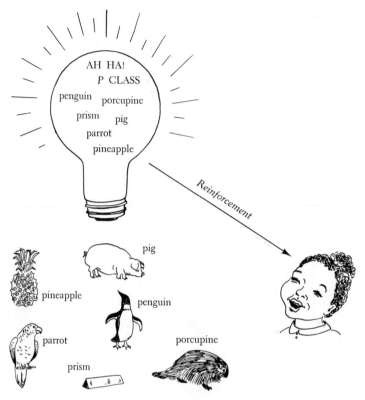

FIGURE 1-8 *Conceptualization of relationships*

sounds of other words that will fit into the established categories, or they will be building new categories for themselves. Many of the youngsters may not tell you about their activities unless you let them know that this is an acceptable thing to do in kindergarten. If this is one of your early attempts to stimulate creative self-direction, you may find it advisable to suggest that they think of other words that begin the same way or other groups of words that all start alike. You are really looking for evidence that they are willing and able to do these things on their own, but somewhere the idea has to be planted that individual initiative is appreciated. This state of affairs is shown in Figure 1-10.

By a planned series of steps you have helped many of your children to master new vocabulary words, to enjoy the success they have in doing so, to conceptualize a relationship among the groups of words, to concep-

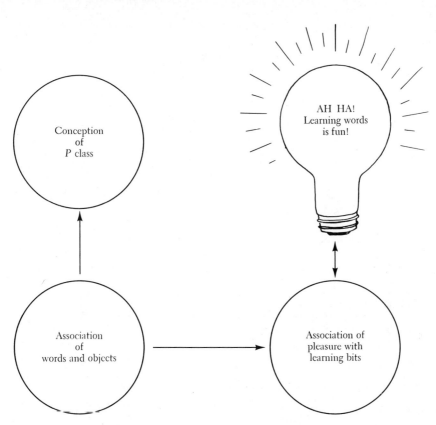

FIGURE 1-9 *Conceptualization of pleasure in work with words*

tualize the enjoyment they had in working in this area, and then to move on to being creatively self-directing in this area.

These children have not become creatively self-directing in all areas of their lives but only in a small segment. However, if they have had this success and go on to have similar success in other and different kinds of activities, it is possible for them to come to see themselves as creative and self-directing in many areas of their lives.

Most of you who are reading this book are not now, and do not plan to be, kindergarten teachers, but the same principles of building associations, adding reinforcement for the successful building, conceptualizing the relationships within both the cognitive associations and the affective associations, and finally moving on to creative self-direction can be developed

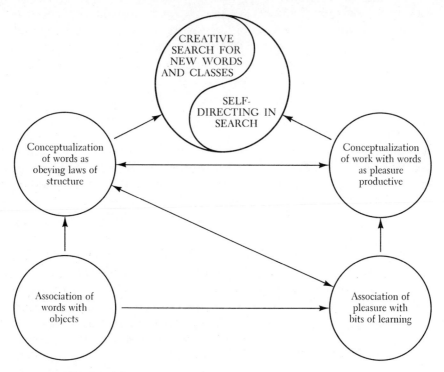

FIGURE 1-10 *Model of a motivated learner*

in any subject area. It requires that you analyze clearly what you are trying to teach so that you can put similar parts together to make it possible for the student to abstract the relationships, to get satisfaction in doing so, and to go on from there. One of the principal difficulties concerns noise in the system or distractors such as words that do *not* begin with the same sound. After a while, when a conceptualization has been made, students can deal with these interlopers and put them aside, but in the beginning, a small number of distractors can destroy the possibility that many of the students will make the basic conceptualizations.

Punishment-related learning

This is a text about learning difficulties rather than learning successes. Unfortunately not all learning programs run as smoothly as would seem possible from the programs outlined in the above section. The young people with whom we are concerned have learned different and more disastrous patterns of dealing with life as it comes to them. Much of their experience is similar to that of the rats who broke out their teeth to avoid the reinforcement system in which they found themselves. Robert G. Heath (1963) tells of one human patient who suffered from narcolepsy and cataplexy—he would fall asleep within a second when falling asleep was not desirable—who had an electrode placed in the mesencephalic tegmentum, which made him alert but was punishing in a fear-producing and intensely discomforting way. He had available two other buttons; one stimulated the septal region, which was alerting and pleasure producing, and the other stimulated the hippocampus, which was mildly rewarding. Shortly after the patient had explored the effects of this button pressing, he devised a hairpin clip so that it was impossible to depress the punishing button. Actually he used the septal stimulator nearly exclusively. The stimulation enabled him to work part time as a nightclub entertainer, whereas formerly his illness would not allow him to hold any kind of a job. We tend to work quite hard to avoid punishing stimulation.

We can trace what happens to some small boys when they are sup-posed to be learning vocabulary and are in the same group described earlier. I suggest that this will probably be a boy rather than a girl, since boys develop reading problems from six to ten times as often as do girls.

When you hold up the penguin and ask what it is, our little boy may be poking the boy next to him, looking out the window, counting his marbles, or doing a great many other things that distract his attention from what you are saying. He may have attended enough to have heard the youngster who said the object was a bird. He may be a little hard of hearing and may have heard only the *pen* part of *penguin*, which doesn't make much sense to him; he knows what a pen is! The associations he forms are shown in Figure 1-11.

Since he is probably being disruptive, you think it would be desirable to pull him into the group by calling on him. You are already just a bit annoyed, so you are just a bit sharp as you call on him. When he comes back with "Bird," obviously indicating that he hasn't been listening, you ask, "What kind of a bird?" He says, "A pen?" You repeat "Penguin," but he doesn't quite get it. By this time you see signs that some of the rest of the class are becoming interested in other things, so you give Tommy a rather wintry smile because you feel you should reinforce him, but you do not feel much like it. This situation is depicted in Figure 1-12.

Tommy may not be at all sure just what he has done wrong, but he has probably gotten the message that something is amiss in his relation-ship with you. The association between the figure of the penguin and his

FIGURE 1-11 *Incorrect or undesired associations*

Punishing action by teacher

FIGURE 1-12 *Negatively reinforcing action by teacher for association*

word *bird* or *pen,* both being tentative, is probably connected to a punishment center (Figure 1-13).

You remember what happened to the rats and to the patient who had connections to the punishment centers? They tried to avoid the situation that was associated with this condition. Tommy is probably trying to do the same thing. He probably is not visualizing the penguin and associating it with the words *bird* or *pen,* but he is also not associating it with the word *penguin.*

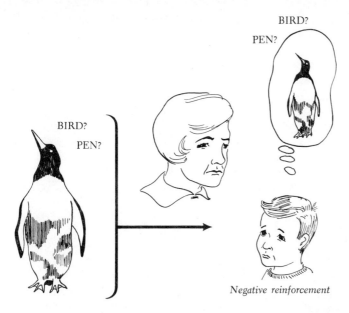

BIRD?

PEN?

BIRD?

PEN?

Negative reinforcement

FIGURE 1-13 *Connection of word and figure to a punishment center stimulated by the teacher's reinforcing action*

When you move on to the word *parrot*, he may pick this up as *carrot*, a word with which he is likely to be more familiar, even though the parrot doesn't look like a carrot (Figure 1-14). Only half attending to the teacher causes fragmentary learning.

If you are human, Tommy is probably starting to get to you by the time you call on him and he makes another "mistake." You tighten your lips and say silently to yourself, "Give me strength," then you repeat as sweetly as you can, "Parrot, not carrot." Again the class claims your attention, and Tommy has seen you as in Figure 1-15. You look threatening to him because you are threatening.

Inside Tommy another connection is being made to the punishment center. The object of a parrot and the word *carrot* is being turned off. Unfortunately the object and the word *parrot* as an association or a vocabulary-building experience are not being turned on as you can see (Figure 1-15).

In particularly unlucky cases, Tommy will hear *porky* instead of *porcupine*, *risen* instead of *prism*, *apple* instead of *pineapple*, *big* instead of *pig*.

bird?

pen?

CARROT?

FIGURE 1-14 *Incorrect
association of new word
and figure*

Of course, by this time you are regularly frowning or tightening your lips at each error.

With each accumulating failure Tommy is building a fine set of negative or punishing associations to all of the vocabulary-learning opportunities. He not only is not making the associations of the words and objects, but he is accumulating punishment connections to the process of trying to learn the words (Figure 1-16).

When you come to working on conceptualization with the group, Tommy has a mixed up bundle of associations rather than the neat and intelligible array that some of the rest of the class have. He is likely to generate a conceptualization, but it will probably be that the work on vocabulary is meaningless (Figure 1-17).

Tommy is also likely to generate a conceptualization about his feelings about work with words. It will be a conceptualization of distaste for this part of school life (Figure 1-18).

Under the described sequence of events, Tommy is likely to become creatively self-directing, but it will be in ways to avoid this business of

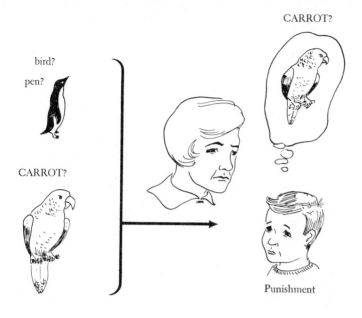

bird?

pen?

CARROT?

CARROT?

Punishment

FIGURE 1-15 *Connection of new word and figure to punishment center stimulated by teacher's punishing activity*

working with words (Figure 1-19). At this point a student with a well-developed learning difficulty has been created.

Most of you will be working with some Tommies who have already built up highly unproductive patterns of behavior in a number of areas. I would like to suggest that the above paradigm covers a substantial part of the learning pattern of many of the young people we are to study in this book. There are a couple of auxiliary situations that should be added if you are to understand some of the dynamics that come out of this learning situation. One is that, after a certain amount of pain in these learning situations, a youngster starts to find positive reinforcements in being the "worst" reader in the class. He has created an image of himself, and he comes close to fitting the image and gains much the same kind of satisfaction that the good student gets out of doing well. You have to remember that none of us can live with a continuously punishing situation, so we find a circuitous way to invert it into a pleasure-producing situation.

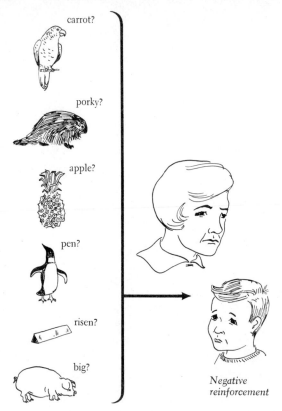

carrot?

porky?

apple?

pen?

risen?

big?

Negative reinforcement

FIGURE 1-16 *Punishment connections for a number of new words and objects*

Just as you can find ways of structuring positively reinforcing patterns of working with students in all areas and at all levels, so too each of us can find ways of building punishing situations for the young people with whom we work. In fact it is very difficult to avoid setting up these undesirable kinds of learning experiences. It is particularly difficult to avoid building these destructive patterns when the student comes with sensory-input difficulties. The partially seeing, hearing, or speaking student can rapidly be made into a turned-off learner in any particular area. Remember that we learn to behave in these ways in small segments of our lives, and it is only with repeated experience in many different learning situations that we finally generalize a self-concept as a school failure. But once this generalization has been made, it is self-perpetuating.

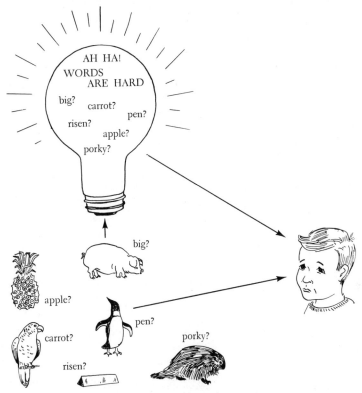

FIGURE 1-17 *Conceptualization of word study as meaningless*

Complex motivation systems

Almost never are learning situations as neat and clear as these last two examples have depicted them as being. Often, punishment leads to motivation, while it should, according to the example, turn the people off. Some people accept difficulties as a challenge, while others find them a reason for withdrawal. Why is there the difference? It has been customary to think that incentives, such as paying students for A's or paying them for learning to read, are highly undesirable and immoral to boot. In real life, a different standard prevails. The most common motivating device used is the prospect of more money. Most of the time, and with people in high tax brackets, this incentive works quite well. Are young people different from their elders? The story of the artist in a garret in Paris, starving as he struggles to paint, is an illustration of motivation that is real and

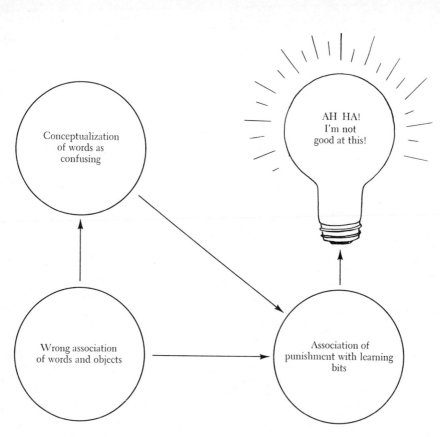

FIGURE 1-18   *Conceptualization of self as failure in work with words*

that exists as motivation in spite of the negative reinforcements. Usually such artists have had a wife or lover who believed in them and in their work, and this belief was enough reinforcement to support the artist.

Earlier, the effect of stimulation of the pleasure centers to erase the disastrous effect of stimulation of the punishment was mentioned. Also the narrow range in which the self-directing creative activity functions was part of the picture presented. Motivation is not a simple all-or-none proposition that can be activated and deactivated carelessly or at will, although it does seem to be subject to governance if the teacher or counselor is willing to put the necessary effort into understanding and operating the vital mechanisms.

In very young children, perhaps even during the period of the

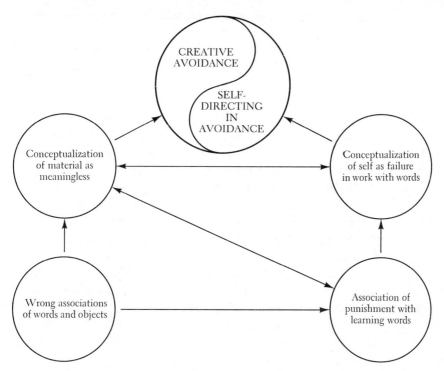

FIGURE 1-19 *Punishment connections leading to conscious, self-directing avoidance*

neonate (the first month of life), success in manipulating people by crying is experienced. These successes or failures are probably the prototype of later patterns of success and failure in interpersonal relations (Wilson, Robeck, and Michael, 1969). People who go into teaching or into counseling have often found that they were good at this task of working with people to get them to do what they wanted them to accomplish. At about the same age as they learn to control people, children are showing the first signs of success in exploring the world of things. They show interest in patterns that show similarity and that are mixed with others that show contrast. At this very young age, they also become bored with always having the same patterns to look at. It is a bit frightening to think of a child a month old becoming bored, isn't it?

Out of these small beginnings, the manipulating of people through crying, the exploration of the physical environment, the feedback of positive reinforcement building to conceptualization and successful self-direction, and finally the winning through obstacles to eventual success, come the patterns of successful motivation. With only small changes from the same directions come the motivations to turn off the world and all its problems.

Babies who are too young to know what they are doing seem to get satisfaction out of being able to make people do what they want them to do. Eventually, out of successes like this come habits of domination of others. It is unclear whether the strength of this dominance comes from immediate success or whether it comes from success after there has been the threat of failure and delay in achieving the goal.

The interest in exploration of the novelty of the environment seems in many ways to be a cooler and more impersonal kind of interaction. It is worth noting that the exceptionally young child will turn away as the objects around him stop conveying new information that he can relate to old information systems. Think of the implications for children from impoverished backgrounds, and think how impoverished many aseptic environments can be. As these patterns emerge of early learning and the needs that are being met in the different cases, consider the changes that would be desirable for full psychological development in early child-rearing practices.

Some groups of children have earned reputations with teachers as being particularly likely to perform well up to their potential. Jewish and Oriental children are expected to work hard and try persistently to master their tasks. On the other hand, other groups, including Negro and Mexican-American children, are expected to be easily distracted. To some extent these expectations become self-fulfilling prophesies, but it is more complex than that. The idea, on the part of the teacher, started through experience, and it has nothing to do with the child being of a different appearance. The Oriental child is more clearly differentiated from the Anglo group than is the Mexican-American. In these various groups, the home cultures have either been similar to or different from the teacher's with regard to the value placed on successful work in school. The Jewish and Oriental parents tend to value education for upward mobility and to reinforce success on the part of the children. On the other hand, the parents in the Negro and the Mexican-American homes have until recently tended not to see formal schooling as a way to a better life and not to emphasize the educational successes of their children very obviously or very vigorously.

The connections to the pleasure centers and to the punishment centers are differentially developed in the different groups.

Establishing new response patterns

When working with children with learning difficulties, many of the causes will be found in the motivation patterns they have developed. Much of the restructuring needed for remediation will come from careful building of needed patterns of success that lead to conceptualizations of themselves as successful in a narrow area. This small beginning of a positive self-concept can be exploited and later expanded until it takes in a more significant portion of the young person's life. Obviously this is going to be a slow process. There are no pep courses that bring success in changing a life pattern in a fifteen-minute interview. However, if the teacher or counselor can visualize the steps that are needed and can understand how the steps can be achieved, eventual success is possible.

As you are seeking ways to retrain students who have become negatively motivated, it will help you to think in terms of avoiding the old patterns, of finding some new and as-yet-unexplored way to handle the learning as far as the young person is concerned. For instance, in reading, if the child has been exposed to an experience-chart approach to learning and has discovered that he is a failure at reading that is taught this way, it would be wise to introduce him to a phonetic approach, a programmed-book approach such as the Sullivan method, an i/t/a/ approach, or something that is sufficiently different so that he knows this is not the same old thing at which he has been failing. Probably a bit of a sales talk about how successful this method has been with other students like him can be an incentive for him to try again. Under these circumstances, it behooves you as the remediator to make sure that he gets the reinforcements and the successes he needs during the early critical hours and days of his new trying. You are literally trying to build a new pattern of responses. It is easy to fall off the new track and have it join with the old failure patterns of responses. If the child falls, it is just one more method that will be very hard to make work. There are not so many alternates that you can afford to waste one, so keep in mind clearly what you are trying to do.

With some students it may be acceptable to structure the learning situation so that some anxiety is aroused, but if this is done, it should be followed by success. This is a tricky operation, and you need to be quite sure of your ground before you use it. One point that is particularly important is that the successes have to be real success. The student knows pretty well if he has missed, even if you pat him on the back, so you need to set the program up to assure his success.

Most of the students mentioned in the chapters that follow have learned poor response patterns. Nearly all of them need the restructuring we have been discussing. I have found this model of learning and motivation helpful. It is by no means the only model, nor is it the only model that will work. However I do commend it to you for your consideration as you try to work with children who have lost their way in our complex school system. Most of the other authors will present other learning models. As you study the material, you will pick and choose among the patterns presented and will accept those you find comfortable. You may synthesize from parts of others, as we have done, and come up with a new model of your own. Let me emphasize that it does help to have some framework from which to try to understand the problems of the young people.

VISUAL PROBLEMS IN THE CLASSROOM

Norman W. Van Donge

2

Dr. Norman Van Donge started his own ophthalmological clinic a year ago. For seven years prior to that he was chief of the Department of Ophthalmology of the Santa Barbara Medical Clinic.

After earning his bachelor's degree in physiology from the University of California, Berkeley, Dr. Van Donge taught for two years in that department. He then went on to Stanford University, where he earned the M.D. in 1958. He was an intern at San Francisco General Hospital for a year, a resident in internal medicine at the University of California Hospital, San Francisco, for another year, and a resident in ophthalmology at the Stanford University Hospital for three years. He is a diplomate of the American Board of Ophthalmologists, a diplomate of the American Contact Lens Association, and a Fellow of the American Academy of Ophthalmology.

Dr. Van Donge has contributed substantially to the well being of the young people of Santa Barbara. During 1967 he was president of the Santa Barbara Eye Society and a director of Sight Conservation. This group sponsors a free clinic for children and also provides free glaucoma tests for adults. You will fiind his presentation very stimulating.

I would like to introduce some of the problems of eye care that, as educators, you will be seeing. You will be counseling young people, their parents, and the community at large, and you should have an idea about the most satisfactory and competent eye care that can be obtained.

FOLK TALES AND EYE PROBLEMS

There are several things that go along with eye care that are really superstitions. I think that I can help you distinguish between fact and fancy. The primary thing that you have to realize is that many people have a preconceived idea about eye problems. For instance, they think that reading in a dark or dim light will hurt your eyes, and they also think that reading in different positions will ruin your eyes. This was demonstrated to me in an incident with my father. After all my training and all my schooling, I was sitting with my feet up, reading the *Reader's Digest*, when my dad came into the room and said, "My goodness, get your feet off there and sit in an upright position and get a good light on your book or you'll ruin your eyes." I said, "Dad, you've been telling me that since I was a child." He said, "Son, you are still wearing glasses, and if you hadn't read like this when you were a child you wouldn't be wearing them."

You have trouble convincing people that there are problems and there are superstitions about the eye, and you must sort fact from fancy. I'll try in this discussion to give you a little basis for discriminating. Position doesn't mean too much, and lighting doesn't mean too much either, for the eye is an adaptive organ and will readily adapt to new conditions. If it can't see, it won't pick up the impulses. You aren't straining or hurting your eyes by reading in a dim light or by reading in an abnormal position. It's just a little harder to read in a dim light or an uncomfortable position.

Another superstition is that if you have one bad eye the other eye has to do twice the work. This isn't true. The eyes do not function like a team of horses. Sight, like an electric light bulb, is secondary to the electrical impulses that activate it. If it turns on at all, it turns on fully, and if it doesn't turn on, it isn't going to make any difference in the functioning eye. The good eye will not be overtaxed or overloaded.

These are superstitions and you want to have them clearly in mind when giving students, parents, and fellow teachers advice.

ANATOMY OF THE EYE

The eye is analogous to a small tennis ball or a golf ball. It is a little smaller than a golf ball. It's outer coating is made of a very tough fiber. It sits in a bony quadilateral box, which we call the *orbit*. This is located in the skull. About three-fourths of the eye is well protected by the bones of the skull and the face, so injuries in the back part of the eye, although they do occur, are rare, and considerable trauma is required to cause them. The outer one-quarter of the eye protrudes beyond the bony orbit. The outer quarter of the eye is exposed, and the lid covers this. The lid actually forms a protective skin layer, and along the edge of the lid is a thick plate of gristle called the *tarsal plate*, which is almost as tough as bone, so you have pretty good general protection of the eye. If you will consult Figure 2-1 you'll see some of these structures.

As I said, the eye can be compared to a small tennis ball. The outer white of the eye, which surrounds or makes up nine-tenths of the eyeball, is made up of a tough, fibrous connective tissue that is opaque to light. This is called the *sclera*. In the center of the eye is an oval that is transparent. We call this the *cornea*. Directly in back of this is a structure called the *iris*, which is colored either blue or brown, depending on your pigmentation. In the center of the iris is a *pupil*, a structural hole in the iris. This is the small black area that will dilate or constrict, depending on the illumination and whether or not you are frightened or have taken various drugs or medications. Directly behind the pupil is a focusing mechanism called the *lens*. The lens is truly a marvelous structure, for when a person is young, he can focus back and forth from far distance to up close with no problem at all. When he reaches age 40 to 45, he has more of a problem in focusing up close. This is why people wear reading glasses or bifocals. Basically, the lens continues to grow all through your life. Because of this, as it enlarges to a critical point, which occurs at around the age of 40, you then have the problem of making it focus light; that is, the lens must bend the light waves so they may focus and enable you to see an object up close clearly.

The lens allows us to bend light and focus the rays when an object is up close. At about age 40 the lens stiffens and hardens and grows thicker so that we can't bend light as well, and we need the aid of reading glasses. When we get to the 60s and 70s the lens has reached a maximum amount of growth, and its growth actually slows down; sometimes the lens opacifies. This is analogous to the white of an egg being fried very slowly

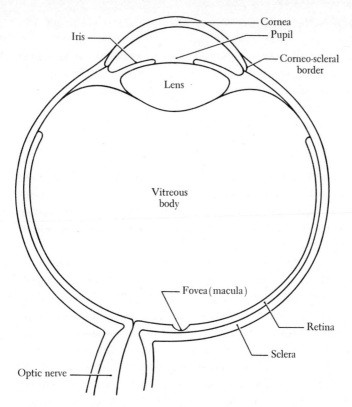

FIGURE 2-1 *Horizontal section of a right eye*

during a period of years. This opaque lens is called a *cataract*. The light can no longer be transmitted through the lens, so the lens has to be removed so light can get inside the eye.

The light passes through the lens and through the major portion of the eye, which we call the *vitreous body* (see Figure 2-1). This is filled with a jelly-like substance, the *vitreous humor*, which fills the inside of the eye. Behind the vitreous body is that marvelous structure that lines the entire inside of the eye. This is the *retina*. This is the photographic plate of the eye that is made up of millions and millions of tiny little nerve fibers or cells that are photochemical cells. When the light gets in, it causes an electrical discharge that is transmitted through millions of filaments that finally collectively form into a large nerve, which is called the *optic nerve*. The optic nerve leads from the back of the eye to the occipital, or back, portion of the brain where the light is subjectively interpreted. I say this because light is truly interpreted, and vision is a subjective sensation. It isn't something that everybody defines in the same way. Because of this subjectivity, there arose a problem in ophthalmology about how we were really going to determine what people saw.

MEASURING VISION

In the old days in Vienna, two hundred years ago, they used to have a person look out the window, and if he could read the writing across the corridor on the opposite window or on the opposite wall, he had good vision. Then they found out that that wasn't necessarily true, because he just had better vision than the professor who was testing him. Eventually, Professor Snellen took a group of "normal" people, and he established a norm in vision. This system, so familiar to us, is what we know as the 20/20 system. Now there are a lot of geometrical ways to figure this. If any of you are physicists you can look it up, but I think the basic thing for you to remember is that when we say 20/20 we are taking an average of a group of normal people, and this is what the normal people should see; they see at twenty feet what a normal person sees at twenty feet. If a person has a problem and sees 20/40, this means that the individual sees at twenty feet what a normal person can stand back at forty feet and see very easily. Thus the individual has some aberration or some deficit in his vision. He's not seeing as well as a normal individual. This is a subjective sensation that we can now measure, and we can measure it on a norm, if you want to put it that way. Some people will have better vision than the norm, and some a little worse; but most of us fall on the 20/20 line, and this is considered average, normal vision. Legally and technically, we say that anybody that has 20/200 or worse is legally blind. They can see to get around if they have 20/200, but they cannot see to read or do fine detailed work. This is the definition of legal blindness.

PERSONNEL IN EYE CARE

Now let us discuss the people who treat visual problems. This is an area in which you are going to have to learn some definitions. The distinctions are very important, and I shall outline them for you so that you'll understand, when you go into a community, the difference between certain individuals. Most laymen confuse these terms and confuse the educational background and the medical and paramedical training that go with the names. Let me give you the definitions and an outline of some things that you ought to know.

An *optician* is an individual who is a lens grinder. In California, which is one of the hardest states in which to become an optician, he has to serve an apprenticeship of three years. He doesn't have to have any formal educational status. If he wants to go into a business as an optician, he has to serve his apprenticeship and then be licensed by the state. These individuals can do lens grinding, lens fitting, lens polishing, and some of them can even fit contact lenses adequately, but they have no necessary formal schooling.

Optometrists are a different group of individuals in the eye-care field. An optometrist can measure and fit you for glasses. This is his function. Optometrists have no medical background. They usually have one or two years of college and two or three years of optometry school. This depends a little bit on the state in which they are licensed to practice. When they finish optometry school, they are automatically given a degree of Doctor of Optometry. This is just what it is called. They have problems with us because, although many of them are sincere and are very good, they may try to overstep their bounds medically. Some of them try to lead patients into treatment that is medically ill-founded. Some may claim they are able to treat reading problems or difficult problems of eye care. You must be wary of these claims, and you must be aware of them in your community. Some of them will be highly regarded. Some of them will have highly satisfactory results on *select* patients, but you need to be very aware of their lack of medical training.

The last individual we will discuss is the one who handles medical problems. He is an *ophthalmologist*. He is a physician who specializes in the care and treatment of the eye, and usually he does surgery of the eye itself. He has a minimum of four years of college and four years of medical school, one year of internship, one year in a specialty of medicine or surgery, and then three years of formal eye training, in addition to his medical training. At the end of that time he's eligible to go into practice. He must be in practice two years before he can take the competitive oral and written examinations to be certified by the Board of Specialists of Ophthalmology. During these two years he has usually been in practice with an older man. When he passes the competitive examinations of the American Board of Ophthalmology, he becomes a diplomate in the American Board or a fellow of the American Academy of Opthalmology. Ophthalmologists have about fifteen years of training in the field of medicine and eye care if they are diplomates of the American Board of Ophthalmology.

These are the differences in educational strata among the three fields.

EYE PROBLEMS

What are the eye problems that you are going to be faced with when you are an educator? What are the problems that you are going to see? There are many, but perhaps I can narrow it down to the basic ones for which you should watch.

Nearsightedness

Probably the most frequent problem is the nearsighted child. Nearsightedness is a condition that is generally hereditary. That is, the trait is hereditary. To understand nearsightedness, you should understand that the front part of the eye, anatomically, is almost the same in everybody. That is, the outer surface in the cornea, the lens, and the focusing mechanism is all about the same, and it has almost the same refractive index. I shall simplify the explanation of what occurs in a developing nearsighted eye. First, the eye begins to grow as does the child. The eye actually elongates. It becomes longer than normal. This means that the light rays coming into the eye, which are normally bent or refracted by the front part of the eye, are focused at a point source in front of the retina instead of a point source directly on the retina. As the child grows, his features grow, his hands grow, and by the looks of some of the students, their hair grows too. As the child's eyeball grows, the child becomes more nearsighted. This goes in stages. The child will usually have the nearsightedness first occur between the ages of 8 and 10, then another spurt will occur at the preadolescent age of 12 to 14, and the final spurt occurs at about 16 or 17. Therefore, these children, if they don't begin to develop nearsightedness at 8 to 10, will begin at 12 to 14, or lastly, they will begin at around 16 or 17. When they grow, the eyeball elongates and the focus of light stays the same. The front part of the eye stays the same; there's no change in it or its focusing ability. It is the back of the eye that grows bigger, and you find that the child ends up having a blurred focus on his retina. We have to correct the problem by using lenses to push this focus back so that it focuses on the retina. This is the problem of nearsightedness. It occurs generally in about 70 percent of the individuals on a hereditary basis, and in about 30 percent of the cases, it will arise spontaneously, with no family history of the problem. You can correct it easily with glasses or contact lens.

These children, when they begin to become nearsighted, will become introverts, so you can spot them. They are often children who have been extremely active and have sat in the back of the room and raised the devil for you in your classes. They may be athletically inclined, particularly the boys, and suddenly they take no interest in girls or athletics or anything else; they just want to sit in the library and read. This is because they can't see in the distance; they can't see at twenty feet very well. They've become nearsighted, and then they become more introverted; they become more studious. As a general rule, nearsighted children, because of their introversion, tend to be a little better students than are farsighted or normal students. They can't see in the distance, and can't play games that require far vision. You can spot the change in children by this change in activity, and, as educators, I think you might be interested in looking for it in some of the students, since the change happens dramatically in many cases. A mother comes in to let me examine her normal child. Three months later the child may be nearsighted enough to require glasses. Nearsightedness can develop that quickly. There's no way of predicting exactly when it will occur. It is a matter of how rapidly the child is growing. Many children have a progressive change that goes on in spurts until full growth occurs—that is, until the child becomes fully mature. In women this is at about the age of 18 or 19; in men it is usually at about 21 to 22.

As I have said, nearsightedness is associated with an abnormal growth of the eye. It is an hereditary error in which the eye, essentially, is too long. Specifically, we can get down to fine scientific measurements, and this isn't entirely quite true, but that will simplify it so that you'll understand what occurs as the child grows up. The eye just elongates, and this really means that his focusing of light rays on the retina is abnormal. The elongation itself is what is hereditary. It's like inheriting brown skin, big feet, or a big nose. There's nothing you can do about it. You can stand on your head, put on contact lens, or anything you want, but it isn't going to change this way of growing. It would seem rational that everyone who is nearsighted would cease to get worse after they've gained their full growth, and yet this isn't always so. The majority of people—about 99 percent—do cease to become more nearsighted when they reach maturity. Not only is there growth in the back of the eye, but there is also growth of the lens-focusing mechanism and the cornea—the entire eye. When people reach maturity, for the most part their eye growth is static, but there are other influences that complicate eye functioning during adulthood. Diseases such as diabetes cause problems, the normal changing of the lens takes place, but usually people who have reached their full maturity have attained their maximum amount of nearsightedness by the age of 22 to 24.

Astigmatism

The second problem that arises is astigmatism. I don't think there's any other term that is so familiar to everybody as the term *astigmatism*, although almost nobody knows what it really is when you ask them. Basically, astigmatism is this: The outer surface, the cornea of the eye (that clear, round window), instead of being shaped perfectly round like a ball, is shaped eccentrically like the back of a teaspoon, so when the light rays come in, they are not perfectly focused on the back of the retina. They are diffuse, scattered, and cannot be put in a point focus. The child then attempts to get them into a point focus by muscle effort. This is the child who squints his eyes and holds his book fairly close to see the print, gets it in view at last, and does pretty well. As he gets a little older, he says, "Ah nuts, let's forget it"; he looks up, and he's got other things he's looking at all around, and he's trying to find other things to do. This doesn't mean, of course, that all students who do this have astigmatism, but these kids have to work hard to overcome astigmatism if it is a measurable amount. I have a large astigmatism in my eye. I can take off my glasses and, without any problem, get 20/20 measurements by squinting, but it becomes very tiring after a couple of hours, so I put on my glasses and it's much easier. From a visual standpoint, with glasses on I don't have to squint or work visually when I am looking for things. I don't have to cone down those light rays into a focus when I have glasses to correct this astigmatism.

The second thing that will identify these children is that they have difficulty in concentrating, difficulty getting print focused, if they have a bad astigmatism. Almost everybody has some astigmatism, but it is the amount of astigmatism that is significant. It doesn't get critical until you have a significant amount. When these children get into high school, they are forced to read for long periods of time, and they do tire easily.

Farsightedness

The term *farsightedness* is a misnomer. Farsightedness is, again, a focusing deficit, and it is a deficit in which you cannot get a clear focus on the retina of the eye itself because of an intrinsic error. In essence, if I can simplify this, the eyeball is too short, so when the light rays come in, they come down into a focus that would occur behind the retina. You would have to have a longer eyeball to obtain a point on the retina. Instead, the retina is forward of the true focus, and you get a blurred image on the retina instead of a point focus. We correct this by a lens in front of the eye. It is a different type, or farsighted, lens. You may have a child who finds it difficult to focus up close. He can't read very well, and he can't see in the distance, so he's squinting at both distances. It is difficult to get him to sit still because he's not interested in reading. He's more interested in other things that are sort of at the intermediate range where he doesn't have to use his eyes too much to really focus in. I think you should realize that farsightedness has implications that are far greater than the problems of nearsightedness or astigmatism. These latter are easily corrected with glasses.

Farsightedness in many children is quite large. We grade in units of diopters, and we run normally from about one to ten units, with most farsighted children falling into the area of about three or four diopters of lens strength, which is a fairly large amount. If you put that up in front of a normal eye, the person probably would see about five feet away, and not very clearly. So when you get four or five diopters of strength in front of you, you've got quite a problem. This can be overcome because children have a great amount of reserve they can correct for by focusing with their lens. They can correct for about eight units of farsightedness.

You are faced with a little problem when these children come in. Because the muscles that are focusing are neurologically connected to the muscles required for turning the eye inward into the reading position, you will find that most of these children who are farsighted to a moderate degree (4 or 5 units) focus so hard on something when they get it up close that their eyes automatically cross. As you realize, when you focus on anything up close, your eyes turn in. When you try to get something clearly in focus at eighteen to twenty inches, your eyes normally will turn in. These children have so much farsightedness that they try to focus at near range, and they focus so hard to get something clearly in view that they just cross or turn their eyes inward too far.

I've simplified this so that you'll understand that when you are focusing up close your eyes will turn in normally. If you also have to overcome a significant error by additional focusing, then your turning in will be much more and you will overturn or cross your eyes. This condition can be easily straightened by putting a lens in front of the child and correcting his farsightedness. He then doesn't have to work so hard to focus. He has the help of the lens to focus up close, so he can easily have straight eyes. However, there's another problem with this. All crossed eyes, or eyes that turn out or in or up or down, are not necessarily farsighted eyes, and the problem is to determine those that are and those that are not. This can only be done by examining the child's eyes under drops that we use to relax the ability to focus, and then we get true measurement. This has to be done medically.

Strabismus

What, then, causes a child who isn't farsighted to have eyes that are misaligned? This condition is called *strabismus*. It means that the eyes are out of alignment. In most cases, as nearly as we can tell, the problem is not an abnormality of the eye muscles; it is an abnormality of the nervous output from the brain. It is actually a neurological problem. In strabismus, apparently the neurological problem or the neurology of the body is such that the one muscle, or a pair of muscles, is enervated more than another, and because of this, one eye turns in or out at a greater degree than the other, forcing the eyes out of alignment. When a child's eyes go out of alignment, the child sees double, and this is intolerable. If you ever had a problem in which you see double, you know what a terribly confusing situation it is. These little children are even more confused because they haven't learned to interpret things as you and I have. To compensate or ameliorate the difficulty, the children neurologically blot out one image. Their nervous system just turns off, and one eye dominates. Usually their good eye will dominate at the expense of their bad one. What happens is that shortly after the age of 5 the full pattern of the nervous system, as far as the visual aspect is concerned, is fully developed. If you don't catch these children by the age of 5½ or 6, you will find that the non-dominant eye has lost vision permanently.

Amblyopia

Amblyopia is not a total blindness, but it is a loss of reading vision, or what we call *macular vision*. Here again, I'll refer you to the diagram

(Figure 2-1). Right by the optic nerve there is a little dip in the diagram, which is the area we call the *macula* or the *fovea*. This is the area of our acute vision. If you knock that area out, or if it doesn't develop, you lose the ability to read and to perceive small objects with that eye. I can best illustrate the loss by having you put one finger directly in front of your eye and look straight ahead. Close your other eye and you'll see just about what an individual who has had loss of his macular vision does. We call this deficit amblyopia. The individual can't see to read with an eye that is afflicted in this way; he has only peripheral vision. This will give you an idea of why we like to have these children seen early when their eyes are turning in or out: when their eyes are out of alignment. They must be seen before they are 4½ or 5, or we can't do anything to restore that lost central vision. There are a lot of people, optometrists in particular, who like to treat these children. The unfortunate problem that arises is that they treat them in all good faith to the best of their knowledge; however, we find that when they come in to us at about the age of 6 or 6½ it is too late, and we cannot then restore good vision to that eye. This correction is a medical problem, and a condition where eyes are misaligned or have some deviation is not a problem for anybody other than a medical doctor or ophthalmologist. It is a problem that does not go away, and it should be checked because, even though a child's eyes may look straight, there may be a slight deviation of three or four degrees. This aberration can really send them, by the age of 4 or 5, from a 20/20 eye that you can salvage down to about a 20/80 or 20/100 eye in which you have a loss of macular or reading vision.

QUESTION: *One child crossed one eye, especially when playing. She would deliberately cross her eyes, and one would go in. She was checked by an ophthalmologist.*

ANSWER: Since she was checked by an ophthalmologist, she should be fairly safe, but she should be checked again.

QUESTION: *A student had amblyopia in one eye; although she was 17 years old, no one knew it before then. They couldn't tell by the tests, because she used to cheat. It seems that her doctor or ophthalmologist told her to put a patch on the good eye, because he wanted to train the bad eye. He seemed to think that something good was going to come out of it.*

ANSWER: You can't always tell with these cases. There are occasional individuals who respond to treatment, and patching may be beneficial.

In fact, I had a 39-year-old man who came in and, because he had an injury to his good eye, I patched it. He wandered around with 20/100 vision, and he came back five days later and he had 20/20 vision. Now this means, of course, that the individual didn't totally block out the nondominant eye. This is a fortuitous thing. What really happened was that he did what we call *alternating*. A very small percentage of people—maybe 2 to 3 percent—alternate; that is, their eyes are out of line, but they will use both eyes separately, and enough vision is used to stimulate full development of the nondominant eye, and the vision in the nondominant eye is therefore developed. There is a chance that patching may help, as in the case of this fellow or this girl. You never can tell, but chances are very much against it after age 5 or 6. However, many times the patient is desirous of trying, and if he wishes we can try.

QUESTION: *In some of these cases can the person be helped by having an operation?*

ANSWER: Actually, in most cases, the main thing you are doing with an operation is correcting the cosmetic effects. After an individual with an amblyopic eye is 6 or 7 years old, you cannot return vision surgically. You are not doing anything except a cosmetic operation. This, however, becomes very important to children, because when they go to class with other children, the other children often say, "Oh, look at Johnny cross-eye." Essentially he is abnormal. The child actually develops a psychological quirk. You see this frequently, and many times you can counsel and guide parents into having their child's eye straightened. Many of them don't buy it; they think it's going to get better. All I can say is that there is a definite reason for correcting, but it isn't a sight reason, it's a psychological and cosmetic one.

Pediatricians who have been trained in the last ten years or so are very alert to amblyopia and the county medical societies now are very alert, particularly throughout Southern California. Free clinics are held, when all the ophthalmologists devote one day during the year to testing possible cases of strabismus that are picked up in a preschool visual-testing program held at all public schools. The optometrists also hold free clinics, and they coordinate, in many cases, with the ophthalmologists. Most of the optometrists here in the Santa Barbara (California) area are very good. In some areas in which I've been, it has been a real problem to see who is going to treat the child. We have preschool visual testing, and we have a free clinic that is put on both by the optometrist and the ophthalmologist in this community, and this is a little bit unusual. There is good rapport between the two professions, and we do interrefer; that is, the optometrists refer to ophthalmologists problem cases that they realize are beyond their scope, so here we have no problem. In other places, however, you may have to realize that there is this problem. I'll just call it to your attention.

The incidence of blindness due to amblyopia is quite high. One report mentioned that as many as one in twenty individuals are damaged in this way. Probably in a routine day I see two or three children with problems such as we have been discussing.

We have discussed amblyopia. I've also told you about astigmatism and nearsightedness, which are simple problems, and farsightedness, which leads to strabismus or crossed eyes, and then to the dominance of a crossed eye and the loss of vision, which is called amblyopia.

Glaucoma

There's another eye problem to which you are going to be exposed that I may comment about. This is not usually a problem regarding children, although very rarely some children do have glaucoma. When it occurs in children, it is an hereditary type of glaucoma, and it is extremely rare. I've probably seen two or three cases in children in the last five years. The frequent kind occurs in individuals who are over 40. Glaucoma is truly a medical disease. It takes a sophisticated set of instruments and considerable amount of background and knowledge just to be able to diagnose many cases of glaucoma. Glaucoma is an increased pressure in the inside of the eye. The eye itself secretes a fluid internally independent of the tears. This is secreted in an enclosed system—the eyeball—to which there is only one outflow route. This outflow route, where fluid can get out of the eye, occurs in a small area where the colored portion of the eye and the white portion meet. There is a little sieve-like mechanism there, and through this sieve the fluid flows out of the eye into the general circulation of the bloodstream. When this sieve plugs up through an aging process, such as hardening of the arteries, the sieve becomes narrowed, and the fluid can't get out. Gradually, over a period of several months or years, the fluid pressure inside the eye rises. When this occurs it destroys the optic nerve, and this destroys the sight function of the retina.

50   NORMAN W. VAN DONGE.

Glaucoma is the specter that threatens 2 percent of all individuals over 40. It is readily treatable today. In many cases it is difficult to diagnose in the early stage, but in the community in which I practice, free glaucoma clinics are held in which all the ophthalmologists devote their time and screen about five thousand people during that day. Anybody in the general public is welcome, and the clinics are publicized in the newspaper. This condition, where increased pressure inside the eye destroys the optic nerve, is the leading cause of blindness in the United States today. This problem is not to be confused with a disease called *trachoma*, which is the leading cause of blindness throughout the world. Trachoma is actually an infectious disease caused by a virus found mainly in the Orient and throughout Africa, including Egypt.

You should urge your families to participate in the glaucoma clinics. This is not so essential for children, as I've said, because glaucoma occurs almost exclusively in people over 40, but families should be urged to participate in the testing program when they reach the age of 40, or sooner if there is a family history of this disease. It's a good idea to go down to one of these glaucoma clinics and have yourself checked, and it is very necessary to advise people to have it done.

Congenital defects

There are other problems that I think boil down to congenital problems. These are problems occurring at birth. You find that tumors arise in the eye. Some are cancerous tumors, which can be a significant cause of misaligned eyes. When we see a child with strabismus, we must suspect an eye tumor. This is why medically we have to dilate the eyes of these children widely and examine them thoroughly. We always look around with special instruments to be sure there isn't a tumor that's gotten into the eye and blocked off a part of the vision, causing misalignment of the eye. If a tumor is obstructing the vision—and this is something that does occur with a moderate degree of frequency—we then must institute appropriate medical treatment. We also have to consider embryological deformities that occur. As you realize, these can occur due to various diseases such as measles or rubella, which can give the child a congenital heart defect, hearing deficit, and cataracts. This is called the Rubella Syndrome. It's a medically characteristic syndrome that occurs when the mother gets German measles in her first trimester of pregnancy. Many of these children have mental retardation and maldevelopment or agenesis (nonformation) of an eye. These are problems that you are going to find and hear about and with which you are probably going to be associated in your community. You should understand that these deficits do occur for this reason. There is a parasite called *Toxoplasma*, which is quite rare, but we do find it; four or five cases have been found here in one local community in the last year or two. It is an organism that lodges in the mother and is transmitted to the fetus. It gets into the eye or the brain and can cause mental problems. It can also lodge in the eye and cause visual problems. These children, again, have their eyes go out of alignment. These are just incidental things, but they do occur, and I'd like you just to be aware of them.

READING PROBLEMS

I'm going to come to one of the most controversial problems involving the eye, and this is a reading problem. This is a problem in which you, as educators, are going to be hotly embroiled. You are going to take sides, and you are going to try to give guidance to children and people and communities on this problem. You are going to be swayed by your friends and by your associations and by various ideas that you'll pick up along the way. There really are so many cults in schools, so many charletans, so many paramedical ideas, and so many bad medical ideas that you are going to be hard put to support whichever theory you think is right, because somebody's going to disagree. Regardless of what you look up and how carefully you prepare, this is a confusing field in which it appears that there is little unanimity of opinion. Pseudoscientific theories, ill-founded individuals giving opinions, and large words make it a conglomerate mass, with few integrating principles. Medical science asserts that there are really three basic reasons why reading problems occur. Medical study shows that children who have poor reading ability may be grouped as follows:

1. The child's difficulty may be due to developmental problems. These are physically immature children who may have epilepsy or unrecognized seizures, such as petit mal seizures, or they may have speech defects, hearing defects, or physical defects. They may be dull normals, and they may be dull normals from bright families who may appear very normal and very bright. Some avoid certain tasks and make intelligent comments that sway you. It is up to you to sort all these factors out and give an opinion, because there are children who can be medically evaluated and can be helped in their reading problems. They can be assisted by careful work and by helpfulness and by kindness and by just a lot of pushing gently and easily on your part.

2. We come across emotional and cultural factors. You are not likely to find that somebody who lives in a tenement or slum-type district and whose parents can hardly speak the English language is going to be an exceptional reader. They don't even know the spoken language, and to try to begin them on a written language is a real problem. Emotional and cultural factors really do play a part, which you have to understand and interpret for your students and parents.

3. The third category is the individual who is born with a specific learning defect. These are very few, but they do occur; and when they occur, they are a problem. They are not only a problem in reading, they are a problem to pick out. These individuals are called *dyslectics*.

Dyslexia is a syndrome that afflicts children who have a specific learning problem. It's like a child being born with a club foot or club arm. This child has a defect, and he's got to learn to use the abilities that are still available. Exercise and work and help are the things that enable a child to use a bad limb. In the same way, exercise and help and remedial reading are going to enable the dyslectics to learn to read. They have a specific learning disorder, but it may not be exclusive to reading. These children can be categorized by saying they have an hereditary family history of this disorder. Usually there is a prenatal problem or a birth difficulty in the mother. There is a minimal, although frequently recognizable, neurological deficit in these children. They are clumsy; their motor coordination is bad. They are emotionally labile. They are hyperactive. You can't get them to concentrate on anything. This is the characteristic problem of the dyslectic. There are many, many ways that teachers try to cure him. I'm sure that you probably will read or have read about the various ways that have been tried.

One of the big theories that has been put out concerns cerebral dominance. That is when a right-handed child is dominant in his left eye. This is said to confuse him or mix him up so that he can't get his words straight to say what he wants to say. He uses his right eye and his left hand or his left hand and his right eye; but anyway, he's crossed, and this confuses him. This theory isn't true. *There really is no medical basis for it.* Cerebral dominance does not enter into the picture of a poor reader or a dyslectic. He is a poor reader because he has a handicap, not because he uses one side of his brain for seeing and the other for throwing a ball or writing. Cerebral dominance doesn't make any difference for reading ability, but this is a powerful theory or cult.

There are studies that show mixed dominance is more common among poor readers than would be expected on a statistical basis, but when you take a group of excellent readers that are really high performers, you find the same percentage of crossed dominance in these people. This has been statistically proved again and again. Jerome Betman (1967) wrote a very worthwhile article, which appeared in the *Archives of Ophthalmology*. It really lays it out and gives references showing statistical documentation that, concerning mixed dominance and reading, there is no foundation for the belief at this time. I think it is important to recognize the name of Carl H. Delacato; he's brought this theory into prominence, and he should have known better. He has some really different ideas, and they are really not bad ideas, but unfortunately he has never published any statistical data on any of his items, so although he is a big man in the field, he's not well substantiated.

You've probably heard of the Delacato Theory—the reading theorist who ties the children's hands behind them, patches their eyes, and makes them crawl on the floor on one side, claiming to evoke primitive reflexes. He has children go on like this for months, and finally, I guess the child gets to the point where he gets so mad at the strictures that he gives up and learns to read. The advocates don't really have much statistical proof of this theory. Delacato has never published any valid statistics that substantiate his claim that this theory really does anything.

Returning to the dyslectic, a child who does have a specific learning defect, to identify and help this individual requires the educator to suspect the difficulty, the pediatrician and the neurologist to look at it, the school psychologist or speech pathologist to analyze the symptoms, and the remedial teacher to help cure it. You have a whole spectrum of problems, but I don't think that anybody else besides these people comes into the picture. The optometrist, nice fellow though he is, will go through a routine—an eye exercising bit; but exercises really do very little for these children except to give them a little more maturity in one of these categories, with the chance that they'll improve.

I had a very bad incident with a patient of mine, a brilliant girl of about 28 who had two children; one of the children was a girl of 5½ or 6, the other, a boy of 6½ or 7. The girl was brilliant, and at 5 or 5½ she could read moderately well. The boy was just a boy, and he could not. The mother got worried and took him to one of these paramedical personnel who charged her $150 for the examination and then told her that she was going to have to have remedial reading at the rate of three hours a day, three days a week, at $25 an hour for a minimum of three months. Being very wealthy she went for about a week of this. At this time she came to us asking for our opinion, and of course we recommended one of the remedial teachers in the public school systems, if anything. We told her that the attention span of a 6-year-old child was approximately seven minutes and to subject him to three hours three times a week was almost totally worthless. The remedial reading teacher found that the child was quite normal, that he read quite well for his age, and she dismissed him within a couple of weeks.

QUESTIONS AND ANSWERS

QUESTION: *I had a 17-year-old student last year who sat in the back of the room and never seemed to have any difficulty seeing the board, reading, or anything else. About three weeks ago he started complaining and sitting closer to the board. He claimed he could not read; he was even having trouble reading papers on his desk. After several days, I asked him what was the matter. He said, "Well, I can't see it." We moved him all the way up to the front, and he still claimed he couldn't see. I sent him in to the nurse, and she checked his eyes and said there wasn't anything wrong. I don't know whether he memorized the chart or not, but there wasn't anything wrong that she could find. He had 20/20 vision. He came back into the room and still complained that he couldn't see. The nurse called the parents. They took him to an optometrist who checked him and couldn't find anything wrong with the boy, although he complained he could not see. He holds the material up close to him and squints all the time. Is it possible there is something that I didn't pick up? Maybe it's just psychological.*

ANSWER: A lot of it can be psychological. Children can have emotional problems. Don't forget that children are under a tremendous amount of pressure to read, not only from the educators, but particularly from the parents. This psychological strain is apparent when you shove a 5½-year-old child into a morass and expect him to do things with which he is unfamiliar; this can cause him to get quite upset. Young children write letters backwards, and the mothers get concerned and call us up in the middle of the night to say that it's an acute emergency and that Johnny is writing his letters backwards. *Strephosymbolia* is one of the terms for this. It is a very nice term for people who like to throw terms around. This is something that is just part of a learning process. Most children beginning school have tremendous psychological problems to which they normally adjust if they are allowed to mature. I think it's not very worth while to have the child's eyes medically evaluated unless a distinct problem seems to exist as far as teacher, pediatrician, and parent are concerned. Writing letters upside down or backwards, unless continued for an extended period, does not in itself indicate visual difficulty.

QUESTION: *What is meant by the term orthoptics?*

ANSWER: Orthoptics is a way of exercising eyes that does profit some children who have a short sequence of these exercises. They are children whose eyes diverge or turn out whenever they attempt to focus on close work. If the problem is not critical—that is, if they can get their eyes normally aligned with a little extra effort—rather than by operating on them, orthoptics or eye exercises are valuable. These exercises basically are about as simple as you can get. Put a postage stamp on the end of a pen or pencil and have a child look at the fine print and bring it up to his nose, maintaining focus as long as he can. This exercise is just like weight lifting. What it does is to increase the strength of the muscles and allow the child a little more muscle reserve.

Eye exercises, aside from strengthening muscles, are almost valueless, except for one other case in which a child's eyes are out of alignment and you align him on a machine called an *orthoscope*. It is something like the machine used by motor vehicle departments. You look in and see a three-dimensional target. Children who have their eyes out of alignment don't see three dimensions, so you want to teach them to do so. If you can help them to learn to see the three dimensions by bringing these targets together, it can be helpful. In the exercises, the targets are moved in various ways. You joggle them back and forth in these machines so that the child gets the idea of what three dimensions are. After this training, surgery is performed on the eye. As soon as the child wakes up, he sees three dimensions. He knows what to look for, in other words, and he'll pick up a fixation; his eyes will be straight in alignment, and he'll hold a fixation.

QUESTION: *Can a person strengthen his eyes by reading up close? There is a theory that claims that people who adhere to this practice can improve their eyesight.*

ANSWER: This theory is a form of charletanism that has come into eye care. This question refers to the Bates Theory, which was popular in the 1920s and 1930s and was published by Aldous Huxley. Aldous Huxley was at the age where he needed bifocals, but he refused to wear them. He went to this fellow who was a cultist, even though he was an M.D. Bates felt that you could, by doing eye exercise, naturally strengthen your eyes. It's amazing what people can do. I have a couple of patients who refuse to wear glasses. They can see very fine print. They have to have just the right light, and they have to have it in just the right position, and they have to really squint. When you reach over and turn down the light, they've really had it. They throw up their arms: "Hey, I need a bright light to see that; I have to get out in the full sunlight." Usually I say, "How do you read at night," and they say, "Oh, I have another trick that I use. I take a pin and put it through a paper, and I look through the hole and I can see very well." You can do all sorts of tricks to get by, which essentially is what the Bates system did. It taught exercises that were valueless and tricks that temporarily helped. Basically they are not solving the problem. Under test conditions they still have the problem. This theory convinces them psychologically that they can do something that they can't, and secondly, it teaches them reading tricks. You can't train your eyes to see better, but you can teach yourself a lot of reading tricks. This is what the Bates Theory does.

QUESTION: *What are the limitations of the Snellen Chart? Some say it can be used to pick up just about any kind of visual defect that the student has.*

ANSWER: Actually the Snellen Chart is good for only one thing. It does not give you a diagnosis; it only gives you an indication of deviation from the visual norm. It does not indicate fusion or the degree of fusion, but indicates only visual acuity. In order to pick out fusion you must have an entirely different test.

The Snellen Chart doesn't pick up either nearsightedness or far-sightedness. The Snellen Chart tests visual acuity, and if you see 20/60, you can be nearsighted, farsighted, have astigmatism, or have an eye disease. All it does is simply define the standard method of grading what you see according to group norms or the norms of your peers. It doesn't have any bearing on what your refractive error or what your disease is. It's purely a chart that tells what you see. That's all you can interpret with the Snellen Chart. Now, when I have a child or an adult read a Snellen Chart, I can tell by the way he puts the letters to me whether he has an astigmatism or is farsighted or nearsighted. I'll watch him try to bring letters into focus if he is far-sighted, or he'll interpret an *F* as *H* if he has a large astigmatism; but these are tricks I know because I work with people with eye problems every day. The Snellen Chart is for nothing more than determining visual acuity. It doesn't diagnose anything.

QUESTION: *What if a person has one eye farsighted and the other eye nearsighted? Will he favor the eye that is least affected?*

ANSWER: People who have a minor amount of farsightedness usually look in the distance because they are not too impaired by the difficulty. Nearsightedness gives them more of a blur. They can compensate easier for farsightedness at distances. A person who is nearsighted will read easier up close. There is some tendency to switch the eye being used, depending on the situation. If a person has a substantial aberration, he is given glasses to correct both these errors, permitting him to see normally at both far and near distance.

QUESTION: *I have glasses to correct this problem, but I usually don't wear them because I find that when I take the glasses off my eyes start to cross. In other words, I can't wear them for a part of a day without being dependent for the rest of the day. Are there any problems that accompany this?*

ANSWER: It won't hurt you at all to go without them. Glasses are only meant for your convenience, and whether you correct a child that needs glasses for a farsightedness, nearsightedness, or astigmatic error, his error is not going to be detrimental to his eye if he keeps his eye glasses off. He's still going to have the same error. Not wearing glasses isn't going to cause it to progress or worsen. This is the problem we get in nearsightedness. The child comes in today, and he refuses to use his glasses until he gets to about age 12. Mother says, "Oh my God, if he'd only keep the glasses on, he wouldn't be getting so bad." But his error will progress with his development and not because he didn't wear the glasses.

I don't think it's necessary to insist that a youngster wear glasses as long as he is performing adequately, even though he has been told he should wear them. Glasses are a convenience to be able to see better. Unless there is some muscle imbalance, it isn't going to hurt the child's eyes one way or the other not to wear his glasses. He's still going to end up with the same error, eventually, that he would get whether he wears them or not.

There are certain exceptions to this, and these you must sort out. It is important to let the mother and the doctor determine the need. The child who has some sort of crossing or the child who has eyes that turn out, and these conditions are being corrected with glasses, are children who can get worse if they don't wear their glasses. So you have to ask the parent and the doctor who is treating him whether the glasses really have to be worn. Is the child doing any damage to his eyes by not wearing them? If it's a refractive error, farsightedness, nearsightedness, astigmatism, it won't make much difference. It's just a convenience for him to see, although by not wearing glasses he may miss some things in class.

QUESTION: *I know that diabetes affects vision, but what does this involve?*

ANSWER: Diabetes is a disease that affects the blood vessels on the eye and the sugar content in the eye itself, which fluctuates abnormally as it does throughout the body. Different levels of sugar in the eye change the refractive index or the bending of light entering the eye. It's interesting to see a diabetic who is well controlled and who then goes out of control. He can suddenly go from 20/20 down to 20/100. This is because the sugar content in his blood and ocular fluid has changed the refractive index in the eye and made him more near-sighted. During the following few days, when he adjusts back to normal and the blood sugar has also been adjusted, he comes right back, and his vision is 20/20 again. Blood vessels are affected by these changes, and they are more affected in people who have had diabetes for a period of years and who are what we call labile diabetics. These are people who go out of control for no apparent reason; they spike high blood sugars for no apparent reason. These are usually people who incur diabetes as juveniles. These are the ones who have most of the problems in later life with blood vessel disease and refraction problems. It's a long-term proposition; it doesn't usually occur in somebody that gets diabetes at the age of 40 or 50. It occurs in people who get diabetes at 16 or 17, and when they arrive at 60 or 70, they have had diabetes for years, with continual trouble over a period of years.

QUESTION: *I've heard people who suffer from migraine say that their vision is impaired by this condition. Is this true?*

ANSWER: There seem to be some visual problems, or at least temporal visual problems, associated with migraine headaches. There are two things that occur. First, there is a nervous discharge from the nervous system. The second thing that occurs is possibly a spasm of one of the major arteries going up into the brain. When this occurs you have a cut down in the blood supply. This is easy to plot; you can actually take somebody who has a migraine headache, and you can plot an area in their visual field. The visual field is what you see frontally and peripherally. These people will usually have an area of temporary blindness. It may be an entire half of the retina that has been partially shut out, although it usually is a quadrant of the retina, it occurs as a *scintillating scotoma*. To the patient, it looks like electric sparks. There are two problems: the nerve discharge and the spasm of the large artery, or one of the arteries, leading into the visual apparatus somewhere in the brain. We don't know exactly where. It's apparently somewhere in the visual track, and it cuts down the circulation to the degree that the person gets this blind spot or scotoma. It's a temporary and transient thing, and vision comes back very rapidly. Amazingly enough, migraine headaches occur in younger people. As you get older they get less and less frequent, but the visual scotoma get more frequent as you become older. You usually outgrow the headaches, but you still can get the scotoma's.

SPEECH PROBLEMS
IN
THE CLASSROOM

3

Theodore D. Hanley

*Dr. Theodore D. Hanley has been professor of speech
at the University of California at Santa Barbara since
1963. His education includes the B.A. from Santa
Barbara State College in 1940 and the M.A. and the
Ph.D. from the University of Iowa in 1942 and 1949,
respectively. For 3½ of the years between receiving his
master's degree and his doctorate, during World
War II, he was in the U.S. Navy. (He had had prior
maritime experience as a bellboy on the S.S. Malolo,
sailing from San Francisco to Honolulu in 1935.)*

*After earning his Ph.D., Dr. Hanley joined the faculty
at Purdue University as an assistant professor. He was at
Purdue from 1949 to 1963 and had reached the rank
of professor before moving to the University of
California.*

Coauthor, with Wayne Thurman, of the book
Developing Vocal Skills *(Holt, New York, 1970), Dr.
Hanley also coauthored, with R. Peters, a chapter, "The
Speech Laboratory," in the revised edition of Lee
Edward Travis's* Speech Pathology and Audiology
(Appleton-Century-Crofts, New York, 1971).

*Dr. Hanley is a Fellow of the American Speech and
Hearing Association and holds the Certificate of Clinical
Competence in Speech Pathology. In 1968 he was
elected to a two-year term as vice-president for
administration in ASHA.*

I propose to carry on with you a modified Socratic dialogue in which some things I say may stimulate you to ask questions, which in turn may lead me to tell you something useful. Thus we may deal with a wide variety of topics, unfettered by conventional classroom techniques.

THE NATURE AND PREVALENCE OF SPEECH DISORDERS

To begin with, let us consider the magnitude of our problem. What is the prevalence of speech disorders?

QUESTION: *Do you mean on the elementary or secondary level?*

ANSWER: Spanning elementary and secondary levels, taking them all together, what's the incidence, the prevalence of speech disorders?

QUESTION: *I'll say 10 percent, knowing that is too high. In the secondary, 5 percent?*

ANSWER: Across the whole grade range, your lower figure is more nearly correct; that is, it is correct, depending upon who makes the evaluation. My first main point is that a speech disorder is a disorder in the ear or the eye, or in both, of the listener. The 5 percent figure that I gave you was a good, solid statistic, provided in a wide survey of speech and hearing clinicians throughout the country. Remember, these are people whose job it is to work with speech and hearing problems, who are alert, attuned to communication problems. I can give you another statistic that is equally sound, equally valid, again depending upon the ear and eye of the observer. This is a statistic compiled by the U.S. Public Health Service. The PHS data collection was done by people who were conscientious and thorough, but they were not speech professionals. This survey revealed a speech-disorder incidence of .65 percent. There is a wide discrepancy in the data. As speech pathologists, we are constantly having to remind ourselves of the role of the listener and the role of the environment in making a determination as to whether or not a child, or an adult for that matter, is in fact someone with a speech disorder.

I have a definition, a guideline, for determining what is or is not a speech disorder. A speech disorder may be defined as that aspect of communication that either visually or auditorily calls attention to itself to the extent that there can occur some loss in communication, based on the listener's attention to *how* the communication took place rather than *what* was present in it. Someone has to make the evaluation.

You notice—this is parenthetical—I refer to the auditory or visual effect. We are becoming increasingly conscious of this latter aspect of communication. Why?

QUESTION: *Because of television?*

ANSWER: That isn't exactly what I had in mind, but it's relevant. What I did have in mind is a new syndrome with which parents are now having to deal. It is new only in the public consciousness of it and the emphasis given it in one of the professions. This emphasis and public consciousness are such that children are being referred for this particular syndrome in numbers that we can't even begin to cope with. What is the syndrome? Do you know?

QUESTION: *Is this involved with orthodontistry?*

ANSWER: Yes, ma'am. The syndrome is *tongue thrust*. This disturbance is so prevalent that estimates of incidence in the population as high as 45 to 55 percent have been made. Now those aren't good, solid figures; they are large-scale, top-of-the-head estimates that sometimes reach public print. At any rate, tongue thrust is a widely observed phenomenon these days—largely, I believe, because more children are seeing dentists more often. The failure of the incisor teeth to make the kind of approximation that is required for good biting is now a matter of great concern to literally thousands of parents. Parents descend, like flies to the honey, on the speech therapist because, seemingly, everyone else disavows the responsibility for tongue thrust. We have inherited tongue thrust to such an extent that one of my highly respected colleagues in private practice in Northern California has wiped out his entire practice except tongue thrust. He calls himself an "oral-deformity correctionist." Well, tongue thrust does manifest itself, and it is observable when it's carried to an extreme. You do have the child who appears to have a speech defect, based on the way he manipulates that useful organ that lies normally just behind the teeth. The abnormality isn't always a speech defect. If you turn your back on this child, you may be unable to detect any difference from normal communication, but when you look at him, he takes on the appearance of what people call a "lisper." Acoustically he can be a very good communicator, but he makes this face, and parents worry about it, teachers worry about it, and he winds up in a speech correctionist's office.

WHEN IS A SPEECH DEVIATION SIGNIFICANT?

Now to return to consideration of the evaluator of a speech disorder. A week ago today we had a cleanup outpatient-evaluation day in the Speech and Hearing Center. (We run outpatient days only one day a week, and we see, at most, four children a day. As you might suspect, our waiting list builds up.) We mobilized all our forces and tried to catch up with this growing body of people who needed to be heard or looked at. We had three staff members, all our graduate students, all our seniors, and two-thirds of our juniors rotating in and out of rooms doing outpatient evaluations on the nineteen children who came to see us.

Two of these individuals stick out in my mind. One was 19 years of age, the other was 12. Both were mongoloids, both of severely limited intellectual attainment and promise. Both had the capacity to communicate bodily needs and a little bit more. They could relate simple experiences; they could relate emotional states, albeit somewhat primitive ones. If lost, each was capable of reporting his or her home address. Both had severe speech problems.

The older of the two, a boy—or I suppose you can call him a man—had, in addition to his other problems, *macroglossia*, a tongue that was so large that it just couldn't fit inside the dental arch. It overlapped so that all his articulation was faulty. He didn't make a single consonant sound with precision. His lips were large and bulky. Approximation of them was difficult because his teeth were large too and his tongue was in the way. It was a difficult job to get a bilabial sound from him. Nonetheless he was, with effort, intelligible. All of the sounds were distorted, but all of them, in context, were sufficiently intelligible that he could communicate these basic things that I've outlined.

The girl, age 12, was considerably better in her vocal communication. Her language was more limited than the boy's. She had principally nouns and verbs, perhaps a few pronouns. But the function words (as opposed to content words), the articles, the prepositions, the conjunctions might just as well not have existed for her. However, in a kind of telegraphese, she was a communicator. On an absolute basis, on acoustical and physiological bases, these were speech-disordered persons. On a practical basis, however, I have a question. Do you have a question or do you have a conviction about the advice that I should have given these parents? One thing more needs to be added; both of these children, I felt, had the capacity to benefit—though somewhat limitedly—from work with a speech clinician. What should I have told the parents?

QUESTION: *What did the parents have in mind when they brought the children to you? Did they want you to diagnose exactly what the difficulties were, or did they want you to advise them as to what they should do with the children?*

ANSWER: The latter. Both wanted their children to realize their ultimate potential. Both of them had the interest of the child at heart. Both of them felt that communication was a part of the overall problem.

QUESTION: *What type of individuals would take the place of these two if you did not include them in a remedial program?*

ANSWER: People more normal in intelligence and with better promise or potential for eventual normal placement in normal employment.

QUESTION: *Since they are mongoloids the time spent on them, although you certainly can do something for them, would be better spent with someone else who would have to be displaced in order to make room for them.*

ANSWER: That is essentially what I said to the students who helped me staff these cases. These children have other needs that are greater than their communicative needs. Since we have more need, more demand, for speech and hearing services than we can satisfy, these were persons much better off if the parents were encouraged to do little simple things at home that would contribute not so much to their communication abilities as to a growth in their receptive capacities, which is an aspect of communication, too. They needed to be read to a little bit more, talked to a little bit more. Both sets of parents were warm, understanding people, but imagine yourself in an environment for twelve or nineteen years with someone who cannot make more than a very primitive response to the kinds of things you say to him. You will find yourself unknowingly, unconsciously, talking above his level to people who do understand. He does get left out of the conversation. It gets turned back to him from time to time. Someone remembers, "Well, we left George out for quite a while. Now let's say something about the puppy dog we saw today."

I suggested to my students and to the parents that these children would benefit from a greater emphasis in the home and in the school environment (as a matter of fact, both of these children were in a special-school situation) on language acquisition through the ear, rather than development of language skills through the mouth.

Can student aides help?

QUESTION: *Can't the graduate students, as part of their training, contribute to helping these children?*

ANSWER: They do. But you raise an important question that goes beyond the limitations of the academic. My profession is very zealous in guarding the welfare of the population at large. The official stand of the American Speech and Hearing Association is that no one who has not clinical certification may take on a patient for private practice. This means the masters degree plus one year, at least, of paid professional experience under the supervision of someone who has the certificate of clinical competence. This means that our students are prohibited, by our acceptance of this ethic, from taking on any kind of private practice. One parent of a child we evaluated recently, whom we had to put on a waiting list, said, "Well, don't you have a student who would like to earn a little money on the side? We don't have much, but we would pay for this service." I had to tell her that we can't let this happen.

QUESTION: *To get back to the mongoloids, how did the parents receive this advice?*

ANSWER: Both of them received it with relief. Conscience, or their neighbors, had told them that the children should be in speech therapy. To have a speech pathologist tell them that the greater need lay in areas where they themselves could contribute gave them, it seemed, good feelings about themselves and what they were doing and could do for their children.

Is an accent a speech defect?

QUESTION: *If one has students who do not really have speech defects but have a very heavy accent, should they be referred to a speech therapist? Some students who come from a foreign country or from another* part of this country have such a heavy accent that they cannot be understood without repeating themselves several times. After a year's time, if they still have this accent and people still have difficulty understanding them, should they be referred to a speech therapist? Could a speech therapist do anything even though it's not a speech defect?

ANSWER: The answer to the second part of the question is yes, indeed, they can. I wouldn't agree with you that it is not a speech defect, because what you describe is an interference with communication. I'm not quite sure of the answer to your first question; it would depend on where that person was going to wind up. We have an exchange student, let us say, from Nigeria, who does not communicate well. He has a good reading and writing command of English, yet he doesn't communicate well vocally, and he's going back to Nigeria next year. What's the gain if he's going to spend only another year here on campus? I don't think we're going to do that much for him, unless back in Nigeria his job will involve contact with English-speaking people and it's going to be important that he communicate well. You must, I think, settle each case on its merits. I've come to this institution from fifteen years in the Middle West—in Indiana to be specific—where we had a large influx of Southern Belles. Believe me, those Southern Belles clung to their southern dialects like life rafts! They were going back to the South. I would have been the last to separate them from what was sometimes substandard speech.

WHEN DOES A SPEECH DEFECT BEGIN?

QUESTION: At what stage in a child's language development should we become concerned about speech correction?

ANSWER: I'm glad you have returned us to the topic with which I intended to stay, which is a much more vigorous examination of what it is we look for in speech correction, and when we should start looking for it. We look fairly obviously at four attributes of speech communication. These are: articulation, the precision with which the individual forms the particular sounds, the phonemes of our language; voice, including pitch, loudness, and quality or timbre; rate, to include rhythm and fluency; and finally language itself. We've had children referred to us, as recently as last month, at age 2½ for defective r's and *s*'s. These sounds were defective; but, you see, the *r* and *s* develop normally at a much later age than 2½. It's considered by some of my colleagues to be normal to have a deviant *r* or *s* up to age 7. Sounds develop in children at pretty predictable rates. The vowel sounds come in early. The earliest of the consonant sounds are *k* and *g*, the back tongue sounds, the nasal *ng*, and *h*, which is formed in the voice box. There is then a rapid progression forward, and the bilabials come in next—*p*, *b*, and *m*. Next, the child develops the lingua alveolars *t*, *d*, and *n*, formed by the tongue making contact with the ridge behind the incisor teeth. At some later dates, not as predictable as those just listed, the labio dentals *f* and *v* come in, followed by the lingua dentals—the two *th* sounds, voiced and voiceless—and the postdental sibilants *s*, *z*, *sh*, and *zh*. The sounds *r*, *l*, *w*, and *wh* will trail along in the same period as the sibilants, the later period at 5½, 6½, 7 years of age. Complex coordinations of sounds, consonant clusters, can still be coming in as late as age 8 without being cause for worry. A final word about time sequence and articulation: the listing I've reeled off for you combines two kinds of data—sound emergence and sound correctness. The data tend to be parallel, but emergence obviously precedes correctness. When, then, do we begin to be concerned about a child's speech? When there is clear reason to suspect that this developmental sequence has been delayed, or when there is some discontinuity in it. We don't consult some abstruse formula in making a decision of this nature. Rather, we inquire into many aspects of a child's development and behavior—more on this later—before deciding whether or not he is a candidate for remedial services.

DISORDERS OF VOICE

Let me now move on to another quite different topic: the voice. The voice, in my view, is the most overlooked of the communications attributes. Voice disorders get swept under rugs, not only by schoolteachers who don't detect them, but by speech clinicians who, if they do detect them, tend to turn a tin ear to them because they are not quite sure what to do about them. We don't do as well teaching about voice problems as we do teaching about articulation problems, which are often mechanical. You may be able to do a lot by teaching the child to place the tongue and the lips in the right position, but to teach him to manipulate his voice so that it's no longer harsh or hoarse is a much more difficult task. One clinician of my acquaintance, worried about this sweeping-under-rugs state of affairs, conducted a survey in one of the counties in Southern California and detected an incidence of uncorrected voice problems of 9.1 percent in a sample of 375 children drawn from grades one through twelve. This was a random kind of sampling of children who had not been referred for evaluation; 9.1 percent had voices that lacked the clarity, the purity, to allow good communication. What's the source of these bad voices?

QUESTION: *Bad examples in the home?*

ANSWER: Sometimes. Not very often. Once in a while you find a child imitating a parent or some loved one who has a strange voice quality.

QUESTION: *TV?*

ANSWER: Rarely. I think Andy Devine, for whom I had the greatest affection and respect, was a very bad speech model, but I doubt that many children imitated him. No, it's not that. You people work in the schools. What causes these bad voices? Playgrounds!

QUESTION: *They strain the children's voices?*

ANSWER: Yes, ma'am, vocal abuse. Playgrounds in big cities, in particular, are offenders. Not only are there the sounds of the other children to rise above in the excitement of the kickball game, but there is the noise of trucks passing by outside the school ground too. In addition to these environmental sources of vocal strain, there are internal sources as well. Emotional tensions are revealed in muscular tensions, not infrequently in the vocal mechanism. You observe the effects of these tensions in your children and, probably, in your adult acquaintances as well. The incidence of vocal nodules (these are the growths, the corns, that develop on the vocal cords of people who abuse their voices) is far greater than is generally known. Because these children don't get referred to laryngologists, often they don't get referred to a speech pathologist. The parent hears the child, is aware of a slight hoarseness, thinks back to his own childhood, and says, "Well I sounded like that; he'll grow out of it." Of course, many children will. You see, the best thing that can happen to a vocal nodule is for a person to develop good vocal habits. If a child moves out of the age of excitement and shouting into a calmer environment and develops a more placid approach to life, then his vocal habits may improve as well, and the vocal nodule may simply dissipate itself.

QUESTION: *Can these nodules be removed surgically?*

ANSWER: Surely.

QUESTION: *Won't they come back?*

ANSWER: As you suggest, within six months, unless the bad habit is corrected, the nodule is right back in place. A parent of one of our graduate students routinely every six months has his vocal cords surgically stripped of the growths on them.

QUESTION: *Might not the person return to normalcy—whatever normalcy is—if, let's say, he lived in a big city all his life.*

ANSWER: It's my belief that even these stubborn cases are capable of being worked with. Techniques are being developed. I know of one private-practice clinic in Monterey, California, where experimental work is being done on vocal nodules that I believe holds much promise for the future. It is dealing with the heart of the problem, not with the periphery. It is dealing with tensions that lead to nodules. It is bringing the client to an appreciation of the things that bring about the vocal strain, that bring about the abnormal pitch level or the abrupt attack, the *coup de glotte* (that means that you bring the cords together hard). We males vibrate our vocal cords 130 times per second in normal conversation. Now if we do that at ten decibels above our average communication level, we're making the vocal cords come together with an impact that's very abrasive. They are beating each other like infuriated middleweights. If the individual can realize what is making him treat his cords in this fashion, if we can bring about an intellectual recognition of the stresses and torments of his daily life and the potential effects on voice, it is possible to reduce the tensions and improve the voice. What these clinicians I have mentioned are doing, actually, is to move their clients through a graded series of imagined situations and talk as though they were in each of the situations. This is a desensitization or conditioning process, going from the placid through degrees of the stressful.

Let me remind you, however, taking you back to children on the playground, that not all the stresses are psychological. Some are simply acoustical. In the latter case, you attempt to change the environment or the individual's behavior in it. You make clear to the person attempting to communicate in a boiler works that either he must get closer to the person he's talking to, must learn to write to him, or must communicate by sign language. He must adopt some means of breaking up his pattern of shouting. In summary, there are acoustical, psychological, and complex sources of vocal abuse. The wise clinician tracks down the sources and tries to eliminate them. Sometimes this is enough to make surgical intervention unnecessary.

QUESTION: *What can you tell us about the incidence of nodules in teachers who consistently have to raise their voice for class?*

ANSWER: I have no statistics, but I think it would be an interesting study. "Clergyman's sore throat," with reference to pulpit speaking, was a common term before the advent of the microphones and public address systems.

QUESTION: *Does this problem of nodules account for the differences in pitch? I assume, for example, that a man's voice probably is deeper early in the morning than it is later in the day.*

ANSWER: Misuse of the voice in terms of pitch often can result in nodules. It brings about a different point of impact. You can bring on nodules that way. But in specific response to your question, the change of pitch in a man's voice has a great deal to do with the way he lives. If he awakens rested in the morning after a good night's sleep, he is relaxed. His vocal musculature is relaxed and he tends to have a considerably deeper voice. As he goes through the day, he gets tired, and the tensions build up generally and in the vocal mechanism. It is tenseness that brings about a change in pitch. The vocal cords get stretched further—not apart, but longer. As they grow longer they grow more tense and, just as in a stretched violin string, the pitch goes up. By the end of the day the man may be communicating at three or four semitones above the level at which he communicated in the morning; then he takes the good dry martini and all is well. He returns to a deep masculine voice for the rest of the evening.

QUESTION: *Are you familiar with the W——— elementary school?*

ANSWER: I've driven past.

QUESTION: *Would you say that this would make a good statistical study— a research project to find out how many nodules the staff and the student body have?*

ANSWER: We had a voice problem referred to us from that school, as a matter of fact. We worked with the individual for a long time.

QUESTION: *You cannot speak in a normal tone inside or outside of the school because of the highway.*

ANSWER: W—— is located in a noisy environment, and it would be interesting to discover whether there are more strained voices there than in other schools.

QUESTION: *Is voice breaking a speech problem? I'm referring to cases where a person is talking and all of a sudden there is just no sound.*

ANSWER: Well, in the case of an adolescent it isn't a speech problem. This is a normal maturational effect. In the case of an adult it is a problem and it needs to be looked at, first of all, I should think, by a laryngologist. If someone comes to me with this problem, I'm going to send him back to a physician and get a medical opinion before I look at him again.

QUESTION: *You've said that voice disorders are not detected very well. What do you do about detecting these disorders? How do you know that a junior-high youngster, or even a person of early high-school age, is not showing simply delayed puberty?*

ANSWER: What about referral? You reach an understanding with your speech therapist. You say, "I've got the word that we may be over-looking some problems. May I send these people to you for evaluation?" I don't know a speech clinician anywhere who will turn down a request to evaluate. Usually the problem is the reverse: the speech therapist worries that the teacher in the classroom is not detecting enough of the problems.

QUESTION: *How does one detect these problems? I sit in a classroom with my students, and I don't notice voice problems, yet I am sure there are some.*

ANSWER: One way is occasionally to listen to *how* the child sounds rather than to *what* he says. Your primary purpose in the classroom obviously is to make sure that the child gets the meat of what you have to present. He must, in recitation, demonstrate some acquisition of information. Nonetheless, it's possible every now and again to tune out the meaning for a moment and just listen to the sounds the student is emitting. Some people have a sensitivity that others do not—a capacity to attend, without conscious awareness, to content and quality at the same time, a capacity to evaluate departures from the norm. Those who do not have this capacity may have perfectly normal hearing acuity; they may be perfectly intelligent people. My wife is among these. She wouldn't detect a speech disorder if it were ringed by neon. She is keen and alert to all kinds of things about the way people behave, but she is not alert to the way they sound. When I point out to her that some prominent individual in politics or somewhere else in the public eye has no more *r* than a wabbit, she is invariably surprised.

WHEN SHOULD SPEECH CORRECTION BEGIN?

QUESTION: *You mentioned the fact that some sounds are still being developed as late as age 8. At what age would you begin speech correction?*

ANSWER: This is a battle that I have with some of my colleagues. Some of them want to go strictly by the book and by the developmental norms. I temper those developmental norms with certain other considerations. If I find a child who is becoming tense and concerned and a parent who is tense and concerned—a parent who will not accept my statement that this child is developing normally—then I will take him on, whether he needs it or not, to get him out from under the gun of the demanding mother. I think this is important. If the parent feels someone else is taking on this load and she doesn't have to be responsible any more and her social status will not be impaired, then the child is going to relax a little bit, and maybe he won't develop even worse symptoms than he has now. In the absence of a consideration such as this, I can offer some rough guidelines that we follow in the Speech and Hearing Center. We may take on a child who has no intelligible speech (but gives evidence of ability to learn) as early as 2½ to 3 years. With articulation problems we'll usually go by developmental norms, basing our final decision on a best guess as to whether the child will have difficulty when he enters school. Many children in the age range of 3 to 5 years are enrolled in our remedial program.

DETECTION OF DISORDERS

Earlier, to an honest and intelligent question, I am afraid I gave a pretty shabby, incomplete answer, and I wish to make amends. A lady asked me, in essence, "How do you know who is a speech defective?" My response was something to the effect, "When in doubt, consult the speech clinician in the school." Well, that's an answer of sorts, and if you have serious doubts, I think that is what you ought to do. However, I also think that one of the functions my colleagues and I serve in coming to you in this seminar-colloquium is to tell you something about how you *do* identify someone whose speech deviates sufficiently from the norm that treatment might be suggested.

Parameters of sound

I recall that I touched lightly on speech in terms of its acoustical parameters. I think now I should like to retrace some of this ground and tell you what you can look for, what you can expect, and what might alert you to speech problems. It's my understanding that most of you are primarily interested in the secondary-school level. I'll talk principally about that level, for a while at least.

PITCH   One of the principal parameters of sound and of speech is pitch. We speak in high tones and in low tones, and if we wish to maintain listener interest in what we are saying, we move from high to low and low to high, rather than remaining always on one note. That one note just might be the best note that we produce, but it gets a little dull after a while. In evaluating the speech, then, of the young ladies and men in the secondary school, one of the things that you listen for and to is pitch. With the boys this can be a frustrating experience, because between the approximate ages of 12 and 18 boys' voices will change, and if you catch a boy in midpuberty, it's going to be difficult for you to decide just what his pitch level is. I think you are in a poor position with a boy who is undergoing voice breaks to decide whether he needs professional help or not. But if you detect someone who shows other indications of having passed through puberty yet whose voice still seems different from the tone that you expect of a person of his sex, age, and size, it might be well for you to listen more carefully to him to decide how far he deviates from normal sound. Cases are not unusual of the persistence of the choir-boy tone, particularly noted among boy sopranos who have been encouraged by their choir directors and their parents to retain that voice for as long as possible. Some are able to carry it through puberty. The normal voice change may take place physiologically—cords thickening and lengthening—but acoustically it does not. This is fine for the choir, but it serves the boy no good purpose when it comes to communicating with his peers and with adults, who may evaluate him as effeminate or at least "different." So the persistence of high vocal pitch in a boy who has otherwise matured is something about which one should be concerned.

Although it is less common now than it was ten years ago, at about this age some of the young ladies take on a pitch level for purposes only they could explain. It has something to do, I think, with the attractiveness of the "sultry" female voice. The girl who adopts this sultry voice runs a fairly grave risk. She lowers her pitch level, which has one immediate effect and one possible long-term effect. The immediate effect is to reduce rather considerably her capacity to inflect, because typically the female phonates habitually at a pitch level about one-fifth of the way up her total pitch range. Now if our sultry voice moves down from that habitual pitch level, which is already fairly low with respect to the lowest tone she can sustain, then the possibility for inflecting downward is markedly curtailed. Monotony of tone is an almost inevitable result. The long-term effect is less predictable, but I suggested earlier that phonating on an inappropriate pitch level can result in damage to the vocal-cord structure, leading eventually to a medical pathology.

LOUDNESS Moving through the parameters of sound, let's take up loudness, or intensity. There are, of course, two extremes—too loud or too soft—in addition to the big middle ground where the communication is adequate. Tendencies toward either extreme may reflect deficiencies in the hearing sense. One type of hearing loss leads the person to hear himself louder than others hear him, hence his voice becomes very soft. The other type reduces his capacity for self-hearing. Trying to satisfy his need to maintain a tone that is understandable to him, he speaks too loudly. Suspected hearing losses surely need to be referred for expert evaluation. I think there are also emotional and environmental causes for voices that are too loud or too soft. An individual who has had to fight all through life to get a word in edgewise in a family of twelve often develops a voice that is strong, strident, too large for the needs of the classroom. The girl from the South, who has been told almost from the day she first puts on her pinafore that young ladies don't shout, may develop the mousy tone that doesn't get beyond the first row in your classroom. These, fortunately, are speech disorders that are pretty readily amenable to correction by simple tactics on the part of the speech clinician. I think probably they are amenable to correction by a quiet suggestion from the classroom teacher. Unless they persist after tactful suggestion, I don't think you need bring them to the attention of the speech therapist. If, however, they do persist, it is time to call in the expert, the one who gets paid for doing the job of correcting the disorder.

QUALITY The next of the parameters of sound, and one that I spend more time on than the others, is that parameter called *quality*. It is determined acoustically by the spectrum of the sound, by the wave form. It is determined physiologically in large part by the relative contributions of segments of the vocal cord that contribute to the total tone. Our cords vibrate in wholes—the complete length of them—back and forth. They also vibrate in halves, in quarters, in fifths, and so on. Each of these small vibrating segments contributes something to the total tone. Then, as the complex tone winds its way upward through the larynx, the pharynx, the mouth, and the nose, these tone components are resonated by the cavities through which they pass. Some components take on added relative strength; others are damped, reduced in total effect. Thus sounds are produced that are discriminable on two different bases: vowel quality and voice quality. Vowel quality allows us to discriminate the $\bar{e}\bar{e}$ from the $\bar{o}\bar{o}$, for example, based entirely upon the quality of the tone. Voice quality is the factor in voice that gives a voice uniqueness, that provides one with a vocal fingerprint. You recognize your friend's voice over the telephone without nominal identification. The voice is familiar to you, and it is familiar to you largely on the basis of voice quality—that particular timbre that is your friend, determined by his vocal structure. Specifically it is determined by the dimensions and vibrating characteristics of the cords and by the size and shape of the resonating cavities and by the way these things interact.

Now this quality for most of us is "normal." There isn't any other term that I know that fits it. It is just a tone that is uniquely us. It is clear, understandable, and inoffensive. But for a few people—and this may be, as I suggested earlier, as high as 9 percent of the children in the public schools—this quality is unpleasant for one of a variety of reasons. It may be nasal, harsh, thin, hoarse, strident, or breathy. It may be even those things that the older voice scientist referred to as guttural or pectoral. These are qualities that are not so pleasant, and they should clearly be dealt with by a specialist. There is no cookbook recipe for a voice-quality deviation. If you detect chronic hoarseness in the speech of a child, you should make sure that a referral is made. Doubtless the school nurse or speech clinician will make further referral to a laryngologist, or at least to the family physician.

Articulation disorders

By the time children reach secondary school, they have aged beyond the upper limit of sound-development norms. All of the sounds are in and ought to be clear, precise, well articulated. You should listen for sounds that are not.

Certain of the sounds are much more likely than others to be mis-articulated, partly because they are more difficult to hear, but more importantly, I think, because they are physiologically more complex. They require finer adjustments on the part of the speech mechanism. You need particularly to be alert to *s* and its voiced correlative *z*. This pair is the greatest offender of all. Errors involving *s* and *z* can persist beyond first and second grades on into high school and beyond. We get *s* and *z* problems in our center. We have two students majoring in our department who have *s* sounds that need a good deal of attention before we are ready to release them to work on the same offending sounds in children. The manners in which *s* and *z* can go astray are many and varied, because the manners in which they are produced normally are many and varied. Test it for yourself. Where do you put your tongue when you make an *s* sound— behind the upper teeth or the lower teeth? I make mine with tongue tip behind the lower teeth, but this isn't the right way. There isn't a single right way. There are just a great many wrong ways. If the *s* is made well, it is made with the tongue grooved somewhat; the better the groove, the better the sound, because the groove channels the air stream against the cutting edge of the incisor teeth. There are children who can't groove. They grow up to be adults and they can't groove, and some lingual compensation is made. I think it may be done by a tongue humping, which, although this doesn't concentrate the air stream in the middle as much as we like, at least concentrates the stream somewhat before it hits the incisor teeth. Now the sounds can be made (defectively) by an interdental tongue protrusion and we get an actual *th* for *s* substitution. This is common. The *s* can be mismade with a firm blockage by the tip of the tongue against one of the tooth ridges, with the air stream dividing around the obstacle, and we have the typical lateral *s*. Once heard and identified, this misarticulation is not easily forgotten. Now what is detectable in the *s* is equally present in the *z* sound, but it is masked somewhat because there is a vocal-cord carrier tone that tends to make the misarticulated sound not quite so readily apparent.

Other articulation problems likely to be found in a young adult and an adult population are *r*, where there is something not exactly like but resembling a *w* substitution, and *l*, where the substitution is very similar to that for *r*'s: something resembling a *w*, sometimes even more like the vowel sound *o*. These four are the most frequently deviant sounds. *Sh* and *zh* sometimes are defective in adults, and it is possible to find an adult who has a persistence of almost infantile consonant substitution. This is a person whose speech is replete with substitutions of one or two of the plosive consonant sounds, or almost any consonant. In my experience *t* is the most frequently used of these substitutions. Someone who uses a *t* wherever there is any consonant provides the listener with an interesting exercise in message decoding.

If you as teachers detect any of the errors I have been describing, which to any extent would also be detected by the lay individual, I believe you should privately point out the error to the student and give him the opportunity to seek remediation. We had two cases in point within the last three weeks in the Speech and Hearing Center. One was a young man, a junior, with a lateral *s*. When he discovered that what was involved was two clinical sessions a week that would probably last well beyond the current quarter and into at least the first quarter of his senior year, he decided that he wasn't too unhappy with that lateral *s* after all, and he departed. That was his judgment, and that was his right. I don't know whether some time in the future the absence of a good *s* sound is going to cost him a job or a promotion or a date. Presumably he weighed the possible consequences before deciding to forego articulation therapy.

The other illustrative case was a young lady, a real charmer, whose linguistic background is French. French was spoken habitually in her home. (It was French, incidentally, from a French-speaking canton of Switzerland. To my ear it was a French-American that may have been contaminated with German, for she had an *r* that was neither French nor German but something in between.) I had the belief that her dialect, although readily detectible, gave her speech a kind of piquancy that was an economic and social asset. It would never cost her a job or a date; it might, in fact, enhance her status in these regards. I encouraged her to go away and forget about speech correction, and she was glad to do this.

Disorders of rate

The last of the vocal attributes that can show deviation from the norm, if I've counted correctly, is the attribute of time. Like the other attributes, there can be too much of it or too little of it: a verbal flow that is sluggish or millrace fast. Moreover, there can be a rate that is between these extremes and still unsatisfactory. A person whose overall utterance in words per minute may be right in the middle of normative values can still be time defective to the point of unintelligibility through the use of short staccato phrases, followed by long pauses.

STUTTERING   A special case in this time domain is the case of the stutterer. Whether or not it is appropriate to lump stutterer in the time category,
I don't really care; you have to lump him somewhere. He is the individual who
has one or both of these characteristics in his speech: either he blocks completely, unable to emit the sound that he'd been saving up, or he buh-buh-
bounces his way through problem sounds and words. In either case, he is unhappy about this way of speaking, and his listener tends to be uncomfortable
too. Some of my colleagues send stutterers out on what are called "situations," in which they go into candy stores and ask for monkey wrenches or to
hair-dressing parlors and ask for life preservers. The attempt here is to prove
to the stutterer that he can say something utterly ridiculous, stutter his way
through it, and nobody will be distressed about it. I think this effort is
doomed to failure. Listeners do not ignore such aberrant behavior. They
laugh at the stutterer, or they squirm. We all are uncomfortable when we
see people who are under tension, regardless of the source of tension.
Stuttering is a tension phenomenon. The classroom teacher, with some
exceptions, tends to deal with a stutterer in one of two ways: by pretend-
ing he isn't there or by oversolicitude. Once the teacher learns the trouble
the youngster has in getting out the simplest kind of utterance, she may
from that point on request of him written communication and simply not
ever call on him, even when he wants to be heard. This I think is a
mistake. If the child shows the least desire to be heard, then even if it
takes a little sweating through, you may count his recitation as your contribution to his eventual ability to live with a disorder that he may never
entirely conquer. On the other hand, the teacher, in her eagerness to provide the child with opportunities to overcome his handicap, may call on
him with greater-than-normal frequency, and this won't do him much
good either. He is constantly faced with the threat that, "She's about to
call on me." Even the normal speaker isn't at his best under this condition.
The sensitive teacher takes the realistic middle ground, first talking
privately with the stutterer. She says, "I recognize that you have difficulty,
that sometimes words don't come out easily. What position do you think
I ought to take about calling on you?" Most stutterers will suggest the
middle ground. They will say, "I'd like to be called on from time to time,
but I'd like it to be when I'm ready." Well, that's fair enough.

QUESTION: *Stuttering is more psychological than physiological?*

ANSWER: That's our current belief. Research in such areas as endocri-
nology, electroencephalography, genetics, and the like, has never
turned up a common factor characteristic of all or even a substantial

minority of stutterers. I believe that not nearly all the necessary research has been performed. Some of the research tools haven't been perfected. If there is a physiological element, I think it does take something environmental to trigger the behavior.

QUESTION: *Am I correct in assuming that you should not feed words to stutterers?*

ANSWER: Yes indeed.

Organic disorders

QUESTION: *What about certain rare instances—for example, where the child had some brain damage that did not affect his mental faculty but affected his speech? Or instances where there had been blood clots, perhaps, as a stroke, and the person just can't seem to grasp the words.*

ANSWER: We have passed over the organics entirely. You are speaking about someone who is dysphasic, which is quite rare among young people. I've also left out cerebral palsy. With this disorder, the child sometimes can work right along with the normal child, straight on through school. But he has a problem. He needs help. He ought to be getting it. The cleft palate is another organic speech disorder. The unrepaired cleft is extremely rare today; early surgery is the rule rather than the exception. However, not all palatal surgery is successful. Sometimes there is not enough tissue for the plastic surgeon to suture together, so the cleft may be repaired for visual inspection, but the soft palate remains nonfunctional. The child no longer is likely to push gruel out through the nostrils, but there isn't enough tissue in the back of the mouth to close off the nasal passages on the nonnasal sounds. This condition may be permanent unless one of two things is done. One additional piece of surgery may be performed. It involves lifting a flap from the posterior pharyngeal wall—from the back of the throat—and attaching it to the abnormally short, inadequate soft palate. With this operation, near-normal function of the soft palate can result, and speech may be improved a great deal. The other answer to the individual for whom early surgery was unsuccessful is one type of prosthesis, called an *obturator*. This is a piece of equipment provided by a dental specialist, a prosthodontist. It consists of an extension off the back edge of a dental plate that protrudes back into the oropharynx. Around this speech bulb, the lateral and posterior walls of the nasopharynx can provide a fairly effective closure and markedly reduce nasal emission of sound. These organic problems are somewhat rare in the classroom, and I chose not to emphasize them, but certainly you should be prepared to meet them from time to time.

QUESTION: *The dysphasics you mentioned earlier—can anything be done for them?*

ANSWER: Yes, we work with stroke patients. There is a rehabilitation center in the hospital where a large part of their patient population is stroke patients. We provide clinical services there, working with language development. It can be a tedious process. They do not regain all the language proficiency they had earlier, but they can make progress. The rehabilitation process may involve an elaboration of the methods that one may use in teaching reading to a child, especially remedial reading to a child who is severely retarded in reading. An attempt is made to relate motor activity, the tactile sense (as in the Montessori use of sandpaper letters), and of course the visual and auditory senses as stimuli for the reacquisition of language.

QUESTION: *I had a child last year who talked as though she had a hot potato in her mouth. The therapist could find no reason for it, but there was something wrong.*

ANSWER: Well, cerebral palsy sometimes reveals itself in this way. The speech therapist must remind herself every now and again that she sees the child in a very restricted environment. Often the child may respond quite adequately to the stimuli she provides under controlled conditions, but it may be another story when the communication situation is normal and unstructured. In the case you cite, it is possible that the child, under the pressure of talking to the "speech teacher," did speak normally, or almost so. It is in the competitive speech situation that the speech starts to fall apart. There also could be other organic or functional causes for the mush-mouth delivery. This child probably should have been given another referral.

HELPING
THE CHILD
WHO STUTTERS

4

John C. Snidecor

*Dr. John C. Snidecor founded the University of
California Speech and Hearing Center in 1940. His
education includes the A.B. from the University of
California at Berkeley, a general secondary credential
from that school, and the M.A. and Ph.D. from the
University of Iowa. Shortly after he came to the
University of California at Santa Barbara, he was asked
to go to Washington, D.C., where he worked for the
National Academy of Sciences and the Psychological
Corporation. Later he served in the Navy and, at the
end of World War II, was head of navy curriculum.*

Dr. Snidecor's most recent publication is the book
Speech Rehabilitation of the Laryngectomized *(Charles
C Thomas, Springfield, Ill., 1968). He is also the
author of a chapter in the revised edition of Lee
Edward Travis's* Speech Pathology and Audiology
*(Appleton-Century-Crofts, New York, 1971). He was
associated early with both Travis and Wendell Johnson
in studies concerned with stuttering.*

*Dr. Snidecor is a Fellow of the American Speech and
Hearing Association, a member of the American
Psychological Association, and a certified psychologist
in the state of California. He is listed in* American Men
of Science *and* Who's Who in America. *Research
reports include five papers before international
congresses. Dr. Snidecor reports that such travel is
subsidized and is the least expensive and most interesting
way of seeing the world.*

In this chapter I shall discuss, in an informal way, the problem of stuttering, which is most surely a problem related to the difficulty of learning to communicate. First of all, however, I must talk about the nature of a speech defect, which varies from person to person and from one socioeconomic-cultural milieu to another. Second, I shall emphasize those psychogenetic aspects of comunication with which you, as teachers and counselors, can assist. Teamwork is the key to the diagnosis and treatment of many learning problems, and not the least of these are those speech problems that, due to their organic or psychological origin, demand the cooperation of several specialists. Finally, I shall allow ample time for questions.

THE NATURE OF A SPEECH DEFECT

Speech defects obviously have to do with abnormalities in voice, articulation, rhythm, note, pitch, and such complex attributes as pronunciation. However, one doesn't really have a speech defect—and this is important—unless it is bothersome to the person who has it, to his audience, or to both. In other words, speech defects are relative to the speaker, the listener, and the society in which the speaker moves. In England, boys are sent to the public schools, which are really private rather than public, so that they may develop the proper cosmopolitan, South-of-England dialect, which will open more doors of opportunity than will a dialect from any other region. In the American Midwest it is, on the other hand, not considered good form to be too precise in grammar or pronunciation. For example, "he don't" is grammatically incorrect and just incorrect enough to prove that one is not the fussy intellectual type. In brief, in some societies if you don't have the correct dialect, you may not really "belong." Generally speaking, speech defects are relatively common in a so-called civilized society, but then I must add that whereas a touch of cleft-palate speech would be acceptable in a university, in the Southern hill country it would, *ipso facto*, be thought to be related to some degree of mental deficiency.

STUTTERING

Today I shall limit my presentation to the problem of stuttering. Although I normally deal with this subject in a graduate seminar that lasts a full quarter, with a mature and motivated audience, such as this one, some important answers about stuttering can be given rather briefly, yet with due concern for the facts as we know them.

Psychological factors

Is stuttering psychological? I am sure most of you would quickly answer, "Yes," and you would be largely correct, but you would have given me an almost useless affirmation of a senseless question. If you have a belly-ache and go to see a physician and he tells you that you have a "physiological" problem, you ask questions or you change your physician. Similarly, when you say that a problem is psychological, you have said nothing. There is such an interplay between that which is called psychic and that which is called physiological that, with humans at least, there will be a component of one within the other whether the basic operations are "good" or "bad." Sometimes the relationships are etiological, that is, causative, and other times merely concommitant. The blood chemistry of a fearful person—perhaps he is a stutterer—at three o'clock in the afternoon may have more sugar and perhaps more calcium than is normal. The simple conclusion is that these blood components cause stuttering or other kinds of fearful reaction. The wise research worker, however, gathers some stutterers together and asks them to come to the laboratory at seven o'clock each morning and at three o'clock each afternoon for a week, and he finds that only in the afternoon is there found anomalous serological data. In this case, he concludes that psychological stress may cause the physiological change. However, might the physiological change cause more stress? Yes, indeed. It is commonplace for physiological stress to be related to psychological problems of all orders.

The male, if he is to stutter, will likely begin stuttering when he is very young, sometime shortly after he begins to talk or when talk becomes especially important to him or to his parents or to both. Little girls almost never stutter, and now is a good time to point out that the female talks earlier, better, more often, and longer than does the male. Only at very high levels of verbal expression does the male equal, and at times excel, the female.

When and how does the stuttering start? As I have said, it begins early, at 3 or 4 years of age, and sometimes in the following manner. Mamma brings Johnny to the Speech and Hearing Center so I can hear him stutter. She says, "Can't you hear him stutter?" I reply that I don't hear him stutter—not, at least, in my office or in the clinic playroom. The mother tells me he talks just the same at home, and she looks at me as though I did not know a stutterer when I heard one—and I have been hearing both real and imagined stutters for well over thirty years. In ten days or so I receive a phone call from a friend who directs a speech and hearing center in another university. He wants information from me about Johnny Jones and his parents; they have an appointment to see him about a problem of stuttering. My friend will tell Mrs. Jones that Johnny doesn't stutter. Then, perhaps three or four clinicians later, Mrs. Jones will find an expert who will agree that her son stutters. This clinician will be either ignorant or a rascal, or perhaps Johnny really has begun to stutter. Johnny probably is not a stutterer. He is a normal male child, and he repeats all of words or part of words; he distorts the sounds in words; he has blank spots when he gets excited and can't say anything at all. If he is left alone and listened to and given time to gradually, very gradually, correct himself, he will develop satisfactory fluency.

Let's take another example with which you may be more familiar. Children are often called "feeding problems." Aunt Mary, grandmother, etc., are told that little Audrey is a feeding problem or a "fussy eater." Given enough of this wonderful attention, little Audrey becomes a fussy eater and uses her gift for attention of a "good" kind; at other times she uses it as a weapon. I know a young woman who was so labeled and, largely on an early diet of bacon and milk, grew into a tall, strong person who, with five feet and eleven inches of height, despaired of finding a husband until a tall, handsome Swede, who appreciated beautiful things in big packages, came along and asked the forever question. Need I remind you that children will eat almost anything if let alone and allowed to do so.

It was the late Wendell Johnson who called this theory of cause the *diagnosogenic* or *semantogenic* theory. There is much of value here and, I believe, more than Johnson actually saw. I propose—and I wish some of you would study this—that those who label people, easily and categorically, are themselves suffering at least minor illnesses. My neighbor down the street calls his next-door neighbor a "goddamn crank." Now his neighbor is nothing of the sort, for he is neat and clean, his house is well ordered, and he minds his own business in a pleasant sort of way. The first neighbor heard that the second neighbor has told a third neighbor that he wished the first neighbor would mow his lawn now and then. As a matter of fact, we all wish he would. Who is having trouble in the social order? Well it's not the man who has things under control. Those who glibly label those who disagree with them as "fascists," "communists," etc., have more than a minor disease. And so it is with those who are unduly perfectionistic, confined, and fussy, who label children as stutterers or as thieves (when they took one orange from the tree).

Now this theory of mine, so far as I know, is new, and I believe it is worthy of study. If you are a Ph.D. candidate, and I know some of you are, you might care to devise a plan to prove my fancy right or wrong.

Organic factors

Now and then one comes across a clear-cut case of stuttering caused, in large part, by birth or other early injury. For example, stuttering may be an overlay on some organic disability, such as cerebral palsy, or perhaps it may exist with the organic disorder but be unrelated to it. I am reminded of a 9-year-old boy who came to see me in a mental hygiene clinic setting. He stuttered rather badly, and his parents were very concerned, so much concerned that one of them drove him a total of two hundred miles each Saturday to see me. On the second or third meeting I noticed that certain speech sounds were distorted, a condition we sometimes term *dysarthric*. Now this is not common in the speech of the 9-year-old, and I suspected that perhaps there had been, early in life, an injury that caused the misarticulation that I heard in certain difficult sounds, such as *l*, *r*, *s*, and *th*. None of these sounds were improved with careful stimulation on my part and careful listening on the child's part. I played a hunch and requested an EEG (brain wave) study, and a pattern was found that, in the opinion of the neurologist and myself, might easily account for the misarticulation of the speech sounds mentioned above. I discussed the matter with the family, explaining that the injury, if indeed such existed, was not sufficient to limit intelligence or other performance, but it did appear to be sufficient to cause part of the speech problem. We went through a brief period of family counseling, during which many facets of family life were covered, but especially we discussed and got accepted the idea that this child might always have a speech defect, although not a serious one.

The end of the story is interesting. Six months after the termination of our counseling sessions, the mother called me by long-distance telephone with the good news that her son had ceased to stutter. I asked if the speech sounds were still in error, and she told me they were. The cure in this rather rare case is so simple as to be quite apparent. Accepting the child's primary problem as permanent served to erase the tensions arising from perfectionistic attitudes that had caused the secondary problem. Most problems are not so easily solved, but it's a pleasure when one has relatively complete and rapid success.

In another sense, stuttering may be organic. Why do we each have somewhat different ways of reacting to pleasure, pain, social stress, and so forth? Certainly many of these differences can be explained on the basis of conditioning and other modes of learning, which may occur even rather late in life. However, you will recall that stuttering starts early in life and usually with the male. I cannot help but believe that we have here both a sex-related and a genetic component. There are no one-to-one relationships, but perhaps we do have something in the germ plasm that leads to stuttering as an expression of stress rather than to enuresis, food rejection, or nail biting. It behooves us as teachers and clinicians, however, to be careful about always accepting such "pat" explanations. To say that stuttering is familial is a far cry from saying that it is hereditary. We do, after all, tend to create families similar to the kind in which we grew up, for we know no other. If my father made me sick, and yet I identified with him, then it stands to reason that I have the capacity to hand this or a related sickness on to my own sons.

Domination and rejection

A few years ago a man by the name of John Moncur (1952) completed a very detailed study about the attitudes and actions of the parents of stuttering children as compared with the parents of fluent children. It is a long study, and the best I can do now is to paraphrase it, and perhaps even have a little fun with his results. Parental domination is the theme of his study. Please remember that there are differences between guidance and influence and domination. If you want a child to stutter (and of course you don't), the first thing to do is get on his back for something about which he is too young to complain. Make him be precise. Bedtime is eight o'clock, not one minute past eight. He is to stop coloring the man blue, red, or whatever the color is, right in the middle of the right leg, or wherever he may be. If his favorite television show goes to the next half hour, never mind—bedtime is bedtime. Another useful procedure is always to insist that he do whatever he is doing the *right* way. You know he will have to do it the right way when he grows up, and so he may as well begin now. Make the assumption that he is too young to learn by himself. If you always tell him what to do and how to do it, he will never face the problem of needing to learn something for himself. He will never get his fingers burned or get scratched by the cat, but it is just possible that he may stutter.

Another facet of the domination complex is the method used to dominate. There may not be any healthy way to dominate, but there are ways that are worse than others. So I suggest that when in doubt, shame him. There is almost no way in which a young child can deal with shame in a healthy manner, but deal with it he will and in ways that may confuse and confound the parents.

As I have hinted before, another mode of domination is through over-channeling of communication: "Think before you speak." "Now start that over again." "Speak more clearly." "Speak more slowly." "Mamma can't listen now." And even, "Stop stuttering."

Guidance and leadership at their best are shared by both parents, usually with certain areas dealt with by the father and some by the mother. Normally it is the mother who is permissive and the father less so, at least in some of the areas of control and guidance. In the case of the stutterer's parents, one often finds a special dynamic situation as regards guidance and dominance. The mother tends to be the perfectionist, and the father may duck his real responsibilities as a father. More than one businessman works overtime, and more than one scientist stays in the laboratory because the working milieu is more comfortable than that at home. It is obvious that the children suffer. Parenthetically, it might be noted that more than one great scientist may have become just that because of a nagging wife and crying children. There are many ways to demonstrate one's masculinity, and they are not all in the home.

The mother of the stuttering child often expresses her perfectionism by being the perfect housekeeper. One mother brought to my office a child so carefully scrubbed and polished that he could have made the cover on *Parent's Magazine*. I asked the mother how often she had washed him that day, and she replied that the child had been very dirty and she had to wash him six or seven times.

The act of being rejected for being dirty leads me to the work of a man by the name of Donald Kinstler (1961) who developed a scale for estimating maternal acceptance and rejection, both overt and covert. He then applied the scale to the mothers of stuttering and normal children. Kinstler's research techniques and investigations of people was never carried far enough, for his study was an exploratory Ph.D. dissertation. The point is that he did hit some pay dirt and opened the way for further study with stutterers and nonstutterers in the degree and nature of acceptance and rejection. If any of you would care to extend his study, I shall be glad to advise you.

To begin with, we should look at the dimensions of the acceptance-rejection dichotomy. First, one can accept overtly. Mother to neighbor:

"We are so proud of Henry. He is getting A's in all of his subjects except physical education, and he is passing that." Now this is overt acceptance, unless of course, mother is an athletics fan, in which case we may have a touch of rejection, probably covert. One can also accept covertly. One case of this type I remember clearly. Some years ago I was in the state of Idaho on an Indian reservation waiting to interview the tribal council in order to obtain permission to study the problem of stuttering among the Indians of this Bannock and Shoshone reservation. It was a cold, clear day, and much of the warmth inside came from the sun that streamed through the windows. A young Indian woman came into the room with a papoose on her back strapped tightly to the "baby board." She unwound the child and played with him very gently and without voicing. She was not aware that I was watching her. There was no overt display. She was simply with her child loving him in a way that was happy for both of them and, quite incidentally, for me. Overt acceptance has in it display, and display implies that others can see it and hear it and do. Giving a boy a knife or a girl a valentine is overt acceptance.

In acceptance, of course, both the overt and covert can be enjoyed. If mother brags about the child (overt), he probably feels pride and satisfaction just as he might if she showed her warmth only to him in a quiet way. In rejection, it is generally more difficult to handle the covert type of rejection, and easier to deal with the overt. Sarcasm, as covert rejection, is difficult for children, as well as adults. A body blow can be answered, often by a body blow. At least it is understood; and perhaps one can take out its sting by directing an overt action toward another object—perhaps the dog, cat, or a younger sibling. Let me make it clear that there is seldom purely overt or purely covert acceptance and rejection. There is likely to be a shading, with one more in evidence than the other.

The real importance of the Kinstler study is that stutterers, by the admission of their mothers, were more often rejected than nonstutterers, and they were more often rejected in a covert manner. Now some of you who are sophisticated in thinking about causes are saying, "Does the rejection cause the stuttering, or is the stutterer rejected because he stutters?" Kinstler did not discuss this point, but the answer is not of prime importance. We can assume, with considerable confidence, that the rejection either causes the problem, at least in part, or the rejection will contribute to the continuation of the nonadjustive behavior pattern.

Going back for a moment to the Moncur study, I should like to bring up a point that seems to be at odds with the concept of permissiveness and acceptance. Moncur found that there were fewer stutterers among the families who developed routine tasks and other routine behavior patterns for their children. Children who take care of their pets, who clean their own rooms, who sweep the front porch each day, seem to have a kind of security that is good for them, and fewer from this group stuttered. Note that we are not including, nor did Moncur, the driven and compulsive approach to routine. I once heard a world-famous psychiatrist state that neurotics reduce their anxieties when they learn to accomplish many of life's demands as automatically and easily as possible. I am not implying that all stutterers are neurotics, but it appears that perhaps their parents have not, in general, appreciated the need for the security that reasonable routine can give.

Recipes with variations

Now comes the difficult part of my task, for I have been asked to state some principles that might guide you in dealing with stutterers, and this I shall attempt to do; but first let me emphasize that if you are not a qualified specialist, then find one as soon as is possible. More about this later.

LISTEN TO THE STUTTERER   More than any other class of speech defective, the stutterer has been denied a sympathetic audience. He has been told to "slow down," "think before you speak," and such other nonsense that helped him not at all. Listening takes patience. I have known more than one stutterer who took sixty seconds to say "good morning." How long do you think it takes such a person to tell you his troubles?

DON'T BE THE EXPERT   Let the person who stutters work out his own problems most of the time. For the last 3½ years I have worked with a college student who stutters. After the first eight months or so, I knew pretty much what he had to tell me in the future, so I have listened for almost three years, with most of the expertise developing in the stutterer as an emerging person rather than by me as the academically educated expert.

BE DIRECTIVE ONLY WHEN NECESSARY   Directions are more important for parents than for the stutterer. A father rejected his family, including his stuttering son, by reading a book at the dinner table. When we had developed some rapport, I said, "Knock it off," and he did.

THROW IN THE TOWEL AT THE END OF THE FIRST ROUND   When a clinician runs out of resources, it behooves him to retreat and find someone who can deal with the problem. I well remember a woman with a voice problem who was sent to me by a physician. After listening for an hour I realized that this woman was desperately ill, that her marriage was breaking up, and that the hoarse, harsh voice was only a symptom of her several problems. I sent her to a psychiatrist who was unable to save her, but he had a better chance of so doing than the general physician or the speech pathologist. There is the right time to refer a difficult case, and frequently this referral should come early rather than late.

DON'T BE TOO SURE ABOUT YOUR INFORMATION Almost thirty years as a speech pathologist and clinical psychologist have made me skeptical about information unless I know the examiner, or at least his credentials and the examining situation. Let me tell you a brief story to illustrate my point. Some years ago I worked in a large clinic and became friendly with a young male stutterer who was suffering a great deal of frustration because he could not communicate adequately with the opposite sex. As a result he spent more than the usual amount of time, even for an adolescent, in sexual fantasy. He was not my client, but one day we discussed a projective examination administered to him by a female clinician. Upon inquiry, the stutterer told me that "all of the pictures are dirty," meaning simply that they were full of sex symbols and in action. A rerun on the test confirmed his informal report. Even a mature and skilled female clinician had not elicited essential information.

SUMMARY AND QUESTIONS

In a brief period I have tried to show you something about stuttering as a problem of learning. I am sure that I have shown you that it usually arises in the family and that it usually is complicated. Some clinicians call stuttering the queen of the speech disorders, and I am sure you can see why this label is appropriate. I promised time for questions, and we appear to have ample time.

QUESTION: *In one of our textbooks there was a case where a teacher assigned a girl a part in a class play, and she convinced the girl she would not stutter because she was going to play the part of a confident and fluent woman. Was this wise?*

ANSWER: I can hardly think of a more dangerous act toward a stutterer. This girl made it, but for every success there would be several tragic failures, intensified by the fact that the failure might come before a large and critical audience. However, role playing in private and with small groups can be helpful.

QUESTION: *Would you please expand on what you said about the desirability of consistent behavior and attitudes on the part of the parent.*

ANSWER: Most of us like to know where we stand in regard to other people, and the child's relationship is especially critical. The child wants to be loved by the parent, and he needs consistent demonstration for his own security. He also has the right to know when he is out of bounds and what treatment to expect when he is not shaping up. If the treatment is consistent, he depends upon it, and if the treatment is wise, he profits by the stability it gives him. There need not be important conflict between the ideas of consistency and permissiveness.

QUESTION: *I believe you implied that at least some Indian groups do not stutter. Would you tell us why?*

ANSWER: Some, and only some, Indian groups are very permissive about communication. You may talk or not and be completely accepted in the social group. As a matter of fact, I knew a chief who rarely spoke, yet he was highly respected and was elected a member of the ruling council. He could communicate, "yes," "no," or "maybe" by a nod of the head or a shrug of the shoulders. On the other hand, Edwin M. Lemert (1962), a sociologist, studied an Indian society in which effective vocal communication was considered so important that speech making was part of the initiation into manhood. He found a number of stutterers. The late Norman Gable, a distinguished anthropologist, looked at a number of Pacific Indian societies, at my request and with my definitions, and found no stutterers. I found half-breeds who stuttered, even in the easy-going American Indian society I studied. There may be some special stresses involved here that have to do with attitudes and rejection rather than with pedigree.

QUESTION: *Do Mexican-Americans stutter?*

ANSWER: We don't know the answer to that question, but if we assume that they do not, then we can assume that they will once they have the opportunities they deserve, for stuttering is the disease of upwardly mobile societies and families. I suggest there is a good thesis here for one of you who is interested especially in the problems of the chicano.

QUESTION: *You have used the pronoun "he" during almost all of your discussion. Only one student mentioned a girl who stuttered. Will you say why?*

ANSWER: The ratio of males to females who stutter is from about eight to one to about ten to one, depending on the sample. I wish we knew why this is true. I could speculate for half, but we probably wouldn't make too much progress.

QUESTION: *Is stuttering hereditary?*

ANSWER: Some authorities say that there is an underlying neurological factor called *dysphemia* that serves as the soil from which stuttering grows. Others have related the behavior of the early stutterer to something akin to epilepsy. In the sense of familial inheritance, one can say that stuttering runs in families. This may only mean that we tend to reproduce the behavioral pattern of the family from which we came. To quote a client of mine: "Well my father was a strict disciplinarian, and we all turned out good enough." This statement justified to him the stern treatment of his son, who came to our speech and hearing center as a stutterer.

QUESTION: *I have been reading about the efficiency of behavior modification procedures with children who are frightened. What does this type of learning theory have to offer the stutterer?*

ANSWER: In my presentation I have stressed the activities that would likely help the stutterer that could also be implemented, at least in part, by the classroom teacher. For this reason I touched upon therapy in depth only as it might be used by qualified psychiatrists and psychologists and speech pathologists. The same reasoning has been followed in my omission of behavior modification as a technique, for I believe that such techniques belong only in the hands of those who are skilled in their use. Yet, I should like to stress that, once learned by the clinician, procedures for the direct conditioning of behavior are not necessarily complex. To get the whole picture, I very strongly recommend to you a book entitled *Stuttering and the Conditioning Therapies,* edited by Burl B. Gray and Gene England (1969) of the Monterey Institute for Speech and Hearing. These men have applied some of the theories of Joseph Wolpe concerning anxiety measurement and modification. In brief but simple, systematic, highly rational procedures, they estimate anxiety and then progressively reduce anxiety levels, starting with those anxiety-bearing attitudes that are easy to approach. Their work has been with stutterers, but certainly these techniques can and have been generalized. My own experience tells me that behavior modification procedures with the parents of very young stutterers can be highly successful.

QUESTION: *I knew a professor who lectured without stuttering, but when he talked with his students in his office, he stuttered. How do you explain this?*

ANSWER: Time is growing short, but this question deserves a brief and rather precise answer. Stutterers have difficulty in situations that pose threats to them, and these threats vary markedly from stutterer to stutterer. Stutterers have told me that the telephone is especially difficult, because the person cannot be seen. Only one stutterer I have known was fluent with the telephone because, as he said, "I can't see him, so I don't fear him." There have been world-famous speakers who were fluent on the speaker's platform and who stuttered in private. More often, the stutterer is more fluent with those with whom he speaks in private than in the more public situation. I once worked with a stutterer who had difficulty with every living creature with whom he associated except his dog. It is interesting that he could talk into a recording machine with fluency, provided he thought I would not listen to the recording.

AUDITORY PROCESSES AND PROBLEMS

5

Sanford E. Gerber

Dr. Sanford E. Gerber is director of audiology in the Speech and Hearing Center of the University of California at Santa Barbara. He received the B.A. at Lake Forest College, the M.S. at the University of Illinois, and the Ph.D. at the University of Southern California.

Dr. Gerber's diverse interests are represented by the broad spectrum of his publications, ranging from clinical investigations of hearing in infants to esoteric studies of digital voice communications systems. In a professional capacity, his service has also been diverse. For example, he served as a member of the advisory board of the HEAR Foundation of the tricounties (Santa Barbara, Ventura, and San Luis Obispo), and he served as an expert research linguist for the federal government. He devoted a sabbatical leave in the fall of 1968 to touring European centers of activity in pediatric audiology.

A chronic joiner, Dr. Gerber belongs to many professional societies, including the International Society of Audiology, the American Speech and Hearing Association, the Acoustical Society of America, and the Alexander Graham Bell Association for the Deaf. His articles have appeared broadly in professional journals such as Journal of Speech and Hearing Research, International Audiology, *the* Cerebral Palsy Journal, *and many others.*

In this chapter I shall talk about hearing, auditory processes, and particularly auditory problems one might encounter within the school environment. I shall also talk about how the classroom teacher might be able to identify the child who has a hearing problem.

When we talk about auditory difficulties in a school-age population, we are in fact talking about a great many children. I cite here a report by the National Institute of Neurological Disease and Blindness entitled *Hearing, Language, and Speech Disorders* (1967), which some of you may have seen. This is a statistical report, and I quote a few sentences from the first page so that you will have an idea of the magnitude of the problem. It says:

> *Among children, it is estimated that 12 out of every 10,000 in the population are totally deaf and that between 150 and 300 of every 10,000 suffer from severe hearing impairment. About 500 per 10,000 have some type of disorder of speech which affects articulation, while 20 per 10,000 suffer from cleft palate, facial malformation, or other organic disorders affecting speech. Cerebral palsy afflicts 13 out of each 10,000 of this population; half of these have some hearing, language, or speech problem. Fifty out of every 10,000 children suffer retardation in speech development not caused by deafness. Voice problems are estimated at more than 60 per 10,000. Stuttering (not necessarily to be considered a speech disorder), affects 60 in every 10,000. In short, this means that 10 percent of the Nation's children suffer from some form of communicative disorder.*

So we are talking about a lot of children when we speak of those who have speech, language, or auditory problems.

A LITTLE ANATOMY

Let's discuss briefly the structure of the human ear, because this is basic to understanding the kinds of problems that may occur. The layman's concept of the ear is that it is the thing that sticks out on the side of the head, the *pinna* (Figure 5-1). The pinna is thought by authorities to be little more than decorative, and it is a useful place to hang earrings. Man does not have, and may never have had, the ability to turn his pinna so as to use it as a kind of receiving antenna. You will observe that most animals have their pinnae on top of their heads, not on the side, and the pinnae are movable. Nevertheless, the human pinna may have some localizing function.

98   SANFORD E. GERBER

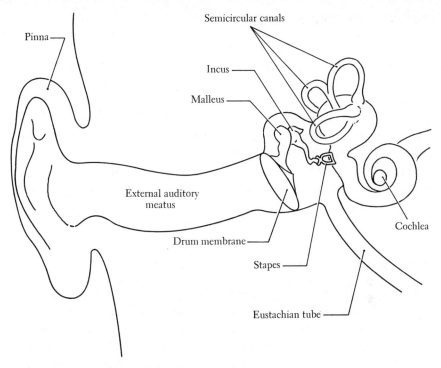

FIGURE 5-1 *Anatomical illustration of the ear*

The pinna opens into the *external auditory meatus,* or the ear canal. This canal ends at the *tympanic* (or drum) *membrane,* popularly called the ear drum. The drum membrane covers the cavity of the middle ear. The middle ear is the site of most of the problems that a classroom teacher would encounter among the children in school. In the middle ear are housed the three smallest bones and the two smallest muscles in the body. The cavity is ventilated via the *eustachian tube* (sometimes called the auditory tube), which opens into the *nasopharynx,* i.e., the back of the throat behind the nose. Children get adenoid problems. Adenoids are normal lymph glands that, when they become infected and enlarged, block the nasopharyngeal opening to the eustachian tube, thus preventing normal ventilation of the middle ear.

Medial to the chain of ossicles (i.e., further to the inside) is the inner ear. Here we find the very delicate organs of balance as well as those of hearing. These are the vestibular organs (the *semicircular canals, utricle,* and *saccule*), which tell us where we are, and the auditory organs (the *cochlear duct* with its internal structures).

OUTER-EAR PROBLEMS

Kids do get things in their ears, and this is a problem. There is an old saying, but it's true, "Don't ever stick anything into your ear smaller than your elbow." If the child has a problem with wax, and some children do, it is not the nurses's place or even mother's place to take it out. An ear, nose, and throat doctor knows how to take it out without doing any damage. Mama likes to clean ears, and the effect of this usually is to make it worse rather than better, because she doesn't get the wax out, she gets it in. The tendency is to push the wax into the ear. The child gets a big plug of wax, and he begins to stop paying attention in class because he doesn't hear any more.

MIDDLE-EAR PROBLEMS

The effect of blockage of the eustachian tube is an unequal pressure on the two sides of the drum membrane. Normally, air pressure from outside arrives via the external auditory meatus and strikes the lateral surface of the drum membrane. Air, which comes in via the eustachian tube, strikes the medial surface of the drum membrane, and in this way a balance of air pressure is maintained. If such balance does not exist because the air pressure is not equalized, your ears may feel "stuffed" and will "pop" when the pressure balance is restored. You have all probably experienced this, for example, in a fast elevator or an airplane. Chronic air pressure imbalance (which has been called *aero-otitis media* and *acoustic barotrauma*) may lead to stretching of the drum membrane, with a concomitant mild hearing loss.

The most frequent source of middle-ear disease is the common cold. As early as 1907 a text pointed out that "causes that act through the nasopharynx by way of the eustachian tube stand first . . ." (Barnhill and Wales, 1907, p. 79). And sixty years later, "The maximum incidence of otitis media coincides with the maximum incidence of acute upper respiratory infections . . . the common colds, infections with . . . influenza . . .," etc. (Mawson, 1967, p. 273). *Otitis media* means simply inflammation of the middle ear. It is very, very common; and it is very, very painful in the acute stage. In general, otitis media is amenable to medical treatment. Chronic otitis media, i.e., recurring ear infection, is not so responsive. If fluid remains in the middle ear, one refers to serous otitis media. An ear, nose, and throat specialist of my acquaintance recently commented to the effect that there is increased incidence of chronic serous otitis media. The reason is that many pediatricians and general practitioners have been treating the acute phase only. Appropriate doses of proper antibiotic drugs will cure the infection but may not cause drainage of the accrued fluid. So, with repeated infections and repeated antibiotic treatments, the fluid continues to accrue in the middle ear. Eventually, this fluid becomes of such a consistency that the condition itself is called "glue ear." And, I suspect that you will, from time to time, get a nurse's report to the effect that some pupil in your room is suffering from glue ear. He cannot hear at all well while that glue remains.

Whether or not the fluid found in serous otitis media is as viscous as glue, it must be drained in some way. Frequently, administration of a decongestant drug is sufficient. Such medication, in conjunction with the antibiotic treatment of the infection, is usually of total effectiveness in combating serous otitis media. If the fluid is so viscous that it cannot be removed chemically, then it must be removed surgically. A common procedure involves the use of a very fine, hollow needle attached to a suction apparatus. This procedure involves making a tiny puncture of the drum membrane and withdrawing the fluid by suction. If this fails, then a *myringotomy procedure* under general anesthesia is indicated, wherein an incision is made in the drum membrane. Sometimes, a drainage heals before drainage is complete. In such a case it is desirable to maintain drainage by the insertion of tiny plastic tubes. Such a tube looks like a spool of thread, because it is flanged at each end to keep it from falling out.

If a child has running ears in school and he doesn't have tubes in them, you had better call the school nurse, because he has probably perforated a drum membrane. The matter of perforation—and you'll see this I guess more at the secondary level than with smaller children—is found in children who swim but are not permitted to swim. You'll get a note that such-and-such a child is not permitted to go swimming. This is a child who for some of the reasons that I've mentioned has chronic ear disease or he has perforated the drum membrane. One way of perforating the drum membrane is with chronic disease: the disease will erode the membrane and perforate it. The danger in the perforation and in the swimming is that something will get into the ear through this perforation: bacteria, viruses, etc. Water is a wonderful thing for transporting disease through this perforation, thus leading to ear disease.

What was, years ago, a major fatal disease of mankind is almost unknown today, and this is *mastoiditis*. Some of you know, I am sure, people who have had radical mastoidectomy—people who have a pocket behind the ear where they have had a piece of bone removed. Mastoiditis is a potential sequel of untreated chronic middle-ear disease. The temporal bone, which houses the ear, and particularly the mastoid part of the temporal bone, is very porous, and the essence of middle-ear disease is the filling of the bone cavity with diseased fluid. The fluid carries bacteria or virus, or whatever is the source of the disease, and gets into the pores of the mastoid bone. The fatal danger is that, by fluid coming up through the pores, mastoiditis can lead to brain abcess. The diseased fluid can come into contact with the temporal lobe of the brain; and years ago, people died from mastoiditis. Today, with antibiotics, we are able to treat them and mastoiditis is relatively unknown. It was once a common and very serious disease. Your reaction to ear complaint should be referral to the nurse. This is something that is usually amenable to medical treatment, and not something that demands special educational treatment as do other kinds of hearing impairments.

INNER-EAR PROBLEMS

Medial to the middle ear is the most complicated structure in the body: the inner ear. I was interested to notice that the syndicated columnist in the local newspaper who gives out medical advice gave some really bad (and, in fact, erroneous) advice on ear diseases three or four weeks ago. It amazes me that people don't go to the doctor: "I have a terrible pain, so I'll write a letter to the newspaper." A parent wrote a letter about kids having earaches. The columnist wrote back: "First send 25 cents for my book on *How to Cure Ear Aches.*" He went on to say, "But you should go to a doctor, who will puncture the inner ear and let fluid out." If the doctor should puncture the inner ear, he would likely get a deaf child, as that would destroy the child's hearing. Now, the columnist doesn't mean that; but he may not know he doesn't mean that. What he meant is just what I've been talking about: he meant he should puncture the membrane to the *middle* ear and permit fluid to drain. Fluid is not normal in the middle ear; however, fluid is imperative to the functioning of the inner ear. The inner ear is essentially a hydraulic system, and the fluid has to be there.

The inner ear contains two sensory systems, which are intimately associated: the vestibular system, which is associated with balance, proprioception, kinesthesia; and the organ of hearing itself. Phylogenetically these are the same system. Fairly high up the phylogenetic scale, in fish and birds, there is one system that serves the functions of man's vestibular and cochlear (that is, auditory) systems. So, if something is wrong with one, the other may also be in trouble. If there is difficulty, for example, in balance, it may also involve an auditory difficulty, and similarly, the other way around. Some of you may be familiar with what is called *Menière's disease*. Menière's disease is due to a swelling of the vestibular system because of infection of some kind. The symptoms of Menière's disease are deafness of rather brief duration (hours, perhaps, or days), intractable vertigo (vertigo is horizontal dizziness like standing on a phonograph turntable), and what we call *tinnitus*, which is simply noise in the ears. You can imagine a patient's reaction to this kind of thing. It is a frightening condition. The only reason for mentioning it is that this is the only condition for which it would be appropriate to puncture the inner ear, and even then it is done very, very rarely. But it also demonstrates that, while this is a disease of the vestibular system, it has these rather gross auditory symptoms along with it. So if the ear, nose, and throat specialist is making a diagnosis of auditory difficulties, it may include tests of the vestibular system to see to what extent it is involved.

In the inner ear is the cochlea, which is curled up and looks like a snail shell. If you unwind it, it is 26 mm in length. In it is the organ of hearing itself, which is called the *organ of Corti*. The organ of Corti is distributed along a membrane, called the *basilar membrane*, which divides this cochlear shell in two. There is another membrane that also runs the entire length of the cochlea, so there are three compartments running through this shell, through this cochlea. The outer two compartments contain a fluid called *perilymph*, which is the same fluid that is found in the vestibular system of semicircular canals and is essentially identical to the cerebrospinal fluid. The inner compartment, the one that contains the organ of Corti, is filled with a different fluid, called *endolymph*. Certain diseases will cause one or both of these membranes to break or to collapse in such a way that the perilymph and endolymph will mix. This will produce a profound deafness. These same diseases may also produce mechanical damage by virtue of the collapse of these membranes. They will fall down upon the organ of Corti, and the so-called pillars of Corti, which support this organ, may collapse. One of these inner-ear membranes, which is called the *tectorial membrane*, has been observed to "roll up and hide" in the corner of the cochlea. *Reissner's membrane*, the one that separates the upper from the middle canal, has been known to break in the middle and fall. A structure that is called the *stria vascularis*, which is responsible for the blood supply in the inner ear, has been known to shrivel up and essentially to disappear. All these may be seen upon microscopic examination or, to be sure, postmortem examination.

One would like to think, "My goodness, these are exotic, terrible diseases that cause this to occur." These exotic diseases are measles, mumps, chicken pox, whooping cough—the diseases that you see in school. To give you a little lack of comfort: A second-grade teacher I know caught mumps from one of the children in her class and lost all of her hearing in one ear. Incidentally, of these diseases, only mumps will affect just one ear; all the others will deafen both. Mumps may deafen both ears, but if one ear goes, it can probably be attributed to the mumps, and not necessarily one-sided mumps. The single largest cause of profound hearing loss, profound sensory-neural, medically or surgically untreatable hearing loss, in children is good old-fashioned measles, the ten-day variety. Until the development of some of the drugs that control the severity of disease (and now, of course, we have both the rubella and a measles antitoxin), it could be demonstrated that over 60 percent of the deaf were cases of postillness-acquired deafness (DiCarlo, 1964, p. 44). This is the kind of thing that you will encounter in your school environment. Measles, rubella (or German measles), chicken pox, whooping cough, and scarlet fever have pretty well disappeared, but all of these so-called diseases of childhood are exceedingly dangerous, and they attack the inner ear directly. They attack in two ways. First, they attack by the high fever—and any disease that is accompanied by a high fever can do damage to the inner ear. Nearly 24 percent of deaf children lost hearing following febrile illness (Vernon, 1968). In the microscopic structures in each ear there are 23,000 nerve endings. These micro-microscopic structures just don't like the heat. So, any time there is high fever, deafness may ensue. Secondly, many of these are viral diseases, and the virus itself has a propensity for finding the inner ear. The measles virus is a nasty little creature. It is a little round ball covered with spines, and it gets into the cochlea and just tears apart those membranes. There are published photomicrographs of postmeasles ears wherein one can see the extent of the damage that has been done (see, for example, Hemenway and Bergstrom, 1967). The result of this is a child with a profound hearing loss.

Other kinds of things lead to deafness in children. There is a fancy word, *iatrogenic*, which means doctor-caused. The most common kind of iatrogenic deafness is a drug-induced deafness. There are drugs that, because they induce deafness, are called *ototoxic*: literally, ear poison. Some of them are well known to you. You'll be pleased to know that aspirin is one of them. People who have arthritis may take thirty, forty, or fifty aspirins a day, as aspirin is specific for arthritis. They will suffer a hearing impairment with tinnitus (ringing in the ears) as a direct result of taking aspirin. Another ototoxin is quinine. It was thought for many years that malaria caused deafness, which is not true. Malaria, you know, is treated by giving massive dosages of quinine; quinine causes deafness. It happens that aspirin and quinine are thought to be only temporarily ototoxic; if you stop taking it, the deafness goes away—if not entirely, most of it goes away. There are other drugs, some of which are given quite freely, that cause irremediable deafness. Many of the mycins are in this class: streptomycin, a very common drug; dihydrostreptomycin, the newest and most wonderful and most toxic of all the wonder drugs; kanamycin, which has sometimes been given in large dosages to children. I have encountered cases of children who had "something" in infancy and were given large doses of kanamycin—deaf children, who may not have been deaf children before they were given kanamycin. We even found a hospital where they were routinely giving kanamycin to all the premature babies. I was startled (the whole audience was startled) by the presentation of a paper with slides showing photomicrographic sections of the inner ear of guinea pigs after an ototoxic dose of kanamycin. There was nothing in that inner ear. It wasn't like measles, where you see the beat-up, collapsed organs. The organs were gone. They weren't even there in bad condition. Another discovery they made with respect to kanamycin was that if you give an ototoxic dose to the animal and then don't give him anymore, he will continue to lose his hearing (Shida and Okamoto, 1967). Kanamycin is given because it's the most general of the antibiotics. The ototoxic dose has been established in cats and guinea pigs, and one assumes that it is the same ratio in human beings. However, an infant may be much more subject to damage than an adult. There have been some studies on the use of streptomycin and dihydrostreptomycin, which are given in cases of tuberculosis. These are life-saving drugs. They should be given only when this drug and only this drug is imperative to the saving of life, and that's true in tuberculosis. Not all the mycins are ototoxic, just some of them. You may or may not encounter this kind of thing in day-to-day school practice. You may encounter it with a child who is ill and is given medication. If the child comes back to school and seems not to be paying attention anymore, it might be wise to have the nurse test his hearing and to find out what sort of medication he has taken. There is nothing you can do about it if he has already had it. It's an interesting problem. We are beginning to learn about the early signs that can enable us to measure in such a way that we can say that this person will be deaf if we continue giving him this drug. Perhaps the drugs will attack the high frequencies first. So, if you can test for those frequencies that are normally higher than our useful audible range and see if there is a change there, this may be a sign of susceptibility, and the medication can be stopped.

IDENTIFICATION

I want to say a couple other things that are, perhaps, immediately germane to the classroom situation. A child who may be suspect of having hearing difficulty may be the child who does not attend, the child who just doesn't appear to be listening to what's going on, the child who withdraws, who doesn't play with the other children, who sits in a corner by himself and does poor work; or, conversely, he may be the child who is hostile, who gets into fights, who is hyperactive, who makes a lot of noise and bangs things around. Small children, small severely hard-of-hearing children, will have a characteristic walk; they shuffle their feet, and they do slam and bang things (Myklebust, 1954, Ch. 6). As they get older they are apt to take on one of two other courses of behavior. Either they are hostile toward their fellows or they withdraw from their fellows. In either case, you should refer to the school nurse for a hearing test any child who seems to be a bright child and is not doing as well as you, as a teacher, think he ought to be doing in the class; the child who is not achieving what everybody's expectations say he should be achieving; the child who is not attending, who is looking into space more than are the other kids; or the child who has frequent colds, who is absent a great deal of the time. If the nurse doesn't routinely test, on his return to school, the child who was absent because he had measles, mumps, chicken pox, etc., the teacher should be sure to refer him for hearing tests. In virtually all schools it is the nurse who does this. Sometimes its the speech clinician, but usually the speech person does it only for the children she is seeing. So, typically, it is the nurse who does the hearing tests. These are the kinds of things of which the classroom teacher should be aware.

THE HEARING-IMPAIRED CHILD
IN THE CLASSROOM

After the child has been diagnosed as one who is having hearing difficulties and something is being done about it (medical treatment, surgical treatment, a hearing aid), the teacher has to deal with that child specially. It is important for the child to be able to see you. (For a good discussion of the importance of visual cues to auditory learning, see Oyer, 1966, pp. 110–113.) Children who don't hear well will lip-read without being taught to do so, and they may not even be conscious that they are doing it; but they will look at you. In fact, this in itself can be a sign of hearing difficulty in a small child. Such a child should have preferential seating, which means that he is up in front of the room and his hearing aid is pointed at the teacher. There is some question as to what constitutes preferential seating: When the teacher gets between the child and the window to talk and he can't see her face because she is back-lighted, he doesn't hear anything because much of his hearing is visual hearing. So, there is a way to behave when this child is in the classroom so that he can get as much as possible with his hearing aid, with his preferential seating, and with his lipreading.

We are talking about a large number of children. Five percent of school-age children have significant hearing impairment. That is a lot of boys and girls! This proportion increases as the children get older. More and more have measles, more and more have ear infections, and so on. What can you do as far as advising the parents? You can ask your school nurse to include these things in her educational program. You can advise the parents a priori: "Has your kid had the measles shots?" "Has he had the rubella shots?" The only other thing that you can do is to be certain, if the kid contracts one of these diseases, that the nurse sees him when he returns to school.

SUMMARY

It is necessary to summarize those things that directly pertain to the role of the teacher in a regular classroom. Such things fall into two categories, which one might call "before" and "after." Before a child is known to have a hearing impairment, it could behoove a teacher to be on the alert for this possibility. That is, it may very well be the regular classroom teacher who first observes that a child is having difficulty. After a child has been diagnosed as one who has trouble, the teacher must deal with him in certain ways.

How does the teacher identify the child who does not hear well? Remember that he is the kid who does not pay attention. He is the one who fails to achieve up to your expectations. He is the one who makes noise, who drops things, who slams doors, who shuffles his feet. He is the one who does not participate in group activities, or if he does, he acts aggressively toward the other children. He is the one who withdraws. These descriptions may also fit children who are not hard of hearing but who have other problems. It doesn't matter. It matters only that the teacher must react to this kind of child, and to react requires awareness.

What if you have a hearing-impaired child in your classroom? First of all, we must believe that this child is in a regular class because that is where he fits. He is not a child whose hearing demands that we have special education. Nevertheless, he deserves special attention in the normal classroom. He should be seated where he can hear *and* where he can see you. Remember that visual cues are very important to him. Remember, too, that he may not always understand and you may have to repeat. Also, you should call upon the school nurse and the school speech clinician for advice; that is why they are there.

NEUROLOGICAL DYSFUNCTIONS

6

Wayland Stephenson

Dr. Wayland Stephenson has been senior neurologist at the Sansum Medical Clinic since 1956. He was chief of staff for the clinic in 1967 and 1968. He earned his B.Sc. and his M.D. from the University of Kansas, did his internship and residency at the Iowa University Hospital, and then served in the U.S. Navy for two years. He taught neurology at the University of Illinois and at the University of Kansas, in addition to carrying on a neurological practice.

Dr. Stephenson has been active in civic affairs since coming to Santa Barbara. He has contributed his services generously to the schools as a member of evaluation teams for assessing the learning potential of atypical youngsters. In 1970 he was president of the Los Angeles Society for Neurology and Psychiatry.

I am a clinical neurologist, and the way I look at some things undoubtedly is different from the way those of you who are going into teaching might look at them. I have to think of the brain as *the* most important organ, the organ that makes us separate and different from any other individual and makes humans different from any other animal.

FACTORS THAT AFFECT BRAIN DEVELOPMENT

A good many things about the brain are determined at conception—that is, genetic things. Teachers have dealt with or heard of such conditions as PKU (phenylpyruvic oligophrenia) and other disorders that are determined at the time of the fertilization of the ovum. Besides the genetic determinants, many other factors are important in the development of the brain, including the general health of the mother, which can't be measured very precisely. Some fertilized ova seem to find a better environment than others, and as a result, the brain, along with the entire embryo, thrives. Specific illnesses such as measles are very damaging. Many of you have had contact with children whose mothers have had German measles in the first trimester of pregnancy. This is a very, very unfortunate occurrence and may produce a variety of disturbances to embryological development, including serious damage to the brain.

If the pregnancy proceeds in a normal way—everything having been normal up to that time—things may go wrong near the time of birth: for example, *eclampsia,* in which the mother is seriously ill and the fetus suffers. In addition, there are the physical events of the delivery of the child. There may be forceps damage to the head, which sometimes injures the brain. The most common difficulty at this time is *hypoxia,* reduced oxygen to the brain. The interference with oxygen may take place in a number of ways and is particularly common in abnormal deliveries such as breech presentations. If the brain is deprived of oxygen for any material length of time, a length of time that will have no adverse affect on other parts of the body, the deprivation may seriously damage the brain. Compression of bones of the head at the time of delivery, the molding that takes place physiologically to permit passage of the infant, may produce bleeding inside the head or may produce compression to cause damage to the brain. These listed disasters are perhaps the most common categories of damage to the brain from conception to birth.

After birth a variety of disorders occur. Fevers of a high degree in early life may produce brain damage. There may be infections in the form of encephalitis at any age, but particularly in the young, that may produce serious difficulties. Injuries are common, and instances of toxic contacts and even tumors and blood-vessel diseases may be seen more rarely.

SYMPTOMS OF DISORDERS

This is only an outline, but given any of these conditions, certain brain symptoms may appear. I will mention them because I think that they are important. Seizures may result. Paralysis, abnormal movements, and intellectual or personality changes may be seen. Academic skills may be affected. Dysphasia may occur. I am not saying *aphasia* but am using the term *dysphasia* because most victims can speak some. Strictly speaking, aphasia means without *any* speech.

Paralysis and abnormal movements

Clumsiness may be part of a mild paralysis or of cerebellar origin. *Cerebral palsy* is a common but poor term for some symptoms of the brain damaged child. *Athetosis* is one kind of abnormal movement. Any of you in your classes may see one of your youngsters, usually with so-called cerebral palsy, make certain writhing movements of one arm, hand, or his face. These movements are commonly a result of brain damage to certain deep structures.

Neurological categories include the so-called minimally brain damaged youngster (I'd put that in quotes myself), the hyperactive youngster, and those with mental retardation and various special sense disturbances. These may be blindness or deafness, and less conspicuously and less handicappingly, loss of smell or loss of taste. All of these may be manifestations of brain damage. You may consider that some cases have resulted, not from a damaged brain that was once normal, but from a defective brain that never was right. It didn't have the right chromosomes in the beginning, and the brain cannot function well.

One child may have almost any combination of these symptoms that I've mentioned. A cerebral palsied youngster may have seizures and very commonly does have seizures. You may expect certain kinds of seizures and I'll discuss these briefly in a few minutes to clarify some of the different types. This person may or may not have abnormal movement. There may be nothing conspicuous other than difficulty in learning to read or difficulty in writing. He may be able to learn to read or write fairly well, and have a miserable time with simple arithmetic. These abilities are just smaller segments or discrete segments of disturbed functioning.

When a person is rather broadly disturbed in terms of his intellectual ability, we neurologists usually call him MR—mentally retarded. Because in all spheres of intellectual activity he may be incapable of functioning up to what we require in ordinary classes, he has to be in a special class.

Probably some of the most disturbing children, for you who are teaching, are the hyperactive kids. They may be bright enough, but they can't seem to stay with you. They can't stay with anything long enough to concentrate.

If you want to interrupt me at this point, and ask questions about any of these problems, I would be willing to answer them as well as I can. If you would prefer, I can go a little bit further on my outline and come back to this kind of difficulty at any point. Does anyone have any questions?

QUESTION: *There was one word you used I would like clarified—athetosis.*

ANSWER: This is probably an area that would have little meaning specifically to this group, but there are a number of movement disorders that we see as a result of neurological disturbance. The sudden jerky movements, with twitches and constant activity, are *choreic* movements. The smaller, more writhing movements are *athetoid*. We see this with some of the cerebral palsy children who are rather markedly paralyzed. The third primary form that might be mentioned are the *dystonias*. This more nearly represents an athetosis of the trunk, and many of the afflicted will be so far bent back and will writhe so with their trunk that they are almost bent double backwards. These states are frequently associated with extreme mental retardation, and the victims are often in institutions; but once in a while you find one in an institution who isn't severely mentally retarded, and this is tragic. Something can be done for some of these individuals—some rather gratifying treatments—with the same type of procedure that is used for the Parkinsonian: needles are placed in the brain to produce small lesions and eliminate these hyperactive movements. In summary, there are the three kinds of movements—choreic, athetoid, and dystonic.

Dysfunction in academic skills

QUESTION: *Did you say that a child may read well and write well but may have some trouble with arithmetic and this could be traced to the brain having some damage?*

ANSWER: You can't always trace it to brain *damage*. When we talk about the problem of brain functioning from the neurological standpoint, the neurologist uses a variety of methods and tools to evaluate brain efficiency. One of his tools is the psychologist, the clinical psychologist, the testing psychologist. We neurologists have methods to determine the presence or absence of certain disturbances of the brain in terms of strengths, coordination, reflexes, and sensation. This is a clinical determination from the standpoint of the physician, if you will. But many times we will find that the youngster is very bright, very agile, and yet there are certain areas where he doesn't function well. These are in the sphere of the clinical psychologists with their standardized tests, which can only be done on humans. Much of the neurological examination, as I am explaining it, can be done on animals—not in precisely the same way—but much of the gross kind of examination can be done on animals. We can't test speech, reading, or writing on animals. In this area we can't work except with man. We can talk about transplanting hearts from chimps to humans and a chimp's heart could function very effectively, but chimps' brains do not work like a human's in higher functions; in many respects, yes, but there are great differences.

You follow this, I am sure. We are left with certain things that only the functional tests will show—the subject draws the diamond, the dots, etc. These individuals can be seriously in trouble in some areas, and yet such a person might still be an All-American basketball player. He might run a four-minute mile but have certain problems that make him have difficulty in adapting as a human. I don't know whether I've answered your question, I'll rephrase it again if I haven't.

QUESTION: *But there is always the ultimate doubt, then, as to whether it is brain damage that caused this trouble. I mean it sounds as though you're saying that you can never be sure, you can never pinpoint it unless there is really gross dysfunctioning in the person.*

ANSWER: We can't, for instance, take an X-ray picture and show it. I could put air in the spinal canal of many cerebral palsy youngsters, have air surrounding the brain and in the normal cavities inside the brain, and see that one side of the brain is shrunken up and one side is normal. They may have a paralyzed arm on the side corresponding to the shrunken brain. The other arm will work fine because, as you know, brain control is crossed. Damage in a certain area may so affect the brain that the youngster can't subtract seven from a hundred and can do very little in the way of mathematical calculation, and yet he may read fairly well and may be bright in other areas. Sometimes we can picture this, in a sense, with electrical recordings which we call the brain-wave test or EEG.

Grand mal epileptic seizures

We have mentioned neurological problems of dysphasics (speech-troubled people), epileptics, and the so-called brain damaged, not necessarily minimally brain damaged. Let me mention some of the features of the kinds of seizures that teachers may see in the classroom. The first and major form of seizure is grand mal epilepsy. This is quite stereotyped. Some instances are more severe than others, but this represents a rather complete discharge, if you will, of the brain, accompanied by muscle movements—first of stiffening, then of twitching, and finally relaxing. The person falls down. He may or may not have a warning that something is getting ready to happen to him—an aura. Some people have a warning and some never do. If they do have, it is a great benefit because they can usually protect themselves. Grand mal attacks last for one or two minutes or so and are followed by a somnolent period. There may be a headache or muscle soreness for a while, and then the child is likely to be quite all right. Some don't feel very well for a day or so, but most people don't have much trouble.

This kind of seizure disrupts the class because it is a very dramatic event. The response of children in the classroom where this happens, and especially when they have never seen a seizure, is rather directly dependent upon the reaction of the teacher. I would hope that any of you, if you have not seen seizures, will maintain your cool in the face of this event. There isn't much that you can do; there isn't much that you *need* to do. You can try to prevent the person from hitting his head and injuring himself—move him out of the way of the radiator or something of this sort, of course—but be *calm*. It's an event that can happen to any of us, and I mean that literally. If you act as though this is something terrible, it is going to stigmatize the youngster.

Petit mal seizures

The little blank spells of petit mal are fairly stereotyped too. They are momentary episodes that occur with no warning in any of the youngsters.

They last for several seconds; the eyes may roll up or they may just stare, and you may see just a little nodding of the head or just a little movement of the hands. This occurs at about three per second and matches with the electrical patterns that come from the brain at that time. The return of consciousness is instantaneous. There is no confusion after a single spell, and the youngster may only realize that he can't account for the time that has passed. If he has repeated spells, of course, then the whole conversation that is going on in the class may be a blur. If you take too much out of context, the rest doesn't make sense, but with rare and brief seizures, there will be little disturbance to the class or in such pupils' ability to perform. They do not fall down with the so-called petit mal lapse, but a few of them will have a different kind of a muscle jerk, and a few of them, rather than lapse appreciably, will slump—just drop very quickly—and then come back. An occasional child will make a sudden jerk, a so-called *myoclonic* attack, and this is all. Many of these people seem not to be unconscious any more than a person who blinks is unconscious. If they do lose consciousness, it's so quick we can't measure it.

Psychomotor seizures

After the grand mal and the petit mal, the third type of seizure we classify is the psychomotor seizure. This is a seizure that lasts several seconds, or maybe a minute or two. It is usually preceded by a strange feeling. This type is not very common in children but becomes more common as you get into the older age group. These people may make grimacing, mouthy, licking, smelling, and tasting movements. You might think it a little like your dog having a chase after something in his sleep. There is often a certain amount of groping or fumbling movement with the hands. The person may respond when spoken to or may seemingly react and yet not be able to answer. He gradually comes out of it, as though coming out of a mental fog, and eventually gets into "focus."

Circle of Willis

QUESTION: *Recently,* Newsweek *carried an article on unexplained cripples who are being linked with neurological problems, specifically in an area called* circle of Willis. *Does this have any significance to us as we see these kids later?*

ANSWER: This has been a problem for a long time. It particularly concerns the pediatricians. I just didn't read my *Newsweek* thoroughly that night. The circle of Willis is the circle of blood vessels that enables the brain to tolerate a reduction of blood flow from one of the vessels that comes up the front of the neck or the back of the neck. These vessels are connected together by a circle of smaller collaterals, but they can become quite functionally important. If one of the vessels gets plugged up, the interconnections will enable the blood to circulate via a detour into the artery of the brain and so supply oxygen and sugar to that area, thus preventing a stroke. The circle of Willis is just that—a circle.

QUESTION: *Like an electric grid system?*

ANSWER: Well, in a sense it is a grid, but under ordinary circumstances there is little flow through the collaterals. If you have two pipes with equal pressure going in one direction and a cross-connection is made, there will be no flow in the cross-connection until there is a pressure differential in the two main pipes. But if you stop the flow in one pipe, then you get flow through the cross-connection. Remember, the brain cannot get along without blood for more than a very few seconds, and collaterals must be immediately available in case the normal source of blood is cut off.

QUESTION: *So this is not basically neurological?*

ANSWER: The circle of Willis is a very important structure from the standpoint of neurology because the brain has to have nourishment and has to get it by way of blood supply; and there may be abnormality in this, including disturbance of vessels in the neck.

NEUROLOGICAL DIAGNOSIS

I don't think it's up to the teacher to attempt to differentiate the type of seizure a child has, but only to recognize the problem and understand that any of these events may occur as a part of a brain problem. They may occur as the *only* manifestation of a brain problem, and this is quite common. On the other hand, there may be any combination of two or more types of seizures. It's rather unusual to have the petit mal and the psychomotor without having the grand mal, but even this combination may occur.

When we are examining youngsters for neurological problems, the neurologist is faced with the matter of establishing whether or not there is something progressive going on. For instance, is there a brain tumor? The history may make it quite convincing that there is actually nothing that's progressive. The problem may have occurred from the very beginning. It may have been quite unchanging for such a long time that it's unreasonable to expect there has been a brain tumor, or a blood clot, or a brain abscess. These things usually have other symptoms that begin to give themselves away—i.e., signs of infection in the cases of abscess, signs of increasing pressure in the case of blood clots and brain tumors that make swelling in the back of the eyes.

Among the studies that the neurologist must perform in his neurological examination are determinations as to whether there is normal movement, normal reflex function, and normal sensation throughout the body. Do the special senses function in a normal fashion? Is this youngster rather smooth, well coordinated, and agile, or is he just a little bit awkward? If he is a bit awkward, is this the result of something that is basically a change in his initial potential, or was he just more awkward than some children? We're not all going to run the four-minute mile, but what is to be considered the normal spectrum? At what point does awkwardness or dullness reflect the pathological state? We know for sure that there are some people with brain damage who are functioning at, let's say, 140 IQ, if you want to use that term. Without damage their potential might have been 165. There are others who never had anything happen to them but were never destined basically to be functioning over 91 IQ, let's say. So there are the abnormal brights and the normal dullards. We must take these elements into consideration.

We go over a routine physical examination, and from the neurological standpoint, we do certain special things, often including the electroencephalogram. This is quite comparable to the electrical test of the heart, though the electrical potentials are much, much smaller and the information is more general and usually not as specific. We may at times, however, find quite specific things, especially in certain kinds of seizures—petit mal epilepsy and to a lesser extent psychomotor epilepsy. Many of the children with cerebral palsy, the ones who may have a shrunken brain on one side and a normal-size brain on the other, may have profound abnormal frequencies coming off the area that is disturbed, and we learn a lot from this.

I've already mentioned the pneumoencephalogram, where we inject air into the spinal fluid space and take pictures of the brain that we cannot see in ordinary pictures of the head. When we take plain X-ray pictures of the head, we take pictures primarily of the box that the brain is in.

It's like trying to see a drop of gin in a glass of water; you can't see it. We also take pictures of the blood vessels by injecting material that circulates very, very rapidly. It requires rapid X-ray sequences, but we can visualize the working of the circulatory system in the cranial cavity, and sometimes we find clogged up vessels. Sometimes we find abnormal formations of vessels or tangled masses that are clearly a malformation. We may find that the vessels are distorted by a tumor or by a scar. The brain, if it is shrunken, will have serious changes in the vascular system. Now to this point I have told you about some of the manifestations of neurological disturbance and some of the things that the neurologist studies. Obviously, we can't go into minutiae, but I shall go into more detail if this is brought up in questions.

FACTS AND FALLACIES ABOUT SEIZURES

QUESTION: *When you were talking about the grand mal seizure, you mentioned that the adult really can't do too much, except perhaps to keep the child from banging his head. I've heard that there is a danger of the child swallowing his tongue. Is this fact or fallacy?*

ANSWER: Well, mostly fallacy. It's desirable, if you can get there, to put something soft between the teeth to prevent biting. Usually the youngster already has fallen out of his chair or fallen down on the floor. Sometimes they let out a cry, and you have time to get to them if you know what is going on. If you had never seen a seizure, chances are you'd be thinking of some disciplinary action until you realized what was actually happening. The most important thing is to see that the child has an air way. Roll him over on his side, as once in a while they will vomit. You wouldn't want him to vomit and aspirate, but don't put your finger in his mouth. Many people will have seizures frequently and never bite, but some do consistently. I should mention that many of these children will lose control of their bladders or have an involuntary stool. This, of course, creates a bit of a sensation in the class, but again, it should be handled with proper recognition of its involuntary nature, and one should not make a lot of it. In summary, you don't have to do much. Children are in very little danger in a seizure.

QUESTION: *Is it true that the worst seizures can be controlled by drugs so that the individuals can function normally?*

ANSWER: In many instances, yes. We see such cases many times for the reason that it is legal requirement in California that these people be reported to the department of motor vehicles. This means that the department of motor vehicles refers them to neurologists, and we examine them and have the opportunity to follow them up rather faithfully, because their drivers' licenses depend on it. I have dozens of people whom I see at intervals and who are legally licensed, having had seizures controlled for many years. The usual requirement is that they be controlled for two years. As a whole, this is a gratifying group of patients to see, from the standpoint of a physician. If you have to see things like brain tumors, that is *really* discouraging. You do run into some discouraging seizure problems, but I'm quite sure that I see more controlled epileptics who are legally licensed to drive than uncontrolled epileptics who are not drivers. There are other seizure cases who are seriously brain damaged, and you find them at such a place as the state institutions for retarded children. Their nervous systems have been nearly destroyed, and they are just vegetables. Many of these people have seizures, but seizures are only a symptom of the other problems. In fact, seizures are always a symptom rather than a disease in and of themselves.

Amnesia and seizures

QUESTION: *What relation is there between amnesia and seizures?*

ANSWER: This question always comes up. This is usually in the area of the so-called psychomotor seizures, which are of relatively short duration. Every once in awhile you'll read that someone picks up, leaves home, wife, and half a dozen kids in Ohio, and comes to California. A year or two later he "comes to" and finally remembers who he is. He is claiming this is amnesia and that it is a psychomotor seizure. These are not seizures, and you can forget them for all practical purposes. They are sometimes alleged for protection against the consequences of criminal acts. You just don't see these "psychomotor attacks" last any significant length of time where there isn't some sort of secondary gain that you can write into it. Everybody who knows he has attacks has nothing of this sort happen. The person who has never had a seizure and then gets on the airplane, flies to New York, takes a bus to his mother-in-law's, hits her over the head with a hammer and kills her, and then says this must have been a psychomotor seizure hasn't had one. This is stretching one's credulity. I don't think we need to be concerned about this.

Socioeconomic status and heredity

QUESTION: *Is there any evidence that these brain damaged conditions are more prevalent in low-income families?*

ANSWER: I think only to the extent that there is an inheritance situation in which the problem makes the whole family constellation less able to compete, and then their low-income situation is probably a reflection of the illness rather than vice versa. In addition, they would beget children like themselves.

QUESTION: *You're saying there is a tendency for epilepsy to be inherited. There are states that do have laws, you know, saying that epileptics cannot marry.*

ANSWER: By and large the laws are getting wiped off the books, but there is something to this hereditary thing—like migraine, if you will. We don't know how migraine is inherited, but we recognize that it is a family affair. There is a certain tendency, particularly for petit mal, to occur in a family. Yes, this tends to occur many times in very bright kids, and it's the one thing that often ultimately disappears. Anyway this is a disease of the little kids, and it almost always disappears in the third decade. It never starts after the second decade, so it's a disease of the young. Some statistical analyses suggested that this seizure incidence is in the range of maybe one in sixty in some families instead of one in two hundred which might be expected in the general population. So it isn't strong. It's not like the specific recessive of PKU. It's not like the strong dominant heredity of Huntington's chorea, mental retardation, and so on.

Occupations for epileptics

QUESTION: *There is one other little area on which we might just touch, and this is a rule or regulation that epileptics are not supposed to become teachers. Do you agree with this?*

ANSWER: I do not. I am a staunch supporter of the epileptics. You know, this is a dreadful thing. It's perfectly respectable to have heart trouble, but if you go to an epilepsy meeting where you're trying to help people learn to have some respect for themselves, which many of them do not have because of society's attitude toward the affliction, nobody shows up—but nobody! And if they do, you find out that they don't want to say that they're coming for their daughter, or their son, or their mother; it's just not acceptable.

There just isn't any basis for this attitude. There is no reason why an epileptic shouldn't teach school. I think it's one of the things an epileptic could do safely. In teaching school, an epileptic is not likely to be cut up by a piece of machinery. It is a rather safe occupation. Incidentally, you have professors at the university who are epileptic. You'd be surprised what a neurologist knows. All of us can have seizures, and it is time we stopped treating people as though they were possessed by demons when they have a comparatively minor neurological dysfunction that is usually well controlled.

TREATMENT FOR SEIZURES

I'd like to mention briefly the matter of treatment for the seizures. It's important from a neurological standpoint to know what seizure type is occurring because medication is so different, and you'll probably have some youngsters in your classes who are taking medication morning and evening and maybe at lunch. This causes a problem at some of the schools because they think that the teachers can't ask the kids whether they've taken their noon pill if they stay for lunch. Dilantin and phenobarbital are the old standbys for grand mal seizures and for psychomotor seizures. I won't mention the newer ones. For petit mal we have to use entirely different kinds of drugs. I'm not mentioning their names, as I don't think they are important to you. It is, however, important that we do not confuse psychomotor seizures with petit mal seizures, because the treatment is so utterly different.

Once in a while the doctor needs the help of the teacher because, strangely enough, some mothers aren't very observant, and while many times we get good history of what's going on from the families, sometimes we can't. Every once in a while an excellent history that just nails it down comes from what the teacher can tell me, because the teacher is with the kids for a long time and watching them carefully.

In addition to the anticonvulsants, I should mention the tranquilizers. Some of these very active kids need tranquilizers, but some of the hyperactive youngsters backfire on them. For several years we've been using medicines, such as dexedrine, that should charge these kids up, but they seem instead to enable them to concentrate. Dosage that might keep us awake at night will enable these children, whose attention is attracted to something different every five seconds, to concentrate on something long enough so they can see what's there. They can figure the arithmetic, see what the word is, and sit on their seat long enough so you can teach the rest of the class. So they are very important medicines. Dexedrine is one of the things used for other purposes with some abandon on college campuses.

QUESTION: *What causes a hyperactive child? Is it that the brain can't close out stimuli?*

ANSWER: First of all I can say that I really don't know, but I can speculate a little. It may have something to do with the so-called reticular-activating formation, which has to do with keeping us awake. It has to be active. When it closes down, our whole brain closes down. There are significant aspects of this problem that are related both to the thalamus and hypothalamus, but these are things that we really don't know much about.

QUESTION: *I read about the drug dilantin. We are using it now as a mood elevator in some instances, and I was wondering what the relation was?*

ANSWER: Well, Mr. Dreyfus was a very successful mutual-fund promoter —and I think almost a one-man fund operator, as I understand it— who was smart enough to get out of the fund-management business when the stock market began to flatten out a little bit. He made a tremendous fortune for himself and other people, and his name was in full-page ads in the magazines with the big lion coming out toward you. Somehow or another, he got dilantin given to him, and this resulted in the big *Life* magazine article, which was then replayed in the *Reader's Digest*. For years all of us in neurology had been using dilantin in not just purely seizure cases. The drug is thirty years old and has been available for physicians' use during all that time and for a while before that for experimental use. This is about the same length of time that there's been any active use of electroencephalography. Correlation between electroencephalographic abnormalities and seizures has resulted in general use of electroencephalography, and many people who are suspected of having seizures or suspected of having something wrong with their head get electroencephalograms. Sometimes the findings are a little bit surprising, and you don't expect to find what you run into; and sometimes without having any frank seizure-like clinical picture, you have an epileptic-like picture in the EEG. This then has resulted in the use of dilantin and other anticonvulsants to see whether this would do anything favorable for the person. A number of people with headaches that weren't benefited by ordinary headache medicines were helped by dilantin or other anticonvulsants when they had an abnormal electroencephalogram. We have been using dilantin on difficult problems of a wide variety for a long time. Every once in a while we find somebody who reacts like this Dreyfus, but somehow or other, if something of this sort happens to me it doesn't quite get the publicity that it got when it happened to Dreyfus. This was just telling what a lot of people in medicine had been doing for a long time, but they had been hiding their light under the bushel, so to speak.

QUESTION: *If it's used with epileptics, isn't it used to quiet the person? Does it enable them to get away from their problems as a tranquilizer would do?*

ANSWER: We really don't know why it does what it does. We do know that dilantin, when it's in a solution, will slow the speed of conduction down a nerve fibre. Incidentally, it has a number of side effects. We are finding, more and more all the time, potentially dangerous effects —and some very serious effects on a very small number of people. But when you give it to millions, of course, you run into this problem sometimes. We know also that, although it doesn't stop the "sparks" that cause an epileptic seizure, it seems to dampen the surrounding brain areas so that the spark doesn't flare up everything and cause a seizure. This we know. Why it has a relieving effect on headaches, for instance, I can't tell you; and I don't think anyone else can, but it does sometimes function in this way.

NEUROLOGICAL DYSFUNCTION AND
CLASSROOM PERFORMANCE

There are many children who are having trouble with reading, which means they are having trouble in learning—and often a greater degree of trouble than their testing results would suggest. It seems that this may have something to do with the lateralizing of functions of the brain. We know, for instance, that the vast majority of people, and even some of those who are left-handed, have predominant language function in the left brain. A small lesion up in the angular area in the left parietal region may make it difficult to calculate. It may also cause a mix-up as far as right and left is concerned. Affected people don't know which side is right and which side is left, and they just don't know whose fingers or what fingers are on their hand.

QUESTION: *Did you say they don't know which finger or whose fingers they are?*

ANSWER: Yes, sometimes they can't identify their own fingers.

QUESTION: *Is this a type of agnosia?*

ANSWER: Yes; but it may not be due to quite such a specific and focal lesion as was once thought. Let me add to this. We know that weird things may happen if we cut the corpus callosum. This has been done on a number of occasions. It separates the two halves of the brain. You may recall that visual impulses coming from the left of center strike the right half of the back of the two eyes. This image then is fed to the right half of the brain in the back. By the same token, what is right of center for both eyes comes into both eyes and goes back to the left side of the brain. You cut this connection between the two halves of the brain (which has been done for experimental, but rather good, reasons in intractable seizure cases). A few people have been materially benefited. These people, with visual stimuli reaching only one half of their brain, have been studied intensively. One half of the brain can do things the other half doesn't know about. This becomes very fancy, if you will, from the psychological standpoint and from the neurological standpoint. I'm only mentioning some of the problems, and I'm not giving you any answers in this regard at all.

We do know, however, that most people, even those who are left-handed, usually speak from the left brain. One way you can tell this is by injecting a barbiturate into the carotid artery on the left side, and most of it goes to the left side of the brain; or it goes to the right side if injected into the right side of the neck. There is some crossover in some people, but this is not great. So we inject a small amount of barbiturate rather slowly, and we find out whether a person loses speech from having one side of his brain, instead of the other, anesthetized. Some of the darnest inconsistencies can arise. Again, I'm not giving you answers, except to tell you that almost 100 percent of right-handed people speak from the left side and a sizable percentage of people who are writing with their left hand will also be speaking from the left side of the brain. This is obviously important when it comes time to lose part of our brain, as with a stroke. I really don't know about my own laterality. Since I am left-handed, I have a considerable curiosity about which side of the brain I speak from and how much speech I would lose from having transient drug effect on one side of my brain.

In any event, we do have laterization, and we wonder why some people are right-handed and why some people are left-handed. Why is it that, when I see a whole group of kids, I see too many who don't know right and left and who throw with one hand, kick with the opposite foot, and sight with a different eye; and why is it that these children often don't read well? Why do left-handers want to write *was* instead of *saw*, *no* instead of *on*, and vice versa. You are going to see that if you are teaching at the early levels where the children learn to read and write.

QUESTION: *Isn't this spelling of words backwards transient and normal at a younger age—at about 4 or something like that?*

ANSWER: It's usually outgrown. It seems to be overwhelmingly, in my experience, the kids who are kind of mixed up as to which side is which. Whether you've had the same experience or not, I don't know, but it seems to me that this is the case.

QUESTION: *Well, my little girl did this for about a year—put her words backwards—and then she stopped all by herself.*

ANSWER: You made a point there. Yes, we agree that children usually outgrow it. Also, why on earth is it so overwhelmingly present in boys instead of girls? We have stammering too, and all these troubles are not exclusively but are overwhelmingly in boys. Did you read in the paper last night about the deep-sea divers who have only girls? This is also an interesting thing. Certainly somebody's going to observe this. It has long been a problem.

QUESTION: *Are little-boy problems not psychological? Do they not tend to get punished by the lady kindergarten and lady first-grade teachers?*

ANSWER: Have you been reading *Today's Health?* In a recent issue they pointed out that young boys are taught to be boys—to make noise, to horse around, to run around, and this sort of thing. Little girls are taught to sit down, to be quiet, to listen, and so forth. Then when they get to school, teachers want little boys to start acting like little girls, and they punish them if they don't. I think this crosses their brains up a little bit. In the article I mentioned in *Today's Health*, it seemed pretty well documented that the boys doing the same level of work get lower grades than the girls.

QUESTION: *Can I back up on something? Is it possible to summarize what you think about mixed dominance? I gather you're leading us to the fact that there is something to mixed dominance in a left-handed person's having reading problems because of neurological disturbance. Do you support this generally?*

ANSWER: Well, I want to say that I don't feel that I have any documented statistical data. I have a strong personal impression, perhaps a prejudice, if it isn't more firmly documented. I do think that maybe I paid closer attention to this as an impression over a longer period of time than some observers because of having this dysfunction rather close at home—having been "mixed" myself and then having the same thing in my family.

QUESTION: *You know there seems to be a great deal of controversy on it; even among neurologists, as I understand, there is controversy. Can you comment on this Delacato, who claims the reading problems occur because the child did not creep as a young child.*

ANSWER: I think that I can speak for most neurologists when I say we feel that this is somewhat akin to the old cosmic-ray business down in Long Beach—that this just doesn't add up to the achievement of human potential as they are trying to claim. I think that they got a great deal of publicity from the business of the Joseph Kennedy case.

QUESTION: *This publicity has created an awful lot of anxious parents whose kids don't crawl, for example. They crawl for one month, and if they get up and walk, the parents are anxious because they are going to be bad readers six years hence.*

ANSWER: I'm not a psychologist, and as an organically oriented person I express my opinion, and I have no objection to continuing to do so. I think it's good, in one way, for you people to be exposed to prejudices and then have to balance it up with your own observations. Sometimes relatively strong opinions make you pay closer attention than if you get some middle-of-the-road answer, but I do not see any systematic relationship between crawling and later reading effectiveness.

QUESTION: *I have in some of my very low classes a few students, quite often boys, who cannot really write or spell. I would say that if they filled a page with a composition they might have no more than twenty words spelled correctly. Would you comment? Also, I am often confronted with a term,* dyslectic. *Do neurologists use this term?*

ANSWER: I think most neurologists use the term *dyslexia*. It's the same word, isn't it? That means nothing except that the person has trouble reading. If you want to say that's visual verbal agnosis, you haven't said anything basically new; you're just made a name for the problem. Dr. Wilson and I have talked about some of these things. I have not been quite as much at an advantage in other circumstances when I've talked to him about this problem as I am now, and I enjoy it. But my completely uneducated guessing is (and we've talked about this, too) that the children have not had, perhaps, in recent years the repetitive stimulation that maybe the kids got fifty years ago. In those days, when they didn't have so many other things around the schoolroom and so many other things when they got home, by the time they had spent a week with *bat, cat, fat, that, hat, mat, pat,* you know, maybe they learned what *A* and *T* sounded like and looked like. I asked Dr. Wilson some time ago, "Do you have any data that would indicate whether fifty years ago there was as much difficulty with spelling, writing, and reading as we have now?" But at the moment he couldn't recall any specific research. I think maybe he has looked up something since. I know it's a bit difficult to answer. I didn't expect it to be an easy answer.

QUESTION: *Would you tend toward the idea that these reading and writing problems are educational handicaps rather than neurological ones?*

ANSWER: I wonder if there are not more of these problems now than there were years ago, and maybe that is a significant factor that indicates the effect of a particular type of schooling. I'm sure that there are some children who are going to have problems of this type as long as we have schools, and some of them will be due to neurological difficulties.

QUESTION: *As a neurologist, do you hold to the theory that the nerves operate on an all-or-none firing principle?*

ANSWER: I think that you're probably referring more to the question of whether the brain operates on the mass principle, the all or none.

QUESTION: *Yes, right.*

ANSWER: It's pretty generally agreed that a single fiber, a single nerve-cell discharge, is an all-or-none kind of principle. But are you asking how this applies to the brain as a whole?

QUESTION: *Well, also, you made the statement that repetition was important; once the nerve in the brain had been stimulated, the repetition was no longer that important because the firing had taken place. The DNA, or whatever is involved, had been stimulated and recorded.*

ANSWER: All right, can you read something the length of the *Star Spangled Banner* once and then give it back to me just as easily as you can give the *Star Spangled Banner?*

QUESTION: *No, because I probably haven't fired all the nerves or brain cells that are necessary to bring this about.*

ANSWER: Somehow or other there is some kind of facilitation for repetition. I think that this even gets over into the neurological literature from the psychological literature. We don't know the exact mechanism of memory. We know that this has something to do with the temporal lobe. There is dreadful impairment of memory when the temporal lobe is destroyed.

QUESTION: *Well, it seems to me that these students who can't write very well don't seem to benefit by any kind of repetition at all. I could give them the same word thirty times, and they'd have to ask me the thirty-first time how to spell it. I don't see any indication in my own classroom where any kind of repetition seems to work. It seems to me they should be able to spell some of the simple words they misspell just by the fact that they're 13 years old and have, I'm sure, asked many, many times how to spell this one simple word. It's beyond me how it could be educational rather than neurological at this age, but I'm sure it could be.*

ANSWER: There are some psychological problems that are motivational in nature that help to feed into this pattern. Now, I don't think they're the whole thing. I think there are some neurological substructures here, too, but I don't know what they are. They're too fine. We're talking now about super-refinements. So much of my work has to do with whether there is a Babinski response here, an abnormal reflex, which probably does not show up unless a good many neurons are out of kilter. We can't measure these things that have to do with spelling. Most of these people will have nothing wrong with the gross electrical patterns off the surface. They won't be having any paroxysmal discharges of such a nature that you can say they get fuzzed up because they're out of contact briefly every few seconds and, thus, can't reorient themselves and get things all back together. We have no explanation.

QUESTION: *What does the future hold for resolving something like this? What are the projections in neurology?*

ANSWER: Again, I don't know. I suspect that with more and more technical refinements we are more and more able to look at one single cell in the brain and we are more and more learning what its effects may be on other cells. The brain is a solid organ, and you can't lay it out flat and look at it as you can look at a gut or the heart. It's going to be the last organ to be understood, isn't it? I can't really look into the future except to predict that a little bit at a time, we're going to find pieces of data. We're learning in neurochemistry. We are learning chemically what goes on in these cells. The chemistry of DNA has been a tremendous stride forward, and this information applies to the brain, too.

Informing classmates about seizures

QUESTION: *We spoke before about grand mal and how a teacher shouldn't make a big deal out of it when it happens. If a teacher knows, because it's on the health record, that a student is epileptic and does have grand mal seizures, do you think it would be best to tell the class at a teachable moment, before, or right after, the first seizure occurs; and, if so, do you do it in front of the student?*

ANSWER: I'm not sure that even the teacher is any better off knowing a child may have seizures. Many times the youngster is going to go through the whole year and the teacher will never see him have one. Teachers are very different, one from another, and some of them are frightened. They shouldn't be, but some people withdraw from something like this. Sometimes, in retrospect, it would have been nicer for the teacher to know, but I just don't know how you're going to tell. Many times parents ask me, "Should we tell the teacher?" and I often answer this partly on the basis of how likely I think it is that the youngster is going to have seizures in that class. It's completely individualized as far as I'm concerned.

QUESTION: *Would we be likely to have one of these people in class who has successive grand mals? They say these are more dangerous than a single grand mal. Would we come into contact with one of these people in the class? Would they even be allowed to go to school?*

ANSWER: Well, you might, because a person may have had only rare seizures and then go into status. When they have one after another, they certainly should be brought immediately to medical attention, should be taken to a hospital. People who have seizures this seriously are not very likely to be a surprise in the class. They're likely to have had enough rather sporadic attacks that their epileptic state is known. It wouldn't be a real surprise; but if he had one after another you'd say, "Let's get him out of here. Get him home!"

QUESTION: *How common are these?*

ANSWER: Quite rare. In the kind of practice that I have, I probably don't see more than one a year. However, I talked recently with the neurological residents down in Camarillo (a mental hospital) and was rather surprised to learn that they wanted me to discuss some aspects of seizures, because their most common neurological problem down there is status epilepticus. It surprised me, as I didn't realize they saw that much of it. So you see, it depends on where you are. If you're going to see first graders, you don't come out to the university.

QUESTION: *Could we return to a question? If a child has a grand mal seizure in the classroom, should you talk to the kids about what happened?*

ANSWER: After a seizure, after the child has gone, I have no objection to the teacher explaining to the class. Yes, I think you should very calmly tell them that "Bill has a certain kind of sickness. He passes out, and when he's passed out he jerks like this; but this is nothing to be concerned about. He probably needs to be treated, and after he's treated for a while he won't do that any more."

QUESTION: *What do you mean when you said a person is gone? Where did he go after the seizure was completed?*

ANSWER: Probably at least to the nurse's office where he can lie down. Most of them, unless they have relatively mild grand mal, are going to have to lie down and sleep for a little while. My experience has been that, even though I don't particularly wish it done, teachers usually rush them home. If the youngster isn't doped up—I mean fuzzy getting over this—and doesn't complain of headaches, and if he hasn't wet himself, in which case it might be embarrassing for him, then I would rather he be kept at school. Does that answer it?

QUESTION: *Would the first grand mal usually occur before the kindergarten age?*

ANSWER: Grand mal can start at any time of life, but it starts from different causes. Remember, I said that this is a symptom. This is like a fever. I often explain to people who come in with a youngster who has seizures that it's like when all the family gets a cold. One kid may run a temperature of 104 degrees, and all the rest of the family will run 99, but they all get the cold; they all get fever. As far as seizures are concerned, we can all have seizures. This is inherent in all of us if we get enough of a "spark." About the timing of seizures, since the seizure is a symptom, youngsters who have something happen to their brain are likely to start seizures in the first few years. After the first few years, it may be that quite a variety of things that can make it happen, and of course, how you treat them depends on the cause of the seizures. Each case is individual. Many will not have any grand mals until they are well into school. They may start having grand mals after they have had a series of petit mals; but when you backtrack on this, you may find that quite a few of these children, in the first year or two, have had a convulsion with fever. So febrile convulsions are fairly common as a precursor to the development of more seemingly spontaneous seizures later—maybe later in the first decade, maybe not until puberty. Puberty is a rather ticklish time for all of these seizures, incidentally. They may start or they may stop about that time.

QUESTION: *Doesn't it take a period of about two or three months to get a child suffering from seizures under control?*

ANSWER: Remember, each one is different. A youngster may come in after having one seizure, and we may feel that the youngster had some particular precipitating cause for that seizure and maybe that cause is not something that is going to recur. There is a certain reluctance, particularly if you don't have anything abnormal in the brain test, to institute treatment that you might have to continue for several years, when perhaps there's not going to be any recurrence anyway. At 6 or 7 or 8 years of age there's no problem with driving, so the only thing you'd suggest is that they be watched, particularly if they went swimming. I discourage them from climbing trees. But other than this, you might find that the best thing in the world to do is to give them no treatment. So you have to consider each one individually.

THE ROLE OF THE SPECIALIST

QUESTION: *If a decision has to be made as to whether a regular school or special school is better for a brain damaged child, do parents rely on you to make that decision?*

ANSWER: No, I can't make that decision because it's the decision primarily of the schools. In the Goleta, California, schools there are those who are having trouble learning who may or may not be brain damaged. They may look all right, and they may not be the kind who are partially paralyzed. (These children are often seen at schools for the trainable mentally retarded.) These youngsters are staffed and are discussed at great length. Usually they are seen by an ophthalmologist, pediatrician, a psychologist (more than one), a psychiatrist, and a neurologist. We have the teacher and the principal there in almost all cases. The students are pretty intensively evaluated. The recommended decision is then made jointly, and not by the doctor. An administrator makes the operating decision after getting advice from all these specialists.

QUESTION: *Are most school systems staffed adequately to take in consultations of all these specialists?*

ANSWER: If they're like Goleta, they are, because they don't pay you anything to do it. This community has numerous pediatricians. It has four neurologists, where most communities of this size have no neurologists. The medical coverage here is quite different than it would be in the average community of 70,000 population. So it's true; many places simply wouldn't have the variety of specialized talents to view these problems in this way.

QUESTION: *What is the distinction between the terms neuropsychiatry and psychiatry?*

ANSWER: Way back when neurology and psychiatry were one and the same, nobody knew very much about either; and as knowledge became more extensive, it became apparent that neurology, being primarily a structural subject, and psychiatry, being medical psychology, should be separated. But for a time the psychiatrists called themselves neuropsychiatrists and they were practicing both neurology and psychiatry. This is getting less and less common. A neuropsychiatrist is likely now to be a man in his 60s or 70s.

QUESTION: *In what proportion do you find a positive neurological defect in the children referred to you by the school system?*

ANSWER: I'm sorry that I can't just go back through a batch of them. I would guess that somewhere between one-half or one-fourth show a significant neurological defect. Though I may not find other things wrong, I'm often impressed that they simply are not educationally agile, that they can't write well, and so on. In terms of playing on the baseball field, perhaps, they might be topnotch. So they are not neurologically defective in the sense of the neuromuscular system.

QUESTION: *Do you feel that a diagnosis that you make is usually acted on by the school and the teacher, so that this child's capacity to learn and capacity to adjust to all the situations of his life are appreciably improved?*

ANSWER: I think that my responsibility is to make specific recommendations. I think that there is usually healthy dialogue, and we usually reach a consensus. The medical group, the psychological group, and the teachers usually reach pretty good agreement on what is the best thing to be done. There may be some minority opinions, such as, "Why don't you try to give this youngster a one-to-one situation, because he seems to have responded better to that than anything else?" There's no real difference of opinion. I think we are rather uniformly frustrated. I think the psychologist and the pediatricians—all of us—are frustrated by these kids who look like they ought to be able to do something that they can't do; and nobody thus far has been able to make them do it. So it's easier for somebody like a neurologist to say, "Well, why didn't the second- or third-grade teacher work harder on the basics?"

QUESTION: *Do you find that teachers and, perhaps, the principals seem to be too much orientated to the social-emotional cause pattern rather than to a neurological cause?*

ANSWER: I wouldn't say that. As I expressed myself a few minutes ago, I wonder whether there isn't much more of this now than there was years ago. If it is true—and I'm wondering if it isn't—maybe when there were one- or two-room schools and the teacher had to control the situation by having a kid write *have* five hundred times, until he learned *have*, the teacher, without even intending to do so, used more repetition because she was so busy teaching the fourth, fifth, and sixth graders. I'm sure the kids didn't put on the fancy musical-comedy productions and so on that they do now in the junior high schools, but I still tend to think that there probably was less difficulty in teaching and learning the basics.

READING AND LANGUAGE DIFFICULTIES

Carolyn Hedley

7

Dr. Carolyn N. Hedley is assistant professor of education at Fordham University of Lincoln Center, New York City. She is a graduate of San Francisco State College and the University of California at Berkeley, and she received her Ed.D. from the University of Illinois.

Dr. Hedley has published widely in such magazines as School Science and Mathematics, The Journal of Reading, *and* Educational and Psychological Measurements. *Presently she is coauthoring, with her husband, W. Eugene Hedley, a book entitled* Language, Meaning and Education, *which is to be published soon.*

Formerly an instructor at the University of Illinois, Dr. Hedley has taught at Roosevelt University in Chicago, as well as at the University of California at Santa Barbara. At present, she directs a reading clinic at Fordham University and is affiliated there with the Institute for Research and Evaluation. She is organizing mother-child tutoring projects in Harlem, New York City, as part of a clinical outreach to literacy problems.

In this chapter, we are concerned with reading disabilities and with disabilities in the area of language. The most important skill in the curriculum in the public schools, reading, is the subject upon which all the other content areas depend—science, social studies, math, English and foreign language studies. Therefore, reading disability is more of a disability than that of being unable to function in the realm of math, science, or history.

WAYS OF ASSESSING READING DISABILITY

When one tries to define reading disability, there is no definition that is generally accepted. One can relate reading age to mental age and determine whether the youngster is reading to capacity; or one can compare and contrast reading achievement level to chronological age and mental age in order to determine whether or not the child is reading to expectancy. This kind of formula is crude, but it can be useful for the classroom teacher. For instance, if the child has a chronological age of 7 years, 2 months, and he is reading at 6 years, 8 months, then one can judge that in first grade the youngster is reading below his chronological age. Is he, however, reading below his mental ability? Taking his mental age (from a nonlanguage intelligence test, if such a test exists in truth), it can be determined whether or not he is reading up to his ability.

There are many formuli to determine the level at which a student should be reading; computers are becoming helpful in determining the kind of performance that we can expect from youngsters scholastically, but the fact remains that no matter what kind of tests you use to test mentality or reading ability, the tests are measuring, in part, a language dimension and are not completely valid. At this point, the teacher readily sees that determining reading capacity by formula becomes a handy labeling process, but it is scarcely fair to the child whose abilities she is measuring.

With regard to reading tests themselves, most give a score on reading speed, reading comprehension, and reading vocabulary. This gives the teacher a measure of the child's reading understanding and his reading vocabulary size. The child who is intelligent should be reading well above grade level. However, the teacher is apt to feel that if he is in the top group, reading at grade level, he is a "good" reader. A problem with developing reading potential is that the youngster uses controlled-vocabulary reading materials, even while studying in the other content areas; therefore, he is not exposed to materials that he is potentially capable of handling. Such a student will read better than his peers but not nearly as well as he should. Individuals do not learn that to which they have not been exposed.

Another simple way of checking reading capability is to read aloud with the student, using materials from the various grade levels. The level of his listening comprehension is a thumbnail index to his potential. The teacher may then test the youngster to determine whether or not he is, in fact, reading at that level. In other words, if I read to you from a sixth-grade reader and you, a third grader, understand what I am reading, the implication is that if you were reading to potential, you would be reading at sixth-grade level.

One readily sees that all methods for determining reading potential, and therefore reading disability, are somewhat gross and that they serve as a kind labeling procedure. In general, they fail to give insight into mental and verbal processes of the cognitive workings of the student.

For practical purposes, teachers often look at intelligence-test scores and roughly judge whether or not the child should be reading on grade level or above it or below it. For instance, if you are teaching a youngster with an 86 intelligence quotient, he is not likely to be reading on grade level; if he is, he is overachieving in a sense, or more important, the intelligence-test score may not be a true measure of the child's mental potential.

TEACHER MOTIVATION IN READING PROBLEMS

Most of the time, teachers are concerned if the children are not reading at grade level. In part, the teacher reaction stems from the inconvenience to her that results when she must organize reading groups for children who are reading below the level of instruction in her class. Also, teachers find that, when youngsters cannot read grade-level materials in such areas as math, social science, and history, the teacher finds herself creating materials for her poorer readers, or she finds that these poorly performing readers are discipline problems. In fact, though he may be a slow reader, the youngster is not truly a remedial reading case unless he is not working to potential. A child who is working nearly at grade level with an 86 intelligence-quotient score is an overachiever; to harass such a youngster by revealing one's own anxieties to him creates problems rather than solves them, since the child probably is working as well as he is able.

A note of caution is interjected here. Frequently, youngsters are given intelligence tests or mental-ability tests. These tests affect the teacher's expectancies and attitudes for children's achievements. However, for the child who is reading below grade level (and presumably about half the youngsters in school are, since reading tests are standardized according to curves of central tendency), these tests are not valid. The child who reads poorly and who gets a low mental-ability score (for instance, a score of 79 as an intelligence quotient) is not being tested for his mental acuity; rather he is being penalized and labeled in a very unfortunate way for reading poorly. He cannot read and, therefore, he cannot pass the test, but this is not to say that the youngster is not intelligent.

CONTEMPORARY READING PROGRAMS

Not very much that is fresh has been said about reading disability in the last forty years. The arguments and clichés about youngsters who have reading difficulty have not changed. Recently linguists and neurologists have invaded the field of reading disability. Though these persons have brought fresh insights into some of the causes of reading and learning difficulties, the solutions applied to the problems defined are disappointingly like techniques used for teaching reading in the 1800s and before. If possible, go to a curriculum laboratory and scan the McGuffey readers and the *New England Primer*. Phonics and linguistics were a rigorous part of both programs, and in some ways these areas were approached with more logical consistency than the garbled presentation that is part of contemporary programs. Here, too, in these programs, one sees the two approaches that are still part of the reading debate today. In some portions the emphasis is on sight vocabulary or what Dr. Jeanne Chall (1967) calls the "meaning approach," and in some parts heavy emphasis falls on the "coding emphasis"—that is, a linguistic or phonic attack on words.

Presently, there is great concern about reading instruction. Having made the cognitive process of reading infinitely more difficult than it is and being increasingly less sure of our methods of teaching it, reading instruction is less well done today than it was before 1925. This is not to say that the children read less well on the whole; they may be less well taught.

Literally hundreds of educational companies are started every year to accommodate this anxiety. At any education convention, one sees a great deal of new material to aid the teacher in her reading instruction. But very little of this material contains new methods, approaches, or ideas about accomplishing the task of teaching reading effectively. Materials may be more graduated, more appropriate for the slow learner, more beautiful in format, but the content is much of the hackneyed information that has been in the possession of the teaching profession for years.

Unfortunately, none of the methodology or the instruction done in reading is too well founded on theory. Consequently, much of the research in reading is a rather goalless activity. Theory in reading is beginning to emerge as the science of linguistics has more to say to us. Moreover, we are learning much more about cognition, language theory, and learning theory. As these sciences develop, the specialist in reading will benefit. Moreover, much more study in these areas should be required of persons working for degrees above the bachelor's degree in the areas of language and reading education.

Without a science of language, research in reading tends to be rather slipshod, and the research tends to be inconsequential in terms of general language and learning theory.

CAUSES OF READING DISABILITY

Having refused to define reading disability, it may seem presumptuous to try to discuss its causes. However, the lack of logic here is only superficial. Legitimately, the teacher can be concerned if the child is much below others in his grade in his ability, and she can measure specific skills with regard to disability. For instance, naming the letters, knowing consonant sounds, and understanding the main theme of a paragraph are measurable skills, and the teacher should be concerned with the causes of not knowing these skills and with their remediation.

Slow maturation, as it refers to cerebral development, may cause poor reading achievement. Along with this same kind of impairment, one may list central nervous system damage and, possibly, minimal brain damage so slight that it cannot be measured although language and reading capacity has been impaired without any loss of intelligence. When one cannot account for a reading disablement in other ways, although the intelligence score is normal or above, more concern is being shown for these other kinds of impairments. However, much of the information concerning such impairment so far gathered is somewhat obscure. Most reading specialists recognize a kind of disability that indicates that the "receiver-connector" system transmits information rather badly (mixed dominance, poor coordination, reversals, poor perception syndrome). This syndrome of factors, which go together, has been dubbed *dyslexia*. However, few in the field of reading are prepared to define this disability with precision; presently the medical profession and the teaching profession are zeroing in on this problem.

Do not, however, be too ready to dismiss the cause of reading disability, dispatched under a handy label, when you find a child with "dyslexia." Many of us have all the variables mentioned in the above paragraph and are reading quite well. When one hides behind a term, it tends to become an excuse to give up on the problem. Persons who have believed staunchly in the idea of mixed dominance, confused cerebral development, a mixed-up neurological system, have alarmed parents unduly with such terms, sometimes misapplied, and relegated a child to limbo educationally. However, a consistent drill program, logically presented under special tutoring, has been known to help these youngsters to the point that they are able to "catch up" and pass other youngsters at that particular grade level.

Readiness

Some of the muscular development and maturational development may be a genuine physical lag. Given another year or so, the youngster's eye muscles may strengthen and his seeming neurological difficulties may disappear.

Other kinds of readiness, such as auditory and visual readiness, sometimes need special work. Some youngsters in beginning reading programs do not have directional awareness, cannot discriminate among the letters visually nor auditorily, and do not see likenesses and differences among letters or hear them among sounds. In these cases training will help, especially if well-prepared materials are used with the children.

However, do not spend a great deal of time waiting for readiness or even teaching for it. Jerome Bruner (1963) has cast a brave stone at the icon of readiness. By asserting that virtually anything can be taught to any student at any age in an intellectually honest form, one can extrapolate that it is better to teach readiness skills and reading than to wait for the youngster to be ready. Give the child practice in the skills he needs and expose him to symbolic activity. The practice can be casually presented and in a very simple way, but get the youngster ready! He will surely not learn that to which he has not been exposed. When one intends to teach an area, the object is to teach it. Not that readiness skills should be ignored, but they can be taught simultaneously with beginning reading. Our logical progressions in learning are not necessarily the psychological progressions embraced by the child. Of primary importance here is a non-anxious, highly positive attitude on the part of the teacher and parent. The despairing parent and teacher pass along their feelings in nonverbal ways; these attitudes are internalized by the child, causing him to feel his own inability to learn.

Visual and auditory problems

Other kinds of disability may be causal factors in handicapping the youngster's reading progress. He may, for example, have a visual problem; this can be taken care of by having the youngster see a specialist. The wall charts to test vision are quite inadequate for most puposes. The Keystone Telebinocular does a more thorough job, and screening tests can be given by the school nurse. The machine sometimes is oversensitive, finding visual difficulties that are not really handicapping. However, I should prefer to use a machine that overdiagnoses to not having a screening mechanism for visual ability.

There is also a matter of lighting when a youngster is reading. It is a bit easier to read in the shaded area than in a glare. Reading eye span is another visual area that receives much attention in diagnostic technique. Probably the concern is not valid. Reading span refers to the number of letters one sees at a fixation. Most of us read about ten letters at one time. Photographs of eye movement indicate that we make approximately eight fixations per line as we read across the page. There are ways in which we may speed this process and ways in which we may skim, but if we are reading for details, for instance, we will make six to eight fixations to the regular page line of print.

We could pause here to discuss the various roles of optometrists and ophthalmologists. The ophthalmologist has more technical training, but each has his function, depending upon what the youngster's visual problem may be.

On the subject of audition, we have two tests that we use with some certainty. First, we give an audiometer test to find whether the youngster hears well in high- and low-frequency ranges; this score should indicate which children have deafness and hard-of-hearing problems.

A second part of the auditing process is that of auditory discrimination; that is, we need to determine if the youngster can discriminate among the many sounds that comprise English speech. There are several auditory discrimination tests. In one for example, the child sits with his back to you; you pronounce words such as *lack-lap*, and the child tells if they are the same word or different words. He must not see your lips while he is taking the test.

You may wonder about the relationship between reading and hearing, but a moment's thought will suggest to you that English is a phonetic language. If the youngster does not understand that there is a relationship between sound and symbol in the reading process, he is confused in a very basic area of learning to read.

Perceptual problems

Other kinds of physical handicaps, such as speech and aspects of perception, can be related to the reading task. Speech is affiliated with auditory and spacial orientation. Presently, the perception skills are getting a good deal of play; for one thing, the perception skills are dwelt on heavily in early childhood education, which has become much more focal recently. Also, a great many tests have come into being that purport to measure these skills, such as the Frostig perception tests (1961) and the Illinois Test of Psycholinguistic Ability (Kirk and McCarthy, 1961).

Subvocalizing

Subvocalizing and lip movement have been stressed as motor activities to be avoided quite early in the reading task. However, these traits may be helpful aids to a child who is having difficulty in beginning reading; they may not become unfortunate habits until the teacher is guiding the child to more rapid reading. Subvocalizing is only slowing down the reading process, but it is natural and may even be helpful at the first-grade level.

To some extent, most of us subvocalize or in some way mentally verbalize while reading; it is this process that most of your speed-reading programs eschew in order to make rapid readers. A first-grade youngster doing this should not alarm the teacher, but when the youngster begins to feel some security, just ask the youngster to read without moving his lips. Some teachers are brazen enough to give the youngster a piece of gum to chew so that verbalizing and lip movement will not be a temptation while he is reading silently.

Environmental factors

Educators should be much more concerned with home, cultural, and social environments and with understanding them. Utilizing the environment to teach language may be a coming breakthrough. Language is a reflection of environment. Frequently, youngsters do not have a rational method for handling language. Our language is highly systematic, but in a sophisticated way. Many youngsters have a very limited vocabularly, as well as an inability to deal with logical sophistication. However, when one begins to study the language of some so-called disadvantaged youngsters, one realizes that there are elaborate language banks and patterns that are understood by that particular community. Very simply, these nonstandard English patterns are not understood by us, as educators and linguists, nor are they accepted by us as legitimate forms of communication.

Moreover, I should like to pursue the study of reading ability in youngsters who speak languages other than English. I recently ran, in a local junior high school, a pilot study that disclosed that bilingual youngsters among disabled readers were somewhat better readers than other youngsters in this same disabled-reader group who were unilingual or spoke a "patois." We have always asserted that a foreign-language-speaking child learning in English is apt to have a disability in reading, since this first language would interfere with his acculturation and thinking patterns. However, we might look at the advantaged youngster to see if speaking two languages gives him an insight into language that ultimately aids him in the linguistic enterprise. In some European countries, children learn as many as four languages; in Sweden for instance, natives speak French, German, English, and Swedish. The cognitive and learning abilities of these youngsters do not appear to be impaired by this experience. However, in this country, we have a real fixation about speakers of other languages who speak English as a second language, partly because we have been made to feel culturally ashamed of being other than "Americans," who necessarily speak English. We ought to adjust our thinking to being more accepting of the great advantages of having several languages with which to communicate in an ever-shrinking world.

Emotional factors

The limits of this chapter cause me to be brief and rather superficial as I deal with emotional factors influencing reading progress. In the classroom, the teacher cannot truly give very much attention to emotional factors if she is working with a class at the thirty-to-one pupil-teacher ratio. Possibly her effort would be *not adding* to the youngster's areas of conflict. First, the teacher is not a psychologist, and she is not qualified to handle psychological problems. However, she may be well aware that the youngster has some reading problems, learning problems, and social difficulties. She may refer the child to appropriate personnel, but in all probability, she may not be able to do more than help the child to feel warmly accepted. In many, many cases this kind of teacher-coping is simply not enough to help the youngster improve his rapport.

Dislike of the reading task can be handled in many cases by presenting the youngster with materials that interest him. Many of the trade companies are producing delightful books that would fascinate the most aggressive and disaffected youngster. However, if one persists in putting the youngster into books that tell about old Granddad and Black Pony when the child is miserably bored, then the negative feelings that accrue to the reading task are to be expected. In spite of the better materials, many books used in the schools are very dated. When time is so telescoped as it is in our era, the datedness of publications makes these books especially tiresome, particularly when the media are producing so much that is sensually interesting and contemporary. At best, much of the material used would put one off—dry, bloodless, unfeeling, mechanical figures moving through vapid, dull, and unendingly moral themes. At least the McGuffey reader offered us literature along with its preachments.

If you are a teacher, you undoubtedly can recall classroom learning situations where the children were not interested, were showing poor attention, and at times, were daydreaming. In some ways this is not the fault of the teacher; you have too many youngsters to care for, and far too many to deal with personally in ways that indicate your interest in their personal development and growth. One does not have the emotional strength to handle all of the cognitive requisites of the school program and to handle the emotional requisites as well. When teachers arrive home from work, they are usually drained. If it were not for summers of rest and disengagement, more teachers would be psychologically imperiled themselves.

When the youngster actually comes into conflict with the teacher, sometimes you will find parental influences at work as well. Many parents have negative feelings toward the school, which they pass along to their children. If parents are even slightly denigrating about the educational system, they can influence the youngster's attitude to the point where the child will not put forth his best contribution in school. This kind of reaction occurs in disadvantaged areas, often when the parent is least aware of his own negative feelings. I have observed the parents who say on the first day of the new term: "All right now, you go down to that school and you behave yourself. Be a good boy, don't play with the bad children, mind the principal, don't forget your lunch, and be nice to the teacher or you'll get it when you get home." Now the child responds to this kind of threat first with fear and then with hatred of the institution that makes him feel so uncomfortable. His mother believes that she has helped the teacher with her task, but in all of her statements, there is not one positive reinforcement of the school. The school for this youngster has become the jail down the street. Frequently, it even looks like a prison, with its grave-gray fences, asphalt yards, and dark oppressive buildings. Thus the child has undesirable feelings toward that school.

Sex factors

There are really far more boys than girls with reading difficulties. It seems to me that, in many ways, the school and the society are not as hospitable to the little boy as to the little girl. In his early years, the boy child is reared in a world largely populated by women—his mother, his teacher. Thus, the significant adults in his life are disproportionately women. He sees his dad running for the train in the morning and coming home at night, but he is with his mother all day long, so that he has few males about in whom he can find a satisfactory sexual role model. Boys may understand how to play house or go shopping, but how do you play dad running to the train?

When the boy gets to school, then, teachers approve quiet classroom behavior. Little boys are expansive. They engage in large muscle activity and pushing, they do not color nicely within the lines, and they do not like the stories in the little book. In short, they are dissatisfying to the teacher. So we see that the school is more rewarding to the kinds of things that little girls are supposed to do. These rewards include educational rewards as well as emotional rewards.

In addition, the materials are oriented to little girls. When baby cuddles up to her teddy bear and her darling kitty and all the other cuddly things that live in beginning readers, we perceive that these characters are sweet, that they are especially appealing to ladies, and that most of the stories were written by ladies, to ladies, and for ladies. Most of these stories suggest that these values are terribly important to people who behave nicely; but these same values do not cater to the interests of little boys. You do not find stories of Dick falling and bloodying himself as he tears down a forbidden cowpath.

Parenthetically, the first year of school, where much of this reading that might be anathema to boy youngsters is presented, is one of the most crucial in the reading program. Should the child be absent or miss much of the instruction, he misses the foundation upon which much further learning is predicated. There is much more teacher turnover in the primary grades; thus you have many beginning teachers instructing in the early grades. Children's reading difficulties can be remedied, but these measures are much less effective than well-taught beginning reading skills.

SOME DILEMMAS AND SUGGESTIONS

In working with children who have reading problems, there are ways in which teachers can help. The physical and emotional climate in which the child must function is unavoidably affected by the teacher; so in many small ways she can work to create an atmosphere that is most conducive to a willingness—indeed, an eagerness—on the part of the child to learn. In other words, there are conditions outside of the child's own internal system that may create blocks to learning, or at least make learning more difficult, and by being aware of these things, the teacher can initiate measures that will eliminate them or reduce their impact on the child. Following are some of the problems that one encounters and suggestions for dealing with them.

Materials interest level

One dilemma facing teachers of reading is that of dated materials, old materials, no materials, or materials unsuited for instructing the particular class population with which she is working. In many parts of the country we have schools that rent materials to youngsters; if the youngsters have no rent money for books or they cannot afford to buy books, they have no books for the children to read! This is one argument in favor of a state textbook system for the schools: under such a system no districts will be totally without books. Whatever one may think of the state texts, they are infinitely better than nothing.

With regard to the visual ability of children to read materials other than primers, most tests show that children can read small print if the space between the words and lines is large. We may thus assume that many materials found in the community can be read by students in the schools.

Pedagogical problems

Pedagogical problems, as they are spoken of here, refer not to faulty teaching techniques, but to such items as overcrowding and class size. One way to help with instruction when the class is large is to work toward having a number of reading groups. In some schools the children come earlier in the morning and read for half an hour at, say, 8:30 A.M.; a second group comes at 9. Then the late-comers stay after school for a half hour longer and study reading. Such practice is hard on teachers, for it involves them in an hour's more instruction per day, but the concentrated instruction does pay in terms of some of the individualized and specialized attention that youngsters yearn for and respond to so well.

The teaching approach

Overdrilling on words out of context can cause learning blocks in a youngster's progress; however, delightful games and activities can be used to reduce the punitiveness of this activity. Youngsters should be able to integrate words into the total reading act soon after they learn them as sight words.

Overemphasis on speed or on such areas as word analysis and phonics can confuse a youngster unless it is integrated into a reading "gestalt." Presently, there tends to be underemphasis on these areas, or at least there exists a lack of understanding on the part of teachers about how to bridge the gap between some needed drill as it relates to meaningful understanding of language and reading. You can have fascinating "word-cracker" activities; usually the fault here is not overemphasis on small reading skills, but dull teaching.

Emphasis on the motor-sensory approach is interesting at this time, because we are becoming more aware of the importance of our senses beyond those of vision and hearing. There are a number of ways of appealing to youngsters. You might, for example, have a listening corner where they hear records and stories or music and where they participate in language activities. When youngsters build a great backlog of language experience, reading is a natural outgrowth of this experience. However, if youngsters rarely communicate, if they never hear language in delightful ways, if they never really enjoy or play with words, reading is a much harder task. Children learn much in language that helps establish speech simply by playing with words and sounds such as *la-la-lala, lalum, la lalum* or, perhaps, rhythms or music. Playing with words or making sounds is a wonderful kind of language game, which brings about awareness, establishes meaning limits, stimulates the senses, and takes away from the drudgery of all of these dreary exercises to which we so often expose children in school.

The story lady who pops out of her box or the puppet shows that implement language games, the slides, the movies, and the field trips are all sensory experiences that encourage youngsters to begin talking about these common happenings. Communication becomes terribly important to youngsters in this generally happy school setting, and it is easy to implement your reading program.

Grouping children

A hindrance to the reading in terms of class morale and probably for your slow learner especially is the classification or promotion system. We have ungraded primaries that are attempting to answer some of the cruelties of labeling, but people being what they are, children often tend to classify themselves. If the child is not in first grade, he is working at Level H. It may take somewhat longer, but eventually children will perceive that they are at a certain level and begin to compare their progress with that of other children.

The idea behind the ungraded primary is excellent, but so often the youngster is not moved up when he is through the materials; he is simply moved along with his group at given promotion periods in much the same way that youngsters have progressed through the grades in other programs. We have yet to work out a prototype for individualized and programmed activity that also allows for individualized promotion without resorting to grade-level distinctions and rigid evaluation in terms of achievement. Psychologically, the promotion plan should involve emotional and interactional evaluation as well, but we do not give these areas the emphasis we should because we do not have ways for evaluating progress in these areas.

Measuring emotional development

There are a number of tests for measuring emotional development of youngsters with reading problems. If you have a child who is reading on grade level or below grade level, these sophisticated tests are liable to penalize him for his lack of ability to read. One test that may be given to children with reading disabilities is the Wechsler Intelligence Scale for Children (WISC) (1949), which is individually administered and measures intelligence as well as emotional factors. However, the WISC must be given by a qualified psychological examiner.

The Bender Gestalt (Clawson, 1962) will give some idea of psychological development; the Illinois Test of Psycholinguistic Ability (Kirk and McCarthy, 1961) has psychological implications as well; but these tests must be given by someone who is trained and not by someone who is simply well meaning. Other tests that may be given are the thematic apperception tests and the Draw-a-Figure Test (Machover, 1959) (which in my experience has been without merit since it is so difficult to get consistency of protocols for interpretation).

Situational and timing factors

Other influences that affect reading performance include attendance at school or transferring from one school to another. The youngster who moves so often that he never makes friends, since he never has time to do so, is often using psychic energy to make adjustments that could be spent on mastering pedagogical areas at school. The size of the class is another factor to consider, as is the entrance age for first grade.

There is considerable question as to when to teach youngsters reading. Teach them to read when they are interested. Many kinds of reading activity can be done in kindergarten or perhaps, in an informal way, even before then. A bright child can handle reading early and, as teachers of the young, you can teach it (where it is not prohibited by law), but you do so at the risk of developing problems for the administration of the school. Usually, when mothers hear that some of the youngsters are having reading instruction, a parade of parents descend on the facility; the principal then tries to explain that the teacher is merely teaching those youngsters who are ready and who have shown some interest in wanting to work with the printed word.

In the school setting, both teachers and parents put about as much pressure on youngsters as they can endure without giving 5-year-olds ulcers. Indeed, some of these wee ones are developing ulcers. In fact, as a society we are becoming quite punitive to little children (in the guise of caring, of course), and I am not recommending that teachers reinforce the pressures that preschoolers already feel. However, if the child is interested, begins to pick up reading while sitting on his father's lap as he reads his newspaper, or is badgering the teacher to tell "what this word is," that seems to me to be a natural flow from one language task to another, and I don't believe it should be discouraged. I believe it can in fact be developed without harm to the kindergarten child.

In many schools there are mountains of interesting things for youngsters to do and a great deal of supplementary material available, if the teacher is not preoccupied with keeping either the children, the materials, or the curriculum in order and tidy by prescription. Although teachers should eschew chaos, schoolteaching is not a matter of keeping the class neat and tidy. At times you do want to take things off the shelves, drag them about for children to use, have a messy little corner that allows the youngsters to be actively busy and, perhaps, making a little more noise than is generally approved.

Personnel, services, and environment

Training of teachers is important, and such concerns as school services and facilities are valuable to help children when they do have problems. One of the first services that all schools should provide is instruction of special nature to all youngsters who have reading difficulty, for the reasons that I mentioned in the first paragraph.

The home environment may be one of the most focal areas for reading ability. Quality of language in the home, the act of reading to youngsters, an appreciation of books and magazines, a great deal of warm exchange of conversation with children is the foundation for learning reading. Recently, fault was found with some of the Headstart programs in terms of preparing children to pass reading tests. Whatever other limitations are found in the study, one can certainly say that, whatever good was accomplished in Headstart, decay would set in, in terms of language programs, if the children were sent back to a very limiting environment.

Simply remarking on physical occurrences when the youngster is present helps to develop a vocabulary and understanding of the world about him. For instance, "Oh, look the sun is setting. It's sinking in the west," gives the child extra points on the WISC in a phrase. A parent who is verbalizing to his youngster and talking to him as though he were a worthy human being and who is also listening to his child when he responds is going to have a child who can handle symbolic concepts, one who will record symbolic kinds of "happenings."

So much for the kinds of factors that influence reading disability. At this point, I would like to discuss some personal prejudices with regard to reading instruction. Many of these observations are not original thoughts of the author, but they bear rehearing simply because they are so ignored by teachers.

First, we have treated reading as a kind of isolated task, instead of treating it as one aspect of the whole realm of communication. We get most of the meaning for our existence from symbolic activity. Part of the symbolic superstructure that gives man his reason for being is language. This includes all symbols—reacting to physical and auditory and feeling cues—but most of the meaning for existence comes from a kind of communicative superstructure that is highly important to the youngster, as it is to the rest of us. If we think of reading as one dimension of communication, we will observe that it is much easier and much more logical than the faculty of speaking. As linguists will tell you, most youngsters are speaking, and speaking quite sophisticatedly, when they come to school. Some few have a very limited vocabulary, but most have been interacting with parents and sisters and brothers, engaging in symbolic endeavor. "That's not your train," "You didn't wait your turn," are examples of this activity. And these youngsters understand equally well. "All right, every one go round in a circle." "Stop your bikes outside the gate." While the teacher is talking, children are understanding. When a child who is told to go to bed says, "You don't love me anymore," he has absorbed some very sophisticated symbolically expressed concepts. In fact, the reading aspect of communication is infinitely more simple than that of speech, because what is achieved in the reading process is merely attaching sounds to symbols.

All meaning and reference in communication have come from a sophisticated cognitive development. The society of the youngster has demanded a great deal of him by requiring him to learn language, but reading is in some ways much more conceptually simple in that it takes the child only one step further by asking him simply to transfer sound symbols to written symbols.

Teachers have, on the whole, ignored the profound logic and system in our own written language. In fact, there are about forty to forty-five sounds used in speaking the English language. The symbols that represent these sounds are fairly consistent in their representation. Artificial alphabets have been invented that are entirely consistent in their representation (for instance, i/t/a/), but even with such contrived forms of print, there is enough resemblance between the two forms of English for children to make the transition to traditional orthography with little difficulty. One may extrapolate that the consistency even in standard English is apparent. Teachers should suggest that there are the forty sounds and that there are symbols, with several variations, that stand for them.

Although they do not sound well when pronounced in isolation, letters or letter combinations can be taught as producing highly regular patterns. The sound-symbol relationship should be emphasized—that is, the idea that letters stand for sounds. Children should understand this relationship. These written symbols are not always accurate or consistent, but they are explainable, and this phonetic principle is the one that underlies our written presentation of language.

Reading is talk written down, to use the cliché. We write the spoken word because we want to store knowledge or to recall it or to spread it or to send it away to others. Before we had television and motion pictures and other media, this was our best way of keeping knowledge until we wanted to use it again, or to convey it to others.

Another principle that should be stressed is that sounds individually can be run together or blended. Again, similar patterns should be taught together; for instance, teach *bar*, *spar*, and *par*, then begin substituting other beginning consonants, and it will not take long for the child to pick up the word patterns and see symbol-sound relationships. Children can be encouraged to manufacture new words sometimes, such as *quar*; now there is no such word, but this indicates that the child has mastered the substitution principle and now needs to separate sense from non-sense.

Work on one skill at a time until the child sees the sense of it, and then try to synthesize this skill into the general reading task.

To teach a great number of ideas in one lesson, for instance, word patterns, compound words, comprehension skills, and oral reading skills, often causes the child to miss the logic of the task of learning just one of these skills. Unfortunately, many of the teachers' manuals have so many ideas to teach in the course of fifteen minutes that the children can not sort out the ideas taught, and so they master none of them.

Anxiety and reading

Teachers' confidence in their own ability to teach reading has been undermined; thus they bring a great deal of anxiety to the reading task. Children, even when they appear indifferent, are very anxious about their ability to read. The child comes to school the first day with deep concern about learning; his concern is reinforced that evening when his dad says to him, "Well, did you read today?" (First-grade teachers should be aware of this and should make an effort to hand out preprimers and go through them with the children so they can answer with confidence that they have. The topic of the child having read will certainly come up for discussion two or three times during dinner, and the youngster should not feel that the school has let him down the first day!)

The point I wish to make is that teachers should try to reduce this anxiety in themselves, in the community, and in the children. Simply presume that there is logic in the reading process and that the children will perceive it. Reading instruction should not have gathered about itself such a mystique that children and teachers are defensive about whether or not the task is being accomplished and about whom to blame in case instruction is not going as well as anticipated.

A way to alleviate this aspect of anxious instruction is to secure a list of the skills to be taught at each grade level and to sequentially and systematically cover them, even if you have to ask parents to help. Teachers who have this kind of systematized approach, especially when beginning as teachers, are often far less harassed about the merit of the program. The children catch the teacher's confidence and learn much more easily. Basal readers and teachers' manuals have not been helpful about presenting the total scope of the program in an organized way; thus the teacher does not see the direction of the total program. A skills list gives it a kind of systematized overview.

The systematization of English has become much more understandable, and in a sense I think that we have the linguists to thank for this. The pattern and the consistencies have been sorted out for us, and eventually instruction should become much more logical.

Finally, when one is teaching the various aspects of the reading skills, some of the youngsters may have gleaned such skills as compound-word analysis or phonic patterns without being exposed to a formal instruction in that skill. Should you find that the child has learned many of the reading skills intuitively, then there is no need to teach them extensively. Ultimately, the teacher wants the youngster to be an aware, competent reader. If he has learned this task on his own, without even knowing the small and detailed areas of the reading task, then do not dwell on his small deficiencies. The objective of the reading program is to teach youngsters to read efficiently; therefore, do not introduce insecurity about inconsequential skills when the greater task has been accomplished.

Teaching isolated reading skills

As we go through the reading skills to be taught at the first-grade level, using the Barbe reading skills list (1960) as an example of such a list, we see the various kinds of reading skills that youngsters should have mastered. However, there is no reason that these skills should be mastered by reading basal readers. The day is coming when we will have enough interesting graded material for children that we can completely change the curriculum of the first three grades and, indeed, that of the elementary school. If enough of the reading skills can be taught in the first three grades in a basal program, then reading can be taught after that as part of the subject matter in the various content areas, many of which are presently being changed and revised.

For that matter, many of the reading materials being published do not stress the reading skills; the intent is that of literary quality and appreciation. Such books are not only enticing to children; sometimes you will find adults reading them as well. In one series, all the content areas are introduced reader by reader, but as a "whole" in book form or as a unit in a book and always in a highly fascinating way.

In such a reading program, the teacher is going to emphasize skills that will augment research, such as using the library, using the encyclopedia, looking through newspapers, learning how to scan magazines and how to develop an approach to reading poetry, reading content, and reading science or literature. There are various kinds of reading abilities attached to reading in the various subject areas. Children should be aware of differences among them: poetry is best read aloud; math has to be read slowly, generally speaking; newspapers can be scanned; and so on.

Students should learn how to use a dictionary (which few adults know how to do well); how to use catalogs, telephone directories, and reference materials; how to take notes.

Eventually students will have to know how to express themselves in many ways as new media are developed. At present, tape recorders, record players, and videotape are standard equipment in schools, yet children do not understand their effective use. In part, this is because the equipment is so expensive to repair and children are hard on materials, but in part, it is because teachers are so loathe to adapt to the use of the new media in a creative way.

High school reading programs

When teaching remedial reading at the high school level, be careful not to blame the elementary school teacher for what has not been achieved by the youngster. Surely, with all that has been said in the first part of this chapter concerning the causes of reading disability, it should be obvious that no one should be held personally responsible in the face of so many things that could go wrong. Do not try to hold the child accountable for what has not been done. It is not a matter of having a checklist of activities to be accomplished; rather, it is a matter of teaching what has not been taught and of building on what has been started at earlier levels. With dropout rates at the high school level as one of education's chief concerns, to take a discouraged attitude with poor readers at the high school level is to ensure that the child will leave school before he graduates. Be as positive and as concerned regarding reading achievement as you would be about the mastery of the content areas.

The high school teacher of content must be a teacher of reading, no matter what her subject. Materials must be much more sophisticated—newspapers, magazines, adult-level books with low-level reading vocabularies—so that students will not be embarrassed and left without personal dignity by having to read "baby-stuff."

There can be much more preoccupation with language itself at the high school level. For instance, study advertising to see how the consumer is being wooed. Study consumer reaction. Teach critical thinking. Study propaganda techniques. Our thinking is being maneuvered. This fact is not necessarily sinister, but children should be aware of how the manipulation of public opinion occurs. Students should be aware of dialect differences and of levels of language, and they should be aware of how to evaluate social-interaction situations. For instance, if I were to talk of lowbrow magazines as material for children's study, many of you would smile. Yet, if I mentioned high-level publications as part of my lecture, you would think me far more urbane. You sense a difference of intellectual appeal here. It is not a matter of telling youngsters that street language is bad and that the intellectual banter of a group of scholars on TV is good, but it is a problem of having youngsters understand that these speech patterns represent different cultural, societal, and educational levels. One must size up the group to whom he is speaking and decide upon which form of English to use. As a matter of communication, not therapy, language can be studied.

Children should be aware of dialect differences. Dialects are not only a matter of geography; professionals of various kinds, the sexes, and persons at the various social levels in our society all have dialects. In some ways dialects are used to exclude others. For instance, teenagers exclude others by developing a lingo. Why is it necessary for them to develop a special and exclusive language? Because they wish to be identified to themselves and others as a group. If you, as an adult, spoke hip teenage language, you would not be accepted into their group; you would be regarded as out of character and out of place. Yet if you do not speak their language, how do you communicate? Such questions become fertile ground for language discussion.

There are, moreover, levels of knowledge, analytical skills, and emotional kinds of language that express feeling; there are ways in which we cue others in to what we are speaking and feeling, which includes symbolic interaction.

CONCLUDING REMARKS

Had I more time, I would include the names of many tests for the measurement of reading disability. However, so much new material comes out between the date of writing such a chapter and its publication that these lists are anachronisms before they reach the reader. On the other hand, many of the most consistently used and better tests are twenty or more years old.

I close with the knowledge that there is a great deal of new experimental material coming out in reading and language. I am happy for it. Publishing companies are so aware of the development, that many companies are mushrooming overnight due to the stress on the area of literacy. I suggest that we are doing much better than we imagine with the task of reading instruction. That there are laggards is inevitable. But perhaps the problems are more statistical than real; bell-shaped curves of model distribution have a way of contributing to our guilt as teachers. Ultimately our knowledge about language and reading will catch up with our good will toward youngsters; when this happens, probably our ways of handling recorded knowledge will be so advanced that we will come to regard reading an infantile form of communication.

IDENTIFYING
AND PREVENTING
READING DISABILITIES

Mildred C. Robeck

8

*Dr. Mildred C. Robeck is professor of education at the
University of Oregon. Her current research activities
include a follow-up study of intellectually competent
students who experienced extreme difficulty in learning
to read. Previously she was consultant in teacher
education, California State Department of Education,
where she was assigned to the Miller-Unruh Basic
Reading Act. She was research consultant to California
Project Talent. She directed the Reading Laboratory
at the University of California, Santa Barbara, from
1958 to 1964. Prior to university teaching, she taught
in the Seattle public schools, including six years at
the Seward Demonstration School.*

*Dr. Robeck received the Ph.D. at the University of
Washington, Seattle. Her dissertation was an analysis
of the responses of advanced, average, and retarded
readers in the fourth grade. She has published more
than twenty articles on reading, including research
reports in the following publications:* Perceptual and
Motor Skills, Developmental Reading, California
Journal of Educational Research, Educational and
Psychological Measurement, Journal of Educational
Research, *and* Conference Proceedings of the
International Reading Association.

With John A. R. Wilson, Dr. Robeck is coauthor of
The Kindergarten Evaluation of Learning Potential
*(McGraw-Hill, New York, 1967), which is an instrument
for teaching and evaluating preprimary abilities,
including readiness for reading. She is also coauthor,
with Dr. Wilson and William B. Michael, of*
Psychological Foundations of Learning and Teaching
(McGraw-Hill, New York, 1969).

This chapter will cover three topics: (1) the intellectual characteristics of students who fail in reading, (2) a procedure for using the Wechsler Intelligence Scale for Children (WISC) subtests for individual diagnosis, and (3) some implications for prevention of reading difficulties.

For our purposes *disabled readers* may be defined as those students who cannot function in the usual school reading situations at their own grade level. Rather precise criteria for identifying "four levels of disability," from simple retardation to complex disability, have been suggested by Guy L. Bond and Miles A. Tinker in *Reading Difficulties* (1967). They recommend a formula to estimate reading expectancy: years in school × IQ × 1.0. A more common, but less adequate, criterion is the number of reading grades the student falls below his current grade placement in school.

The students in the research I shall report ranged from first grade to the senior year of high school. With a grade range of this magnitude, one needs to know more than the number of years of retardation. By the time a student gets into high school, two years reading disability might not handicap him very much in some subject areas; by then reading ability in particular subject-matter areas might be more relevant. Without going into the complexities of how disabled readers were identified in the reading laboratory, I can report that all subjects included in these studies were extremely handicapped as readers.

Here at the University of California at Santa Barbara we began accepting primary children into the reading clinic in 1959—a time when this was extremely uncommon in California. By trying to start early with remedial teaching, I became interested in prevention. By 1965 a statewide program for primary-age children had become available through the Miller-Unruh Basic Reading Act. The purpose of the legislation was to prevent reading difficulties and to identify for early correction those children who were having difficulty in learning to read. When we attempt to prevent reading difficulties, a consideration of readiness characteristics seems to be the most promising approach. Some of the readiness characteristics often used in kindergarten and first grade are irrelevant, if not misleading. Later in the chapter I shall discuss prereading abilities that are crucial if a child is going to succeed from the beginning in learning to read.

INTELLECTUAL CHARACTERISTICS

In the reading laboratory an analysis based on the subtests of the WISC was used to evaluate intellectual functioning. The WISC subtest scores

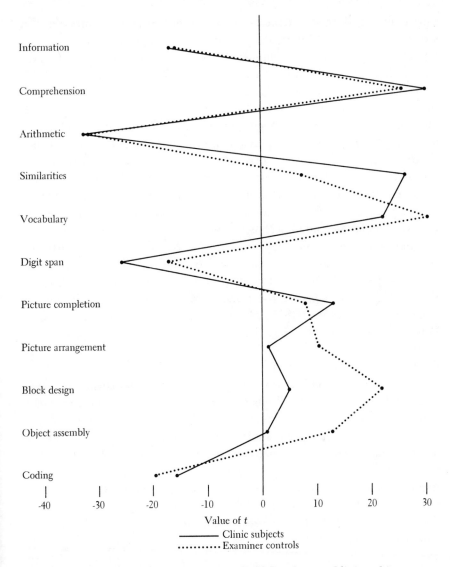

FIGURE 8-1 *Intellectual functioning on WISC subtests: Clinic subjects compared with examiner controls*

of a reading-clinic population were computed and graphed (Figure 8-1). Over a five-year period we completed reading case histories, including WISC profiles, on nearly two hundred children. The data shown here summarizes part of a comprehensive study of the first subjects to enroll (Robeck, 1964a). In subsequent studies I found them similar in intellectual functioning to the group represented by the dotted line. The abilities you see as very low are Information, Arithmetic, Digit span, and Coding. Several investigators have obtained this syndrome for students who were having difficulty in learning to read (Altus, 1956; Burks and Bruce, 1955; Kallos, Grabow, and Guareno, 1961; and Neville, 1961). Some minor inconsistencies reported in the literature appear to have been due to differences in the selection of subjects. For example, the investigator who includes slow learners in his sample is not likely to find they function like children who have shown a discrepancy between reading capacity and reading achievement. One of the purposes of our research was to see where the intellectual strengths were and to capitalize on these strengths in clinic teaching. You will note the high areas are Comprehension, Similarities, Picture completion, and Object assembly.

Before we leave this graph, I'd like to tell you why this particular comparison was made. I wanted to try to use the WISC for diagnostic purposes. I needed someone to teach me how to administer it. Dr. John A. R. Wilson, who had tested some of the children in the beginning, taught me to give the WISC and supervised me during the initial studies. When I came up with the wild profile you see here, Dr. Glenn W. Durflinger, then chairman of the department, said, "Well, how do you know you aren't creating a bias?" I said, "Because I had a good teacher." The chairman's comment was valid, however, so this comparison was made to check for examiner bias. We had a few referrals from various elementary schools who already had WISC's on file. It was a simple matter to pull their data and compare the subjects I had tested with those tested by others. The solid line on the figure represents the controls—the group used to see whether a consistent bias in the technique of giving the test was responsible for the deviation. The profiles run very similar except in Picture arrangement, Block design, and Object assembly. We found great variability—a flat probability curve—for these three subtests within all clinic groups (Robeck, 1960).

PROCEDURE FOR INDIVIDUAL DIAGNOSIS

Now, let's consider the technique for deciding whether an individual's score deviates significantly from normal. I was fortunate in that an important factorial analysis of the WISC by J. Cohen was published about the time we started the intellectual-profile studies (1959). Cohen concluded that WISC subtest scores, when applied to individual students, must be considered in terms of the student's overall intellectual ability because of the high positive correlation he found between the different subtests and the total IQ score. Therefore, if you are interpreting strengths and weaknesses by comparing the subtests, you must first partial out the general intelligence.

I can give you an actual example of how general intelligence operates, in a test situation, to influence subscores. Dr. Wilson and I used the Stanford Binet Intelligence Scale (Termin and Merrill, 1960) for testing kindergarten children in the development of KELP, the *Kindergarten Evaluation of Learning Potential* (1967). During the research phase I gave a good many Binets to kindergarten children. One 5-year-old, who was functioning at about a 9-year-old level, was shown the design cards she was supposed to look at and draw. One of the designs is quite difficult; the other one is much easier. The examiner says to the child, "This card has two drawings on it. I am going to show them to you for ten seconds, then I will take the card away and let you draw from memory what you have seen. Be sure to look at both drawings carefully." Well, this 5-year-old showed me that she knew about how long ten seconds is, among other things. She looked at the complex design for about seven seconds, looked at the simpler one for two seconds, then looked back at the first one for about one second. When I handed her the pencil, she said, "I'm going to do the hard one first because the other one's easy to remember." Many abilities were being tested besides the child's ability to remember and reproduce designs perceived visually. This is a practical, clinical example of why you need to partial out, or compensate for, the student's general intelligence when looking for particular intellectual strengths and weaknesses.

One two-part calculation that is really very simple allows for general intelligence when you wish to compare the subtests of an individual's profile. The information that appears on the cover of a WISC test form is shown in Figure 8-2. These data are taken from an actual diagnostic report, although the names of the student and the referring person have been changed. This profile is characteristic of those one sees over and over in the reading clinic. Note the Verbal tests, including the alternate test, Digit span. The sum of the Verbal tests has been recalculated to show what the sum would have been if only five subtests had been given instead of six. A sum of 65 has been entered as the Verbal scaled score, instead of 78. Mark's Performance tests have shown a sum of 63 for the five Performance tests administered. I never did find the Mazes subtest useful for most clinic children, so we usually didn't give it. We always used the

WISC RECORD FORM

NAME ____________, Mark AGE 10 SEX M

ADDRESS Oak Hill Rd.

PARENT'S NAME ____________

SCHOOL Central GRADE 3

REFERRED BY M. Simpson

	Year	Month	Day
Date Tested	61	5	2
Date of Birth	51	2	19
Age	10	2	

	Scaled Score	IQ
Verbal Scale	65	* 119
Performance Scale	63	* 118
Full Scale	128	120

*Prorated if necessary

	Raw Score	Scaled Score
VERBAL TESTS		
Information	13	11
Comprehension	18	16
Arithmetic	10	12
Similarities	20	18
Vocabulary	38	13
(Digit Span)	8	8
Sum of Verbal Tests		6/78 13 (x5) 65
PERFORMANCE TESTS		
Picture Completion	11	10
Picture Arrangement	43	17
Block Design	28	12
Object Assembly	26	14
Coding	33	10
(Mazes)		
Sum of Performance Tests		63

NOTES

Friendly, vocal.
Manipulates with both hands. Writes left handed.
Says he is allergic to animal hair.

mck
Examiner

The Psychological Corporation
304 East 45th Street
New York 17, N. Y.

Printed in U. S. A. 0070 57-200 AS

FIGURE 8-2 *Sample of the cover of a WISC test form (By permission of the publisher.)*

Digit span subtest, however. The scaled score for the full battery shows a sum of 128, with allowance made for the alternate test. Essentially, this is the sum of ten subtests. To find the scaled-score mean, you simply divide by ten. At a glance you mentally calculate 128 divided by 10 or 12.8.

The second step in allowing for, or partialling out, general intelligence is to find out whether each scaled score is higher or lower than the subject's own mean, and how much. On Information, is Mark lower or higher than his own mean? He is lower. You subtract 11 from 12.8 to get a minus 1.8. In Comprehension, what is the deviation? It is plus 3.2. And so on. This gives you an easy way to partial out, or allow for, the child's general intelligence.

According to Cohen, you must also allow for differences in the reliability of the different subtests. In looking at the published reliability coefficients in the WISC manual, page 13, you will note differences in the reliability and the SE_m (the range beyond which a measure is significant) at the different age levels: 7½-year-olds, 10½-year-olds, and 13½-year-olds (Table 8-1). By using the particular standard error of measurement for each different subtest in the appropriate age column, we are able to arrive at what can reasonably be called significant deviation. Let's look again at Mark's WISC Record Form (Figure 8-2). His scaled score for Information is 11. The usual interpretation would be, "Well, that's very close to the mean score of 10. He's okay in Information items—above the average." However, we get a different picture of his functioning if we recalculate from his own scaled-score mean of 12.8 to get the minus score of 1.8 on Information. But is minus 1.8 significant? We assume that deviation greater than one standard error of measurement is significant. In what age group is Mark? The SE_m for the Information subtest at age 10½ is 1.34. In other words, if Mark's score deviates more than 1.34, we consider this difference greater than chance deviation and probably significant. Mark is varying a little more than a standard allowance for errors of measurement. We consider him low on Information items, even though he would not be considered low by the usual criterion score of 10. In dealing with each case according to age, and each subtest according to the reliability of that particular subtest, we rescore—one might say—in numbers of standard errors by which the child deviates from his own scaled-score mean. Essentially we convert scaled scores to sigma scores, but you need not concern yourselves with the statistical terms. You can see what simple arithmetic it is: (1) to partial out the general intelligence, (2) to allow for the differences in reliability at different ages and on the different subtests, and

TABLE 8-1 RELIABILITY AND STANDARD ERROR OF MEASUREMENT* OF THE WISC TESTS (N = 200 FOR EACH AGE LEVEL)

	Age 7½		Age 10½		Age 13½	
	r	SE_m	r	SE_m	r	SE_m
Information	.66	1.75	.80	1.34	.82	1.27
Comprehension	.59	1.92	.73	1.56	.71	1.62
Arithmetic	.63	1.82	.84	1.20	.77	1.44
Similarities	.66	1.75	.81	1.31	.79	1.37
Vocabulary	.77	1.44	.91	.90	.90	.95
Digit span	.60	1.90	.59	1.92	.50	2.12
Verbal score (without Digit span)	.88	5.19	.96	3.00	.96	3.00
Picture completion	.59	1.92	.66	1.75	.68	1.70
Picture arrangement	.72	1.59	.71	1.62	.72	1.59
Block design	.84	1.20	.87	1.08	.88	1.04
Object assembly	.63	1.82	.63	1.82	.71	1.62
Coding**	.60	1.90	—	—	—	—
Mazes	.79	1.37	.81	1.31	.75	1.50
Performance score (without Coding and Mazes)	.86	5.61	.89	4.98	.90	4.74
Full Scale score (without Digit span, Coding, and Mazes)	.92	4.25	.95	3.36	.94	3.68

* The SE_m is in scaled-score units for the tests and in IQ units for the Verbal, Performance, and Full Scale scores.
** Based on correlating Coding A and Coding B, 115 cases. See text for explanation. For age 8½ the value is .56 for 91 cases.
SOURCE: David I. Wechsler, WISC Manual: Wechsler Intelligence Scale for Children, The Psychological Corporation, New York, 1949, p. 13. Reproduced by permission of the publisher.

(3) to decide when real deviation is likely. Look at Mark's Vocabulary score, for example.

Vocabulary tests are known to be very good indicators of IQ, at least for middle-class children. The standard error of measurement is only .90 and .95 on the Vocabulary subtest; less than one scaled-score deviation from the child's own mean can mean strength or weakness in vocabulary, whereas items like Object assembly or Digit span seem to require a deviation of almost two scaled scores to be significant, because of the SE_m's for those particular subtests. We now have taken the steps necessary to justify an interpretation of the WISC subtest scores as an individual diagnostic profile.

In the research studies, the procedure used for a sample of one was also used for the groups of clinic subjects. The decisive trends that came out of the first study led me to think that, as far as intellectual functioning was concerned, a sample of twenty should yield consistent trends, if such existed, in a clinic group. We began at once to identify groups according to the symptoms of reading disability they revealed when reading orally. Readers responded very differently from one another in a reading situation. At that time about half the kids who were turning up at the clinic had serious problems in decoding. These kids seemed otherwise to be bright and relaxed, to have good speech, and to relate well to adults and other children. As soon as we had identified twenty clinic subjects who showed a lack of word-attack skills (and didn't have physical handicaps or emotional disabilities to account for their reading problem), we designed a procedure to describe their reading behavior and analyzed their intellectual functioning as a group. Their combined profile on the WISC subtests is shown by the solid black line (Figure 8-3). Note that Information, Arithmetic, Digit span, and Coding are very low. Unless the deviations are characteristic of the group, summing will produce a flat curve; the individual deviations cancel each other.

The children who were poor decoders were compared with a different group of twenty clinic subjects whose most apparent symptoms of reading disability were associated with extreme tension in oral reading situations. It took about 2½ years to find twenty children who showed these extreme tension reactions. Their combined profile is shown in the dotted line (Figure 8-3). I had expected that the intellectual functioning would be very different from the previous group because their reading symptoms were so different (Robeck, 1962). The similarity between the two groups is almost weird. I don't have space to report the full analyses for these groups, but I could indicate a suspicion that emerged. Tension associated with reading may be environmentally caused to a large extent, while genetics may be an important influence on the child's intellectual functioning (Jensen, 1969). The mean is indicated in the broad horizontal line. The narrow lines indicate the range beyond which a measure is significant, or two standard errors of deviation (SE_m).

Comparison of young children with adolescents

At this point I began to suspect we ought to enroll clinic children at a younger age. To check this out, we did a comparison of the youngest and oldest clinic subjects. The more important parts of the study had to do with motivation over a long-term basis, but we are looking only at the intellectual functioning in this chapter. All of the youngest children happened to cluster around the age category of 7½ in the reliability table.

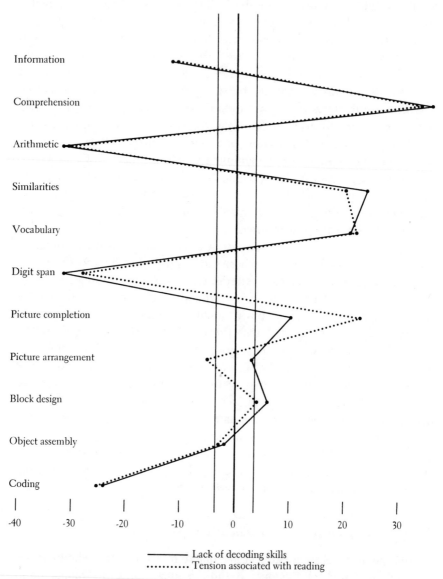

FIGURE 8-3 *Intellectual functioning on WISC subtests: Lack of decoding skills compared with tension associated with reading. N = 20; probability at 0.001 = 3.85*

The older group clustered around 13½, but ranged up to age 17. The young children are represented by the solid line and the adolescent children by the dotted line (Figure 8-4). Notice again that the syndrome of strengths and weaknesses is quite consistent for both groups. Differences in intellectual functioning, at least in part, occur as a result of learning. Note the Information subtest; young children, as a group, are a little low in the first place. After six to eight years in school, the scores of disabled readers are much lower in Information than are the scores of the younger group. This could be explained in part by the lack of information they get from reading, as compared with normal students who read more and at higher levels of content.

QUESTION: *How do you account for the difference in the Vocabulary score?*

ANSWER: The differences in Vocabulary scores could be explained by the same reasoning. You see, the younger children have a good vocabulary compared to their age-grade peers. Vocabulary is partly a cultural thing. The children in this particular reading-clinic population are rather selected—at times a fourth of them were professors' children. The point is that vocabulary of itself does not assure them reading success. Note the combined Vocabulary score for the adolescents. They have lost most of the superiority they may have shown once in Vocabulary. Again, you could expect this deterioration to occur with a combination of little or no reading and low achievement in school. Without exception, these students had low grades in school, and many were assigned to slow classes. As you might expect, adolescents also showed a progressive falling behind in Arithmetic as well as in Information.

The Coding subtest showed the adolescents to be much less disabled than their younger counterparts. If Coding difficulties are related to some borderline neurological problem, you might anticipate this finding that young children do more poorly than older children on this subtest. Children tend to lose the symptoms that go along with minimal neurological dysfunction as they near puberty. In other words, the symptoms may have been there earlier and, perhaps, may have given trouble at the beginning of reading, but by adolescence you have a hard time to diagnose minimal impairment as a cause of reading difficulty. You would consider any difference as great as the difference between these groups in Coding to be statistically significant. Whether the deviation is high or low, the difference between the younger and

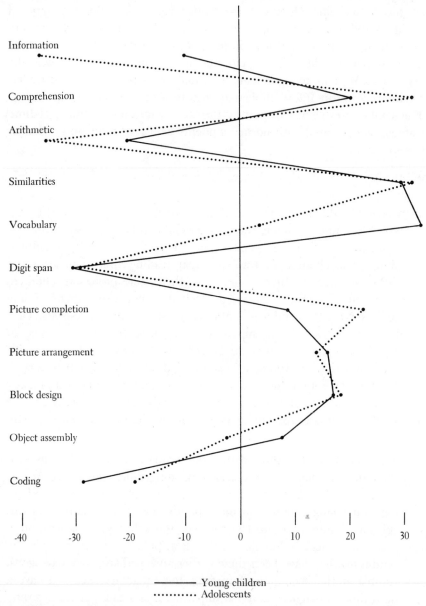

Information

Comprehension

Arithmetic

Similarities

Vocabulary

Digit span

Picture completion

Picture arrangement

Block design

Object assembly

Coding

| | | | | | | | | |
-40   -30   -20   -10   0   10   20   30

——— Young children
·········· Adolescents

FIGURE 8-4 ~~Intellectual functioning~~ on WISC subtests: Young children compared with adolescents older groups is greater than two standard errors of measurement (SE_m), and therefore significant, on Information, Comprehension, Arithmetic, Vocabulary, and Coding.

Comparison of high-IQ and other clinic subjects

What do you think the profiles will be like if our experimental group consisted of the high-IQ subjects? The first twenty children enrolled who registered IQs of 120 or above were studied as a separate group. Their IQ range was from 121 to 145, in spite of the fact that all had been given the alternate test, the Digit span, which depreciated the IQs from 2 to 7 points.

The high-IQ children are shown by the dotted line (Figure 8-5). Except for certain performance tests, the groups again look very much alike when the general intelligence has been accounted for.

QUESTION: *What is the solid line?*

ANSWER: The solid line is the clinic population—the basic-line group that was used in the first study. One of these days I'm going to do an analysis of the girls. The incidence of girls in clinic populations is usually quite small—from 1 to 6 or 1 to 10 in different clinic populations reported (Spache, 1968). I have looked at enough of these girls individually to think their intellectual functioning will be similar to that of the boys who have similar learning problems.

IMPLICATIONS OF THE WISC PROFILES

Several years ago I read the first of these reports to the California Education Research Association. One of the people there, whom I didn't know at the time, was Jack Holmes, former professor of educational psychology, Berkeley. I was trying to suggest some commonalities within tests on which the clinic subjects did well, as compared to tests on which they did poorly. In fact, all the tests on which clinic children were high gave some freedom to the subject to work from generalizations. Dr. Holmes spoke up, "Are you hinting that this group is better in dealing with generalizations than they are in specifics?" I said, "Well, the results seemed to show this, but I was afraid to say so." He said, "I think you should say it." With such clear reinforcement for this particular suspicion, I continued to interpret the data in this way. The next step was to apply the observation in the clinic situation.

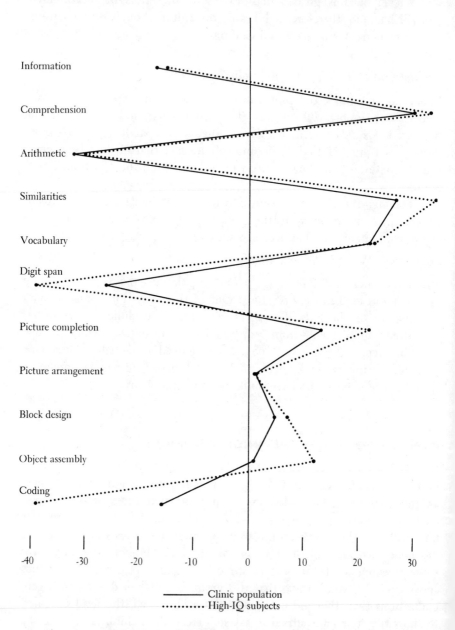

Information

Comprehension

Arithmetic

Similarities

Vocabulary

Digit span

Picture completion

Picture arrangement

Block design

Object assembly

Coding

-40   -30   -20   -10   0   10   20   30

——— Clinic population
············ High-IQ subjects

FIGURE 8-5 *Intellectual functioning on WISC subtests: Clinic population compared with high-IQ subjects. IQ held constant, N = 20 and 20*

Teaching students to conceptualize

You are familiar with the distinction between inductive and deductive teaching. Inductive learning takes place when the student discovers relationships between bits of data or information, while deductive learning results from being given information step-by-step up to and including the principle, the rule, or the generalization. Dr. Wilson calls this discovering of relationships *conceptualization*.

In working with clinic children, we found them to be very good conceptualizers—as the WISC profiles suggest. One of the techniques that was successful (if the student could discriminate auditorily) was to give five or six examples of a phoneme-grapheme correspondence and let the student figure out the relationship or common element in all the words. Of course, the clinic teacher must decide which part of a sequence to introduce and how big the steps shall be.

At Christmastime, while visiting in Texas, I was reading with our granddaughter, Elyse, who is in second grade. She was having trouble with the two sounds of *c*. She didn't know when to use the hard sound and when to use the *s* sound. This is easy to teach. Select five or six words from the sight vocabulary, if possible, or from material being read at the time: *cellar* (the problem word), *cent, cereal, center, cedar*. Make selections that will get you back into the story material for the application of phoneme-grapheme principles—a step that doesn't always happen when decoding instruction is isolated from comprehension instruction. Pick out a group of words that are in the forefront, as it were, of the reader's needs. Go down the list with the child. If he doesn't know them all, help him identify and read them. Next, say, "What do you notice about this list?" or, "Do you notice anything alike about these words?" or, "In what way are they all alike?" The child looks for and formulates the generalization. Bright clinic children were unusually good at this, because of the intellectual characteristics we have seen on the graphs. In this particular example, you may need to say, "Yes, the words all begin with *c*, and what letter comes next? Yes, it is *e*. In all the words? Tell me the generalization (rule, principle) in your own words." Another day you may follow with another list: *cider, circle, city, circus, cigarette*. Later the *ca, co,* and *cu* groups are analyzed. Finally the child makes the generalization that a *c* followed by an *e* or an *i* usually takes the *s* sound (or the soft sound, if you want to use that terminology), and *c* followed by *o, a,* and *u* usually makes the *k* sound. This generalization is useful, even in the study of the Romance languages.

Many of your pupils will be good at this kind of thinking—even though they are poor readers.

To teach decoding this way may take a little longer, but when you go back into the story, the student will be able to see how the rule works. We want the student to get payoff, and soon, for all that he learns in decoding, so we teach only generalizations that are reasonably consistent. (Small wonder they get confused with phonetic rules that have many variations!) Can you think of exceptions to the generalization about beginning *c*? Exceptions are not very numerous. Students need to learn to insert "usually" into their statements. Depending on the age and goals of the student, the teacher may want to say that this rule works for Spanish or French, too. For you, as a clinician or a tutor, it is much less frustrating to teach a sounding principle just once than to teach it over and over again to students who continue not to know it.

QUESTION: *How many clinic children have this intellectual profile of good generalizing abilities?*

ANSWER: If you rule out the partially seeing, the partially hearing, and the extremely handicapped emotionally, then this intellectual strength is characteristic of most reading-clinic children. About nine out of ten are low in both Digit span and Coding. By traditional reading-clinic procedures we were supposed to teach by the strongest sensory avenue: if the child was weak in the auditory modality, we were to use visual methods, such as sight word recognition. Our research showed that most children are weak in both visual and auditory modalities. The sequence is critical in this procedure of conceptualizing phoneme-grapheme relationships: (1) auditory discrimination of the phoneme, (2) discovery of the phoneme-grapheme relationship, and (3) application in the context.

QUESTION: *Can you do the same thing if the c is not followed by a vowel?*

ANSWER: There is a vowel in each pronounceable unit.

QUESTION: *So, it doesn't matter that the second letter is h?*

ANSWER: We would have previously taught *ch* as a digraph; the child will be cued to sounding *ch* (as in *child*) at an earlier step in the decoding sequence.

As you get into medial positions of a sound within the word, these are harder to discriminate. The student makes the transfer if he has learned the sound-letter correspondence at the beginning of the word correctly. In medial positions, a lot of other cues will help; but most of the time, the principles hold in the middle of the word. Usually we don't bother to teach the phoneme-grapheme correspondences that do not occur frequently.

Another advantage of teaching the child to attack decoding problems by conceptualization is that he can start making his own independent generalizations of other principles for decoding. One tendency clinic children have is to overgeneralize. I recommend helping them through the exceptions in the beginning so the generalizing they do does not break down and cause them not to trust themselves in the reading situation. Teach them to say "usually" or "most of the time." Talk about why our language has variations—how we get words from many different languages and many different places. With young children, I've often used tally marks to show roughly the proportion of times a rule will work: "The rule gets you through this many out of ten words, so is the rule worth knowing?"

QUESTIONS AND ANSWERS

Are there other questions about the intellectual functioning? Or the techniques for using the WISC to diagnose the functioning of individual students?

QUESTION: *I want to make sure that I have the graphs right. The charts that you use were graphed from the standard error of measurement of the scaled scores?*

ANSWER: Yes, the dotted line represents the distances in SE_m's that a measure deviates from the scaled-score mean. The first step is to find the student's own scaled-score mean. The second step is to find the direction and amount of deviation on each subtest from the subject's scaled-score mean. (This has the effect of partialling out his general intelligence.) The third step is to say, "How far is this score from his mean in terms of the standard error of measurement?" You simply take the standard error of measurement for the appropriate age and the particular subtest and divide to see how many standard errors of measurement are contained in this distance from the mean. Then you're back to the score of 1, 2, or even 4 plus or minus, which is really a sigma score.

QUESTION: *The −40 is . . .*

ANSWER: Minus 40 is the combined deviations, or sigma scores, for the clinic population. I'm glad you brought that up. The reason this score got so large is because the individuals in the group were so consistent in the direction of their deviation. We have already divided the deviation by the standard error of measurement, so the -40 is actually a test of significance. Deviation beyond the horizontal lines above and below the mean (Figure 8-5) indicate significance at the .001 level. Usually only one or two of twenty students from the clinic samples would fail to conform to this pattern on specific subtests other than Picture arrangement, Block design, and Object assembly. When the scores are added algebraically, minuses cancel out the pluses, or those that do not follow the pattern. Statistically, this sum is essentially a t-test of significance because it is divided by the deviation by the standard error of measurement.

QUESTION: *I'm still missing that last set. What does that -40 represent?*

ANSWER: I have been presenting a procedure that would justify your using the WISC subtest scores in individual diagnosis. For group studies the results of the individual analysis were combined. Minus 40 shows the extent to which a reading-clinic population was low in coding ability. A normal population would fall near 0. For research on groups we combined the individual sigma scores, because theoretically they could deviate up or down from the mean with equal probability. You can imagine how simple this procedure is for clinical diagnosis or group studies. Each child has these scores calculated and recorded. All I have to do in analyzing group data is to select the cases that meet the criteria, then add the sigma scores.

QUESTION: *That dotted line represents the entire two hundred kids?*

ANSWER: It represents the first eighty. I used them as a comparison group because the data were already deposited for these eighty with the American Documentation Institute where it could be examined. For this graph, the totals were corrected to an N of twenty.

If this sample were like Wechsler's norming population, the sum of the deviations should be 0, because the highs and lows would cancel each other out. In the reading-clinic sample we found consistent deviation in all but three subtests. Deviation beyond 2.86 represents a 99 to 1 chance that the difference is real.

Studies of intellectual functioning have been done with the Stanford Binet that show similar results (Rose, 1958). When using the Stanford

Binet, you need to run a factorial analysis of the items to identify clusters of related functions—a process that tends to get complicated. Most of the WISC subtests require similar kinds of functioning from one item to the next (Meeker, 1965). In California, eight out of ten psychometrists use the WISC for individual intelligence tests in situations where students are having learning difficulties. There's a tendency to use the Stanford Binet for prediction of school success and for early identification of gifted children. There was a tendency also to use the Stanford Binet for younger children until the Wechsler Preschool and Primary Scale of Intelligence (WPPSI) was published (1967).

QUESTION: *Did the children with tension symptoms show reversal problems?*

ANSWER: The reversal problems were related more to the age of the subject than to any thing else (A. Cohen, 1969). The younger children showed reversals more often than older students. Our high school subjects usually didn't show reversals or confused dominance, even though we suspected from their folders that they might at one time have had reversal problems.

QUESTION: *What happens to the motivation of tense readers as they get older?*

ANSWER: Well, we haven't checked that out, yet. I have been trying to interest Dr. Wilson in helping me do a follow up study, using counseling techniques to get at this question. We found some clinical evidence that those who continue to lack word-attack skills either develop tensions associated with reading or a lack of motivation for reading. The elementary-age children in our clinic groups were more likely than were secondary students to show simple lack of word-attack skill, without there being obvious avoidance or lack of motivation (Robeck, 1965).

QUESTION: *Apparently the tension doesn't show on the WISC?*

ANSWER: We excluded children from this study who were generally tense or emotionally disturbed. We looked for students whose tension became obvious in the reading situation but was not apparent in non-reading interpersonal situations. For these children, tension wasn't apparent when the WISC was administered.

One of the things that I did check out was the proportion of tense readers in different age groups. I found that at about second grade the incidence of children who showed tension symptoms related to reading was higher than in the upper elementary grades; then the incidence of tension went up again at junior high school level. I interpreted this observation to mean that in the fourth to sixth grades the kids had learned to live with reading disability. They had learned other ways of meeting status needs in school. When in junior high, the pressure to read was increased and the tension associated with reading went up again.

QUESTION: *How could you describe the tension—just extreme nervousness in trying to read, or what?*

ANSWER: Well, the most extreme of these cases was a very polite, verbal, outgoing boy. When his classroom teacher would insist he read a book, he would pass out. We said this was "tension associated with reading." He would get beads of perspiration on his forehead, he would turn pale, and he would get faint. We didn't ever actually have him pass out in the clinic, but this information was in the cumulative folder. An awareness of this problem induced his parents to bring him to the clinic. They claimed he would pass out when he had to read. Other students showed high-pitched voices, fidgeting, and paleness. By identifying these children and analyzing their reading error patterns, we were able to describe their reading behavior. From this description we could identify what we called "tension associated with reading" from tapes, without seeing the outward manifestations. We picked up additional cases, particularly among older students who could be classified by trained professionals as tense readers. One of the basic symptoms is that the error ratio deteriorates as soon as the student starts making mistakes. You can take this kind of reader—a ninth grader, for example—who reads quite well at sixth-grade level. When you increase the difficulty of the material to seventh-grade level, his error ratio may double. The reader who lacks motivation for reading, on the other hand, may actually improve his error ratio with an increase in the difficulty of the material. We have many tapes of poor readers who actually improved their performance, their error ratio went down, when the difficulty of material was increased. In tense readers, the opposite happened. They typically would make a few mistakes and then would start a deterioration of error ratio, even though the difficulty of the material remained constant. When the number of errors increases markedly within a level, you immediately suspect tension is associated with the reading act. This finding is useful in working with older children. To summarize, we found and described the characteristic patterns in the young children, whose tension mechanisms were apparent because they had not learned to mask them. The kind of errors made, however, were found to be the same in some older students.

QUESTION: *What I find hard to understand is why the pattern of tension is restricted to reading, for example, particularly in cases where the children are exceptionally bright. Because reading is so important in society and in school, I'm surprised that the overall image is not affected. I find it hard to picture a boy who passes out when a book is presented to him who doesn't otherwise exhibit a pattern of emotional disturbance.*

ANSWER: I think this is a good question, and I think in a school situation the tension may become generalized. We might expect negative effects to be generalized to reading at first. This affective conceptualization might not transfer to playground activities, however. You see this syndrome is very complex. The boy I mentioned had learned to get payoff from helping the teachers. He happened to be a fourth grader. His teachers typically had found him delightful to have around. He cleaned the chalkboard; he picked up paper; he was always doing things for people. In the clinic, the other children liked him. One day we were painting word boxes. He was there first, did the best job, and stayed with the painting the longest. If I needed anything carried, he'd say, "I'll take that for you, Dr. Robeck." He had learned to be successful in gaining favorable recognition in these ways. As frequently as possible, he was meaningfully employed elsewhere when the reading time came.

The WISC was a fun test for these kids because we didn't ask them to read, you see. I learned a quick way to establish rapport at the beginning. The kid already knows he's on the spot; he knows he's being tested. I would simply say, "We think you're a good learner, and we need to find out *how* good you are. This is going to be fun for you, because I'm going to do the reading, and you're going to do the thinking." This approach gave no specific help, but usually it was all that was needed to put the clinic subject at ease. When we took this type of student into the reading situation, however, his responses changed. I'd say, "Now, let's go to reading." The student's voice would start going up. Some students would stammer, even though they had not done this before. There are many ways that people show tension—coughing as contrasted with yawning. On the other hand, children who lacked motivation for reading were not bothered at all when asked to read. (Of course, yawning can be a tension mechanism, too.) It's not all as simple as I'm indicating here, but you look at the child in different kinds of situations within the clinic, and you can tell when he is at ease as contrasted with an increase of tension when he is reading. We found an identifiable reading-error pattern in this group.

PREVENTION OF READING DIFFICULTIES

Let's turn to some of the problems we face in developing a program for the prevention of reading difficulty. It seemed obvious to me, when studying clinic subjects, that if a child could be successful in reading from the beginning, there should be no reading problem. Almost everybody believes this, but people differ in how the beginning instruction should proceed in order to assure success for the reader.

Readiness and reinforcement

One ready answer to the question of how to help the child to succeed is that you postpone reading to a later age, particularly for boys, because they seemingly have more trouble in learning to read. This advice is simply to admit the boys to school six months later; give them a chance to mature, and then they won't have any trouble. This theory has been shot down recently by studies showing that children learn much more much earlier than we had suspected previously (Pines, 1966). We now suspect that 4-year-olds learn some things as easily as do 6-year-olds; that some kinds of learning take place easier at age 4 than age 6; that the neurological aspects of intellectual development of the child is half complete by the age of 4 (Bloom, 1964).

The approach that consists of merely waiting has been challenged by research, especially by those persons interested in physiological explanations to learning. Of course, those who still insist that the mental age of 6½ is the best time to begin reading don't accept the research reports from neuropsychologists, so you won't find it difficult to get into an argument on this subject. There are school districts that hold children back from promotion to a higher grade or postpone reading instruction for 50 percent of the class. They believe in waiting for children to mature as the means to their becoming more efficient learners.

On the other hand, some of us suspect that children could learn the visual symbols of language as easily as they learn the auditory symbols of language at about age 2, provided that the system of reinforcement were as effective for learning to read as it now is for learning to speak. Many people are saying that biologically and intellectually the child is just as capable of learning to read at age 2 as he is to speak. When he is in difficulty as a learner in school, this may be related to many conditions, including his social characteristics, the methods of teaching, and the systems of reinforcement used. You can perhaps think of some important differences between the reinforcement systems the child encounters in learning to speak as contrasted with learning to read. In learning to speak, the feedback to the child is immediate. If he asks for a drink and somebody understands him, he gets a drink. That is very reinforcing. In school, we tend to expect him, from the beginning, to find the reading situation inherently reinforcing. In group reading instruction, the teacher doesn't always know exactly where the child left off the day before or what is successful performance in his own terms. My daughter-in-law, who has a 2-year-old in the house, knows exactly what her son can accomplish from day to day. If he assembles a toy for the first time, Nancy will say, "Oh, Michael, I saw what you did! Jay, did you see what Michael can do? He put all the rings on the spindle by himself. Yesterday I had to help him with the last one." Because the child is an individual in an individual's environment, his needs are satisfied; the feedback comes to him promptly. Michael is noticed when he practices saying names of things or for getting closer to a correct pronunciation. Most children learn to speak very rapidly and well from age 2 upwards. Some people have the notion that children could learn to read as easily under similar reinforcement situations. In beginning reading, we bring thirty children together. Some of them spend a great deal of time doing things they already know how to do, while others struggle along trying to imitate responses that don't make sense for them.

In setting up prevention programs, we need to find ways to organize the lessons so that each child gets feedback, from moment to moment and response to response, whether he is correct or not. Day before yesterday I heard a report at AERA (American Educational Research Association) in which the differences were studied between mothers in a college community and mothers in a slum community in how they responded to their preschool children while they were learning language (Scott, 1969). The investigator found that mothers of the inner-city children were reluctant to give either feedback or praise. They would ask, "What's this?" But when the child said, "Spoon," these mothers wouldn't say anything. The mother from the college community typically would say, "No, that's not a spoon, that's a fork," which seemed to be better reinforcement for learning than not verifying, not confirming, the child's effort to communicate. In the classroom, immediate feedback requires an organization in which the groups of children are small. Teachers are finding that the paraprofessionals—the extra persons in the classroom—although untrained, can be taught rather readily to interact with children. It helps the untalkative child to have somebody there to listen, to respond to conversation, and to hear him read. If we're going to prevent reading difficulties, we will need smaller groups, more adult interaction with the child, and better patterns of reinforcement. Also we need to know the levels of ability a child needs in critical areas before we expect him to associate spoken and printed symbols.

QUESTION: *About the feedback aspect—it sounds as though you are assuming that the task will be inherently reinforcing if the child gets the correct feedback.*

ANSWER: The situation gradually can become inherently reinforcing by giving direct, personal reinforcement in the beginning. In other words, I would teach the child to have pleasure working with words. At first the pupil may need attention and feedback to make reading activities rewarding. The pleasure-punishment aspects of the situation need to be controlled. I think discovery learning is reinforced intrinsically. There must be inherent pleasure in finding a solution to something that has bugged you. William James claimed it was characteristic of human beings to need to relate the bits and pieces of one's environment. Piaget suggests a similar need in human beings; the individual, the organism, needs to accommodate, cognitively, to whatever is assimilated via experience. People have this necessity to organize experience cognitively, which Piaget has differentiated as seriation, consolidation, causality, and other operations (Wilson, Robeck, and Michael, 1969). Dr. Wilson and I call the grasping of relationships conceptualization. When different bits and pieces of the environment are related to make structure or sense, this learning is satisfying. If you have been curious about something, have been working for a solution, and have had some tension along with the involvement, you must have sensed pleasure to have the puzzle fall into place. Sensory-motor learning, as well as verbal learning, can be inherently rewarding, but sometimes the learner needs help to identify the source of his reward. I would not rely solely on the reading material itself to provide the reinforcement to the child from the beginning. I would teach him that it is important by the way I react to his reading. This idea varies some-what with advocates of "responsive environment" in early childhood education. I think that in sensory stimulation there is pleasure, but I wouldn't rely on this exclusively in beginning reading.

Critical abilities for achievement in reading

Let's go into the research on critical abilities for learning to read. Obviously, the problem-preventive reading environment will need to be based on an analysis of a minimal level of functioning in critical prereading abilities. These abilities are: (1) visual perception, (2) auditory perception, (3) sensory-motor integration, (4) language development, and (5) intellectual potential.

Visual perception has been given a great deal of attention in schools during the readiness period, although most children who come to first grade do not need further special teaching in this area. Some children do, however, so how do we determine whether a particular child has developed adequate visual functioning for reading? Many readiness programs require all pupils to go through pages and pages of visual discrimination exercises in a workbook. Kids who don't need this can be utterly bored by six or eight weeks of this—either in kindergarten or first grade. Some children in the 4- to 5-year-old group—about 12 percent of the children from suburbia —are not able to pick out the "one that's different" in a row of pictures or symbols. Over half of the 4- and 5-year-olds from a slum environment are not able to do this. However, if you change the instructions to "find the one that is not like the others," you immediately add a small percentage of the advantaged children and a large percentage of slum children to those who are successful in making these kinds of visual discriminations. You are left, then, with a small percentage of children in both groups who do not have the visual perception needed for reading. Apparently, the Frostig materials for teaching visual-motor coordination are very helpful for these children. I suspect one of the reasons that some programs have shown less gain from Frostig materials than the project directors had hoped is that many children were included who had already developed the visual-motor skills that were being taught, so naturally they did not show significant improvement. Marianne Frostig (1966) developed a screening test to find out which children need the visual-motor practice. Approximately 10 to 20 percent of the kindergarten age group need special practice in visual discrimination or perception or both.

When Dr. Wilson and I were developing the *Kindergarten Evaluation of Learning Potential* (KELP), we decided to teach and observe the kinds of visual discrimination that are needed for beginning reading. The Safety Sign item, in which children reproduce familiar signs with precut letters, both teaches and tests this ability. If a child can select and turn the letters correctly, we assume he doesn't need exercises in finding the "figure that is different," and the "letter that is the same" in the reading readiness workbooks. Like many people today, I once thought that no particular harm was done to children by having them go through reading readiness pages. I have changed my mind about requiring any activity that lacks novelty and stimulation. Apparently, we can teach displeasure in a school situation quite readily by keeping a child at a task that is not challenging and therefore is not fun. Also, if the child can write his name, turning the letters correctly, we can then assume his readiness for writing.

The second critical ability for reading is *auditory perception*. The child must be able to hear the phonemes—the sound parts in words— before he can make the correct associations with the graphemes of printed words. Most of the reading readiness tests do not include an adequate sampling of this ability to discriminate letter sounds in sequence. Dr. Wilson and I put an item into the KELP material to help the kindergarten teacher screen for auditory discrimination. If children can sort a group of toys by the beginning sound, you know they are able to discriminate that particular sound. In the literature on reading, a noisy argument continues about whether children should be taught vowels first, or whether one should begin with the consonants. If the child discriminates both classes of sounds within a word, it doesn't make much difference which order the teacher follows. Another argument ensues over whether to begin with the long or the short vowel. The short vowels are harder to discriminate. It is difficult to hear the difference between short *i* and short *e*, short *o* and short *u*. If the child is hazy in his discrimination of short vowel sounds, you had better start with the long vowels because they are so much easier to hear.

Tests for this kind of auditory perception are available for older students, including college students. Some college students are unable to make a number of auditory discriminations. Small wonder, then, that they were not able to associate particular sounds with particular letters, as one must do in both decoding and encoding. When the teacher chooses to deemphasize the phonics program, he shifts the responsibility on the child to build his own sets of phoneme-grapheme correspondence. In other words, he must discover his own relationships as he goes along, which is what sight methods require. The highly intelligent child, who learns to

182   MILDRED C. ROBECK

read primarily on his own, has learned to make the generalizations he needs for independent word attack. All learners are highly dependent on good auditory discrimination when not given systematic instruction in decoding.

I want to warn you away from overuse of a wide variety of auditory perception tests that have little or no relationship to reading success—tone discrimination, for example. The child needs to hear phonemes in order to make sense out of beginning reading instruction, particularly in decoding.

The third ability for beginning reading is the *integration of the sensory systems*, and Phyllis Katz and Martin Deutch (1963), in their studies of slum children, compared the good with the poor readers among Negro boys. They found no difference in visual perception, as such, between the groups. However, they found some difference in favor of the good readers in auditory perception. They found even greater differences between the groups in their ability to shift from one sensory modality to the other. Readers need to take in visual stimuli and make auditory responses, or vice versa. The poor readers took longer to make this shift, even when the stimuli for the responses were nonreading materials.

R. Held and J. A. Bower, Jr. (1967) studied visually guided reaching in infant monkeys. The investigators deprived infant monkeys in ways they would not dare to deprive human infants. They put a plywood apron around the monkey infants so that they could not see their hands. Their monkey subjects became severely retarded in reaching and grasping. When one of their hands was revealed, the subject spent a lot of time looking at it. Very little transference was made from the right hand to the left hand. Research on learning is showing that the separate sensory systems are highly developed at birth through learning that takes place prenatally.

Much of the learning during the sensory-motor period (ages 0 to 2) and in the preoperational period (ages 2 to 4), as Piaget would define them, is the integration of the different systems (Wilson, Robeck, and Michael, 1969). Speech and reading require interaction of the visual, the auditory, and the kinesthetic systems. The coordination among the six pairs of eye muscles is required constantly in seeing the printed page. Many fine motor skills are involved in speaking and in handling a pencil. In reading readiness evaluation, we need to observe the child at the pre-reading level and to be sure that these kinds of sensory-motor integrations are developed before expecting the child to succeed in reading. Left-to-right spacial sequencing, for example, isn't something with which a child is born; it isn't genetic. Some Oriental languages are printed in columns from the bottom of the page; Hebrews begin on the left and read to the right.

Reading from left to right is a characteristic of our culture that the child needs to learn. As a way of establishing left to right, the Safety Signs in the KELP illustrate a procedure. We start with play. We want the child to have fun using these signs. To reinforce affective and cognitive learning, the teacher might say, "Did you have fun?" or, "You were a good worker today. How would you like to try this again some day?" Perhaps the child thought this activity was not for him. The teacher needs to observe this and to try to think why the child was less than enthusiastic. The next time he is given the Safety Signs, the teacher should involve him in activities that are stimulating and satisfying. With many such experiences, the habit of working from left to right with letters is established. Many other experiences can be used also: the child writing his name, listening to stories from books, and interpreting series of pictures. Some reading-clinic subjects revert at times to reversals of words or letters as late as age 10.

Some kindergarten guidelines recommend "training in auditory perception" that consists of teaching the pupils to listen for rhyme words in poems. This emphasis can result in confusion to the child who is simultaneously trying to learn the beginning-to-end sequence of phonemes in words, because children cue their listening to the end of the word at a time when they should be learning to hear word parts from the beginning. If we spend a lot of time teaching kids to listen to the ends of words and don't teach them to listen to the beginning of words, we need not be surprised when they attack words in reverse. I soft-pedal the listening for rhymes in kindergarten and early first grade. (Anyway, it doesn't take a rhyme to make a poem!) Children can have fun hearing the euphony and rhythm of verse without being drilled on rhyme endings. During the stage where the child is being taught the left-to-right ordering of words and pages, I would avoid training him in listening for rhyming.

A number of subtests within the readiness tests indicate sensory-motor integration. If the child can write his name reasonably well or can learn to write it quickly when we show him, I see no reason for spending time in readiness workbook pages on eye-hand coordination. Some 3- and 4-year-olds have extremely fine muscle coordination and learn to write their names easily. The matter of muscle coordination in children within the age range of from 4 to 8 may be more closely related to their rate of growth at the time than to their chronological age. Many 4- and 5-year-olds come to nursery school with very adequate muscle coordination for such things as turning pages, accommodating to the printed letters, writing, and following the line. Some children appear to have better muscle coordination at age 4 than others do at age 7.

QUESTION: *Are these children the ones that are growing more slowly than the ones that are shooting up?*

ANSWER: At the times a child is making a growth spurt, he must make many adjustments to the physical environment he has been manipulating habitually. You may notice more difficulties in motor response from the child who is growing rapidly than from the child who is growing slowly at the time and, presumably, is having to grow in neurological integration.

The fourth of the critical areas of readiness is *language development*. The knowledge of syntax may be more critical than size of vocabulary. The linguists are beginning to demonstrate the importance of basic speech patterns as more critical than vocabulary. We saw that vocabulary scores were relatively high in reading-clinic children. Other evidence might be cited to show that an extensive vocabulary does not assure success in beginning reading. The numbers of words that slum children know— Spanish-speaking children and black children—is approximately the same as the size of vocabulary middle-class children used in the 1930s and 1940s. The size of vocabulary did not keep middle-class children from learning to read then, nor did we delay their reading instruction. However, between the slum child's language and that used in books, there are differences in word sequence, in syntax, in what some call a deep sense of language. This problem raises another argument about whether or not we should teach minority-group children to read their own dialects. Those who advocate teaching children to begin reading standard English argue that time is being lost, developmentally and chronologically, for efficient learning of language; but the numbers of words that a child is required to know in beginning reading is not extensive. Probably he does need to have internalized the patterns of speech that are used in the reading material.

The fifth concern in evaluating readiness for reading is rate of learning or *intellectual potential*. I would discard the notion of a chronological age of 6½ as an appropriate criterion. Children with IQs in the 50s can learn to read if they are not started too soon and their program is built on success. On the other hand, you saw the records of children with IQs of 120 to 145 who were severely retarded in reading. The boy who was highest in our clinic sample is currently assigned to the slow classes in his high school. Once a pupil has reached fourth grade, the group intelligence tests he gets in school usually require him to read. In vocabulary items, particularly, he is restricted in his responses to his achievement level in reading. If the candidates for remedial reading are not identified early, they are difficult to find by the usual school screening procedures. By the time they are in junior high school, their low-achievement patterns are spread throughout their classroom behavior.

QUESTIONS AND ANSWERS

QUESTION: *I trust you are not too enthusiastic about the Ilg-Ames placement methods. What do you think they do in their screening devices? Do you think they test the integration of all skills, or do you think it is really a maturation thing?*

ANSWER: I would like to see the Ilg-Ames Developmental Scale (1964) used in further research on the relationship of this syndrome to beginning reading and on determining how we might change beginning reading programs to fit the child, rather than to delay the child's entrance in school or retard him as to grade placement. Whenever 25 to 50 percent of a class are not "developmentally" ready for their grade placement, change the curriculum!

QUESTION: *They don't mention that.*

ANSWER: Well, they do not pretend to be knowledgeable about curriculum; in fact, their first chapter is quite specific about this point. They are from the Gesell Institute. Gesell's purposes in his initial research were to describe typical growth patterns for particular age groups so that children who were mentally retarded could be identified by their parents and brought in for early treatment. Gesell was not trying to describe the variability within an age group, nor was he trying to suggest procedures for teaching. He was trying to identify retarded children. If you put the Gesell research in context, it has limited applicability to older children and to those who are above the norm in intelligence or development. Putting pupils back increases the chances they will drop out of school and decreases the chances that they will ever get into the professions. When large numbers of children are involved, I simply would adjust the curriculum to the children instead of putting them back or retaining them. The child who is developed mentally should do what he is developmentally ready and eager to do. I object to holding down a child to the lowest point of his developmental profile—to using a wastebasket term like "immature" as the rationale for a curricular decision. If we are going to identify the child who is immature, the solution is not to send him back home for another year to an environment that has already denied him full development. When he returns one year later, he is worse off—still further behind. If a child is mentally retarded to the extent that he needs training with exceptional children, that is a different matter that should be reflected in the diagnosis.

QUESTION: *Although right now the children are being put into a lower group or a slower group.*

ANSWER: I think there are tremendous possibilities in transitional programs.

QUESTION: *But is it not important to do something—not merely to wait for the kid to get older, for him to do only the things he can do already, or for him to spend his time developing the skills that aren't really going to help him when he gets in first grade? If a kid is frozen in a junior or primary class, then I think it is very bad. I have seen many such programs in operation.*

ANSWER: If the identification is good, if the instruction is based on needs, and if the teacher will move the child upward as he achieves, the transitional program can prevent early failure for some children. Dr. Wilson and I started the development of the KELP after sitting in on a case study during which a child was selected as immature and put into a junior-primary class. The child had a Binet IQ on file of 124. He was little, and he was in the younger half of his class. To us, he appeared more ready to learn to read than many who were assigned to first grade. This question brings us to the criteria that I would not use for beginning reading: chronological age, physical size, sex, size of vocabulary, or social maturity.

QUESTION: *What about the reading-levels program? At some schools the entire population has been divided into gradations with regard to their grade level of reading; so all the children are dispersed throughout the morning to different reading classes at their level. It sounds as though it has some potential in a way, but are there traps? Are there some real pitfalls?*

ANSWER: This kind of sectioning has potential for dealing with more children at various instructional levels for a higher percentage of the day than is possible in traditional age-grade placement. The pitfall is in assuming that a group of children whose reading achievement scores are the same, or nearly the same, need like instruction. I started an article once, which never got finished, about three fourth-grade pupils who came out exactly on the grade norm—4.6. But how they differed! (The names of the students have, of course, been changed.) James, who was intellectually gifted but had taken three years to start reading, was advancing rapidly and joyously. Pamela, who had allergies and eczema, was absent so frequently her skills checklist was full of holes. Jeffrey had contracted "sports fever" to the extent that only careful selection of materials and regular attention to comprehension skills kept him from becoming a reluctant reader. Readers differ in many ways other than total achievement level.

CONCLUDING REMARKS

Before we adjourn, may I also make a plug for grouping. I don't want to leave the impression that you must always teach every child by himself. This simply is not feasible; we seem always to have about thirty pupils and usually only sixty to ninety minutes for reading. We can teach one pupil at a time for two or three minutes, or we can teach ten at a time for twenty to thirty minutes. The crux of the problem is to use a class organization that utilizes frequent regrouping according to learning needs.

We have talked about improving reading instruction. May I close with a reminder: "There is a relationship between IQ and success in learning to read, and between chronological age and beginning reading success. Within the kindergarten–first-grade groups, however, I am quite sure we in the schools have overapplied the research on groups to the disadvantage of many of the individual students we teach.

THE CULTURALLY DISADVANTAGED CHILD

9

John A. R. Wilson
Mildred C. Robeck

Dr. Mildred C. Robeck was introduced at the beginning of Chapter 8 as a specialist in reading. Her list of credits in that field are impressive. She also has earned distinction in working with the disadvantaged.

Dr. Robeck was one of the original training group for officials from districts where Project Follow Through was being established. For two years she directed an advanced study institute for teachers, principals, and central-staff officers from districts where programs for the disadvantaged were being funded. She has been a consultant on Indian education both in Oregon and in South Dakota. One of her current research projects is concerned with the potential for and the nature of language development of American Indian children.

Dr. John A. R. Wilson has also been closely identified with programs for the economically disadvantaged. For four years he has been an official evaluator of Title I projects of ESEA (Elementary and Secondary Education Act). He served on the instructional team working with teachers, principals, and central-staff officers from districts where programs for the disadvantaged were being funded.

Dr. Wilson's background includes working, teaching, and counseling with both rural and urban poor.

This discussion stresses the necessity for personalizing and individualizing the school programs for the disadvantaged, beginning with the child's initiation into the school community. Adult sensitivity to the cultural strengths of children from different ethnic backgrounds ensures that their previous learning will be utilized as a base for further learning. A selective focus on individual potential helps to avoid the conflicts between the cultural values of the family and the goals of the school. A shift to learning opportunities that are structured on individual strengths could rescue some of the doubtful programs now offered for disadvantaged children and youth.

Each ethnic group has cultural advantages that distinguish it as a group. These culture patterns are learned by the child before he enters school. The traditions of any people can become disadvantageous when new or different modes of life become desirable. Cultural disadvantage is the inhibition, reactive or proactive, of past acculturation on a present learning situation.

Some culture-oriented learnings are more likely to become barriers to change than others. A mother tongue, when different from the national language, interferes progressively as the individual advances in age before beginning to learn a new language. Because of a passion to fulfill the "melting pot" interpretation of democracy in the United States, a temptation has persisted to eliminate or even destroy the assets of the first language in order to teach English. The compulsory discarding of a person's language, whether dialectic or foreign, may make him feel that his whole culture is being discarded and that he is being downgraded. When the first language is valued and encouraged as an asset, words and grammatical forms of the second language can be related to patterns already learned. In this way the school can expand rather than diminish the learner's feeling of his own worth.

Some ethnic groups have desired integration and have themselves rejected "old country" ways. But others, most notably the American Indians, needed to retain their cultural identity in a hostile environment. Recently many Negroes have recognized their exclusion from the melting pot and have attempted to reconstruct a cultural identity that includes all black groups. An attendant hostility toward the central group is likely to interfere with otherwise effective reinforcement schedules in school.

Cultural disadvantage can result from any marked deviation from the social or economic mainstream. Ralph (the name is, of course, fictitious), age 6, was at a disadvantage when his first-grade class studied family roles. He was confused by the discussions about mothers making beds, preparing meals, and driving the kids to school, since at his home these things were done by the maids, the cook, or the chauffeur. His account of his mother's activities, such as building a historical museum, was incomprehensible to his classmates. At first Ralph's teacher was uncomfortable in his home because she didn't know how to respond to the butler or how to approach Ralph's mother.

Within each ethnic or cultural group is a full range of individual competence, uniqueness in intellectual functioning, and extreme variability in affective strengths. The overlapping in the range of human strengths is far greater than mean differences in these strengths among groups of people. Teachers who see a child as John or Juan are more likely to see his potential as an individual than is the teacher who sees him as a black, a chicano, a Puerto Rican, or an ADC kid (referring to a form of welfare, Aid for Dependent Children). There is no doubt that the intellectual efficiency of individuals from any group can be improved by education. We propose that improvement happens only to individual persons. We believe that significant improvement in school learning can occur only when teachers move beyond appreciation of cultural characteristics to valuing students as persons and believing in them as learners. Such teachers can help significantly if trusted to diagnose the learner's needs and individualize his learning programs.

R. Larson and J. L. Olson (1963) developed a method for identifying culturally disadvantaged kindergarten children. They found a wide range of abilities in all groups sampled and concluded that membership in a cultural minority group did not necessarily mean a child was educationally disadvantaged. From their data, Larson and Olson established a multifactor criteria for selecting individual students for special programs based on language development, self-concept, social skills, and cultural difference.

HANDICAPS RESULTING FROM CULTURE

A culture, by definition, results in intellectual inbreeding that sets the individual apart from other cultural groups. Communal living, as practiced by one subculture in the United States of 1970, is likely to result in cultural disadvantages for the children who are reared there.

While keeping in mind that each individual is unique, we will focus on some learners whose disadvantages are duplicated many times in contemporary America. The names of the individuals are, of course, fictitious.

Nina

Nina Martinez was a 4-year-old we observed in a Headstart class. She was dark skinned, had long, straight hair, neatly combed. She had two dresses, one faded blue, the other bright pink, which she wore on alternate days to the school. Nina came to the attention of the teachers because she refused to eat, either at snack or lunch time. She usually drank her juice but never her milk. Even with the urging of a Spanish-speaking aide, Nina continued to refuse the food. She conformed to other classroom expectations, but the teachers were not sure whether she was imitating the other children or whether she understood the instructions to the group.

Because of her concern that Nina wasn't eating, the teacher asked the parent coordinator, Mrs. Smith, to give priority to Nina's parents in her visitation schedule. After her visit, Mrs. Smith reported that Spanish was spoken in the home except in conversation directed at herself, at which time the father did the talking. Nina had an older sister and two younger sisters who watched and listened quietly. Mr. Martinez said several times that he had brought his family to California so that his daughters would have advantages like the girls in the United States. It was apparent that Mrs. Martinez understood English when she responded to questions about Nina's not eating in school. She said, "Nina, she like frijoles, tortillas, cakes, coffee. She like bananas." During Mrs. Smith's entire visit, Nina, like her sisters, watched and listened but did not speak. The visitor left both her telephone numbers and asked Mr. Martinez to phone if she could help Nina in any way.

Nina's cultural differences include her language, the vague aspirations her parents have for her, and the kind of food she has learned to eat. Probably she has learned to identify with her mother, whose interest is centered in the home, whose communication is in Spanish, and who accepts the fact that the male has the dominant role in family affairs. Had Nina remained in Mexico these patterns of living would have facilitated her growing up.

Tommy

Tommy Talltree, age 6, was enrolled in kindergarten. He came fifteen miles on the bus each day from his grandparents' farm in the foothills. His mother had died in childbirth when Tommy was 4 years old. His father had gone to the city to find work and turned up at the farm occasionally for a few days. When Tommy was 5, his father and uncle had taken him and four male cousins to California to see Disneyland. Tommy's grandmother questioned him occasionally about the rocks and pine cones he collected at the overnight campgrounds where they had stayed. She advised him to remember all these things so he could tell about them when he went to school. Tommy listened with great interest to her stories of Indian heroes. He had won a blanket in the dance competition for boys, age 6 and under, at a recent Indian festival.

Tommy's grandfather leased most of his land to a white, small-grain farmer who paid a share of the crop each fall. A treaty allowed Indians to hunt venison in the national forest whenever they needed meat. The family's only other income was the occasional sale of a horse to another white man who contracted a bronco string for the rodeos.

Like his cousins, Tommy's acculturation was consistent with Indian ways on his reservation. He was never punished verbally nor physically, but a look from any adult was interpreted as approval or disapproval. He watched television but was discouraged from imitating the commercials or practicing the roles. His family enjoyed being together, but hours sometimes elapsed without a word of conversation being exchanged.

Tommy's particular culture was disadvantageous to him in the school because of his Indian economy of speech and his intense involvement in Indian culture. His isolation on the farm had given him little opportunity to learn the kinds of social interaction that characterize the classroom learning. His varied and extensive patterns of nonverbal communication at home were lost on his teacher, who was frustrated by his nontalking. However, she noticed his alertness at story time and the alacrity with which he chose and worked puzzles.

Robert

Robert Jackson, age 10, was enrolled in grade three after transferring from the city one hundred plus miles away. He was an extremely handsome boy. He had curly (not kinky) hair, dark skin, and even white teeth. In the classroom Robert wandered from desk to desk annoying other children. Before his first week was out his teacher, Mr. Marshall, referred him to the counselor saying, "That kid is driving me up the wall. He hasn't worked as much as ten minutes on any assignment I have given him. I think he understands what I tell him to do, but he doesn't listen. I don't know whether to go easy with him or start laying down the law."

Mrs. Jackson came in for a conference at the request of Mrs. Whitney, the counselor. Mrs. Jackson, smelling faintly of scotch, wasted little time in pleasantries before launching into a history that seemed to have been told several times before. She said, "Fred, my husband, drives a garbage truck and lives with his black parents, who never approved of me because I am white. My father pleaded with me not to marry Fred. Father always talked about the blacks being just as good as the whites, but when I wanted to marry Fred his fine theories evaporated. At first Fred was proud of our baby, but now he wishes Robert could wear an African haircut. Every vacation they drive down to get Robert, or they send a bus ticket. I'm left all alone. Robert has never done well in school, even though he was very bright as a little kid. The teachers have never really challenged him."

The counselor saw that here was a mother who had verbalized her own problems and escaped from any need to resolve them. Robert was torn between the expectations of his father's black community, with all its present turmoil, and the weak, ostracized, alcoholic home life supplied by the mother. He literally did not know who he was and spent his days looking for himself. He was disadvantaged by his lack of cultural identity.

Manuel

Manuel Juarez, age 14, attended classes for slow grade-seven students. He was the fourth of eleven siblings, who ranged in age from 18 to 2 years. His oldest brother, Pedro, attended a work-opportunity program for mentally retarded boys. Pedro spent four hours each day washing dishes in a supper club. He had been arrested and treated for heroin addiction. Manuel's two older sisters went to school on a very irregular basis. Both had dossiers in the police files of known prostitutes. Manuel was absent from school two or three days each week. The family, as a whole, had acquired the highest absence rate in the history of the school. Manuel had been picked up twice for stealing rock records. The four younger siblings who attended school had thick files in the elementary counselor's office. Their records were characterized by truancy, low achievement, and undeveloped intellectual potential. A 4-year-old sister was enrolled in Head-start. Two youngsters were still at home.

Mr. Juarez was second barber in a small shop that catered to Puerto Ricans and Negroes. Mrs. Juarez, who was concerned about her poor health, attended evening classes conducted by Catholic Welfare. When the school social worker, Harriet Dawson, first visited the Juarez's home, she was impressed by the mother's apparent interest in the children and her high level of articulation. Miss Dawson was accustomed to families of this size crowded into a flat and normally living in rather untidy conditions.

After several visits to the home, she realized the family was intricately involved with numerous agencies and was making no visible progress in solving their problems. Only after several more visits did she conceptualize the problem as centered in the mother. Mrs. Juarez used fear of illness to rationalize keeping her children home from school and dependent on herself.

Leroy

Leroy Scott, age 22, was recruited in Alabama for Upward Bound studies in a North Central university. The principal of his high school (for Negroes) had recommended him for undergraduate work. Although he survived the special summer-training program, Leroy found himself with three F's on midterms. He experienced the cultural shock of moving from a high school where he felt competent at the top of his group to college classes where he was unable to keep the pace of the lectures or complete the assigned reading. His reinforcement as a student came primarily from the black studies discussion group where he felt he had as much to offer as anyone else in the section. In his frustration, Leroy turned to activities sponsored by the Afro-American Club. These extracurricular activities, which seemed so real and vital, cut heavily into his study schedule. Basically, he was disadvantaged by poor academic preparation for a highly competitive degree program. A program in compensatory education is available to Leroy and a small percent of the culturally disadvantaged.

PROGRAMS FOR DISADVANTAGED CHILDREN AND YOUTH

Programs for the culturally disadvantaged have expanded rapidly since public attention became focused on poverty groups and on the importance of the early years in human learning. Much of the financial support for these programs has come from the federal government, although most state legislatures provide money to supplement national programs or to initiate others. For example, California has a compensatory education program that predates the federally funded programs. Private social agencies, particularly church groups, offer child care and rehabilitation services designed for disadvantaged persons. Most federally supported programs are contingent upon some local funding.

Preprimary education

Most prominent of the preschool programs for the culturally disadvantaged has been Headstart, which is offered throughout the country under the auspices of the U.S. Office of Economic Opportunity (OEO). The purpose of Headstart is to prepare disadvantaged young children for successful schooling. Each project incorporates health care, family involvement, supplemental nutrition, teacher and aide training, community action, and opportunities for cognitive and affective growth. Services are restricted to areas where large numbers of families live in poverty. This economic criterion has involved large numbers of minority-group children who were also culturally disadvantaged by the definition used in this chapter. Individual children who live within designated areas may be included even though their parents do not come within the poverty definition.

Headstart programs are characterized by a favorable adult-child ratio, the recommendation being a teacher, an aide, and a volunteer for each fifteen children. Guidelines for the projects have tended to reflect the developmental point of view, which focuses on the whole child. Individualized health and dental care is provided each child, including diagnostic examinations, preventive and corrective treatment, with record keeping and follow-up. Unfortunately, the instructional programs usually have not diagnosed and followed the cognitive growth of the individual children. The early programs have generally assumed that children from a particular age and cultural group needed the same kinds of learning experiences, the model being the traditional nursery or kindergarten setting for mainstream white children.

Headstart agencies have required increasingly objective evaluation of the effectiveness of the educational aspects of the programs. As a consequence, substantial data are available from the ability and achievement tests used for evaluation (Cicarelli and Granger, 1969). In general, results have shown limited improvement at the end of the program, and the improvements were usually no longer discernible after the children had been in school for two years. These findings have been a bitter disappointment to those connected with Headstart, who uniformly saw the work as highly stimulating and substantially effective with the children.

The conflict between objective and subjective evaluation has resulted in various interpretations of the value of Headstart. One of the most notable explanations has been that the competencies children developed in Headstart have been ignored when the child entered regular school classes; he has been forced to wait for his peers to catch up (Scheuer, 1969). A second interpretation has been that intellectual progress is genetically determined, and the improved environment of the Headstart program was a waste of time (Jensen, 1969).

We would like to suggest that the difference between the individualized program for health improvement and group-oriented education programs explains some of the difference between the success of the health programs and the limited improvement shown by the educational programs. We also stress the point that whole-group instruction in kindergarten or first grade tends to minimize the child's emerging capacities. Dentists know that children from poverty backgrounds have more DMF (decayed, missing, or filled) teeth than children from affluent homes, but dentists spend most of their time with the children who need fillings and not with the group as a whole. Likewise, pediatricians and nurses keep records of diagnoses, treatment, and followup of individual physical programs. This chapter recommends practical ways of focusing on the educational development of the culturally disadvantaged individual.

Follow Through programs

Follow Through was initiated by those who saw the importance of providing continuing training in primary grades for children who had made initial gains under Headstart. Follow Through projects are geared to the first three years of the child's school programs—kindergarten-to-second grade or first-to-third grade, depending on the local organization of the school. The guidelines from the U.S. Office of Education, which is the funding agency, require continued attention to physical and mental health, nutrition, community involvement, parent participation, and in-service education for teachers and aides.

Recently (1968) proposals from school districts have been designed to fall within one of four different educational emphases: traditional or child centered, intensive stimulation or structure centered, theory centered or behavior modification, and community controlled. Like Headstart programs, objective as well as subjective evaluation has been required. At this writing (1970) no study comparable to the Westinghouse Learning Corporation evaluation of Headstart (1969) has been published.

Title I of ESEA

The first section of the Elementary and Secondary Education Act (ESEA), P.L. 9110, provides federal funds for compensatory education. School districts must survey their populations to define areas of poverty. The schools in these areas become target schools in which children who are most educationally disadvantaged are selected for intensive remedial instruction. Originally the criterion for educational disadvantage was performance two or more years below grade expectancy. Recently (1969) the importance of identification of high-risk pupils and the establishment of a prevention program has become a major factor in these projects. When the programs were first established, it was anticipated that children and youth could be pulled out of certain classes for intensive individualized instruction over a short period of time, after which they would return to the regular instructional program on a full-time basis. Experience has led to new directives that anticipate the individuals will need to be in a program for at least a year and continued in the program for subsequent years until grade expectancy has been reached. Most of the programs have stressed basic skills, particularly reading. In some states, at least, programs are required to have a mathematics component. Funds for teaching English to students whose culture is based on another language has been of particular value to children in districts where such opportunities had been limited previously.

A wide variety of other innovative opportunities for atypical individuals have been supported under Title I, ESEA. For instance, classes to allow unwed mothers to complete high school have helped many girls to escape a particularly disabling subculture. In-service education for teachers frequently features interaction with leaders from minority groups. They help teachers understand the aspirations and the prejudices of culturally different persons. Most of these projects are characterized by low student-teacher ratios, community involvement, in-service training for staff, objective evaluation of results, and built-in correction on the basis of results.

High School Equivalency Programs

High School Equivalency Programs (HEP), initiated by the OEO, provide a second chance for young adults who have dropped out of high school. Generally the programs are situated on college or university campuses where, with other young adults, these individuals receive counseling, class instruction, and tutoring. Combined with this experience is usually a teacher-training program for upper-division or graduate students who are preparing to teach in disadvantaged communities. Most projects are designed to serve particular groups, such as Indians, black ghetto residents, chicanos, or a combination of these groups.

HEP students are selected for academic potential, which is in line with the goal that through this program participants will become prepared for higher education. If they are successful in passing high school equivalency examinations, they are awarded high school diplomas that admit them to college, often on the same campus where they attained eligibility.

The many frustrations of compensatory education are converged and intensified in HEP programs. The campus differs from the outside world by the nature of its function. Added to the usual adjustments that all college freshmen must make, the HEP student is handicapped by failure associations with school itself. The typical high school dropout brings a storehouse of past learning that is negative. Classes are remembered as uninteresting, threatening, and punitive. The classroom and books are certain to retrieve many feelings of inadequacy and failure, from which the student escaped when he left school. A great distance exists between the place at which the dropout is, in terms of self-understanding, and the place he must reach affectively to participate fully in a college community, even one that is sympathetic. If the student is also handicapped by past language differences, cultural discrepancies, and economic discrimination, his enrollment in HEP may be the school's final chance to help him.

The instructor usually starts the HEP assignment with dedicated zeal. The experienced teacher comes to the program with well-established patterns of interaction, which other students have reinforced in the past merely by learning from him. Whether aware of it or not, the experienced teacher has learned to rely on feedback from students to plan the next steps in teaching. The older the students, the more classroom teachers depend on language for this feedback of what has been learned. The larger the class, the greater the teacher's necessity to obtain this feedback in written forms, such as term papers and examinations. Most culturally disadvantaged students have learned to resent papers, because they maximize the importance of their weakest skills, and to reject tests, because they assume them (usually with justification) to be discriminatory. To ease both the problem of identity with the campus and the nature of class instruction, many programs have recruited tutors to work with HEP and Upward Bound students on a one-to-one ratio. Tutors have helped many students, particularly by being someone who is at home in the academic world and to whom the student can learn to relate. Many tutors, however, are not successful. They lack skill in teaching and find that their own experience in learning English provides few clues for teaching it as a second language. The typical tutor lacks the training to analyze his student needs and to provide the immediate success that dropout students need desperately.

Upward Bound

Upward Bound is a college program jointly financed by the federal government and the university that offers the program. Private contributions are often needed for student transportation and other incidental expenses. Usually faculty and regular students of the college or university raise funds for these purposes. The aim of Upward Bound is to give enhanced opportunity to academically able, culturally disadvantaged college-level students. High school graduates without sufficiently high grade points to enter a particular institution or students who come from secondary systems that normally have a negative index applied to their graduates are brought to the college campus for a summer of intensive instruction as preparation for entry into the regular fall classes. Summer instruction is usually supplemented by assignment to class sections that are smaller than normal, by tutorial help in courses the student finds difficult, and by special individual counseling with regard to financial and adjustment problems.

Many major universities conduct regular recruiting programs to attract particularly suitable candidates from culturally disadvantaged groups to their campuses. High school teachers can often do a service to individual students and to the local university by contacting the Upward Bound coordinator to draw his attention to students who would profit from this kind of help.

Job Corps Training Program

The Job Corps Training Program has been funded by the federal government through the OEO. As this is being written the future of this program is uncertain. The program is designed to help young people from poverty and dissident cultures obtain industrial training that will enable them to establish themselves in gainful employment. Most of the training centers have been operated by industrial concerns, such as Litton Industries, rather than by school systems. The programs have been expensive, costing in the neighborhood of $10,000 per year, per student. Communities in which corps training centers have been established have frequently been unhappy with the trainees. Often the corps centers have been located on surplus army training bases, and invidious comparisons have been made between the corps trainees and the army trainees.

Many of the young people who enter the Job Corps Training Programs have dropped out of school, many of them have already established police records of one kind or another, nearly all of them need basic instruction in reading and elementary mathematics. Many of them come from inner cities and find the isolated rural setting of many training centers somewhat dull. A moment's consideration will make the reader aware that these are young people whose school systems have failed them dismally. Even the partial success of the Job Corps program may be a notable achievement when one considers the alternate future of the typical trainee.

Counselors and teachers at the secondary level should check to see whether Job Corps training opportunities are available to their potential dropouts and provide information to students for whom this kind of experience would be valuable before they go through a disorganizing and destructive period of unemployment.

Career Opportunity Program

The Career Opportunity Program (COP) is a priority program with the Educational Professions Development Act, through which nonprofessional or paraprofessional workers may become professional, usually in some aspect of teaching or counseling. Projects usually combine classroom experience as aides, in-service workshops, and college courses that lead to degree and credential.

Other programs

Many other educational programs are especially designed for culturally disadvantaged children and youth. The Ford Foundation has supported experimental attempts to establish local ways of overcoming handicaps of this type. Rosenburg Foundations have been particularly active in research for improving the educational programs for the disadvantaged. Many of the programs for handicapped students, which are mentioned in other chapters of this book, are particularly important to the culturally disadvantaged. In many school systems, conflicts develop because of overlap between regularly established programs, such as reading, and federally funded programs, such as Title I of ESEA, which have a large reading component but different administrations and emphases.

Work-experience programs, established under the George-Barden Act, may provide opportunities for culturally disadvantaged youth that are the more valuable because they are open to all students and no stigma is attached by being set apart. Teachers need to steer a discreet course to get the best possible help for each child or youth in his charge.

SPECIFIC KINDS OF CULTURAL DISADVANTAGE

While there are many different kinds of handicaps to learning, problems that are physiologically caused, such as vision and hearing disabilities, are distinct functions that can be precisely defined in terms of discrepancy from an established norm. Discussion of cultural disadvantage is much more complicated, because there is no agreement upon definition concerning the culture for which an individual is disadvantaged.

The culture of poverty

In many instances the culture of poverty and cultural disadvantage are considered synonymous, even though the cases presented earlier indicate that cultural disadvantage is a much broader term than is poverty. However, there are disadvantages that seem peculiarly debilitating in a poverty environment. Some of these are materially related to existence. Poverty does not ensure, but makes more likely, a badly balanced diet. Poverty does not foreordain more dental caries, but it is likely to lead to neglect in repairing those that occur. Because of these close associations of poverty with neglect in diet and health care, the Headstart and Follow Through programs have had nutritional and medical elements.

Administrators rather than teachers usually coordinate the work that is done through nutritional or medical programs for children or youth. Although the teacher is often the person who discovers the child who comes to school hungry, health services are becoming a function of experts (North, 1968). Whether programs are available to alleviate poverty or not, the teacher is responsible for school instruction. As far as learning is concerned, the primary disadvantage of poverty is one of the spirit. A feeling of defeat before one begins is characteristic of the affective world of the poverty child. This spiritual malaise is one that the teacher can observe and help to remedy, often enough, by her own encouragement. A persistent low-energy level on the part of a particular child is a symptom that should cue the teacher to seek available special services for the child or his family.

Language disadvantage

A mother tongue that is different from English is an educational problem the teacher quickly observes when a non-English–speaking pupil enters the class. There is no problem of identification in such cases, even though the alleviation of the handicap requires a good deal of time and effort on the part of both the teacher and the child. In some parts of the Southwest, most of the children entering school have Spanish rather than English as the background language. Many Indian, Pureto Rican, and Cuban children speak only their own language.

A controversy is raging about the extent of, and the proper way of dealing with, the language difference of poverty or ghetto children and youth. Carl Bereiter and Sigfried Engelmann (1966) claim the speech of black ghetto children lacks substance, logic, and breadth. They have established and popularized a system of specific, intensive, highly structured training in small groups to get the children talking and to improve both their speech and their feelings of worth. M. Black (1968) claims that ghetto children have limited vocabularies and limited models for, and ability to use, sentence patterns common to middle-class families. Walter Loban (1963) classified the speech patterns of elementary school children, then analyzed the choice and arrangement of language within these patterns. He found evidence that the nonstandard dialects of his low socioeconomic subjects had comparatively few options within grammatical constructions, lack of single words to substitute for groups of words, limited variety of nominals (names for things), and limited arrangement of movable syntactic elements.

On the other hand, Jean Kuntz and Joan E. Moyer (1969) conducted a study to test a number of opinions shared by two or more experts on the language and learning characteristics of Headstart and middle-class children. When comparing the language skills of disadvantaged and economically advantaged children, they found some difference in knowledge of words selected from the Gates word list (1935) but no difference when words from the disadvantaged child's environment were used. When these words from a familiar background were the stimuli, the sentences used were equally long for the disadvantaged and the advantaged groups. The contention of M. Deutsch (1965) that disadvantaged children would not persist in problem-solving activities if the solution were not immediately apparent was also rejected by Kuntz and Moyer when they tested and found no difference between the advantaged and disadvantaged children. In a third part to their experiment Kuntz and Moyer found no difference between advantaged and disadvantaged children's abilities to choose a delayed larger reward over a smaller immediate reward. This finding was contrary to that of W. Mischel (1958). A. Pearl and F. Reissman (1965) claim that the language of the poor is richer and more vital than that of the middle class and that schools should teach poverty children to read and write in the patois common to their family groups. On the basis of an intensive review of intercultural language differences, Courtney B. Cazden (1966) concluded that children who are disadvantaged economically and socially show retardation in language development. She suggests that those who describe lower-class child language as rich and expressive may be revealing a romantic view in which the clichés of a subculture are perceived as creative expression by someone from a different culture. Or perhaps the vitality of language, cited by Pearl and others, is ethnic in origin and not characteristic of the lower classes in any group.

It seems apparent that many of the generalizations concerning the children from poverty need to be reexamined. Probably all of them have an element of truth and apply to certain children and youth. Certainly the findings about groups are not true of a great many individuals within the subcultures, and the stereotype of a poverty child tends to obscure his real needs as an individual who varies subtly from each other child.

Ethnic cultural differences

All groups of people have a culture that includes language(s), religion(s), modal behaviors or practices, valued technologies, diets, and systems of social relationships. Culture develops within an environment and over a period of time, usually many generations. When the social environment changes, individuals within the ethnic group differ in their desire to adapt to new cultural patterns or to adhere to the social heritage. Some examples of the stresses that have developed within the subcultures of the United States may help the teacher understand the personal struggle of individual students with the forces of acculturation.

MEXICAN-AMERICANS The pachucos of Los Angeles are boys and girls lost between the outmoded traditions of their Mexican parents and the American world where their way of life is not quite accepted. Graduate students who come from chicano homes cite at least four reasons their culture causes difficulty in adjusting to "Anglo" schools.

First, is their traditional belief in La Raza, "The Race." The Mexican-American thinks of himself both as a citizen of the United States and a member of La Raza, the mystical concept of all Latin-Americans, united by cultural and spiritual bonds derived from God. The spiritual aspect is perhaps more important than the cultural. The spirit of the Spanish-speaking people is taken to be divine and infinite. As one Latin expressed it, "We are bound together by the common destiny of our souls." They believe that if they live by God's commands, they will be so strong no one can block them. They recognize that Anglos take advantage of their weakness, but they blame their weakness on themselves, not the Anglos (Mullanix, 1969).

A second component of Mexican-American culture is the cult of masculinity. The Mexican family is patriarchal and authoritarian. There is a double standard in which education is for the man, sexual liberties are for the man, material comforts are for the man, and politics are for the man. The woman is subordinate. She must be faithful to her husband and her children. She is controlled by her parents until she marries; then she is dominated by her husband. The girl's life at school is influenced by woman's role in life as wife and mother, and nothing more. In the culture of Mexico, the man is head of the household and the dominant figure of the family. He generally decides if the wife is to attend a PTA meeting or if she is to participate in a community or civic activity. Usually neither he, nor she, becomes actively involved in the school community. When the Mexican-American moves from the ghetto into areas more heavily populated by Anglos, the cultural factor of masculinity becomes dysfunctional. Mexican-American women compare their relationship with their husbands to that of their Anglo neighbors, and marital unrest and increased alienation often results.

A third cultural difference that affects the child's relationship with the school is the Mexican's special emphasis on the immediate and extended family. The effects of this dichotomy between the value systems is devastating on the educational opportunities of the children. The Anglo family is child centered, while Mexican life is family centered. The schools can't understand why a mother will keep her child home to tend her brothers, sisters, and cousins while the mother takes an aunt to the hospital. The middle-class parent considers his child's education more important than competing activities; but the Mexican parent sees family welfare and family solidarity, including the extended family, as more important than school. The teacher usually does not understand or accept his viewpoint. In addition, the school is a symbol of Anglo authority—a force that Mexicans see as tending to dissolve family ties. The school demands that the parents obey its wishes. If Nina's mother wants to have her stay home from school and tend her sisters, the school can seek a court order that demands that the child forsake his family obligations for the needs of the child, a demand that conflicts with the values of their culture.

The fourth barrier is the affective power of the native language. The symbols that maintain a culture are best communicated through language. Many members of the older generation of Mexican-Americans speak no English and live and die in the ghettos without realizing that the rest of the world is not a run-down slum. From the Anglo viewpoint, the use of Spanish is a hindrance to the progress of the Mexican-American. For the Latin, Spanish is the primary symbol of loyalty to La Raza. The Mexican-American who speaks English in a gathering of conservative Latins is mocked and regarded as a traitor to La Raza. Spanish allows the culture to flourish and permits the Mexican-American to maintain ties with his family in Mexico. English is the language of authority, spoken by the cop on the beat or the social worker who controls the family's allotment. When Spanish is spoken in the homes, it is easier for the child to express himself in Spanish; however, many Anglo teachers seem to believe that the child is trying to be difficult.

AFRO-AMERICANS Many, but by no means all, black students find themselves set apart because of the color of their skins. Often this separateness is associated with poverty and, in some cases, with sufficient difference in language to effectively bar communication. Some inner-city schools are inadequate for any child and destructive of both the students and their teachers. One of our graduate students described the school where he taught for three years (Janofsky, 1969).

> *This de facto segregated elementary school has over one thousand pupils in grades K through 6. Of the over 98 percent black children, most come from lower socioeconomic-class families. The neighborhood around the school is run down, buildings are dilapidated and yards unkempt. Broken glass litters the sidewalks and the streets. Rather than make any repairs, families who are able to improve their economic situation move away to a better neighborhood. Rat infestation is a problem, and children report that cockroaches run over them in bed at night. Clothes collected in a recent drive were covered with lice. A number of the homes are without hot running water. . . .*
>
> *About one-third of the children in the school are born illegitimate, but this carries little or no stigma in the black culture. There are five children in the average family. The father is absent in about 30 percent of the homes, and many of these families are on welfare. Even where there is a father or father-substitute present in the home, the family structure is highly matriarchal. . . .*
>
> *Only one of the six classrooms at each grade level is doing school work appropriate for that grade level. The pupils drop further and further behind academically each year they are in school. Three years ago the school employed only six nonwhite teachers, and none of the teachers lived in the local neighborhood. The school was like an island in the community.*

There was a lot of aggressive hostility expressed by the boys at the school. Fist fights would break out in the classrooms, in the halls, as well as on the playground. Those involved would be sent to the vice-principal's office to be punished. The vice-principal, a large and powerful man, would hit the children with a gigantic wooden paddle with air holes. Children who were especially difficult would receive the paddle on bare skin. . . .

The fight would usually begin the same way each time. One boy would pick on another boy by calling him names and teasing him. The name calling would continue back and forth until one boy would make a derogatory remark about the other boy's mother. Such an insult is the last straw and calls for physical retaliation. Similar types of fights go on between girls also, but they usually end in kicking, biting, scratching, and hair pulling. . . .

The teachers at the school were afraid of the larger intermediate-grade boys. There had been incidents in which an upper-grade boy would resent being disciplined on the playground and would take after the teacher with a baseball bat. It was also not uncommon for boys to chase girls and even follow them into the girls' lavatories. . . .

Pupil-teacher relations at the school were quite strained, apart from the physical aggressiveness of the pupils and the vice-principal. Many children had a wealth of second-hand sexual experiences and developed a large vocabulary of four-letter words. New white teachers would react to the children's language with shock at first, but experienced teachers soon learned not to pay attention, as otherwise the frequency of this language increased. The black teachers, all middle-class, were much more punitive when the children used four-letter words, and the standards they set for their pupils were generally higher than those set by the white teachers. It was evident that the children were unable to live up to the middle-class standards set by both the white and the black teachers. . . .

The family of the inner-city black child is very different from that of the typical middle-class white or black child. The inner-city black family is often quite economically unstable. Frequently, with the father absent, there is no successful male role model for the boys in the family to pattern themselves after. Typically, the black children become peer-oriented several years before their white, middle-class counterparts. This is because much of the child care in these large black families is provided by older cousins and siblings. Since the black children are not accustomed to considerable adult supervision, it is understandable that they rebel in response *to teacher discipline, which is often administered in a dogmatic, authoritarian manner. . . .*

At home when the black children misbehave, corporal punishment is the rule rather than the exception. Thus, it is not surprising that the children usually react to teasing and insults by peers with physical retaliation. The punitive measures of the vice-principal only antagonize the child and add to his sense of low self-esteem. The differences between the inner-city black subculture and the white, middle-class culture are clearly reflected in the social interactions of black inner-city school children. These children come to school unprepared to behave according to the expectations of the educators.

When children live in this way at home and at school, it is not surprising that investigators have not fully untangled the cultural, economic, and genetic factors that cause failure in school learning.

AMERICAN INDIANS   Although the culture of American Indian tribes has remained visible, the poverty in which they live defies analysis of their problem on ethnic grounds alone. According to Peter Farb (1968) housing is inadequate for 90 percent, unemployment ranges from 40 to 75 percent, and overwhelming proportions suffer from communicable diseases that were unknown to them before the white man came to America. Many of the children suffer from hearing loss due to ear infection (25 percent) or a handicapping eye infection, trachoma (61 percent). Indian education is the worst of any minority group. The Indian averages 5 years of schooling, compared with 11.2 years for other Americans. Farb's most devastating criticism was that the longer the Indian stayed in school, the greater was the gap in achievement between himself and the white children. When the U.S. Bureau of Indian Affairs was founded one hundred years ago, its explicit aim was to alienate Indian children from their culture and integrate them into the white society. The white society has stripped the Indian not only of his land, but also of his identity, making the Indian embarrassed about his heritage. From 1830 on, many Indian tribes were driven out of their homelands and forced to relocate in new environments, bringing about an alienation from their own land and geographic culture. One implementation of this policy occurred in Eastern Oregon, where eight tribes with different languages and divergent cultures were relocated on one parcel of land—the Umatilla Indian Reservation. This kind of move implies many shifts in the roles of the adult family members, new responsibilities of the children, and generally, a new emphasis on physical relocation rather than maintenance of the prevailing customs.

Some of our graduate students work with Indians on campus or at one of two reservations. They become cognizant of the Indian's dilemma and supportive of his cause. A sample reaction is shown in the following quotation (Collins, 1969).

> With regard to the predominant religious difference, the Indian has unjustly suffered under American systems for not being an adherent to the Judaeo-Christian ethic. That the whites have desperately attempted to Christianize the Indians is still evidenced today, where, on a recent visit to the Warm Springs Reservation, I counted seven churches. Many of the Indians on this reservation live in middle-class suburban homes and work on the "Indian Motel," since Warm Springs has been turned into a posh resort area where wealthy white tourists may camp out in "genuine" teepees, complete with electrical appliances, a heated swimming pool, and a variety of vending machines. . . .

> Other attempts at making the Indian desire the glories of the American Dream included such laws as making all Indians (males) cut their hair, despite the fact that many Indians believed their long hair contained supernatural powers. . . .

> As for the children, many were at first taken from their families and sent to boarding schools for eight years, where they received dietary changes, store-bought clothing, and a white education. They were then simply released, and they either remained outcasts in the white society or strangers when they returned to their own families and culture. This problem still exists today, for even if we do give the Indian a white education, he is socially restricted to the reservation. . . .

> Since they have been stripped of their own culture and deprived of being a part of the white middle-class structure, they really lack any strong identity and therefore are alienated, in a sense, from all culture. An education does not help the Indian compete for a job, since he is socially barred from such competition. . . .

> Most Indian children have the additional problem of learning English in school as their second language, as well as learning new ways of life and operating in them, including switching from a barter system to a wage system. . . .

> When he enters school, the Indian child brings with him a set of values from his family, which often do not work for him in the new school. In one instance, four boys were reprimanded severely for stealing fruit from a

neighboring orchard. They became very indignant at being called thieves, and they explained that, yes, they had taken the fruit, but there was no fence around the property, and to them, a fenceless property meant no individual ownership. The Indian child must learn in school to merge two cultures into one meaningful value system. Where conflicts in two opposing values occur (the home versus the school), confusion of loyalties may result. . . .

Even basic terminology, which teachers assume the white child knows from his out-of-school cultural experiences, must be interpreted for Indian children and made concrete to their understanding. Because of their communal way of life, for example, the concepts of private ownership must be defined and dealt with before other learnings that presuppose this knowledge can occur.

Another graduate student, a nun, related an incident that occurred on the first day she began teaching at a school for Indian children. The children, first and second graders, were sent outside for recess while she got the material together for the next lessons. Suddenly she was aware of silence—an unusual soundlessness from the playground. Thinking that the children had run away (perhaps out of fear of her black habit) Sister rushed outside. They were all playing there, running and chasing each other without the shouts and laughter she had been accustomed to hear during recesses.

Table 9-1 summarizes the cultural conflicts that Indian children of Northwestern United States experience when they move between home and school.

Social interaction between minority groups and the dominant culture is a reciprocal process. There are intangible obstacles as well as obvious hindrances. Educational progress, on an equitable level, will depend on the elimination of poverty, prevailing prejudices, and injustice. Hopelessness and despair can then be replaced with hope and confidence.

TESTS, LEARNING, AND THE DISADVANTAGED

In most of the chapters in this book, specific tests are suggested to confirm or refute the existence of a suspected disorder. We would like to draw attention to research indicating that great care needs to be exercised in the interpretation of tests of intellectual functioning that are effective with children in the mainstream of American culture.

TABLE 9-1   SOME CULTURAL TRAITS OF INDIAN CHILDREN AND CORRESPONDING
IMPLICATIONS FOR THE SCHOOL

Aspects of acculturation	Educational implications
Speech is idiomatic English or native.	Intelligence could be masked.
Time is not important.	May seem indolent or inefficient.
Prefers rural life, although may live in cities or towns.	May lack enthusiasm for "city things."
Emotionally reserved, nondemonstrative.	Child masks emotional reaction; may seem lacking in empathy or sympathy.
High degree of control of interpersonal aggression within group.	Seems to endure much without fighting; seems stoic or unfeeling on surface.
Pattern of generosity; shares.	May be seen as unconcerned about the necessities of tomorrow.
Ability to endure pain, hardship, hunger, frustration, without external evidence of discomfort.	Teacher must be alert to these conditions; child will not complain.
Positive valuation on bravery and courage; highly aggressive bearing in military exploits.	Reacts to accounts of bravery; responds to patriotism and stories of courage.
Fear of world as dangerous.	Reservations about volunteering for unexplored or unknown adventures.
Practical joker.	Teacher may need broad sense of humor.
Attention to concrete realities of present in contrast to abstract integration of long-range goals.	Teacher should proceed one step at a time. Child may seem to lack appreciation for distant future.
Dependence on supernatural powers outside one's self that determines one's fate.	May seem to lack initiative for reform or change.
Disdain for any semblance of boasting; avoids spotlight.	Should be praised judicially, quietly.
Values basic virtues of bravery, generosity, fortitude, integrity.	May be confused by culture that values material accumulation; own values may be disfunctional in modern society.
Belief in imminent justice.	Fairness essential in control measures.
Lack of retentive traits.	Must be taught to save money, keep appointments, attend to maintenance of possessions.
Absence of fear of heights.	Can work on high buildings, bridges.

SOURCE: *Adapted from Bonnie Koreiva, "Educational Implications for American-
Indian Children," Curriculum Bulletin, 25:19–20, University of Oregon, Eugene,
October, 1969.*

Richard J. Rankin (1968) reported an experiment in which Navajo children were given a Draw-a-Man test (Goodenough, 1926) and, in most cases, failed miserably. He pointed out that in this particular culture undue attention to one's person was considered vanity and was systematically discouraged. When the test was altered to Draw-a-Horse, the Navajo children had a much more normal distribution of scores, while a sample of American children tended to bunch at the failure end of the Indian children's norms.

H. M. Clements, J. A. Duncan, and W. M. Taylor (1969) cite the subjective elements in the use of objective measures with culturally deprived students. They review research that shows a valid interpretation of scores is strongly dependent on knowledge of the cultural background of the minority group being tested. An important element is the examiner's sense of responsibility toward the individual student. Scores on tests are influenced, also, by cultural values of the counselee, which influences his performance effort. The authors conclude that good instruments, responsibly interpreted, help to provide a better diagnosis than is possible with subjective data alone.

A. R. Jensen (1961) was impressed with the apparent discrepancy between playground intelligence and classroom performance, confirmed by IQ scores, for Mexican-American children in Southern California. He devised three tests to measure the speed with which children could learn a series of "immediate-recall," "paired-associate," and "serial-learning" tasks using familiar and unfamiliar materials. The criterion was the number of failures before mastery.

The tests he used were new learning experiences designed to examine the time it took different children to learn in a new setting. The familiar materials consisted of groups of twelve objects: wristwatch, bar of soap, spoon, rubber dagger, toy gun, comb, toy car, plastic toy airplane, water glass, paint brush, candle, ball. Jensen had an alternate group of similarly familiar objects. His list of abstract materials included seven plastic forms 1¼ inches in diameter and ½ inch thick: yellow triangle, blue triangle, yellow diamond, green diamond, red circle, blue circle, and a green square.

In the recall test the subject named the objects and was given ten seconds to study them, after which they were returned to the box and he named as many as he could. As the child named the objects, the examiner took them out of the box and put them in front of him. When he couldn't name any more, the rest of the objects were taken out of the box and named. The process was continued until the youngster could name all of the objects without help. The score was the total number of objects requiring help.

In the serial-learning test, the examiner covered each object with a box. The subject had to learn which object was under each box, working always from left to right. The process was continued until the child could name all the objects from left to right. The score was number of errors before complete naming was accomplished.

The paired-associates-learning test required the child to learn to associate an object from familiar Series A with an object under the box from familiar Series B. There were twelve combinations. The subject's score was the number of errors before guessing all objects correctly.

Unlike most intelligence tests, which tap the learning already completed from a range that is assumed to be equally available to all testees, this series of tasks required the student to do the learning during the task. Using these materials, Jensen found that low-IQ Mexican-American children in his sample, which was small, did as well as high-IQ Mexican or high-IQ Anglo-American children. However, low-IQ Anglo-American children were poor learners on these tests.

Jensen concluded that the IQ tests used to form the groups did not discriminate between bright and dull Mexican-American fourth graders. The Mexican-American and Anglo-American slow learners, as selected by an intelligence test, may need very different kinds of instruction. Jensen recommended direct-learning tests to diagnose which Mexican-American students could profit from a school program that differed from that used with mentally retarded.

In a related experiment with adult retardates Jensen (1965) found that some retardates became fast learners after they were given intensive practice in verbally mediating the parts of the learning tasks being undertaken.

A need exists for differential evaluation that is coupled with developmental experiences designed to build on the present strengths of the child. We developed *Kindergarten Evaluation of Learning Potential* (KELP) to meet this need at the prereading level (Robeck and Wilson, 1967).

In order to analyze the child's functioning in English, the child is taught and observed in the following categories. (Quoted by permission of McGraw-Hill Book Company.)

ANALYSIS OF FUNCTIONING IN ENGLISH *The KELP items involve a wide range of language experiences. Observations of the child's classroom performance on KELP can be analyzed to determine his functioning in English according to the following categories: (1) performance items which can be learned by watching the teacher's demonstration and by seeing other children play the game; (2) items which depend for successful learning on the child's understanding of the teacher's explanation in English; (3) items in which the teacher can identify children who are relatively accomplished in the semantics of English; and (4) items in which progress in learning vocabulary can be noted accurately and reinforced selectively. Not all KELP items were classified in this way. Rather, the authors selected a cluster of five items which the teacher might use to analyze the strengths of bilingual children and disadvantaged children.*

Probably none of the items in KELP is entirely culture free, but certain levels of learning on selected items enable the school to evaluate the child's intellectual functioning, apart from competence in the English language. If a child speaks a language other than English, his efficiency in learning the new language can be observed in his success on selected items of KELP.

PERFORMANCE ITEMS   *The items color coded in red on the cover of the pupil's edition are relatively independent of background in English. They can be learned in the kindergarten setting by children who speak little or no English. Items which give the teacher an evaluation of the ability of children from limited backgrounds and experiences include the following: Skipping, Bead Design (L-1), Block Design (L-2), Bolt Board (L-3), and Writing a Name (L-3). [L-1 means Level One Learning, or association learning, in the KELP items; L-2 means Level Two, or conceptualization; and L-3 means Level Three Learning, or creative self-direction.]*

These items are explained and demonstrated by the teacher. The child can perform them successfully at the level indicated without having to speak. Also, the use of the devices can be observed in the performance of other pupils; if the child is shy, he can learn from other children by watching them. Some alternate items which might be used are the Block Design (L-1), the Bolt Board (L-1), and the Safety Signs (L-3). They would be used instead of, rather than in addition to, the items suggested for this appraisal.

UNDERSTANDING SPOKEN ENGLISH   *In this category, the nature of the task must have been understood in English by the child. Items were selected which were explained verbally by the teacher and must have been comprehended in English in order to be learned at the indicated level of success. Items which sample this ability are shown in orange on the pupil's Summary Test Booklet and include the following: Bead Design (L-3),*

Block Design (L-3), Safety Signs (L-1), Writing a Name (L-1), and Auditory Perception (L-2).

Item success does not require speaking in English on the part of the child, but item success does require the understanding of the nature of the task as explained by the teacher. Alternate items are the Bead Design (L-2), the Safety Signs (L-2), Writing a Name (L-2), and Social Interaction (L-3).

COMPETENT ENGLISH EXPRESSION *Success on certain items requires competence in English, and children from homes with much conversation, educated speech, and discrimination in semantics have an advantage. Items which show relative sophistication in English expression are represented by the yellow coding and include the following: Bolt Board (L-2), Calendar (L-3), Auditory Perception (L-3), Social Interaction (L-1), and Social Interaction (L-2).*

Quite likely, the kindergarten year will not show the development of English in the non-English–speaking child, which success on these items requires. However, the teacher can observe the child's aptitude for learning English. The items selected for observation of special competence in English demand an explanation from the child which goes beyond the typical speech level of five-year-olds.

POTENTIAL LANGUAGE DEVELOPMENT *When the teacher observes a child who learns the performance items easily and does not seem to function as well in the other items, she may discover that the language or English background in the home is less adequate than the child's overall potential. In this case, extra attention to language development by the school can compensate for deficiencies in the home. Items which are cues to potential language development are identified with red stars on the Record Book Summary.*

> *Learning color names*
> *Learning to speak in simple sentences (Calendar, L-1)*
> *Learning the names of the days of the week (Calendar, L-2)*
> *Learning the names of the numerals and counting in English (Numbers, L-1)*
> *Learning the names of the toys (Auditory Perception, L-1)*

These are typical skills encountered in the early stages of learning a new language. Direct teaching is indicated for the bilingual child, as well as for

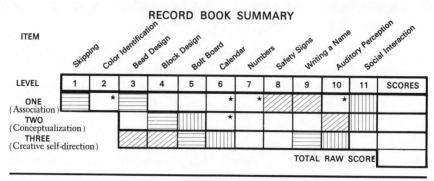

RECORD BOOK SUMMARY

FIGURE 9-1 *KELP Summary Test Booklet (From Mildred C. Robeck and J. A. R. Wilson,* KELP Summary Test Booklet: Teacher's Edition, *McGraw-Hill, New York, 1967. By permission of the publisher.)*

the child who has had limited experiences and a poor language back-ground.

By counting the scores entered in the color-coded boxes of the Record Book Summary and recording the totals in the corresponding boxes of Analysis of Functioning in English, the teacher can see whether the child's growth pattern appears to be consistent or whether his successes are weighted by English language factors. (pp. 2–3)

A comparison of two American Indian boys who attended the same school will clarify the procedure for analyzing the children's functioning in English.

Tommy Talltree had grown up on a reservation where English was the dominant language. His best friend, Joseph Standing Bear, had entered the school from South Dakota, where his family and friends spoke Sioux. The scores earned by the two boys are shown in Table 9-2.

Tommy's performance on KELP was exceptionally high for any child and confirmed his teacher's subjective evaluation that he was a very bright little boy. He showed both high potential and high competence, even though, if he followed the normal pattern of school success for Indian boys, he might later be a school dropout. Joseph, whose background in

TABLE 9-2 ANALYSIS OF THE ABILITY OF TWO AMERICAN INDIAN BOYS TO
FUNCTION IN ENGLISH, AS MEASURED BY KELP SCORES*

	Tommy Talltree	Joseph Standing Bear
Performance items	5	5
Understanding spoken English	5	3
Competent English expression	4	0
Potential for language development	5	4

* *Mildred C. Robeck and J. A. R. Wilson*, KELP Summary Test Booklet: Teacher's
Edition, *McGraw Hill, New York, 1967.*

English was limited, showed strengths in items that were independent of
English knowledge, listening and understanding spoken English, and potential for learning the language. The fact that he was successful on none of
the items that required sophisticated explanations in English does not mean
he was unable to master the concepts. At this point we know he was able
to learn the names of colors, to count, to use a complete sentence in a
limited situation, to name the days of the week, and to learn the names of
objects.

The evidence suggests that Joseph could readily learn to read if his
instruction were structured to use his already present strengths and to help
him expand his knowledge and use of English. However, he would probably
fail in a language-experience approach to reading instruction, which would
punish him for his inability to express his ideas in English.

Tests are useful tools, but they need to be used with discretion. Many
of them give false positive or false negative scores when used with culturally different children. The instruments that give a student a chance to
show what he can do in a novel situation seem most likely to pick out the
children who have the greatest promise of future learning ability.

CHANGES IN ETIOLOGY WITH AGE

For a great many of the culturally disadvantaged the school years have
been unkind. High proportions of the high school dropouts come from
minority groups—individuals who have decided the punishment they were
suffering outweighs the possible good school might do for them. The
remedial programs funded by the federal government have not yet been
in operation long enough to provide data concerning the post-high school
success of children for whom intervention was made at the preschool level.
Informal observation indicates that for some of the children the intervention was damaging. A child in a small group—say five pupils—that is

gathered to remedy difficulties in learning to read can see his failure more plainly in the same way the successful child comes to see his gains. When sharply focused failure occurs, it is probably more damaging than more diffuse failure, which allows an indefinite hope of eventual success.

On the whole the federally funded programs are improving with the experience, the research, and the self-correcting features of most projects. The teachers are learning by their past mistakes and from their failures. The requirements for evaluation are forcing a great many people involved in these programs to look carefully at what happens to the children. For many of us this has, at times, been extremely painful, but it has ensured modification in the program, with the hope of eliminating the failures that occur. A real danger exists that premature appraisal of the value received from the funds allocated will be based on what was accomplished in the early years of the programs before effective operating techniques evolved. There is some indication that a judgment has already been reached about Headstart that minimizes the emerging successes of the program.

When a state gathers data from many projects in many school districts, it must summarize the data before it can be sent on for further summarization in Washington. The process of extraction and tabulation ensures that countless individual successes are lost in the statistical treatment that reduces all to the least common denominator of the mass effect of the projects across the nation.

HELPING AND HURTING

It may help to look at the individuals sketched earlier and to note ways in which they may be helped rather than damaged as they progress through school. Each child is an individual. School failure is the culmination of many small disappointments that lead the student to feel he cannot cope successfully with the school situation. Teachers, counselors, and specialists can improve the success rate of disadvantaged youth as they become more skillful in seeing the sensitive points that destroy the integrity of learners.

Sensitivity to affects

Nina Martinez, the Headstart child from Mexico, didn't eat or drink her milk at school. To some adults this is no big thing, but it can be the beginning of acceptance or rejection of school and all that it stands for. By not eating, Nina was being denied the pleasurable associations with school that lunches and snacks provide for most children.

Attempts to force Nina to eat the things she had already rejected almost certainly would have failed if attempted directly. With failure was likely to come rejection associations of the teacher along with the food. The spreading associations could readily incorporate the school in all its phases. This rejection would have been much more likely if Nina failed to understand some of the teacher's instructions and failed in her own eyes to perform tasks she saw other children being reinforced for performing. It is easy for teachers, whose responsibility is learning, to be quite oblivious to simple stress situations that start trouble by negative conditioning. Once under way, negativism is self-feeding and becomes more and more impervious to positive reinforcements. No one need *do* anything wrong; the error is one of omission. To prevent Nina's self-withdrawal, someone had to perceive the problem and know enough to reverse the pattern. We have thousands of Mexican-American children in school who are failing because no one has seen what was needed to draw them into full participation in the school environment.

Nina's teacher picked up the remark in Mrs. Smith's report that Nina liked bananas. When the teacher stopped at the supermarket for her regular shopping, she bought some bananas, which she took to school the next day. When snack time came, she quietly asked Nina if she would like a banana to eat with her juice. Nina silently accepted. It took several days before it was possible to have tortillas served at lunch. They turned out to be the corn tortillas the Martinez family preferred. Gradually, through her concern about Nina's food, the teacher communicated her concern for Nina. It was some expense to get the bananas and extra work to convince the lunch staff that tortillas should be served, but trust is built from small considerations such as these.

By the end of the year Nina was using her teacher as a second model. She still thought the way her mother did things was good and right, but she also identified with her teacher and gradually preempted the role of teacher when playing school. She accepted school as a pleasant place where she should try to do the things that were suggested to her. It is too early to say that Nina will make it in school, but she has a better chance because she learned that someone outside her family cared about her.

Attention to unusual potential

Tommy Talltree, the brilliant little Indian boy, if he follows the normal course of school development, will not even enter high school. Most of his life will be spent in extreme poverty, with occasional periods of affluence when a crop is sold or a temporary twinge of congressional conscience brings an unexpected windfall. If Tommy follows the pattern of his people and is average in stamina, his life expectancy is 42, denying him an additional twenty years he might expect as an Anglo-American.

Tommy is fortunate in being in a kindergarten with a teacher who believes in him as a competent learner. With KELP she has objective evidence to support her contention that Tommy is bright and should be given real opportunities for success in life.

In years past the tribal idea of success in life and the teacher's idea have been at cross purposes. A life of study and books has not fit into tribal values for the good life. This pattern is changing among Indian leaders, who are concerned about the future earning power of their people. Tommy's teacher helps to close her end of the cultural gap by living out her genuine appreciation of Indian culture. She encourages Indian children to wear their costumes to school at festival time. All the children learn the dances, with Indian children as models. Portraits of Indian heroes are displayed on the walls, and Indian artifacts are exhibited in the showcase. She also visits the homes of all the children in her class.

Some of the men of Tommy's tribe have broken into twentieth-century life in a major way by becoming high steel construction workers. This work first became a tradition among certain Canadian tribes, where the men left their homes on the St. Lawrence River to join construction crews. Similar physical challenge, although quite different in nature, is the operation of heavy earth-moving equipment. Some Indian boys have become successful aides in primary classrooms and remained in school beyond the usual dropout period. Others have become successful teachers. Indian mothers who serve as Headstart or Follow Through aides often demand more of the Indian pupils than do teachers in charge of the programs.

How do you associate Tommy in kindergarten with a female kindergarten teacher and a future job as a cat skinner? The answer is that you don't, without some outside intervention. Intervention, however, is what this chapter is about. Various career opportunities would be more likely to come about if they were inserted into tribal thinking now as a possibility, not only for Tommy but for other boys as well. Job-experience training would be needed, as well as programs for career ladders to the professions. Ways would have to be found into tightly closed unions with high pay scales. But most of all, the glamor and romance of the work would have to be conveyed to the tribal elders. We have stressed the point that you look at individuals and teach individuals. All this is true, but in some tightly knit cultures the way to touch the individual is through the controllers of the culture. Thus it seems if Tommy is to be freed to become an able person within two cultures, changes will be needed. The school will need to recognize and support his qualities as a person and as an Indian. His elders within the tribe will need to reinforce his successes in the extended community.

Positive behavioral reinforcement

Robert Jackson, the handsome boy of 10, is almost a classic example of the children described in Chapter 11, "Educationally Handicapped Children." His mixed parentage, his vacillation between cultural worlds, and the weak maternal control all made successful remediation very difficult. Conflicting pressures had operated on him in every aspect of community life to aggravate his frayed self-concept. He'd had no consistent cultural relationship to provide an anchorage on which to build conceptualizations about himself as a person or as a learner.

Following the conference with Robert's mother, the counselor sat down with Mr. Marshall to identify the constructive aspects of the boy's situation from the cumulative file that his former school had transmitted. Robert was intelligent, approximately a standard deviation above the mean on several tests that sampled different kinds of learning. He apparently had had a favorable infancy—adequate nutrition, personal care, and a reasonably stimulating environment. His language development was better than typical in his school, including both vocabulary and syntax. His distractability seemed to be socially or emotionally based, or both, rather than physiological. On the negative side was Robert's poor achievement in basic skills. He could manage teacher-guided reading of first-grade-level (1.8) materials. He knew the addition combinations and most of the subtraction combinations, but he mixed these responses with little attention to the process indicated in the symbols. He had never finished a paper by himself. The counselor and Mr. Marshall decided that Robert's relationship to the rest of the class, particularly the boys, was critical. Mr. Marshall said he was too busy with the total group to observe when and how Robert's disruptive behavior was getting started and to what extent other children were reinforcing it. The counselor, Mrs. Arnold, agreed to observe his interactions for a week, thirty minutes each day in preselected classroom and playground settings. An analysis of these observations showed the teacher's interactions as corrective-negative seven times out of eight. The remaining interactions were instruction, usually help with desk work, following, "Robert, why haven't you started your work?" On the playground, the boys used schemes to box him out of the games. "Robert's always cheating." "You were too tagged; you're out."

A strategy was planned in which Mr. Marshall would reverse the pattern of teacher attention that Robert was getting, and the boy would be recognized for in-desk behaviors, particularly for even a gesture toward doing his assigned work. Robert worked with a cluster group on individualized reading. It was decided to see him first each period and to introduce him to programmed reading, where he could show maximal output with minimal writing. A reward system was arranged by which he would receive tokens that could be cashed with his mother for a modest supplement to his allowance. Two boys who starred in the social structure of the class were appointed to "read with" Robert from the storybooks that followed the remedial reading program. The PE teacher checked out the basketballs several weeks earlier than usual and organized shooting practices to give Robert and several other boys a chance to be involved in activities where their mistakes would not reflect on a team of players.

This strategy, as expanded, was arduous for Mr. Marshall. He found it difficult to be consistent in reactions toward Robert, because he could not give each class member equivalent treatment, such as seeing all of them first at reading time as he did Robert. He was surprised, however, that most of the children understood that Robert needed this kind of help, and the socially perceptive children smoothed some conflicts for him. When Donald complained that "Robert always gets to be first," the teacher openly discussed this with Robert, who offered to take his turn and to start his reading on his own. The reading improved, but Mr. Marshall was forced to seek a tutor in mathematics. Robert overreacted in his need for peer identification and often did foolish things to gain favor with them. Mr. Marshall maneuvered seating arrangements and study groups to bring him into contact with boys whose tolerance for atypical behavior was high and to help him avoid children who had hostilities of their own to act out. By the end of the year the teacher and the counselor felt good about Robert's progress, but they were extremely concerned when Mrs. Jackson decided to move to another area. Robert was not yet ready to make his own way, either academically or socially. There is a chance he may find a place for himself in a group of atypical youngsters who reinforce each other for antisocial activity.

Providing structure and authoritarian direction

Manuel Juarez, the overage junior high school youngster seemed likely to follow the family pattern from juvenile delinquency into more serious social difficulties. The mother's destructive way of life made intervention by the schools very difficult. Any continuity in remedial instruction is destroyed by excessive absence. Teachers cannot teach children who are not in school. A glimmer of hope emerged when Manuel was committed to a boarding school for wayward boys.

Mr. Thompson, the administrator, is a very strong character who believes that all boys can become decent hard-working men no matter what their past may have been. He insists that each boy assume responsibility for some of the chores on the farm home, and he insists that the work be done in a thorough and orderly way. Manuel had a difficult time adjusting to Mr. Thompson's requirements when he first went to the home, even though his cultural background assumed a strong male dominance. His experience of being babied by his mother had not prepared him to get up early on a cold and snowy morning to clean out the milking barn. He used all of the techniques he had developed to defy teachers who had tried to insist he learn something. None of these techniques worked with Mr. Thompson, and gradually Manuel started to take pride in doing a good job of cleaning the barn. He had little choice about doing the work, but as he succeeded he felt better about himself.

Before Manuel was put into classwork he was given a series of interviews intended to help him choose a vocation after leaving school. He had no idea what he wanted to be and was not very cooperative in the interviews. He did see that he would need to be able to read better and to handle basic arithmetic no matter what he might do. The school program was organized as a highly authoritarian operation, with insistence on completing the tasks assigned. While this approach would be undesirable for most young people, it proved very beneficial to Manuel. He learned almost in spite of himself.

Underneath Mr. Thompson's sternness, he respected the boys for what they could become, and he was able to convey his faith in their essential success to each of the boys in his charge. The rest of the staff agreed with Mr. Thompson's philosophy and supported the program energetically. For Manuel the regimen was very constructive. He learned to work hard. He was given a variety of different farm experiences, and by the time he was 18 and ready to leave the school, he had become a well-trained and efficient farm laborer. He had decided that the open-air life was pleasant, and he was content to find a job on leaving the school that made use of his training.

Mr. Thompson placed Manuel with a friend who operated a large farm in upstate New York, and the young man found himself a respectable member of the community. He had enough competence in reading and arithmetic to meet his needs. He had a salable skill, and he had a habit of systematic work. By going directly to work from the school, he avoided the temptation to slip back into the crippling ways of his old home. For Manuel, removal from home and a completely new and rigorous regimen gave him the strength to escape from almost certainly squandering his life without benefit either to himself or anyone else.

Positive counseling and individual help

The belated stirrings of middle-class conscience, prodded by riots and student demands for justice, have sent universities looking for capable black students to color their largely white campuses. For many young people these new openings have been an opportunity for upward social mobility. However, not all of those appointed to scholarships have found it easy to transfer from an easy-going school environment into the competition that energizes the highly selective university. Some students rise to the challenge, some become discouraged and return home, and some are able to survive through the help of special tutors, most of whom are recruited for particular subject areas from the student body.

The old-fashioned way to deal with Leroy Scott would have been to dismiss him for having failing grades. This approach is not very viable when the student has been sought out and recruited to come to the campus in the first place. Today, Leroy's failure would be regarded as a failure of the people who conduct the program. Another way is to point out to the instructors that Leroy is a special case and that the grading system traditionally used for other students is unfair to Leroy's group. Some instructors interpret this to mean he should be given a courtesy pass even though he has not done the required work. In the long run this is an unsatisfactory way of meeting the challenge, either for the institution or for the student. The institution erodes, by a small amount, the prestige that made it an institution worthy of being sought out by scholarly people. The damage to the student is subtler and erodes his confidence in himself as a scholarly person. A similar kind of erosion occurs when the student initially selected for racial membership is excused from the required courses that act as screening devices for major emphasis. The student may need black studies to develop pride in his own background, but narrow academic programs restrict his opportunities for graduate or professional study.

In Leroy's case, as is true with all of the culturally disadvantaged, the problem is to find ways to strengthen the student's skills and aspirations sufficiently for him to meet the challenges posed by the new competition. A counselor, provided by the program, advised Leroy to drop, without penalty, one of the courses in which he was failing. (Most university students quickly learn the drop dates and various other techniques for passing the courses for which they lack aptitude.) In addition, Leroy was given prompt tutorial help with two courses. The counselor taught him to budget his time, gave friendly supervision, and pushed him into learning the library facilities. At times Leroy resented the limitations on his time in the Afro-American Club. However, he did improve in his ability to study. His grades were passing at the end of the quarter, and he was in a position to attempt the next quarter with more assurance. He had done the work, had gotten through, and had the foundation for the next courses in all but one of the sequences he had initially selected. Two further quarters of close and careful help were needed before Leroy was able to function without a tutor, but he knew one would be found for him if needed. He had succeeded; he was pleased with himself; he was a stronger person. If any of the "easier" ways had been taken, Leroy could have been weaker, rather than stronger, as a result of the experience.

WHAT THE TEACHER CAN DO

Regardless of the cultural orientation of their homes, all children need to master the skills that enable them to capitalize on their strengths. In school terms this means that they need to learn to read, to spell, to write coherent sentences, and to compute in mathematics efficiently. They need also to understand social relations, to appreciate the art and music of many cultures, and to understand scientific relationships and many other things that are taught in school. However, if the culturally disadvantaged master the skills of communication and mathematics, this other knowledge is open to them through books and papers. If they have not mastered the basic skills, many sources of vital information are closed to the disadvantaged student, and the knowledge of his lack can of itself make him feel inadequate in the larger community.

In terms of affects and self-concept there is an interaction between failure, poor self-concept, and inability to learn. We may argue about which comes first—the failure leading to the poor self-concept, or the poor self-concept leading to the failure. As teachers, we have the necessary control to prevent failure. If a child already has a poor self-concept, one of the best ways to help him improve his feelings about himself is to arrange his school situation so that he can perform adequately in his own eyes as well as in the eyes of his classmates. Several teachers have described their own experiences in trying to change the lives of disadvantaged students (Kohl, 1967, and Herndon, 1969).

For a long time it has been fashionable to teach all children as if skills were learned incidentally, while the class studies more "vital" and "interesting" community-related projects. For many years, training programs for elementary teachers included no course on how to teach reading as such. The reading was part of the social studies block or the language arts block, for both prospective teachers and their future pupils. This emphasis may have been necessary some years ago in order to escape from a highly formalized and lifeless drill approach to learning the skills, at least for pupils who had already learned the speech and language patterns used by teachers and in readers.

Today the level of competence needed in basic skills is much higher than formerly. Many children from advantaged and from disadvantaged homes are not learning to read well enough to succeed in high school or college, and many are not learning to compute or write well enough to conduct the daily transactions of an industrialized society. It is not necessary to go back to the old drill procedures. Improvements are taking place as teachers learn to specify sharply what the child needs to learn and to plan ways to see when the skill has been learned. Mastering school skills is intrinsically interesting for most children. The lessons become hateful when persistent failure accompanies a child's attempts to master new learning. The skills adults attempt to master are different—golf shots, bowling stances, or dance steps—but their reactions are like the child's when he is learning to read. If you succeed you are pleased with yourself, and if you fail often enough—not just once or twice—you come to avoid this line of endeavor. If the instructions are sufficiently specific so that you can understand and achieve the desired results you know you have succeeded. But if the instructions are buried in extraneous detail, you may find it impossible to understand what the task is all about and what you need to do to get started. You will likely fail.

For the advantaged and the disadvantaged child alike, teachers need first to recognize the importance of teaching the basic skills. After that, the essential subsystems that make up the skill must be specified. Many published materials are now designed this way, but the selection, timing, and follow-up are the responsibility of the teacher. This emphasis on the skills should be as closely related to vital living as possible, but when the choice becomes one of achievement or amusement, the mastery of communication skills is more likely to sustain the student's needs.

In-service programs for teachers emphasize behavioral objectives at this point in history. They are learning, through workshops and seminars, to state the goals for teaching the skills in behavioral objective forms; that is, they specify the behavior, the level of success, and the conditions of the learning.

The culturally disadvantaged child needs more help from the teacher than does the middle-class child because his prior learning has not been as useful to him in the competition he faces. However, the teacher's task is the same for the disadvantaged as it is for all children—that is, to take the child where he is and to help him reach the next level of accomplishment. Skill is needed in this teaching, because so often school has meant punishment, and these connections need to be erased and replaced with constructive attitudes toward learning. This is a difficult, but not impossible, task. Although the United States suddenly has more teachers than the schools employ, more teachers are needed who are willing to do the work required if culturally disoriented students are to succeed.

THE EMOTIONALLY DISTURBED CHILD

10

W. Van Spanckeren

W. Van Spanckeren is director of clinical services for
the Devereux Ranch Schools of Santa Barbara. This is
a complex of schools that provide residential care to
severely emotionally and mentally different children and
adults. He did his graduate work at the University of
Missouri and the University of California, Berkeley
and Santa Barbara.

For more than fifteen years Mr. Van Spanckeren has
worked with an unusually wide range of emotionally
disturbed individuals at the Devereux schools. In
addition to his diagnostic work, he has spent countless
hours relating to and learning from these children
and their parents. He has a practical approach to the
treatment of even the severely disturbed. This has
made him believable to those teachers who must cope
with children who have emotional problems.

Mr. Van Spanckeren has helped many teachers develop
success-oriented programs for individual students and
small groups. He conducts training sessions for the
teachers who work with the children. In addition, he
works with both pre- and postdoctoral interns in
clinical psychology and in education. He was president
of the Santa Barbara Association of Clinical
Psychologists in 1968.

Because the more disturbed the child, the more he needs support, I am going to discuss in detail the idea of *dependency,* and the strengths and failings of dependency networks around the child. I believe *an emotionally disturbed child is one whose behavior consistently arouses negative feelings toward himself from those upon whom he is emotionally or physically dependent.*

MEETING NEEDS

The baby learns who is important to him in that they meet his dependency needs so he can survive. His mother provides relative freedom from distress through giving him protection, food, warmth, and stimulation. Generally, she provides relief from discomfort and fear and gives pleasurable sensations that generalize into a feeling of well-being. She becomes important to him. He learns how to summon and keep her near him for a time. If he can't do this, he will almost certainly be emotionally detached, and he may even die. His relationship with his mother is his first, and it should be satisfying.

If persons other than his mother make him happy, they then become important; he learns to depend on them. If a mutually satisfying relationship can be set up with them too, then he's more secure. Generally, this broadening circle will include father and grandparents, and later, other siblings who sometimes ignore or compete with him. By age 4, he is usually forced into at least minimal interaction with peers. One useful function of the nursery school is to facilitate the child's interdependence with other children. The child also learns that the significant adults will treat him better if he shares the swing with that "horrible boy" over there.

As the confusion of childhood gives way to expectations or an understanding of the system in which food and other basic needs are met routinely and predictably—"I've always had breakfast in the morning," and, "No one here will hurt me, probably!"—the youngster begins to consider his agemates as important for many reasons. Some of these are: "Sometimes another child helps me have fun, like on the seesaw or pulling me on a wagon or giving me part of his cookie"; "Sometimes I enjoy watching another child laugh, and I play with him"; or "He cries when I hit him;—I am strong"; "Grown-ups may do special things for me when I'm with a bunch of kids"; "If I'm alone and quiet, the grown-ups don't pay much attention to me, then I become afraid." The average child finds his agemates gaining in importance to him and programs such as 4-H and Scouts help the child learn he can exist, for a time, without adult help.

As a preadolescent he can, in some ways, behave as an adult. At this time, he obviously considers the peer group almost as important as his parents in meeting his needs. At age 12, most of his conscious needs are socially oriented, since he's come to be so sure his physical needs will be met that he doesn't need to worry about them any more. He mimics his friends in dress and behavior, and these are necessarily different from the accepted standards of adults if he is to prove to his friends that he is becoming independent. He's not like his parents in dress or in his attitudes toward adult mores. He often wishes to prove he's no longer a mama's boy but, instead, is a man who thinks for himself. This is a frightening time for the 12-year-old because he's so terribly vulnerable if he tries to push his comparison to a man; he doesn't *really* earn a living, he doesn't *really* drive a car or vote. These are activities usually associated with adulthood. As he goes through his teens, he's more like a man, his peers are more manlike and he considers them increasingly important, and his parents are even less popular with him, because loyalty to them may cause him to lose his individuality and status with his peers.

DISTORTIONS IN NEED SATISFACTION

Now we can go back and see what can go wrong and why some of the children's behavior can be so different from that which the teacher and, less often, the other children want it to be. As indicated above, a child's first significant relationship is with its mother. If for some physiological or other reason it's not rewarding—usually the mother's and the infant's needs for each other are so very great—then there's extremely serious trouble ahead. The child may fail to have a positive attitude toward anyone and be labeled schizophrenic or autistic, terms that include the idea of preoccupation with oneself.

The schizophrenic child seems generally out of touch with the people and the larger aspects of his surroundings. He may be able to cope only with small objects, such as the spinning wheel of a toy car, a twig, a piece of lint. The failure of his relationships are so complete that he may not speak at all or he may obey only a few simple commands. The student who does not communicate with others, who is withdrawn and apparently emotionless, though irritable and perhaps bizarre in some ways, may be schizophrenic. He may be paying attention to internal feelings, sensations and fantasies, to the apparent exclusion of stimulation from the outside. Children with this type of problem are not often seen in the public school, although any child may behave in this way when he's been under severe stress for a time. If a child has the foundation of a satisfying infancy and early childhood, then any later emotional problems will be superimposed on that basic strength. The roots of his personality will be well placed, regardless of the brief continuing stresses he meets. With an auspicious beginning, we can assume that he will nearly always be in touch with others and be able to, even if imperfectly, receive and send verbal and nonverbal messages. Schizophrenia is sometimes termed a breakdown in communication.

Now some children have, for a variety of reasons, formed strong attachments to their immediate family, but when the time comes for them to widen their circle of satisfying relationships, they cannot do so. They are aware of their surroundings but are in active conflict with the people and even the objects in it. They may be more trouble to you, as teachers, because their problems show and demand your action. A word to the wise here: If you just say "Stop" you will only temporarily alter the child's behavior, and there will be little lasting effect. *Do tell him what to do that will please you* (pick something he can and will do immediately) *and will please him, too.* If you can nurture a mutually satisfying relationship with this child, you can expect him to improve in conformity to classroom policies. Children diagnosed as having "personality disorders" and as "neurotic" often have exceedingly strong ties to one or another parent, but their histories are barren of other continuing relationships.

UNDERSTANDING AND HELPING DISTURBED CHILDREN

Now there are two keys to the understanding of a child's behavior: First, there are reasons, always complex, never fully known, but logical and rational for the behavior we see; second, behavior that is rewarded will tend to be continued. If we consciously use these two keys, we will be more likely to learn *why* the child behaves as he does, rather than merely reacting spontaneously to his actions. Sometimes, the problem with the second key is to find out what is rewarding the child. What you assume is rewarding may be what will be rewarding to you but may be quite different from what is rewarding to the child. To see you break out in tears, or leave the classroom, or have him leave the classroom may be the reward for which the child is looking. If you can determine what is basically rewarding to the child, you can change the system so that desired actions are supported and undesirable actions are less frequent.

You will have emotionally disturbed children in your classroom. Your treatment should include protection from further stress and regular satisfaction of basic needs. Reassuring physical contact, such as a hand on the shoulder, a pat, or a squeeze, may mean much more than you know to the child. The child who is in reverie may have an excellent system for blocking out speech and nonverbal communication of many kinds. He may impair his vision by concentrating on something small, or he may impair his hearing by humming to himself or making noises to block out sounds; but if you go over and put your hand on his shoulder, you will get his attention, and you may stimulate a feeling of warmth and regard in *both* of you. Comforting words telling of the child's safety, his importance, and his individuality are also significant to both of you.

Encouraging positive behavior

The physical setting should be one in which the child cannot easily get into trouble. The adult can then give the rewarding smile or the pleasant sound or taste or feel when the child has behaved in a desirable way. In the classroom, the child may be seated away from aggressive children and the "don't touch" articles. He should be given simple instructions and tasks that he can complete successfully at his own pace and within his attention span. Longer tasks must be broken into components with rewards for completion of each. If the teacher can maintain a relationship with a child in which the child knows the teacher likes and cares for him as an individual, then she will do the child a great service.

Another technique that aids the disturbed child in the classroom includes letting him walk outside (or inside) the class when he finds it necessary. The child will be able to tolerate a great deal more in the classroom if he feels that he has a choice, that he can escape when he needs to. This option of leaving the scene is as great a solace to them as it is to us. If you've ridden with a poor driver, you know the feeling of panic when you feel that you can't get out of the situation. You are trapped. By allowing the child to leave the scene for a time you are acknowledging his independence. You can also put him first in line. If you have things to be punched, kneaded, torn, smashed, or carried, he can be a winner! These have the advantage of being short-term tasks and are things that he can do successfully. You can keep him next to you. This is a way of making him feel safe, because you can then assure him of physical protection; and often, the more disturbed the child is, the more he fears for his physical safety, his very physical survival. The child who is terribly disturbed may often talk of death, violence, and destruction. By *your* acceptance of a disturbed child, you are setting a pattern that the students who want to get along with you will follow. They will pick up by your nonverbal cues whether you believe that the child should be "teased to help him get over this bad habit" (not recommended) or whether he should be respected as somebody who is a worthwhile human being in his own right but who has an unfortunate mannerism, habit, or attitude at this time.

You should give the emotionally disturbed child a face-saving excuse for behaving the way you want him to. Try explaining to him that *you* accept him with his problems, but it's necessary for him to make an effort to behave reasonably when he is with you in the classroom situation. You understand that it is easier for him to sit on the floor or lie down or sleep, but tell him that in the classroom it is necessary for him to do other things and, as a favor to you and as a mark of his esteem for your relationship, he can stay in his chair for you for a time. Sometimes, in order to reinforce this feeling of closeness between you and the child, you can have him keep something of yours for the duration of the day. If you are a woman, maybe you can have the child keep a scarf or a comb; if it's a boy, perhaps he can keep some key or be in charge of the erasers. These are old techniques, but perhaps you see them a little bit differently if you see them as a token of a helping and mutually rewarding relationship between you and the child. Another thing you can do, of course, is to isolate the child or the external stimuli.

Ways in which teachers can help

It is important for the child that you make accurate notes of his behavior for his cumulative folder, because the child headed for trouble is generally detected by the time he reaches the fourth grade. I have been told that teachers can pick the first-grade child who is going to be in trouble in high school. The more precise your observations are, the fewer generalizations you make, the more help you are giving a child as he and his record go from grade to grade.

The disturbed child depends upon routines to find your door, to get through your door, and to find his seat. These may be the only things for him that are really the same from day to day. What goes on in the classroom is not precisely the same as it was the day before. Like the neurologically handicapped child, the disturbed child is often upset by small changes, so you can help him to feel comfortable and be successful by having well-established, predictable routines for him and by proceeding at a slow pace. A slow-paced program is right for most of the emotionally disturbed children. For others, you'll have to move rapidly in order to keep them in contact with you. It will be up to you to decide for which child the pace should be fast, for which it should be slow.

QUESTION: *How do you tell which should be which?*

ANSWER: I often notice quickness of speech and try to walk somewhere with the child. I know a medical internist at a local clinic who always comes out to a large central waiting room to greet his patients and to walk back to his office with them. I think that by the time he has said "Hello" and walked the first few steps with the patient, he's done about half of his important diagnostic work. The experienced diagnostician picks up, responds to, and catalogs cues from your general demeanor, your speed of movement, the strength of your handshake, the temperature of your hand, whether you meet his eye or not, or what your clothes look like.

QUESTION: *What is most often the best place to look for trouble in the classroom?*

ANSWER: Most of the time when I'm called in to see what has gone wrong in a program, I find that someone has verbally or nonverbally—sometimes without being aware of it—told the child to try harder: "Now let's see if you can do it at this level." They have expected too much from the child. This arouses in the child the same feeling you had when you were learning to skate. If someone took your hand and started to go faster than you wanted them to, perhaps you could stay on your feet for a little while, but you surely were not comfortable, and you weren't receiving stimuli very intelligently. You were panicked to quite an extent. You would rather have the person support you than pull you too quickly and thereby frighten you.

QUESTION: *How much ahead of time should you tell the child of changes?*

ANSWER: I said earlier that routines are good for the emotionally disturbed child. Changes should be discussed generally well in advance and specifically a day ahead of time. Put a ring around the date on the calendar (then he can be sure), and then you tell him as accurately as possible exactly what will happen. Let him ask questions. Tell him how he is going to feel about it and how he is going to react to it. If you tell him what he is going to feel like and what he is going to do, the odds are good that he will feel and act as you predict. Talk it over afterwards, too, and make him proud that he did well.

Jackie was an 11-year-old schizophrenic boy who suddenly began to scream and cry uncontrollably. When this had persisted for several minutes and the staff could not determine the cause of the outburst, they asked me to help. It was immediately apparent that Jackie was not receiving any more messages of any type from the people around him. He was busy expressing his response to a chaotic situation—as he saw it. Since he was in his usual place for that time of day and there were no new staff members there and he had his usual type of clothing on and there were no new students nor activities, I wondered if there was some physical problem bothering him. He looked healthy, but I saw that his hair had been cut recently. I asked if he had had his hair cut that day and was told that he had just had it cut. I asked if there was a new barber or if anything unusual had happened, and I was told that everything was as Jackie had been accustomed to having it when he had his hair cut, which happened approximately every two weeks. I asked who had taken him to the barber shop, waited for him, and brought him back. The usual staff member had done this. I then asked if he had returned to this particular classroom by the usual route and was told that the staff member had received word that there was a message for him at another office, so he had taken Jackie from the barber shop to the office and then to the classroom. The staff member and I then took Jackie from the classroom to the office and to the barber shop. The staff member then, alone, took Jackie from the barber shop to the classroom. As soon as the return to the classroom from the barber shop was begun, Jackie quieted down, and by the time he reached the classroom, he appeared quite comfortable, though still somewhat flushed from his exertions.

Relating to the emotionally disturbed

QUESTION: *How can you help the child relate to you if he has trouble with adults?*

ANSWER: Develop a difference so the child can identify you. MacArthur had a corncob pipe; some people call attention to physical differences between themselves and others. You could have a different-colored door on your room. This would help, too. The child would then know, "Well, this is the right room." In a long hallway with just a number on the top of each door, it is kind of nice to know by some other method whether or not it is the right place. The child who is quite disturbed doesn't trust his memory, so having several cues readily available helps him. His eyes may be telling him something is there, but he has been fooled before, so he touches it, or if no one is watching, he may smell it. You have seen children, usually the younger ones, smelling things as they get them. If you see an older person smelling something—this chalk, for example—you might think, "Aha, perhaps that person is not in very good shape." If you saw someone tasting it, too, you would have even more reason to wonder about him. So, you can help the child by giving him many cues to identify you, his room, and his own chair—particularly the first few days of school.

By putting his name on things, you help him identify himself. A child who is disturbed sometimes doesn't know who he is. This afternoon, a girl told me, "I don't know who I am, and I don't know where I am. I don't know whether I'm in hell talking to the devil, and I don't know whether I'm up in the clouds. I don't know whether I'm dead. I don't know how I'm supposed to feel. I don't really know who I am." I have had a number of young disturbed adults tell me something like this. Everyone of us, here, has in a pocket or purse several cards with our name on them, but how many of the children in school, through the sixth grade, have anything with them to tell who they are. This is very meaningful for the child. I think you should have his name on his desk so he better knows who he is.

QUESTION: *What can you do about it when you just plain don't like a child?*

ANSWER: The passive-aggressive technique is one that is often used by children and adults. If you find yourself angry and you don't know why—you just feel frustrated but you can't put your finger on it— chances are good that someone has been using passive-aggressive techniques on you. The person who is being passive-aggressive is the one who knows a banana peel is there, sees that you are coming and can predict that you are going to slip, and then doesn't do anything about it. The passive-aggressive person is the one who often makes you wait and says, "Wait, wait, I'll be right there." In our society, you punish, often with feelings of virtue, the person who does something overtly wrong, but rarely are we expected to punish the person who doesn't do anything at all. So, if you are feeling guilty or angry, you can look objectively at the child, and sometimes you will see that the child has been hostile toward you. Children can load us with pity, too. Perhaps he's learned that he can make you feel pity by displaying his withered hand or telling of the trouble that his parents have had, by telling of the operation he is going to have or about the terrible teacher he had the year before, or whatever. If he does, perhaps then he can manipulate you into bottling up your anger because of one of his misdeeds.

Helen had a mild case of cerebral palsy, and she believed this caused people to be prejudiced against her. This, she thought, was the reason she got poor grades in high school, had no friends, and was rejected by all except her loving father. Though a photograph of Helen would reveal a well-proportioned, dark-haired teen-ager with attractive features, her real-life presentation of herself was quite different. Her clothes were usually dirty, inappropriate, mismatched, improperly buttoned, and they seemed to fit poorly. The writhing athetoid movements of her left hand caused her to crumple up whatever schoolwork she handled or to disarrange her skirt. Her speech was sometimes incomprehensible because of the straining mouth movements and head tossing that accompanied her efforts to communicate. Nearly everyone who met Helen was touched by her plight and went out of their way to help her have her share of the good things of life.

It was only after some weeks that it was discovered that she was putting her clean clothing into the dirty clothes hamper and was intentionally soiling the clothes she had on. It was then learned that she could control her fingers well enough to play the piano passably, and she never crumpled the sheets of music. She could read her mail from her father quite easily and could remember material well enough to approximate an IQ of 110 on intelligence tests. Other students were keeping up her room for her until she became so obnoxious to them that they rejected her. This gave her further proof of the fact that she was rejected because of her handicap. She arranged to be left out "accidentally" by being late and was usually in the foreground, obviously miserable, when there was a visitor to her group.

In a physical education class one day, measures were being made of the students' ability to bat a softball. All the girls participated, and

Helen was in the outfield helping to return the balls to the pitcher. When the activity was apparently over, the staff member in charge asked a number of times if everyone had had their turn. It seemed that everyone had. The outfielders and infielders went to get on a waiting bus, the staff collected the materials, and then, as the bus was half full, Helen wailed that she had not had her turn. She had the staff member in charge neatly trapped. He had the choice of hurting Helen or inconveniencing the group of three staff members and eighteen girls. He chose to add to Helen's list of injustices. She passed this on to her father who telephoned the unit administrator, again, to find out why Helen was, again, mistreated.

Fortunately, Helen's father supported the treatment effort, though with many fears, and the secondary rewards for her physical handicap were increasingly reduced. Instead of seeing herself as *the cripple* who was rejected, Helen began to see herself as Helen *the student* who, incidentally, was crippled. As this shift occurred, her appearance, speech, and mannerisms improved, and she was soon able to make a satisfactory independent adjustment to college.

Nonverbal communication

If you just can't get along with a particular child because you are confusing the child with someone else, then you should, in all fairness, suggest that the child go to another teacher. You should also consciously decide what behavior you will accept. It is likely you are more tolerant than you think. Certainly your placement of limits will be different than those of other teachers, since in some areas you will be relatively more or less strict than in others. We confuse the child when we say, "No, no!" and smile and nod. You may be conveying the message to the child, "I know I'm not supposed to let you do this, but I thing it's kind of cute, so go ahead." You are also saying, "Read my gestures, not what I say."

Because our actions most often reflect our true feelings, the child learns to trust his sight at least as much as his hearing. You have all heard of how "children can really tell who likes them." This is how they do it. You give cues by the way in which you touch others, nod at someone, smile, frown, turn away, change the volume of your voice, and by your bodily attitude and the placement of furniture in your room. I know a teacher who is most comfortable separating herself from the children in the class with her desk—and she is a splendid teacher. I know others who are always with the children, are close to them and want the children close. On the other hand, you may know, perhaps, a teacher who is even closer to the child than the child wants her to be. This is a teacher who is meeting her own needs more than the child's, just as is the aloof teacher. Again I say, your needs are real also—and at least as important as the child's. Your displays, the material on your bulletin boards, and the clothing you wear tell the children about you. Harry Harlow's studies with monkeys teach how important our clothing can be. If you come to school dressed in clothes that will quickly show dirt or will be unrewarding to touch, it tells everyone, "Don't touch me!" If you are dressed in brown terrycloth, you should be attractive, I suppose, to monkeys and the children. It says to the children, "I am someone who expects to be touched and who can be with you." If you come to work in combat boots and a field jacket, this tells how you expect to behave. I know an administrator who is feared when he wears a red sweater: "Watch out, he's angry today." Your hygiene, your tone and accent, your choice of words, and your tempo are all shouting who you really are to the children; and they mistrust phonies. The word *congruent* was used to describe people. If you are what you seem to be—if you are internally consistent, honest, square, true-blue, all wool and a yard wide, a brick, or a solid citizen—you are predictable and to be trusted. If your verbalisms are parallel to your nonverbal communications, then the children will have quite a bit of confidence in you.

QUESTION: *What did those monkey studies show?*

ANSWER: I recommend them very highly. Some beautiful studies of monkeys' interactions appeared in *Life* magazine four or five years ago, as well as in professional journals. Harlow, et al., found that a monkey, when raised with other little monkeys, usually grows up to be a healthy, happy, normal monkey, whether or not there are parent figures. On the other hand, a monkey without peers isn't particularly well adjusted. If he's raised without anyone at all, he tends to be terribly distressed; he's withdrawn, autistic. They found that monkeys would rather have a mother figure to whom they can run and cling rather than one that has been feeding them but feels cold. The children of schizophrenic parents are often themselves schizophrenic because the interaction between them, the verbal and nonverbal communication, is unsatisfying; there isn't a real response between the two. I saw a movie showing a schizophrenic mother nursing her baby. The nipple came out of the baby's mouth, the mother was not aware of this, the baby struggled, smacked its lips, and to the best of its ability said, "Give me some attention, please"; but the mother was out of contact, so the child gave up and learned to be passive and just wait.

QUESTION: *When you get these children later in life, will they ever become normal?*

ANSWER: Sometimes when they do, it is almost like watching a wooden Pinocchio come to life. I've known a number of children like this, and I know they are becoming a person rather than a robot when I feel an empathy with them. I'll give them a playful sort of a shove, and they'll shove me back *spontaneously*. Sometimes I will tease them, and they tease me back playfully. Often, it is the timing of the act that gives you the clue as to whether it is normal or abnormal. If you say "Thank you" to somebody and they look at you a moment and then say, "You're welcome," you can sense that something unusual was going on in them.

Incidence of emotionally disturbed children

QUESTION: *Is there a significant difference between the number of boys and the number of girls who are emotionally disturbed?*

ANSWER: By this definition of emotional disturbance, which stresses interdependency (but is not the usual definition), I would guess that there are about the same number of each. You find girls tabbed as "emotionally disturbed" less frequently than boys until they are in their late teens or their twenties. It seems that parents become upset quicker about the boy. About the girl, "Well, she'll be a nice quiet girl, and she'll get married and everything will be well." The boy, however: "If he's beginning to act up now, it may get worse, and he'll never be able to make a living and take care of himself. We should give him treatment now." When the girl reaches 18: "Why she's never going to get married unless she stops this thing she's doing and starts doing something else. We had better get her in to see the doctor." So you find younger boys and older girls in treatment.

QUESTION: *Would you estimate what percentage of students in secondary schools would be termed emotionally disturbed children?*

ANSWER: The figure of 10 percent is often given in the public schools—called the troublesome 10 percent.

QUESTION: *Do you think, then, that all the emotionally disturbed children will make their disturbance known to us?*

ANSWER: No. As I pointed out, some of them will be passive-aggressive. Some of them will be too dependent and terribly emotionally disturbed, but they won't necessarily make you feel sorry for them, cause you to notice them, or make you angry. Perhaps the best definition of a well-adjusted person is that he contributes more than he takes.

THE EDUCATIONALLY HANDICAPPED CHILD

11

William J. Elliott
Raymond Bauer

William J. Elliott obtained the B.S. in education and the M.A. in educational psychology at the University of Nebraska and the Ph.D. in education and psychology at the University of Denver. He has been involved in special education as a school psychologist in California for the past twelve years. At the present time, he is director of pupil personnel services in Goleta, California.

Raymond Bauer received the B.S. and the M.S. in elementary education and special education at the State University of New York, College of Education, at Buffalo, and is a doctoral student in educational psychology. He is presently the coordinator of special education in Goleta.

This chapter is actually a dialogue between a school psychologist, Dr. Elliott, and an educator, Mr. Bauer. It demonstrates the differences in points of view attributable to the different perspectives of the school psychologist and the coordinator who is responsible for maintaining his special education program.

ELLIOTT: Ray, before we begin a discussion of learning disabilities or programs for the educationally handicapped, I should like to introduce myself and present an historical perspective of the area of learning disabilities. Before I ever became professionally interested in education or the problems of learning, I learned about learning as a student in the public schools. From those experiences, I think I developed a two-factor perspective of learning and learning problems; the two concepts in my system were those of intelligence and motivation. If a student were intelligent, he would learn; if he were not intelligent, or if he were less intelligent, he would fail to learn or would learn at a slower pace. If the student was obviously intelligent enough to learn and yet failed to do so, then he either was not interested or was somehow resisting and had to be forced to learn.

Later, as a student in educational psychology, I learned a bit more about how to measure intelligence without being too concerned about its definition. I soon became much more sophisticated in the area of motivation, however, since that was a period of time in which the research in self-concept was coming into vogue, and the effect of depth psychology on education was causing us to focus on the emotional factors involved in learning. I have never regretted this initial emphasis on self-concept and its roots in early object relations, for I still place social-emotional factors high on the list of the concerns of the school psychologist in diagnosing learning problems. However, as I look back on those first years of work as a school psychologist, I realize my theoretical formulations and resultant daily behavior were too limited to help teachers to deal with many kinds of learning problems.

My first experiences as a teacher, a counselor, and a psychologist taught me much about the importance of social-cultural factors in learning. In fact, some of us in Goleta, California, were moving toward the development of compensatory education programs before legislative provision was made for such programs at federal and state levels. Actually, I think exposure to the Child-Study Program, developed by Daniel A. Prescott at the University of Chicago in 1939 and carried on by the Institute for Child Study at the University of Maryland, strongly reinforced my awareness of the importance of social-cultural factors in learning and of the complexity of the learning process itself.

I remember clearly two of the assumptions stated by Prescott to underpin his child-study approach: that human behavior is caused and that its causes are multiple, complex, and interrelated. I have developed a strong appreciation for the meaning of that latter assumption in the last few years as I have attempted to understand, in even a crude way, the neurophysiology of learning and the fascinating interweaving of perceptual-motor and emotional processes in the young child.

I think Prescott's six-area framework (1957) for the analysis of human behavior can still be used in developing a diagnostic model for the area of learning disabilities or for testing the adequacy of prescriptive formulations. The six areas of the framework are:

1. Physical factors and processes
2. Love relationships and related processes
3. Cultural background and socialization processes
4. Peer-group status and processes
5. Self-developmental factors and processes
6. Self-adjustive factors and processes

I am embarrassed that the area of physical processes received so little attention in my own diagnostic model until quite recently. Once I determined that the child could, indeed, see and hear and exhibited no evidence of gross neurological or other physical defect, my interest in the physical area was satisfied. Now that I am involved in more detailed study of perceptual-motor development and the relationship of perceptual-motor efficiency to later cognitive learning, I feel much better satisfied with my approach to the diagnosis of learning problems.

In the physical area (item 1 above) one would be interested in information concerning growth rate and maturity level, energy level, state of health and nutrition, health history, handicaps or limitations, perceptual-motor efficiency, and physical appearance and feelings about appearance.

In the affectional area (item 2) one would seek information concerning family relationships and other close personal ties that influence behavior and learning. From these relationships grow many self-referent ideas and feelings that facilitate or inhibit learning.

From the child's social-cultural experiences (item 3) come many attitudes, and these attitudes determine what he will be interested in learning, how he regards himself as a learner, how he regards the school and its values. The teacher's own socialization processes have much to do with how well he and the student will work together. The peer group (item 4) as a self-culture may be considered worthy of consideration in itself.

The psychological factors (items 5 and 6) defined by Prescott represent the individual's internalization of external forces from family, peers, etc., into a fantastically complex set of ideas, attitudes, and feelings that we call self-concept. These self-referent ideas become autonomous as behavior determinants themselves. By understanding how the individual sees himself and how he characteristically protects himself from perceived threat, one improves the opportunity for successfully helping him modify his behavior (learn).

At the same time that I was developing a bit more sophisticated approach to the diagnosis of learning problems in children, I became increasingly aware that learning disabilities are as much a function of the nature of the school as they are the characteristics of the individual learner. I now hold strongly that one must be as concerned with diagnosis of the needs of the system as with the needs of the individual student and that often it is the system that needs "fixing" rather than the child.

To conclude this personal reminiscing, I must report that these years of study and experience in schools have left me feeling more ignorant than before concerning the nature of human learning and learning problems. It was much simpler to assign a child to the diagnosis-for-placement category than it is to generate useful prescriptive hypotheses to guide the teacher in his work with the child; I must now work with other learning specialists in order to develop a sufficiently complete picture of the child to guide the teacher. Happily, however, working as a member of a multidisciplinary team is more exciting than working alone, and the shift from diagnosis for placement to developing a basis for prescriptive teaching holds much more promise for being helpful to children.

BAUER: It is interesting, Bill, that you trace your own professional development in the fashion you do. William M. Cruickshank and G. O. Johnson, in their history of special education, *Education of Exceptional Children and Youth* (1958), trace a similar path of program development over a longer period of time. Actually, my own experience was a bit different. At good old Buffalo State I was taught that educators had already found many of the solutions to the problems of handicapped children. I would say that my training was based on two or three principles that were unquestionable. First, that "special education" classes were the answer for children who had learning problems and we should do all we could to sponsor more programs. Second, all that was needed was a confirmation of a suspected problem and a ready-made program could be brought to bear on the child. Third, that intelligence was fixed and there wasn't much that could be done about it. Let me tie these principles together to give you some idea why I was so uncomfortable as a classroom teacher for about the first two or three years of my teaching.

After I entered teaching I began to get the feeling that not too much effort or concern was being expended for handicapped children. If a district had a special education teacher, a classroom, and plenty of equipment, then society had fulfilled its obligation to these handicapped children. In fact, special education classes were almost sacred ground for many years, before some educators began to question the value of these classes (Johnson, 1962). I don't believe anyone really felt that these classes were harmful to many children and that much of the expenditure of time, money, and effort was unjustified.

A companion concern I began to develop was that of the assigning of children to existing programs. All too often, diagnosis became merely "suspicion confirming." As an example, many teachers I worked with had children who were suspected of having limited intelligence. A referral was made to the psychologist, and testing was done. If the score was low enough, the suspicion was confirmed and the child was placed in a class. My concern was not with the procedure but with the assumption that everything the child needed was offered in that particular class. No extensive diagnosis was made or prescription for remediation written that was tailored to the needs of that student. I believe we can call this "pigeonholing."

Finally, the idea of the permanency of IQ was further justification for special classes. If a child was "retarded" and a program was available and the concept was valid, it was just about the end of the future of that child. All the teacher had to do was use the mandated curriculum, and there wasn't much of a problem—yet.

My discomfort began when many of the students began to make phenomenal growth when I least expected it. I treated them like normal students, gave them work that was modified and intellectually above what the curriculum called for, and using this as a base, begged many of my colleagues to take them back into their classrooms for short periods of time. It was from this period on that I began to see the need for individual prescription writing for all children, the injustice of labeling and pigeonholing, and in many cases, the danger of a hasty diagnosis. It seems to me, Bill, that you were saying that your diagnostic model was considerably modified by your experience in the schools and that I am saying that in teacher training I was given a teaching model that proved inadequate when I started to use it with kids. Can you deal with this question of a diagnostic-learning model for special education?

DIAGNOSTIC-TEACHING MODELS

ELLIOTT: We both agree that a learning model is necessary for both the diagnostician and the person responsible for teaching the child. My beginning model was a two-factor model dealing with intelligence and motivation, while it seems to me that your prescribed curriculum guide dealt with a single-factor (intelligence). According to such a model, a child with a mental age of 7-6 and a chronological age of 9-5 will automatically be at *this* point in your curriculum guide. Since both models are obviously inadequate, we need to begin to define some of the basic dimensions of an adequate model.

Rather than define a completely new model, I should like to point to one that I ran across recently in the literature. I suspect, since you think of the classroom teacher, that this model will be more satisfying to me than to you, because it is a model used to structure the work of a diagnostic and research center. This model is presented by Keith E. Beery (1968a) in an article entitled "Comprehensive Research, Evaluation and Assistance for Exceptional Children." Beery presents a schematic model and some brief definitions of the model's dimensions, which I should like to quote in their entirety.

RESEARCH AND DEVELOPMENT MODEL
The diagram of the Child-Study Unit (CSU) Research and Development Model shown in Figure 11-1 is an outline of a design to give comprehensive, integrated, manageable, and generalizable direction to research and

clinical work with exceptional children. The major dimensions which have been considered in this model are:

A. Age. *Since we are considering organisms as they are developing in childhood, static concepts of perceptual and other functional attributes are inadequate. All investigations emanating from the model should be designed within a developmental framework. On the basis of the model, normative levels of development should be specified according to each of four major dimensions, to their subcategories, and to their interactions.*

B. Object relations. *Many theoretical models are exclusively physical, cognitive, or affective in their dimensions. In the field of learning disorders, most of our formal models have not included sociopsychological factors of an affective nature, despite the likelihood that proponents of all these models would agree that there are important reciprocal relationships between sociopsychological development in relation to learning and other factors (Pearson, 1952).*

Since these reciprocal relationships have not been examined adequately, the interaction of the object relation dimension is thought to be an important characteristic of the CSU model.

C. Process modality. *This dimension is familiar in both education and medicine (Bateman, 1965). Every child is an information processing organism and his growth is highly dependent upon learning. This information is derived from and expressed through various sensory-motor channels, so that each modality, for its reception and transmission, should be considered in assessment and in planning an assistance approach.*

D. Information processing level. *Although our present conceptualization of their interrelationships is undoubtedly imperfect, a hierarchy of levels of behavior presumably exists. More precise description of this hierarchy should increase the efficiency of our efforts to evaluate and assist children in their development. For example, relative activation levels are frequently overlooked even though these levels presumably mitigate all of the physical, perceptual, and cognitive abilities which affect information processing. Neither the hypo- nor the hyperstimulated child is able to utilize his physical, perceptual, cognitive, or affective capacities fully. There are, undoubtedly, optimal levels of activation which are modality specific and can be regulated experimentally and therapeutically.*

This dimension incorporates the highly important factor of integration among the functions represented in dimension C. Many children develop adequately within modalities but are unable to coordinate these functions sufficiently to meet the demands of many learning tasks (Beery, 1968b).

E. Symbol level. *Many children function adequately as long as they are not required to deal with words and other abstract or arbitrary signs. Recognition of the hierarchical stimulus relationship which seems to exist among objects and their pictorial and symbolic representations is of great significance in planning effective education for normal children as well as for those with learning disorders. These relationships, as well as their interactions with other dimensions, require definition and experimentation.*

I like this model, Ray, because it has several dimensions that our models lacked. It emphasizes the dynamic *age*-related nature of learning behavior. Diagnosis and remediation must take developmental *sequence* into account in order to be effective. Remediation must begin below the level of difficulty in any area of development.

For school use I would emphasize and elaborate the "object relations" or sociopsychological dimension. In a recent discussion of symbolic learning Dr. Robert Oyler, coordinator of Psychological Services for the Claremont, California, Unified School District, described the child's acceptance of a symbol to represent concrete experience as an act of faith mediated by the student's trust of the teacher. For the educationally handicapped (EH) student, the support of an understanding adult must be even more critical than for the child without learning problems. Will it ever be possible to establish teacher-pupil compatibility as a criterion for placement?

In his process modes, Beery has presented the three sensory modes through which most information comes to the organism. However, I would want to elaborate on those three basic modes, not so much in diagnosis as in looking at prescriptions for perceptual-motor problems. A. Jean Ayres (1963), in her work with children, strongly emphasizes the need to be concerned about the vestibular system and simultaneous stimulation of the vestibular and tactile systems in remedial activity. Beery feels that the levels he presents in his "processing-levels" dimension may require some elaboration or reordering, but he has gone far ahead of many of us in presenting that

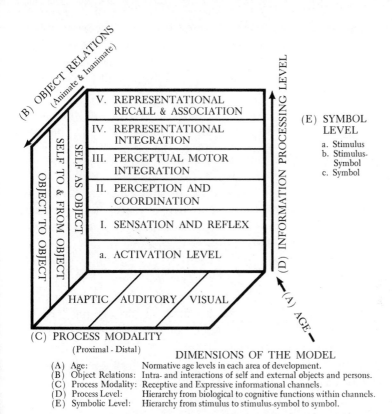

V. REPRESENTATIONAL
RECALL & ASSOCIATION

IV. REPRESENTATIONAL
INTEGRATION

III. PERCEPTUAL MOTOR
INTEGRATION

II. PERCEPTION AND
COORDINATION

I. SENSATION AND REFLEX

a. ACTIVATION LEVEL

(B) OBJECT RELATIONS
(Animate & Inanimate)

SELF TO & FROM OBJECT

SELF AS OBJECT

OBJECT TO & FROM OBJECT

OBJECT TO OBJECT

(D) INFORMATION PROCESSING LEVEL

(E) SYMBOL
LEVEL
a. Stimulus
b. Stimulus-
   Symbol
c. Symbol

HAPTIC / AUDITORY / VISUAL

(A) AGE

(C) PROCESS MODALITY
(Proximal - Distal)

DIMENSIONS OF THE MODEL

(A) Age: Normative age levels in each area of development.
(B) Object Relations: Intra- and interactions of self and external objects and persons.
(C) Process Modality: Receptive and Expressive informational channels.
(D) Process Level: Hierarchy from biological to cognitive functions within channels.
(E) Symbolic Level: Hierarchy from stimulus to stimulus-symbol to symbol.

FIGURE 11-1 *Research and development model (From Keith E. Beery, "Comprehensive Research, Evaluation and Assistance for Exceptional Children," Exceptional Children, 223–228, 1968. By permission of the author and publisher.)*

hierarchic sequence. Anyone who wants to understand this dimension in any depth should consult the original article to see how Beery elaborates any one of the levels presented in that hierarchy. Each level is extremely complex in itself and requires much study to understand and to make useful for either the diagnostician or the teacher. I certainly will translate this dimension of Beery's model into other terms, and I will probably have to simplify it in order to make sense out of it as I diagnose children now. Five years from now, I may be able to deal with it in its entirety.

I guess I present the model in use at the Child-Study Unit because it is more exhaustive in defining basic dimensions than most working models. I know very well that as I express inadequacy in being able to diagnose along those five dimensions, I am admitting to being unready to give the teacher information in some of the areas that will help her to teach the child. One of my major problems will be translating information on some of these dimensions into material that is immediately useful to her. Maybe I would need to know the model employed by the teacher as well as my own model before I could consider translations across from the one to the other. Would you like to pick up at this point?

BAUER: Bill, the concerns that I have as an educator about any theoretical behavior model is that it provides only part of the picture needed by the classroom teacher concerned with the education of EH children. An article by Robert Valett (1968) that appeared in the *Journal of School Psychology* illustrates my concern. Valett mentions specifically that one of the needs of the child who has a learning disability is for highly specific instruction. In my opinion this is the weakest part of any theory or model. I have seen hundreds of monographs, articles, and books dealing with the philosophy of diagnosis, the psychology of diagnosis, techniques of diagnosis, etc., but I have seen no more than a dozen books in the past ten years that dealt specifically and entirely with teaching techniques to be used with children with learning disabilities. The need for information dealing with specific remediation is acute.

Although a theoretical model is a necessary part of the process, I would be more interested in research related to techniques of remediation and more trained teachers able to combine the two. Generally, teachers are prepared to teach normal children and to provide them with knowledge and skills necessary for integration into our society. Most universities and teachers colleges provide introductory courses to exceptional children, but these are not sufficient to provide any real basis for competence in working with these children. With the exception of the graduates from special education programs in certain universities, we simply do not have enough teachers adequately trained or sophisticated enough in psychoeducational diagnosis and remediation to service the needs of these children. If the university and college systems do not expand programs and recruit more candidates to fill these programs, the task will have to fall to local districts and special education departments. Therefore, the theoretical model should be the starting point for training of in-service teachers, but the model should include more training in specific remediation techniques.

One educator who has made this effort is Dr. Robert Valett, director of the Learning-Resource Center for Exceptional Children, Sacramento, California, Unified School District. Valett's rationale (1969) for his program is simply stated in the following passage:

The primary objectives in educating children with learning disorders are the identification and remediation of specific disabilities. To achieve these two objectives, all disabilities need to be operationally defined in educational and behavioral terms. While medical and psychological terminology is of supplemental value in clarifying etiology and in specifying diagnosis and relevant treatment goals and plans, the primary model must still be educational. p. 5

This rationale serves as a basis for what I consider to be a "working" program for the remediation of learning disabilities. With the publication of his book *Programming Learning Disabilities* (1969), Valett has attempted to integrate his concept of basic learning abilities with theoretical constructs of four other theorists and researchers: Benjamin S. Bloom, J. P. Guilford, Jean Piaget, and Frank M. Hewett. The importance of this work to educators is that Valett has attempted, in my opinion, to complete the continuum from the theoretical foundation of the structure of intelligence to the philosophical question of the goals of education. To be sure, there have been many authors who have published their works outlining their theories and methodologies to remediate learning disabilities, but they have either embraced one small fragment of relevant research or ignored the research completely. I believe Valett has given the educator a complete program of educational objectives, development and structure of intellect, and strategies of teaching, and all in relevant behavioral terms. This program also provides for the assessment of where the student is developmentally, and for those teachers and administrators concerned with records, Dr. Valett's program has all of the profiles, report sheets, etc., necessary for the continuation of evaluation and programming.

In short, Bill, I suppose Dr. Valett's program appeals to me in two modes; one as a teacher and the other as an administrator. As a teacher, the program speaks to me in terms that are meaningful to teachers—that is, behaviorally and developmentally. As an administrator, the program provides for testing and remediation that can be done by classroom teachers, with necessary record keeping being kept to a minimum. In addition, underlying all of Dr. Valett's work is sound research, which aids the administrator in assuring teachers and other professionals that the program will provide meaningful results. These meaningful results might provide us with additional data for our diagnostic-teaching model.

ELLIOTT: In summary, then, we agree that both diagnostician and teachers need a diagnostic-teaching model that enables them to translate their assessment of the student into specific remedial experiences that give some promise of improved performance. These models are eternally subject to modification as we learn—in fact they guide our evaluation of experience and make improvement more likely.

Enough of this theory. Speak to me of reality, Ray.

THE PRESENT STATE OF EH

BAUER: With the passage of AB 464 in 1963, California became one of the first states to attempt to do something legislatively about children with specific learning disabilities. Although the initial allocation was small, it was a step in the right direction. I'm sure that many educators felt, as did politicians, that a large expenditure of funds into a program was all that was needed to alleviate a problem. As I view it today, the problem that arose was not in the intent, but in the implementation of that intent. First of all, the majority of school districts weren't prepared to comply with the law, either in trained personnel or in facilities. Second, the guidelines for operation of these programs were loosely defined, both in the law and the state department of education regulations. This is illustrated by the following excerpt taken from Section 2, Article 27, Subchapter 1 of Chapter 1, Title V of the California Administrative Code, which reads:

. . . whose learning problems are associated with a behavioral disorder or a neurological handicap or a combination thereof, and who exhibits a significant discrepancy between ability and achievement.

This looseness was indeed unfortunate for two reasons. First, the districts that were sincerely interested in helping children expended a lot of time, money, and energy and were not too sure that they were heading in the right direction. Secondly, many districts used this lack of clarity to establish programs that deteriorated into "dumping grounds" for many problem children. I'm not attempting to fix blame, Bill, but let me explain further the point I made about the implementation of the philosophy, because I should like to contrast this with the way Goleta is attempting to meet this need.

Generally speaking, the historically accepted approach to the diagnostic process begins with a concern by the teacher for one of her students. She makes a referral to another professional for assistance, and some form of a prescription is written that is to remediate the situation. During this process certain assumptions are being made, namely, that the problem can be defined adequately, that specific remedial techniques are available, and lastly, that there are trained personnel who can carry out the recommendation. During the initial phases of the EH program in California, I don't believe these assumptions could be made with any degree of certainty. Although progress has been made in the past few years, many districts are still fumbling for the right combinations. I also believe that an historically accepted approach to diagnosis is probably a detrimental factor to growth in EH programs. School districts generally cannot afford too many specialists, and therefore many schools share one psychologist, nurse, speech therapist, etc. This forces many of these specialists to work alone and merely read reports of the other specialists before making their final decision. This inhibits the exchange of information, points of clarity, or ideas. In my mind, there is a real question of doubt as to whether we have all the information we could possibly gather about a particular student. As a consequence, some of the programs written for the student are of a fragmented nature, and when you couple this with ill-equipped classrooms, inadequately trained teachers, and poor guidelines of operation, your program is in trouble.

In Goleta, the process of identification begins in the same way, i.e., a concern for a student and the original referral, but now there is a person at each school who is responsible for the coordination of all data and personnel. It might be a nurse, a resource teacher, or some other special-service person. I believe that there are some unique features of this arrangement in that through planning all of the interested parties are brought together at the same time to discuss findings and plan a program for the student. All pertinent data is available; schedules, telephone calls, etc., have all been done; and the precious time of the specialists is conserved. The main strength of this Child-Study Team is that the person responsible for the coordination of the team is also the person responsible for the necessary follow-up services and evaluation. In addition, the coordinator serves as liaison between the school and other schools, special-service departments, and community agencies. If we believe that evaluation is a continuous process, the Child-Study Team serves this function beautifully.

Before I talk about Goleta's program for EH children, Bill, I think an article by Dr. Alice Thompson (1968), which appeared in the *CEC State Federation Journal,* illustrates and summarizes more clearly some of the concerns I experienced earlier. I think her title, "A Crisis Report and Some Opinions," is more than appropriate for this discussion. Her opinions about EH programs are as follows:

1. *That the problems are much greater than had been anticipated.*

2. *That the cost is far beyond expectation.*

3. *That the numbers of children who need at least some special help far exceed the expectation—perhaps 25 to 30 percent of the total school population.*

4. *That children are not being habilitated and returned to regular classes as had been hoped.*

5. *That there are no "miracles" available to the EH teacher.*

6. *That the load of responsibility and preparation for EH classes is too heavy for a single teacher, or even a teacher and an aide.*

7. *That EH children are multiply handicapped.*

8. *That half the teachers who undertake the teaching of EH children leave the field within five years.*

9. *That most academic and conduct learning problems are more severe than had been assumed. It was once anticipated that when inattention and hyperactivity should be overcome, learning could take place at the normal rate.*

10. *That even severely involved EH children can be contained and taught in orderly classroom procedures.*

11. *That distinctions between EH and EMR (educable mentally retarded) children in the marginal ranges are arbitrary and controversial.*

12. *That a pleasant, purposeful, learning-focused atmosphere benefits almost every discordant child, regardless of his particular condition.*

13. *That there are wide district differences in assignment of EH classification to children.*

14. *That there are wide district differences in assignment, makeup, and policies of admissions and discharge committees.*

15. *That the state financial structure will not permit unlimited EH expansion.*

I am forced to agree with Dr. Thompson, and therefore I'm excited about the fact that Goleta does employ the Child-Study Team concept and, also, that it serves so effectively. The data provided by the Child-Study Team serves as the foundation for the evaluation and placement of the student by the EH admission and discharge committee. It also provides the guidelines for the implementation of the committee's recommendations for the possible remediation of the learning disability of the student.

At this point I would have to introduce a personal bias that does influence the operation of our EH classes. I believe, just as Dr. Thompson does, that a student can learn, regardless of his particular condition, if he has the opportunity to be a part of a pleasant learning-focused atmosphere. This philosophy is an integral part of the remediation process of the educationally handicapped program in Goleta. In the majority of the cases the student can be successfully integrated into a regular class on a part-time basis within two months after his initial placement in the EH classroom. The length of regular class placement during the first trial depends on the degree of disability of the student. If the initial trial is successful, the length of the regular class placement is increased until the student can participate for an entire school day. This placement will last until the EH teacher has conclusive evidence that the child can successfully withstand the expectancies of the regular program.

The success of this integration depends considerably on the degree of participation in the EH program by other teachers and the principal of the school. There is no question that the addition of another student, especially a problem student, is a burden to many teachers and, in many cases, certainly unfair. In order to make this trial placement less traumatic, it is not unusual for special class teachers to make certain professional "deals" with their colleagues. The special class teacher in Goleta is provided with a trained aide, plenty of teaching aids and materials, and additional services. It is not unusual for the special class teacher to send the aide along with the student who is being integrated into a class for the first time. The aide may assist the regular class teacher until the student feels secure enough to be left alone. In many cases, the regular class teacher may exchange the EH student for one of her class who she feels could benefit from some specialized help. The encouragement of the principal does much to facilitate such placements, and many of the successes of such placements are primarily due to the principal's willingness to continually evaluate and make recommendations for better utilization of his staff.

This continued working relationship is providing us with some new insights into the possible benefit of this type of programming. It remains for future research to provide us answers to some questions about the reality of the special classes.

I am happy to say, Bill, that some of the concerns of such eminent researchers as Dr. Thompson, as well as myself, are also the concerns of educators at the state level. I believe you, as well as some of your colleagues, have some feelings about the future course of special education.

THE FUTURE

ELLIOTT: Ray, in bridging from present to future, I should like to quote the recommendations in a "position paper" on supplementary (special) education prepared this year by a committee on special education of the California Association of School Psychologists and Psychometrists (CASPP). These recommendations spring from concerns closely related to those stated by Thompson.

CASPP proposes the following directions for the education of children with unique requirements:

1. *The present single-definition categories of special education should be reassigned under one classification—"Supplementary Education."*

2. *Supplementary Education should include all currently defined classifications, i.e., physically handicapped, trainable mentally retarded, educable mentally retarded, educationally handicapped, gifted, deaf,*

hard-of-hearing, blind, partially sighted, dysphasic, Miller-Unruh Reading program, Compensatory Education, and other groupings of children in need of special help.

3. *All programs under the Supplementary Education umbrella may be integrated into/with regular classrooms of a school district, and students would be involved in the regular activities wherever and whenever possible.*

4. *Supplementary Education would provide three types of programs: the supplementary integrated classroom; the individual and small-group instruction program; home instruction.*

5. *One Admission-Discharge committee should screen all applicants for all classes and decide on placement based on the student's needs based on multiple criteria (school reports, psychological studies, and medical recommendations). The child would be placed in a group or class, depending upon his needs rather than pre-set, rigid criteria, such as measured intelligence, physical disability, or emotional instability. These criteria would all be considered in the final placement, but would not be limiting factors.*

6. *In practice, a school district or county office would continue to provide a program for physically handicapped children, with specially trained teachers and special equipment; however, Supplementary Education criteria would not preclude an educationally handicapped student from entering this program if there is some educational technique offered in this program that would not be offered elsewhere. An educationally handicapped student could be placed in a program especially designed for gifted students for part of the day if this program meets his special needs, etc.*

7. *Supplementary Education would be offered to students with special needs from the ages three to eighteen and, in some cases, twenty-one years of age. Early education has been demonstrated to be a method of prevention of regression.*

8. *Under Supplementary Education the role of the school psychologist will be one of assessing functional abilities and disabilities with prescriptive educational recommendations. His services would be an ongoing process of evaluation, consultations, and involvement after placement. These roles would be pursued by other support-specialist personnel as well.*

9. *Several pilot programs should be activated throughout the state in representative schools so that specific recommendations could be developed through research. Adequate financial support guidelines and other program requirements (such as guaranteed services for the identified pupils) could be evolved through controlled experimentation and research.*

Therefore, in summary, CASPP recommends that the present structure of Special Education, which concerns itself with placement of children into single categorized classes, be abolished and in its place a set of multiple processes be coordinated into a specific Supplemental Education Plan for a specific child when and for as long as the child's need is less adequately met by the regular classroom procedures. Under this new procedure the moral separation of children into "acceptable" and "rejection" would be ended or lessened, as most children at times need supplemental planning and programming. This new procedure, or Supplemental Education Plan, with its flexibility and individual design, also provides for more adequate control of transitional anxieties which result from shifts from or to regular class routines.

Selection, diagnosis, program planning, programming, and regular and periodic reevaluation of program and child would be accomplished by: (1) psychological and other specialist professions, (2) appropriate evaluation and consultation, (3) an interdisciplinary Evaluation Committee, (4) an Advisory Committee, (5) supplemental education programs, (6) administrative policy and supervision of the process, and (7) consultation by state and county personnel.

I certainly agree with the CASPP viewpoint, and I think that their concerns have already been heard by those responsible at the state level. Although they are not final as of this writing, some profound changes have been made in the new Title V of the California Administrative Code. Without going into a long item-by-item description of these new changes, I'll attempt to highlight those I think are really important.

First of all, the descriptions of students eligible for the program have been more specifically written. The descriptions have become more inclusive, but also they have become more exclusive as well. Second, the types of reports presented by specialists must include a prognosis as well as a diagnosis. A further requirement is that broad terms such as "reading deficiency" are not sufficient for identification, but must be described in such a way that a relationship is established between the specific disability and school achievement. Thirdly, the admissions and discharge committee of the district, established by the law, is made responsible for many more functions than under the previous regulations. It has been given greater power to perform these functions, and specific requirements in the form of membership, types of reports necessary, priority lists, etc., are but a few of the new facets of this committee's work.

As you can well imagine, much of the work and many of the changes in the regulations are the result of the efforts of the state department of education consultants who operate throughout the state. These people are in a prime position to view existing programs in operation, and they can be of immeasurable assistance in establishing or maintaining programs. In addition, the many interested professionals who are conducting research projects throughout the country are providing much-needed research data. Dr. Alice Thompson, who was cited earlier, has been conducting a very interesting project at the California State College at Los Angeles. This project has been in operation for at least five years, and some interesting methodologies are being utilized. I would say that Dr. Thompson summarized the present concerns and future problems that need to be solved in the same article I quoted earlier (1968). This brief passage could be considered a preamble to future planners of educationally handicapped programs. Dr. Thompson comments that:

Before proposing some suggestions for reconsideration of the EH program, it seems in keeping to mention that the special class of deviant children, self-contained and continuing, is steadily decreasing in state, national, and international use. The arguments against special classes are that combining "like" children (according to some established formula or category) tends to perpetuate and reinforce both the category (as an almost specific entity) and the behaviors it assumes to represent; that removing a child from his normal peer group emphasizes his differences in his own perceptions and requires some measure of "building back" in order to overcome the ego reduction; that the special class has no magic for improvement that is not susceptible of duplication in the regular class; that removing handicaps from general visibility increases rather than decreases intolerance of handicaps among normal children and additionally deprives them of opportunity to develop their own potentials for helpfulness and compassion toward misfortune; that fully half of teachers trained to work with disturbed chil-

dren leave the field of special education within a few years because of the rigors of the experience; and lastly the exorbitant expense. In order to accomplish our goal of adequate education for all children, we must carry on a two-pronged program; one for the very serious disablements where school performance is continually tenuous, and one for the huge group of apparently normal children who are not profiting optimally from the procedures of the regular classroom.

CONCLUSION

In light of these looks to the future, Goleta's program seems to be moving in the right direction in its development. In our multidisciplinary Child-Study Team we have the potential for generating broadly useful diagnostic data and the prescriptive hypotheses that give the special teacher a beginning point with the child. The team would be delighted to be released from the obligation of classifying children in single-category placement pigeonholes, but the members of the team will need to learn from each other and from other sources more about gathering prescriptively useful data. Even more important, they must learn to work closely with parent and teacher in translating diagnostic findings into meaningful educational experiences for the child.

At the same time, the special education teacher must take the next step up to a more fully professional effectiveness. He must learn to consider the members of the Child-Study Team as colleagues who are available to him *in* the classroom as well as outside. By involving in his classroom the psychologist, the nurse, the speech therapist, and others, he can keep them reminded that their diagnostic studies and prescriptive statements need to reflect the teaching style and idiosyncratic nature of this particular teacher in his class.

It is probably a mistake to focus these remarks concerning the future upon the improvement of the special education program and its auxiliary services as such. Much more important is a school district's attempts to upgrade its basic or regular program. A child defined as educationally handicapped in one classroom will not be so defined in another. The child who fails in one school or school district may succeed in another. In other words, diagnosis of learning difficulty should identify weakness or need in the school system at least as often as it identifies need in the child.

12

PATTERNS
OF
THE SOCIALLY MALADJUSTED
CHILD

Robert E. Barry

*Dr. Robert E. Barry has been director of pupil personnel
services for the Santa Barbara City Schools since 1957.
He has taught junior and senior high school classes
and has been a faculty member at many institutions in
the United States and Canada. He earned his bachelor's
degree at San Francisco State College, his master's
degree at the University of Southern California, and
the Ed.D. at Stanford.*

*As director of pupil personnel services, Dr. Barry is
responsible for the work of the counselors in the schools,
the school psychologists, the school social workers,
and the welfare aides. He is also responsible for group
testing and research programs, as well as for attendance
and the allied responsibilities of work permits and
continuation education. In other words, if socially
maladjusted students do not come to his attention
through one of his duties, they get to him on another
basis.*

For some years Dr. Barry has been listed in Who's Who
in the West *as a recognition of his contributions to
state and local professional and social service agencies.
In 1967 he was awarded the Distinguished Service
Award by the Council on Social Agencies, composed of
health, recreation, educational, legal, correctional,
welfare, and allied private and public organizations.*

I want to think through with you some of the background of the socially maladjusted child, to look at what the socially maladjusted youngster is, and to consider some of his peer relationships.

TABLE 12-1   BASIC NEEDS OF THE HUMAN PERSONALITY

Biological needs	Biosocial needs
Food and water	Security
Warmth and comfort	Emotional support
Air	Sense of achievement
Elimination	Contact with other humans
Shelter	Motivation
Balanced nutrition	Affection and attention
Light	Communication
Physical activity	Model
	Self-worth

In Table 12-1 are listed a number of basic needs of the human personality. I have divided this outline into the biological and biosocial needs. We think of the personality, if you can go back to the time of birth of a youngster, as having certain requirements that come into being with the arrival of a person on this earth. These we regard as biological needs.

BIOLOGICAL NEEDS

Food and water would certainly be two of the basic needs of a child in order to exist; not far behind would be the need for warmth and comfort in order to continue the existence that he has established. Think about other biological needs required by the young child. Oxygen could be one, although you might classify it along with air since it is part of the mixture that is air. Elimination has been emphasized in many of the TV and magazine ads. Without this help people might not be so aware of this particular need. Shelter could be considered part of the need for warmth and comfort, although shelter might be classified as a need in its own right. Balanced nutrition is necessary, at least to a degree, for survival. Light and physical activity could be added to the list. There definitely are biological needs that do exist.

BIOSOCIAL NEEDS

As a youngster gradually grows up, he gets involved in what we might call biosocial needs. For instance, there is the combination of his own biological needs—his own growth pattern—interacting with the impact of society upon him, thus creating needs as he gradually develops. I have listed here, for instance, the sense of security, the ability of the child to go back and find that his parents are still sustaining him when the outside world impinges upon him too much, the security of knowing that there is always someplace to which he can go. Robert Frost said that home is where they always have to take you in. This is a basic part of security—that there is always someone on whom you can rely. I don't know that we ever actually free ourselves from this particular need. Some people use the term *security* in a different sense, that of removing themselves from all social contact with humanity so that they are free within themselves. A person who is totally secure within himself, who needs no others, is very rare today. Most of us are dependent upon someone else. This dependence on others is brought home when you find there is a bread strike in Los Angeles and a hundred miles away people are alarmed because no one has ever learned how to bake a loaf of bread. This experience of dependence has been foreign to us. The fact that some incident is taking place in a remote area disturbs us because we rely unconsciously upon one another for services and have come to accept these services as part of normal existence. In our complex society, these biosocial needs impinge upon us much more than they did in the days when people did not rely on others to fill their needs. A farmer, for example, was self-sufficient. He raised his own crops, his own animals, and he could survive with little in the way of support from the community. It is pretty hard to be self-sufficient now.

The dependence on others is not limited to material well-being. Very frequently we lean on another individual to give us the emotional support that we require, including a sense of achievement.

The biosocial needs involve the idea of need for being in contact with other human beings. Is this a true need? There are hermits. There are individuals who walk away and hibernate. Perhaps they had family situations they found untenable, so they removed themselves from the contact with others. There is a story that goes back to World War II when infants in England were removed from their mothers and were taken where they would be safe from the bombing. This separation, in many cases, reduced the intelligence and, in some cases, brought on the death of the infant.

Even though the children were surrounded by human beings, they were not human beings of the close, intimate family, and as a result many infants pined away. The French children, too, suffered because of the bombings, but they were kept with the family because there was no safe place to send them. This contrasting treatment had a decidedly different effect upon the children. The French children survived the physical danger better than the English children survived the deprivation.

Another biosocial need is motivation. All of us need some sort of a goal. No matter how short the goal may seem to other people, most of us are looking for some reason for continuing to struggle, other than just to stay alive.

We also need affectionate attention. We have a need to provide for the well-being of others, which results in affection for ourselves. This need is most clearly evident in the satisfactions of raising a family, although sometimes the need is not satisfied.

Marriage usually is a culmination of experience in which two people find that they satisfy the need in the other to be wanted as people. This deep need explains many happy marriages where those on the outside say, "I don't see what she sees in him."

Everyone needs, at times, to be able to withdraw to a retreat. This need is not for a total lack of communication. Rather, it is a need to escape from the continual pressures of others who make demands. Executives suffer from unsatisfaction of this need if they do not take time to escape the pressures of their jobs. In a way, the need for withdrawal is a mirror image of the need to be wanted. It is possible to get too much of a good thing.

Children need someone after whom to pattern themselves. These models may be adults or peers. There are many choices that have to be made, and a model gives a reference point for making a decision. The number of possible choices is reduced, and the pressures are relieved. The models may be close at hand and include parents, teachers, older brothers, or they may be more remote and include movie stars or other prominent people. Bob Dylan and the Beatles have been models for many, many young people. Religious teachers are potent models for some of the young. Peers are also potent models, particularly among teen-agers who may be copying a remote model second hand. Two major elements seem to be present in the modeling: the first is reduced tension in decision making, and the second is a reflected being wanted. Imitation is a form of flattery that often brings acceptance.

The thing that probably drives most people close to the borderline of insanity is a feeling of being worthless. Most people most of the time feel they are worth something to someone else, but many people have periods of depression when they are sure the world would be better off without them. This feeling has very little to do with any reality. It is as likely to afflict a great achiever as it is an alcoholic who causes misery to most of those around him. On the other hand, the sense of achievement and of worth that comes from success in one's own eyes is very buoyant and enhances many of the other biosocial needs.

There are certain biological needs and certain biosocial needs, and the combination of these is very important to an individual. The model that is followed, the people with whom you live, the kind of warmth and food available to you, and the kinds of communication you receive all go together to make you what you are. There are an infinite number of possible combinations, because everyone comes out a wee bit different. The genetic influence even in twins is always tempered by a myriad number of environmental forces. It is not only the forces that act on people that are important but also how the individual sees these forces as acting. Some people seem to be natural optimists; they see the forces as benign. Others seem to be natural pessimists, seeing the forces as malevolent. One person can look at a glass and see it as half full and another can see the same glass as half empty. As we look at social maladjustment, we'll be looking at some of these forces and the way they are interpreted.

FAMILY INTERACTION

I am indebted to Virginia Satir, who works with family counseling, for Figure 12-1 and for some ideas about personality organization. You start as a self—whatever that self is—you have an individuality, you are a personality, you are unique. You are a boy or girl, and as you grow up you become either a "man" or a "woman," with one of these names as a title or a sign of maturity. These titles are supposed to be granted to you at a certain phase of existence. At some particular time in existence, if the pattern follows in the normal way, man and woman meet. That is the dashed line between the words at the top of the diagram (Figure 12-1). To know just what the circumstances of the meeting will be, you have to read *True Romance* or *Love Story* or some other magazine devoted to this topic. Anyway, there is a contact, the man and woman meet eyeball to eyeball, and all of a sudden, there is interaction. Then, after love, they go through a particular ceremony, which is called marriage. Out of the marriage they have a new title. They are now called husband and wife. They have gone through another progression, and another title has been given after they have achieved a changed state. In time these two are blessed by progeny, and at this time their son or daughter is given a name. Until birth the expected infant has been known as "it." The husband and wife have thought of various names, but on the arrival of this particular first child, "it" is called a son or daughter, and right away these two individuals, who have been man-woman, husband-wife, now have a new set of titles in recognition of their new status. They are now called father and mother. As time goes on, there is a second child to bless this union, and there is another set of titles—brother-sister—because there is relationship between the first child and the second child. The arrows in the diagram indicate the complications that the second child brings to the relationships of the first child.

In the beginning we had a simple relationship between the man and woman, although calling courtship simple is a matter of comparison. After courtship, the man and woman transfer to a complex relationship called marriage, and all of a sudden the most intimate relationship of their lives begins. They try to adjust to all of the complications of living with another individual. She hadn't realized that he threw his nightclothes under the bed each morning when he dressed, went off to work, and left the clothes there. People don't ask before the marriage contract, "Do you throw your clothes under the bed when you dress?" But it is something that you discover in a hurry after marriage. You also discover other things such as that he squeezes the tube of toothpaste in the middle. Of course, "he" may be "she" in any of these situations, but it is customary to assume that he does the undesirable things. All of the unexpected differences in lifestyle must be surmounted by both partners to the marriage. The relationships that seemed fairly complicated during the courtship, have become more involved.

When junior is added to the situation, junior being either a son or daughter, notice all the arrows that suddenly jump into the picture. We have husband and wife, with a straight arrow indicating an adjustment between them. Now wife has to adjust to the child, and husband has to adjust to the child. Don't think that this is easy or simple, because up to this time, husband has had a monopoly, he's had the sole attention of the wife. All of a sudden the wife has become a mother, and now her attention is distracted. There is an arrow going to husband, but now there is also an arrow going down to junior. As a consequence of the divided interest, many men have feelings of jealousy. The basis for the jealousy is the fact that he has to share the attention of the wife with the child. Strange as it may seem, he is jealous of this helpless little infant. He talks about *your* child, etc., as though spontaneous generation occurred. In the beginning junior has a relatively simple adjustment to mama and papa because he is helpless, but a relationship develops with the mother-father combination, shown by the arrow. This relationship becomes more and more complicated as the youngster gets older. He tries to emancipate himself from the husband-wife combination by joining teams and similar things. Tension arises as the emancipation drive causes the mother and father to see separation is imminent. They want to keep junior tight to this particular association, while junior, on the other hand, wants to go out into the world to find himself.

When you put brother and sister into the situation, not only does the wife's attention, which she has to share with father, go to the first child, but it goes to the second child as well, and her attention is split three ways. In turn, the father has to share in the same relationship, and of course junior and the second child have to arrive at a sense of interrelationship. This can be very severe competition unless junior number one has been prepared for the new arrival. In other words, if the first child has monopolized a mother and a father, and if all of the sudden a second child arrives on the scene, the first child is likely to be jealous because he must now share some of the parents' affections and attentions. This jealousy can cause a great deal of turmoil. Under these circumstances, you can understand how this organization can become very complicated. I'm trying to show you that the organization that sounds very, very simple in a family—husband and wife, the added child—can become extremely complicated as you add more children. Think of the complicated interrelationships, as an example, that the individuals had in the book *Cheaper by the Dozen*. They not only had arrows all over indicating relationships among the twelve children but also from mama and papa to the twelve. Even if there are only two children, little variations can occur, as shown in the small diagrams of Figure 12-1.

Emotional acceptance

Does mama accept the fact that she is about to have junior, or is this an unhappy surprise? Until now she has been the center of her husband's existence. They have gone out to shows, have gone dancing; it's like the courtship all over again. Then all of a sudden on the horizon looms the possibility that she is not going to have all of this gaiety. She is going to

Family organization

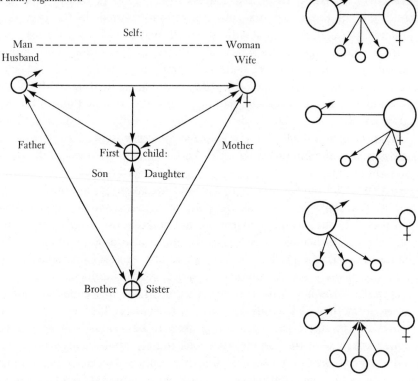

Variations

FIGURE 12-1 *Adjustments within early personality organization* (*After Virginia Satir.*)

have to stay home and take care of junior. It has already been pointed out that papa may be quite jealous and upset over the arrival of junior. After all, the living-room furniture is not paid for, and the car has only had two payments, etc. This can become quite difficult, depending on just how much is accepted and anticipated.

Patterns of authority

There are variations in family organizational patterns. These are shown in the small diagrams in Figure 12-1. In one, mama and papa are equal in size, indicating apparent equality in relative authority and status, with arrows pointing from the parents toward three juniors. This is a family that has not yet abdicated parental authority or given it to the juveniles.

The second pattern is that of the dominating matriarch. This is the family where mama is the big circle and papa is the little circle—Mr. Milquetoast—where papa takes very little leadership in the family. All the arrows come from mama. She is the boss, isn't she? We could even put an arrow over to papa to let him see who is boss. Have you ever seen a family like this?

The third example is the patriarchy, or the traditional family. Father is the predominant member of the family. Mother even asks father if she may leave the table, as do the kids. *Life with Father* depicted this kind of family; "Father Is Law," the story of the Dutch families in Pennsylvania, also showed this family pattern. It is the old German tradition. Father is everything and mother is nothing. Mother is a chattel, so to speak, and has no authority. The children are directed by and obey father.

The fourth example is the child-dominated family. The parents act like children too and are not able to give directions. It is difficult to tell which are parents and which are children. In Figure 12-1, the children are the bigger circles. This kind of family is seen more and more commonly these days. The parents have abdicated, they are run by the kids. Kids are making the decisions, and actually, the parents are looking to the children for leadership. The children also are looking to parents for leadership, but there is no leadership for them. The lack of leadership by the adults creates a real problem family. This is the kind of family where the youngsters run wild. Children can also easily get out of control in families where one parent dominates. They maneuver the nondominant parent in order to get their particular whims satisfied.

In some families, mama makes certain decisions, and then papa comes home, hasn't seen the kids all day, and immediately vetoes the decision. Mama says, "You can't go to the dance over the weekend," and papa says, "Oh, go on, let her go." He hasn't seen the situation that brought about the ruling that sister can't go to the dance this weekend, but he makes a reversing decision. This is split authority. It is most likely that this will cause problems in a family, because youngsters from babyhood, almost from the time they are born, sense whether or not they can maneuver adults. If you have had little children around you, it doesn't take them long to find out how they can get around you. They have their own particular little ways. They haven't studied psychology; they were born with it.

Expectations

The expectations held by mama and papa often set the stage for later problems to develop. For instance, papa wanted a son—after all this is a sign of masculinity. If he got a son, he could go down and tell all the rest of the fellows, "I had a boy," whereas if he gets a girl, his expectations are not satisfied, and he is disappointed. A sign of these disappointments is seen in names children are given—for example, combination names, where the name was obviously meant for a boy, but when the girl showed up, they stuck an *a* on it. My name happens to be Robert, but it could have been Roberta. Sometimes these disappointments persist to damage the self-image of the children. Some families pick names such as Robin, which can be for a boy or girl. The parents can't go very far wrong, but the child may suffer. The expectation can be for a girl rather than for a boy, as in a family, for instance, that has had three boys in a row, and they are just praying for a girl, when another boy comes along. They are thoroughly disappointed. This becomes a very damaging expectation. Almost as big a disaster is the situation in which the parents want a girl so badly that when she does arrive she gets much more than her share of attention. She can turn out to be a tyrant who demands her own way all of the time. One way to balance the family composition is by adoption, although in many cases adoptions are arranged before birth, so there is no more control of the sex than is true in the normal family situation.

Reward and punishment

The situation of the father who comes home and countermands the punishment imposed by the mother can be damaging, because the mother loses authority. This conflicting ruling may get more complicated with a grandma, a grandpa, or other relatives living in the home. Mama and papa may see eye to eye, but grandma says, "Oh, honey, here's a quarter; you can go down and get anything you want at the store." She knows the allowance has been cut off, but she sees a chance to buy status in the eyes of the youngster. It is not that grandparents are undesirable, but complicating reaction patterns do exist when groups of people live together. What may seem a simple thing in this matter of interaction between human beings can be extremely complicated.

Family rank

Family rank has a decided effect on the kind of pressures that are exerted on a child. William Altus, at the University of California, Santa Barbara, has studied the rank of youngsters and their relative intelligence, adjustment, and other psychological characteristics. The first child who arrives is usually the model, the second gets by with a little more, the third one a little more, and by the time number twelve arrives, he gets by with murder in comparison with number one. As a consequence of this factor, parents expect more of number one than they do of the children who follow because it is the first time they have gone through the routine. When number one comes along, parents try various things on him. Some of the things work, and some of them don't. On number two, parents try the things that worked and forget about those that didn't. On number three, parents have kind of forgotten what worked with number one and two; by and large, they are getting blasé. By the time they get number three, they sort of roll with the punches. In other words, they become imperturbable about some of the things, often just simple little things, that were earthshaking with number one. For instance, shall the girl wear lipstick to school? At what age were knee pants exchanged for long pants? In my day, we wore knee pants to school, and how I hated them! My whole goal was to get rid of those blankety-blank things and get long trousers—corduroys. Young male teachers today don't identify with these vivid memories, because they weren't raised in that era. Another source of strain for me was asafetida. Asafetida was a piece of material that smelled to high heaven. A hole was drilled through it, and it was worn around the neck. The idea was that you wore this around your neck under your shirt, and it kept you well. Why did it keep a person well? Nobody would come within fifteen feet of you if they got a smell of this stuff, so as a consequence of that you never got an infection. My main idea as an adolescent was to get rid of this asafetida and get long trousers.

Conflict areas

In Table 12-2 are listed a number of conflict areas, both within the family and between parts of the family and the wider society; an example is age difference. An age difference of fifteen or twenty years between marriage partners may not seem important at ages 30 and 50, but the difference between 50 and 70 is a great deal. It makes more and more difference as you get further up the scale. The age difference may make a decided difference in how the partners react to youngsters. Someone who is 60 may react quite differently than one who is 40. The 40-year-old may be quite amenable to certain things that go on, while the 60-year-old puts a damper on the same things. This difference in reaction can cause conflict between the

TABLE 12-2   CONFLICT AREAS WITHIN THE FAMILY AND BEYOND

Factors	Life situations	School-social demands
Age differences	Economic insecurities	Study
Sex	Class divisions	Home obligations
Race	Group criteria	Money
Associations	Vocational dissociation	Restrictions
Competitions	Handicaps	Scheduling
Ideals		
Education levels		
Experimental levels		
Religion		

parents and between child and parent. Even the normal spread in age between parent and child creates strain. The fact that the kid is just 15 and the parent is 45 means there is a difference of thirty years between them. Papa has forgotten just a little bit of what happened or how the world looked at age 15. Perhaps he, the devil, got away with things that his son wants to do at 15, but he has forgotten all about it by the time he has gotten older. This age difference can cause a lot of family conflicts. Basically this is the so-called hated generation gap. It is the cause of a great deal of strife. There is always going to be a generation gap, because there are always going to be age differences. The first time that the youngster and the mother or the father are the same age, we are going to have a peculiar world. When this begins to happen, spontaneous generation or something of this sort will have to be operating.

SEX FACTORS   The very fact that a boy is a boy and a girl is a girl can cause conflict. The father sides with the boy or with the girl, depending on what book he has read, and this may make a difference in the way he regards the other. Mother thinks that the girl should help with the housework and that the boy should help out in the yard. The girl likes gardening. She doesn't like doing dishes. That doesn't matter—tradition. You do the dishes and you learn to cook. So we have nasty names such as "tomboy." There are certain names for the boys, too, but we won't go into that.

ETHNIC MORES   There are race or ethnic mores that cause strains within families. Certain mores, or ideas of proper behavior, are held by members of particular ethnic groups, although these concepts of what is proper are being seriously challenged. The black people, especially the young black people, are demanding a different status. This group is not unique, and demands for new approaches have been voiced over the years. The second generation of immigrant families have nearly always demanded changes. The older generation often does not go along with these modifications of the old mores. The result is conflict between parents and children over and beyond the normal conflict between the generations.

PEER-GROUP ASSOCIATIONS   "I don't like your friends. Don't bring them to the house." That dictum is a red flag for youngsters. They meet the forbidden friends outside the home. The youngsters are then accused of going behind the backs of the parents. The youngster says, "You don't trust me," and the parent says, "No, I don't trust you. I don't like your friends. I don't want them around." Stresses of this kind are often counterproductive from the parent's point of view. Stubbornness can lead to continuing associations that would be dropped as unsuitable in a less tense atmosphere. The association with peers with antisocial habits can be a very damaging experience. A great deal of the current drug addiction is spread through peer associations, when one of the group starts to experiment with dangerous medicines.

COMPETITION   Some mothers try to compete with their daughters. This kind of competition seems incredible, but there is much more of it than would seem likely. Mothers compete with daughters for the same boy. The miniskirts were started by the young. They were copied by knobby-kneed women of middle age who wanted to be young again. Articles in the newspapers tell of situations where a daughter brings home a boyfriend and immediately the mother makes a play for him. She uses her wiles on him and establishes an unhealthy competition. Somewhat similar competitions may be set up between a boy and his father. The father is, perhaps, a skilled auto mechanic, and junior would like nothing more than to get his hands in the grease, get into the car, and imitate his father; but father pushes him away. He's afraid to have him working on the car, perhaps, for fear the young one might do too well. As another instance, the mother working in the kitchen pushes her daughter away: "I have to get dinner." "But, I want to watch you." "Oh, no, don't get in my way; you make me nervous." There are perversions of one of the best forms of learning. Shared work experiences are a golden opportunity, actually, for the mother and daughter or the father and son to have a good relationship. The relationship becomes disastrous when it becomes a matter of competition rather than cooperation.

EDUCATIONAL AND EXPERIENTIAL LEVELS   Educational difference between mama and papa, between the youngster and the parent, may cause strains. One difficult relationship is the situation in which junior goes on to get a college degree and neither mama or papa has finished high school. These strains are developing in some minority groups that traditionally have not valued education highly. The father's place and role can be threatened when his son changes his social status by means of a college education. Often the father's status within his peer group declines because his son is no longer subservient. In the Anglo culture, the father's status nearly always improves as a form of reflected glory from a son's achievement. This gain in prestige is not as likely in some minority cultures.

Family strains can also develop when the parents are college educated and sons or daughters do not wish, or are scholastically unable, to get a college degree. In spite of the best intention on the part of the parents, there is likely to be a subtle form of rejection that enters the parent-progeny relationship.

Young people today have many experiences that their parents did not have as they grew up. Many young people have gone to Europe, around the world, and to far away places that their parents have not seen. Peace Corps experiences, education-abroad programs, charter flights, and the youths' willingness to hitchhike in strange places have helped build knowledge that their parents do not have and cannot share.

RELIGIOUS AND STATUS CONFLICTS The young are religiously more mobile than were their parents. Changing away from the family religious beliefs can be a factor of difference or strain. This has a tendency to cause conflict whether there is too much or too little religious interest.

We have the ladder-climbing family, the ones who are trying to get into society and who are too busy with material gains to have time for the family. At the other end of the scale we have the poverty family that does not have enough for existence. These varying strains can be sources of difficulty. In one case, the material needs seem so important that the kids get pushed aside because their parents are trying to compete with the Joneses. In the other case, families don't have some of the things that youngsters need in order to hold their own in competition with their peers.

Most families, except those in the upper-upper class, more or less resent a classification that makes them less than "the best." The reaction is varied. One approach is to try to pull yourself up by your bootstraps from one level to another. Often the children suffer as a consequence. This desire for upward mobility is part of the problem faced by black families. They feel pushed into a class below what they have earned and resent the class distinction they feel is based on color; consequently, they feel discriminated against. They are trying to rise on the social scale, and this rising aspiration is creating a conflict within the family as well as in the ethnic groups.

DISSATISFACTION WITH ONE'S LOT Frequently a person may have vocational goals that he has set for himself but has not attained. The failure is damaging to the family relationship because it is damaging to the individual. For example, a fine watchmaker lives in town. He has done a good business, raised a fine family, and been a good member of the community, but he has always wanted to be a violinist. He is certain that he would have been a master violinist, but his father, who was a watchmaker, trained him to be a watchmaker. He practiced the violin on the side, but he was certain that if he had had enough lessons, he could have been a virtuoso. He has eaten his heart out over what might have been. He is doing a good job in his work and with his family, and he might have had a much richer life if he could have accepted this. Instead, he sees himself as a failure, largely through causes beyond his control. Not only does the rejection of his life make him an unhappy person, but he has created unhealthy and largely unnecessary strains on his family.

Physical handicaps often lead to effects similar to those shown in the example of the watchmaker. The short foot, eye trouble, or hearing difficulties are often seen as unfair afflictions. The limitations of the handicap are bad enough, but when they are compounded by a natural rebellion against fate, the suffering and the conflict in the family are likely to be increased.

DEMANDS AND DISCIPLINE   Study or homework requirements is a common cause of conflict. Readers of this book will have memories of questions. Did you do your chores? Have you taken the garbage out? Did you do the dishes? The chores were not so onerous, but there was a tension between family demands and school demands that made the student feel caught in the middle.

Money is a major source of conflict among members of the family. "I need money to buy a book," or "I need money for this or that." The result is that the parent feels pushed and harassed, and the young people feel demeaned to have to ask for the money.

Parents frequently say "No, you can't stay out till two o'clock in the morning. You have to be in by eleven like most of the kids." These restrictions are a source of conflict.

A similar and related argument evolves in the family when a parent points out that the youth is going out on Saturday, so he has to get his school assignments done. This is, therefore, the time to study; but it's also the time that Rowan and Martin are on TV. "No," says the parent, "this is the time for your study, so you must put the television program aside." When the young student hears all the chuckling going on in the other room and his family whooping and hollering, he feels discriminated against because he is supposed to be studying over and above it all. So there are many conflict areas.

SOCIAL MALADJUSTMENT

Let me review quickly. We have certain needs if we are to develop a healthy personality. Certain adjustments are made within our personality as we mature. Many activities facilitate or impair harmonious development within the family. From outside the family, biosocial pressures and certain affects have an impact on development. The growth situation is dynamic, with outside distractions, outside emotions that impinge upon us, and organic symptoms such as headaches, knee aches, toe aches, and pains of various sorts. We are discomforted because it's too warm, too cold, too moist. We stayed up too late, or they changed daylight-savings time at the wrong time for us, so we lost an hour's sleep. We have a fantasy, we are going to do great things if given a chance.

In the center of one's existence is work, which means work in a broad sense. It may be housework, the work of a student, work that one does with a machine, but it is something that occupies the center of your existence. Once you become occupied with your work, whatever it may be, the aches and pains are forgotten. Once you have gotten out of bed, washed your face, gotten your clothes on, the aches and pains that seemed overpowering at 5:30 or 6 in the morning are dissipated. Whatever monopolizes your time takes most of your concentration. In some cases, due to disease, exhaustion, criticism, failure, deprivation, obstruction, or conflict, the attention balance is overturned. Something happens to the proportion of attention we give different areas of our lives (Figure 12-2). Work may assume a very minor role and other preoccupations start to take over. These outside forces may take a disproportionate amount of your attention, so you have moved from a work-oriented life to a new situation with a new focus. In other words, some of these conflict areas have caused you to change your primary attention from a healthy emphasis centered on work, and you become socially maladjusted.

Social maladjustment has been defined as an inability to meet the demands of the social environment or to satisfy normal needs for companionship and social relations. In other words, instead of having normal relationships with people, you let pain, discomfort, fatigue, or other outside concerns distract you to the point where you snap at people. In one cartoon series, Rex Morgan had the future President of the United States

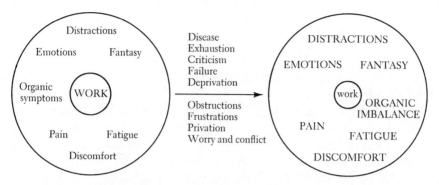

FIGURE 12-2 *Biosocial pressure and its effects*

kept out of office because he didn't go to see Rex Morgan who was the only M.D. in the United States able to prescribe something for him that would restore his balance. This sort of thing can happen. Distorted attention can cost a job, a marriage, a promotion, or it can cost happiness. This is social maladjustment. It used to be called various things. Most people try to the best of their ability, according to the theory, to resolve this conflict (Figure 12-3). In other words, a person should recognize that certain things can cause him to get out of kilter and lose the normal balance of life. All of us have tensions, guilt feelings, or a number of other difficulties, but usually we do not let them get out of hand.

Reactions to distorting pressures

There are three possible ways in which you may adjust to distorted attention. One is adjustment, one is partial adjustment and another is maladjustment. Maladjustment is the least satisfactory approach. Most of the people in the state hospitals for the mentally ill are suffering from maladjustment. In maladjustment there is no resolution of difficulties. The person actually goes to the point where the personality that he started with is completely shattered and he has become another individual; or he is in a position where it is going to take a tremendous amount of therapy to get him back to an acceptance of himself as an individual. Psychoses and neuroses bedevil him. Mental illness occurs as a result of this displacement of attention, when it becomes a shattering experience. Fortunately, only a

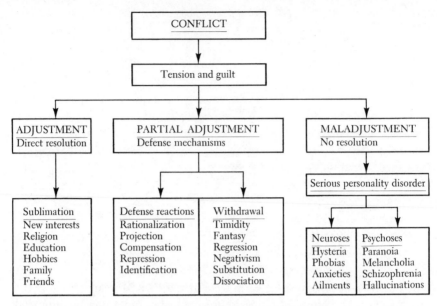

```
                    ┌──────────────────────┐
                    │       CONFLICT        │
                    └──────────────────────┘
                                │
                                ▼
                    ┌──────────────────────┐
                    │   Tension and guilt   │
                    └──────────────────────┘
```

┌─────────────────┐   ┌─────────────────────┐   ┌──────────────────────┐
│ ADJUSTMENT   │   │ PARTIAL ADJUSTMENT │   │ MALADJUSTMENT   │
│ Direct resolution│ │ Defense mechanisms │   │ No resolution   │
└─────────────────┘   └─────────────────────┘   └──────────────────────┘

Sublimation	Defense reactions	Withdrawal	Serious personality disorder
New interests	Rationalization	Timidity	
Religion	Projection	Fantasy	Neuroses	Psychoses
Education	Compensation	Regression	Hysteria	Paranoia
Hobbies	Repression	Negativism	Phobias	Melancholia
Family	Identification	Substitution	Anxieties	Schizophrenia
Friends		Dissociation	Ailments	Hallucinations

FIGURE 12-3   *Patterns of conflict resolution*

relatively small percentage of people go in this direction. Most either make a direct resolution of problems or settle for a partial adjustment (Figure 12-3); and frankly, most settle for a partial adjustment.

DIRECT RESOLUTION   In a direct resolution of the problem, for instance, if a person is thwarted by a particular difficulty, he may develop a new interest. He may possibly turn to religion, seek education, develop a hobby. He may turn to family or develop friends. Let us look at these possibilities quickly. Let's take the violinist. He is interested in the violin. In fancy, he pictures himself as a virtuoso and playing before thousands of people. In order to forestall worrying himself sick over the fact that he might have been a virtuoso and commanded thousands of dollars for a performance, he seeks new interests. This might be watchmaking, a blonde, a religion, or a hobby club. It might be any number of things that he could do to distract himself. This is a type of adjustment. In other words, if a person can't solve the particular problem, he can turn to something else and sublimate this unresolved problem. In *sublimation*, a person puts the problem to one side and concentrates on another facet of life. If this unfulfilled desire keeps bubbling to the surface, the person is still going to be faced with a conflict between wish and reality, but if the new interest is strong enough—if the religious conviction is strong enough, if the hobby is engrossing enough, if your new friends are distracting enough—this conflict will soon fade into the background and will no longer be a consuming passion. This approach is called direct resolution. It is more feasible for some people than for others and for resolving some difficulties than for resolving others.

PARTIAL ADJUSTMENT A person who is in high school may be extremely overweight. She has failed to lose weight, and so she throws herself into her studies and gets all A's; but in doing so, she has lost out in the social areas and has become maladjusted sexually. This would be partial adjustment. *Defense mechanisms* are ways of protecting one from disasters. *Rationalization* is the old fox and the grapes; the fox jumps for the grapes and can't reach them so he says, "They are sour, and I didn't want them anyway." No readers of this book use that particular excuse! *Projection* is illustrated when you get up to bat and you swing three times violently and in none of the swings does the bat make contact with the ball. The cause is projected by the player from himself to outside causes: The pitcher must be using an unfit ball or he's using a spitball or the bat had a hole in it; something of this sort is the cause of the batting failure. Some people try this type of adjustment when the officer stops them and pulls them over to the side, and they say, "But, officer, all of the cars are speeding," and the officer says, "But, I want you." The speeder knows he has no answer, but he tries to distract the officer and to project the cause of the speeding onto somebody else. *Compensation* is the kind of partial adjustment used by the stout girl who can't get friends but who makes up for it by becoming a good student. In other words, she is able to achieve in another area. Some boys want to become athletes, but they can't, so they become students. This adjustment is not necessarily bad. It is simply the person's recognition of the fact that he can't get something, so he makes a partial adjustment. Most people don't make a total adjustment, but thank heavens, most people don't sink into a maladjustment. Most of us are still walking around outside the barriers of the state hospital.

Repression means to put something down underneath. This is an adjustment mechanism that is often used. The fact is that everyone represses many things. Everyone has problems that keep bubbling up to the surface and distracting them, so they push them below the surface of consciousness.

Identification means that a person identifies with somebody else. For instance, the bat boy on the baseball team visualizes himself as being Frank Merriwell. Frank was the one who had the up and down curve. He always came in at the ninth inning, out of breath, and substituted for the last batter. When he came into the batter's box he knocked the ball over the fence. This is the sort of fantasy that James Thurber had in mind when he wrote about Walter Mitty, the great surgeon, the great physician, emancipator, the great everything. This was identification. This is a type of fantasy. People have some of these fantasies where they make a partial adjustment.

Everyone has needs in the personality. Satisfaction of these needs are blocked in various ways, sometimes from within the families, sometimes from the outside. In trying to adjust to these particular pressures upon themselves, certain adjustments are made by everyone. Everyone has had some of these defense mechanisms and used them at various times. At certain times, many of us have gotten a splitting headache on the day of a dental appointment: "But, I will phone you again one of these days when it is hurting again, but in the meantime it has stopped, so I won't come in." Have you ever done that? That is a defense mechanism. I am sure that none of us has used any of these particular devices, such as saying, "Gee, it wasn't my fault. Look what he did." These are devices that we have all used at one time or another.

MALADJUSTMENT The earlier it is possible to identify some of the adjustment problems that youngsters have, the more quickly the children can be helped with these problems by recognition, remediation, and referral. First, it is necessary to identify the youngsters who are having adjustment problems (actually, it is the rare youngster who doesn't have some adjustment problems). Next, measures should be taken for remediation: What to do about it? Sometimes it is very simple. The teacher sees the youngster who has difficulties; he always wants to be the center of attention in the class. Down in the preschool, the little primary kids hold onto the teacher's skirt. They want attention. Frequently, by giving them something to do, it is possible to satisfy their particular need for having attention. This is the wonder of the monitor system—selecting a monitor to clean the goldfish bowl, to clean the chalkboards, to do this, that, or the other thing. Otherwise the poor teacher would be driven frantic trying to take care of all of these kids who want her sole attention.

This is a very simple level of remediation. Problems are not all solved that simply. Sometimes the youngster is so thoroughly rejected that making him monitor has little or no effect on him. He wants absolute attention and does all in his power to get it. At this point, referral may become necessary, because it may be necessary to have outside concentrated attention to assist this particular child or to help a family try to reconcile the damaging situation. Take the instance of the father who was vetoing what the mother had in the way of control. This situation was much more than can be handled in a normal school classroom. The older girl was beginning to show absolute rejection of the mother because she was the source of all the discipline. Father had become the center of all the good things; mother had become the center of all the bad things. As a consequence, there was rejection of the mother; there was defiance. Under these circumstances, the counselor recognizes that remediation is much more complicated than it would be with the child who wants attention. It is necessary, to get this family pattern back into some sort of balance, to refer to some place where concentrated help can be given to father, so that he can see what he is doing to the family; to mother, to help her become reinstated in a position of at least some approval; and to the youngsters, to help them see the picture of the mother and father. Frequently it is necessary to use outside sources.

Many of the kids who are maladjusted are what are called *socio-paths* (Table 12-3). People used to use the term *psychopath*, but this term was a little bit confusing. Sociopaths are simply those who have a disorder in their relation to society, and as such, they have an inability to adjust to the social environment in order to satisfy their normal needs. Common characteristics of sociopaths are inadequacies. They can't do the sorts of things that normally they would be able to do. Teachers have heard over and over again about youngsters who fit these descriptions: "He has good ability, but he is not working." "He is an intelligent youngster, but he is not able to make friends," etc. There is an inadequacy, and frequently there is a misdirection. The youngster, instead of going off in a direction that might be anticipated and that would lead to a constructive, positive solution, goes off onto a slant where there can only be disaster or unhappiness. This particular maldirected adjustment showed up in the hippie movement. Rather than functioning in a way that allows for the possibility of positive, constructive achievement, some of these youngsters have gone off in a direction where they are not accomplishing anything. They are not making any contributions. Their particular aspect is negative. From that viewpoint, this is misdirection. They are identified as sociopaths. In other words, they are having difficulty in adjusting to society. I think that all you have to do is pick up a paper or a magazine to find instances of sociopaths.

Ineffectualness means that the person may want to do certain things, but he is unable to do them. He doesn't accomplish things that he sets out to do. This is the person who starts two dozen tasks and never finishes any of them. This is the person who has an investment in any number of

TABLE 12-3 CLASSIFICATION OF THE MALADJUSTED AS SOCIOPATHS

Definitions
Those who have a disorder in their relationship to society and to the cultural milieu Inability to meet demands of the social environment or to satisfy normal needs for companionship and social relations

Characteristics	Broad categories
Inadequacy	Sexual deviates
Misdirection	Antisocial, overt action, open revolt in view of reachable goals
Ineffectualness	Dissocial, subtle (Figure 12-3, "Partial Adjustment")
Unpredictability	
Irresponsibility	

things, but he actually never cashes in on any of these things. He is ineffectual. He doesn't get the things done that he feels he wants to do. *Unpredictability* and *irresponsibility* are characteristics of such sociopaths, of people who are at variance with society and with themselves. Sociopaths as a group could be divided into three types. We are not going to go into detail about the first, the *sexual deviate.* This is a sociopath who is at odds with society and with all the variations of society that are possible. Too many volumes have been written on sexual deviations to warrant further elaboration.

The second type, the *antisocial,* are in open revolt. Usually they can see the goals, but they don't want them, or they don't want to expend the effort necessary to reach them, so you have an antisocial type of action. These are the youngsters that teachers will see. They are the youngsters who throw things, the youngsters who slug somebody. They are the ones who write on the walls, etc. They are the antisocial.

The third type, the *dissocial,* may be as much in need of help as are the antisocial, but they are very subtle. They remove themselves. They will not associate with others. They live in fantasy. They have an extremely difficult time accepting anyone's assistance. These are the youngsters who are largely overlooked in the schools. Teachers can't miss the antisocial. They are right in front of them, and if they miss them, the antisocial will hit teachers in the nose to be certain that the school is aware of the fact that they are there. The dissocial one, who is the quiet one, removes himself. He may actually steal and do things of this sort in order to gratify his particular needs. I don't think of this as being antisocial. I think of this as being an indicator of problems.

People want a cookbook about how to deal with problems. Dr. Spock attempted to do this for parents raising children. For numerous reasons, I

TABLE 12-4 A GUIDE FOR IDENTIFICATION OF SERIOUS MALADJUSTMENT
AND FOR AVAILABLE RESOURCES

General symptoms	Identification	Extra-school help
Chronic misbehavior	Teacher	Psychologist
Deliberate, willful acts	Parent	Psychiatrist
Rejection by peers	Peers	Mental health clinic
Disregard for consequences	Family physician	Family counseling
Worsening cyclical actions	Supportive personnel	Family service
		Catholic Social Services
		State or county child welfare services
		Legal resources
		Probation departments
		Holding facilities
		Hospitals
		Observation
		Extra-parental placement

don't intend to be Dr. Spock, but over and over again the question is raised: "How do you know when this problem is serious?" I am tempted to set down just a few things to give us a guide (Table 12-4).

Significant behaviors

Many youngsters develop chronic misbehavior patterns. At first the child is tardy. He then starts to cut classes. While cutting classes, he starts to lift things from the dime store downtown—little things. Next, he advances to records from the local record shop. After records, he graduates into company with youngsters who are in difficulty, and then he goes "whole hog" and takes someone's automobile. At this point, he is up for grand theft, auto. This is a series, and I have telescoped it because it usually takes a fair amount of time. These boys or girls are gradually getting worse, and it becomes chronic. There seems to be no end. There is no short-circuiting of this behavior. At some point, it is apparent that the symptom is not only going to lead to a maladjusted youngster, it is going to lead possibly to law violations, to the recognition that this kid is going to be in reasonably serious trouble.

In spite of the fact that a teacher or counselor sits down with the youngster, counsels him, talks to his parents, keeps him after school, tries to be a buddy with him, right in front of you while you are watching he deliberately does things over and over again that will get him into trouble. This is simple out-and-out defiance. He is challenging you. It is an attempt to make you respond to him in some way. These *deliberate, willful acts* are among the first steps toward serious problems, I have noticed.

Rejection by the peers is probably one of the most apparent things that the teacher can observe. The other kids don't like what the misbehaving kid is doing. They try to correct him. They try to intercede and keep him from doing things that will cause trouble, and he couldn't care less. This is one of the most obvious symptoms. When a person's own peer group rejects him, this is cause for concern, and when the kids get down on a student, the problem is really serious.

Another sign that a youngster may be headed for trouble is an apparent *disregard for the consequences* of his acts. As a teacher or counselor, you try to spell out what might happen, and the youngster almost flies in the face of this warning and challenges you to prove it. To prove the point, you go through all the sequences, trying to help him to see all the consequences that might result from violations of the law—the effect on him and his future record, as well as the effect on his parents. You pull out all the stops on a description of the dangers, and the kid couldn't care less. He goes right ahead and does things that will get him into trouble. This is a disregard for consequences.

I have already mentioned the *worsening cyclical actions*. It is sort of like dropping a stone in a pool, with the circles getting bigger. The stone is the first difficulty, and as it gradually widens, it starts to make more and more circles. If you have ever watched these circles go out, you have noted how there are involvements with other circles, and pretty soon the situation is quite complex. Thus, in the beginning a kid might do very minor things, but gradually the depredations become bigger and more chronic, and a pattern begins to emerge. However, even with the help of a child-rearing cookbook, I don't believe you can neatly categorize these patterns.

W. C. Karvaceus (1959) of Boston University has a checklist that he suggests you can use. You go down a column, and if the kid is so many years behind the other youngsters in reading, check it. If there are so many years difference between his parents' ages, you check that. If he is the third sibling, you check that. You add up all these points, and if the total is so many, the youngster is a potential delinquent.

I think this is oversimplifying the diagnosis. I think this is useful as a guide, but many of the kids who have high scores on a checklist like this will grow up and won't have any problems, and yet another kid, with almost precisely the same sort of pattern, will grow up and end up in San Quentin, Folsom, or some other prison. Exactly how you distinguish between the two is still unknown. We have no method of diagnosis that enables us to distinguish precisely between the youngster who is going to go completely off the beam and the youngster who is going to have the same kind of headaches that many of us have had in growing up, but who is able to keep his balance and survive. However, one of the significant factors that we can't avoid is the fact that we can go down to the lower grades and identify patterns that have been in existence for older members of the family, and we can note that the environment has been such that youngsters in the family over the years have, one by one, toppled over the edge. You have to be a betting person to pick out some little darling in kindergarten or first grade and say that his chances of winding up as a juvenile delinquent are about 70 percent. This is tragic. In spite of a high probability of delinquency eventuating if the child is left in the home, the authorities do not know what to do about it. You just can't take children away from their families. In Russia you can. You can't here.

Identification of the deviant child

Who identifies the child who may be socially maladjusted? The teacher should be at the top of the list. Frequently the teacher will see something in the classroom that could be a warning. The parent is so close to the child that when the teacher tries to explain to the parent about his concerns, the parent says, "But we don't see that at home." The parent doesn't see it at home because the associations involve only two, three, or maybe a dozen people in the family; the child doesn't have the pressures of thirty or thirty-five kids in a classroom, where he has to make an adjustment to the whole bunch of youngsters of the same age. These stress situations bring out the interrelationships you didn't see at home. So the teacher is frequently one of the first to see some of these signs. An alert teacher can observe some of these symptoms and refer the matter on to someone else, if he is not in a position to solve the problem himself.

Usually, the parent is the second to notice that the child has problems, although peers will identify this deviant child very early. "I don't want to play with Johnny. He's not nice." You hear kids saying this sort of thing. Family physicians sometimes are helpful, but supportive persons will be the last to identify deviant behavior.

Services

All of the readers of this book distinguish between a *psychologist* and a *psychiatrist*. Most older people don't. The psychiatrist is a doctor of medicine, while a psychologist usually has an M.A. or Ph.D. in psychology, designed to enable him to understand people and their problems. The psychiatrist, in addition to the training that he has had as a psychologist, has had extra training as a doctor of medicine and is able to prescribe medicine. Some of the rare ones have both an M.D. and a Ph.D. These terms are frequently used interchangeably by people who do not know the difference.

A *mental health clinic* is a resource designed to give psychological and psychiatric assistance to one or more members of a family. The family that goes in may need outside help for group counseling, individualized counseling, or assistance with members of the family. More and more it is becoming apparent that it is not only the individual that should be treated, it is the whole family constellation. An individual usually cannot be separated from a family pattern. With a youngster who is having temper tantrums and rolls on the floor and becomes blue in the face, it is necessary to know what the family situation is, because chances are this pattern of behavior didn't just originate with the child. There are usually situations that have led up to this behavior.

For family counseling and other family assistance, there are family service agencies, Catholic welfare bureaus, child welfare services, and county welfare agencies, among other resources.

Family service agencies, organizations made up of social workers, are available locally and nationally. These are people who do everything to assist families, from helping with the family budget to helping children understand their lessons or determining what to do with a drinking parent, etc.

Catholic Social Services is an agency that is supposedly designed for Catholics. I don't know how it operates nationally, but locally it doesn't matter whether you are Catholic or not. The workers will take you in and help you because you are in need, rather than because you are or are not Catholic. This is one of the wonderful things about our local agency as a referral source.

Child welfare services provide casework service. The social workers will go out and help any family, whether they are receiving public assistance or not. In California, child welfare services were set up by the state legislature with the idea that families frequently need help. For instance, many anonymous calls come to the school office to say a particular child is being beaten. "Won't you come down and investigate?" Or a child is wandering around on the streets, "Won't you please come down and investigate?" And you say, "What is your name so I can get the details?" "Oh,

I don't want to get involved in this. You just come down and you'll see. You'll hear the child being beaten," etc. So you go, and you try your level best to find out in which apartment you will find the child. Anonymity is one of the great American vices. People don't want to get involved. People in my position will get these anonymous calls from individuals who are very much concerned about the welfare of these children, but they don't want to be dragged into the fray.

The child welfare service was set up with the idea that they would go into a home to investigate the possible neglect or mistreatment of children or to investigate a case where someone should act on behalf of the children. Unfortunately, the law is pretty strict in regard to the fact that you have to have absolute proof that the child is being mistreated, but mistreatment does happen. In the local paper now is a story about a parent who is being tried because of the death of his child. You have probably read such an article in a metropolitan paper in the last six months. Of course, the authorities must have had absolute proof, because there must be evidence that children have been manhandled in the family. In one local case, the family claimed that they were bathing the child and the child slipped out of their hands, but the head was partially bashed in and the brain damaged to the point that the child would never be normal again. The police were unable to take any action because there was no proof of the fact that this youngster was actually beaten and abused. There is a state law now, belatedly, resulting from the fact that many of these children have been beaten into insensibility for relatively minor things, very simple things.

One child came to school with both eyes blacked. After talking with her, the teacher was quite concerned and talked to the principal. The principal called me. I sent the doctor over to examine the child. He found, in addition to the blackened eyes, bruises all over the back of this girl. It turned out that the father wanted to teach the child to tell time. When did daddy come home? Daddy came home, of all things, at a quarter to five. Imagine teaching a kid of first-grade age "a quarter to five." I mean five o'clock is difficult, or six or eight. At what age do they start telling time? About second grade. A quarter to five is a very difficult concept. If he came home at four o'clock, or at five o'clock, maybe the child should be expected to learn that, but a quarter to five is a difficult time, and the big ox had beaten the kid. Well, the physician called the police, the police came, and the child was put in juvenile hall for custody. Thank God we can do that sort of thing. One of the police officers and the physician then visited father at his place of work to give him more than

Dr. Spock would give him in his book. You wouldn't believe this sort of thing could happen. This happened in Santa Barbara, California, in one of our very high socioeconomic areas. This is the same man and woman who had a courtship, went through the marriage ceremony with stars in their eyes, came floating down the aisle—then it turns out that he beats the tar out of the wife and kids and all the rest of the family. There is a strange metamorphosis in parents that kids suffer through, and it is very difficult for an outsider to find out what is happening. Frequently we see a youngster who has all sorts of the screaming meemies, and when we talk to the mother and father—they are two of the most charming individuals—they can't understand the child's problems.

I have had hundreds of cases, but I will give you this illustration. This kid was cutting school. He had been doing quite well. He was a teen-ager in high school, and he was starting to get failing grades, was having all sorts of difficulties. The family was perfectly charming. The mother and father came in. The father had a good steady job as an auto mechanic, and the mother was a teacher, so they had an above-average home in the suburban area, and the family could give no reason for this youngster acting this way. He was insubordinate, he was talking back to staff at school. This seemed to have come on all of a sudden.

We finally got them to go to a family service agency—for the boy's problem, of course, not their own. This happened in the spring of the year, and by the time the youngster came back in the fall (we gave him another chance in school), there was a complete change. The school picked a certain student each month and put his picture in the hallway. This was the student of the month. The year after the treatments, the boy achieved this award, and he graduated—not outstandingly, but he graduated.

The boy's brother had graduated from California Institute of Technology and had a scholarship there; he was a brilliant boy. We thought this was the clue, but it wasn't at all. The problem was that father would go out and get drunk every once in a while because of the educational gap between him and his wife. He had gone only so far through school, and his salary as an auto mechanic was erratic; but here was mother bringing home a larger salary, steadily, because she had gone through college. There were certain times when his income was down, and hers was still up. She had a uniform plateau of a good salary coming in consistently, whereas his went up and down. He was kind of second place in this family, with this education gap and the erratic income. He would go out and hit the bottle, and he did this so often that his driver's license was finally taken away.

Buddy Boy knew all about what was going on. The other boy was away at college; he had made an adjustment to this strife and had gone away. Buddy Boy, however, couldn't adjust to this difficulty because he wanted like mad to get a driver's license. His parents wouldn't let him have a driver's license. Father, whose license had been taken away for drunk driving on two or three occasions, was stealing out at night, when people supposedly didn't know he was doing it, and driving the car all around. Buddy Boy knew this was going on. They were living this life of sham—on the outside they were a very resolute family. They were doing all the things that society was expecting of them, yet underneath was all this turmoil.

I didn't learn about some facts of this situation until a long time later. One day the mother saw me in a conference and said, "Do you remember so and so?" I never bring up these situations out of the past, because usually the parents don't want to be reminded. I said, "Yes, now that you remind me of it, I do, and I was wondering if you would speak to me," and she said, "I want you to know he is now a fisherman. He has his own boat, and he is married and has two kids. Everything is wonderful." The boy had gone on to junior college, but he didn't want to go on to become an engineer like his older brother. He was making good money, the mother said, and everything was settled down. I said, "And how's home?" She knew what I meant without my saying anything further, and she said, "That's all settled, too."

Well, this is one of the success stories, but for every five successes, there are ten with which you don't succeed, and you never get to the root of it. My point here is that the parents in this case were somewhat honest. They at least said they could use some assistance, even though they presented the outward face that "We don't know what this problem is all about." They honestly might not have known what the problem was all about, but at least they faced up to the fact that there was a need. Too often in our school situation we will have problems, and the parents will refuse to face up to it. "I don't know why you should be having problems with our child. We don't have any problems at home," and this sort of thing can stop therapy right at the start.

Facilities

Under certain circumstances there are facilities and procedures that can be used to help the child who is having problems. These include such things as juvenile-hall, private-school, or extra-parental placement, as well as observation or hospitalization. California's juvenile-hall facilities used to be free, but we found that the kids went out and rang the doorbell and said, "My parents just beat me, and I want to stay overnight," or something like that. It turned out that they were staying out until 2 A.M., and they were afraid of what the parent was going to do. They were due back at 11 and it was now 1:30 or 2 in the morning, so they thought, "I'll go to juvenile hall, and my parents will be sorry that I am in custody." These kids were taken in, but after a while the authorities found out that it was a cost to the taxpayers, so now, if the parents can pay, the cost is prorated at about $10 per day. The same thing is true of the forestry camp and the girl's home. The California Youth Authority, to a certain extent, charges according to the ability to pay.

Our local *girls' home*, La Morada, is a minimum-security facility for court wards. There are no bars on the windows. There is no attempt to hold the youngsters there. To be accepted, girls must be of school age, but there are some types who are not admitted. Girls who have made overt suicide attempts are not admitted, and promiscuity cases are not very hopeful, but you could name on one hand the reasons why girls won't be taken in; consequently, the home gets practically everything. There are runaways, children who are out of control of parents, cases of school misbehavior, narcotics users, and many others.

La Morada is as close to a home as can be set up. Fifteen girls is a maximum load. They live in, do their own cleaning, cooking, and bed making. It's that sort of plan. Primarily, the quarters are designed with the idea that many of these youngsters have not had a normal home situation, and it is an attempt to give them a normal home life. In such circumstances, there are always going to be kids who, when they first come, will not adjust. In theory, they come because they want to come. Of course in the back of their minds there is always ambivalence, because they could be home or elsewhere—wishful thinking—and sometimes they run away.

A girl may be classed as a runaway, depending on how this is defined. She may be called a runaway from the girls' home because she goes to the root-beer stand a block and a half away and is not available for roll call. She may be in the nearby cemetery, which is a favorite place for the girls to meet boyfriends. I hadn't thought of this as being such a cozy place, but it seems to be one of their favorite places. Girls are classed as runaways if they are not available at lockup time.

A middle-aged woman is usually the head of the girls'-home facility. At one time it was felt there should be a man and a woman as joint heads of the operation. Some authorities wanted a father figure in there, but these girls had had enough father figures, and they didn't need more of the same. A twenty-four-hour staff provides supervision, and psychological counseling is a standard procedure. The girls attend neighboring public schools.

Some of the girls naturally will run away, and they may be picked up in Texas or some such place, but these are the extremes. By and large, the runaways are short-term runaways, girls reacting to either a real or an imagined grievance.

The home has a merit system in which the girls can earn a certain number of points, which helps them to get out a little bit early; and for particular offenses they are docked a certain number of points, which may become a grievance. Even though the girls developed the rules themselves, the designated girl may, for example, refuse to cook for tonight, so consequently she is docked two points. This is a grievance, and the girl takes off somewhere that evening to punish somebody in the house for this alleged wrong that is done to her. The girls' home is no security prison. The girls can walk out the front door. Success is measured by a willingness to conform to peer suggestions, to accept adult help, to earn commendations. La Morada has had remarkably good results as a unique service to girls.

Forestry camps for boys are also minimum-security facilities. There are runaways because there are no fences around the place, no bars on the doors; but of course, if the kids want to run they usually have a long way to go, because the camps are located up in the mountains. In a sense, though, youngsters can leave because, basically, the whole philosophy of this program is rehabilitation rather than punishment. There will always be runaways from these centers. By and large, there are more successes than failures.

First of all, both boys and girls are placed by the courts; they both must be in violation of a juvenile court law. The boys in Santa Barbara and Ventura Counties (California) are more-or-less isolated in the Santa Ynez Mountains. The Los Prietos Boys' Camp holds around one hundred boys. This facility is shared by the two counties, who divide the expenses on a prorated basis. The parents pay as they are able to. By and large, the girls' homes have a more sheltered atmosphere in comparison to the forestry camps for boys. The boys, for instance, are used frequently for fire fighting and are paid, incidentally, by the U.S. Forest Service. These are volunteers. The boys also work outdoors around the camp, and there is a lot of construction being done and things of this sort. The girls cook, sew, clean house, clean windows, and so on, but it is a relatively sheltered sort of atmosphere.

In response to a question as to the similarity of the problems that get boys and girls into these places, it should be said that in some cases the female of the species is more deadly than the male. Some of the situations that the girls come in on are real humdingers. Of course, some of the boys do something equally as bad, so you might say that the offenses are fairly equal.

As far as living conditions are concerned, the boys sleep in dorms, whereas the girls have bedrooms. The senior girls have their own room, while the junior girls share a double bedroom. There is a certain amount of distinction between the sexes when it comes to things like bedrooms and showers.

Juvenile hall is a temporary holding institution. It was never designed for long-term holding, as were the girls' homes or the forestry camps. Usually, in the forestry camp and the girls' home, young people are held from nine months to a year, but at the juvenile hall, the average stay probably is somewhat less than two weeks. There are two distinct divisions in juvenile hall. One is for the neglected youngster who is not at fault. His problem is the fault of an adult, and the child has been neglected, has been deserted, or has been abused. These are called *dependents*. The other division is for the predelinquent and delinquent young people. The dependent and the delinquent are kept separately. They live separately, they eat separately, they sleep separately. There is a barred door between the two. The youngsters who are in the dependent unit may stay in juvenile hall for a considerable period of time. The youngsters who are classified as delinquents are disposed of as soon as possible. They are supposed to come to court not more than forty-eight hours after they have been detained. At that time the officers have to show that there is a petition on file and that there is legal evidence that justifies holding the youngster, otherwise he is released automatically. This presentation of the reason for retaining the young person is made before a referee or a judge. The exceptional youngster in trouble stays for a longer time, but by and large, they are let out very quickly. Some people in the school business think they are let out too quickly. Sometimes a youngster will be in trouble in the community, and before we are able to file our school report to verify the fact that we are having our hands full and would just as soon have a vacation for awhile, he is back knocking at our door. Often it would be more convenient if we could have him stay in juvenile hall for a few days. Sometimes this detention is good rehabilitation.

The youngster in the dependent unit may be there for any number of things. Here is a mother who has been found forging checks. She goes to jail. What do you do with the three kids when there is no father in the home? They go into juvenile hall for protective custody. Someone reports two crying babies in a car downtown. The windows are rolled almost to the top, and it is a very hot day. A policeman looks inside. There is moisture on the inside of the windows, so it is necessary to have someone break the window to get inside. Those kids are taken into custody, and you have a frantic mother coming after them. "Well, I was just in the store for a few minutes. I was just about to come out." "I guess the time slipped up on me," etc. The strangest thing is that parents will leave kids and go off for two days down to Tijuana, Mexico, or down to Palm Springs, and old Buddy Boy, age 12, is supposed to take care of the two younger kids, and something may happen. For instance, there may be a fire. Well, the fire department moves in, and there is no adult around, so the children are placed in protective custody. In another case, a baby may be abandoned on a doorstep. The people at juvenile hall thus take care of children from practically newborn infants up to adolescents. These kids may stay in juvenile hall for a considerable period of time before a home for them is found.

Another facility for taking care of children with problems is the *foster home*, but there is a desperate need in this country for these homes. There is an outfit called JEFF Joint Effort for Foster Families), which is organized to try to find people who will take children into the home on a boarding and rooming basis. Unfortunately the pay is not very large. The pay runs somewhere between $75 and $95 per month, and many people don't want to go to the trouble of taking care of youngsters for this kind of income. The most difficult age to place, of course, is the teen-ager. Who wants the teen-ager? He brings with him problems of using the telephone and wanting to go out at night and dating, and all sorts of complications. There are few, if any, homes for teen-agers who are in difficulty, not because of what they did, but because of what an adult did—neglecting them, deserting them, or otherwise abusing them. Finding foster homes for these children is a real problem.

Another problem is finding schools for these kids, because these are few and far between. The school that wants to take a youngster who is an emotional problem or a sociopath, as defined, is very rare. Most of them want the elite. They want the high-caliber, excellent, intelligent youngster who is college material. Anybody can run a school on that basis. All that is needed is to run a test on the prospects. If they come up with 130 IQ, they are welcome. If they behave themselves, fine; if not, kick them out! It is not hard to run a school like that. The young people who are not wanted by anyone—including, in many instances, the parents—are the bright, capable youngsters who are striking out against authority and who are a real challenge. Even some private boarding schools specializing in the maladjusted are no longer equipped to handle the sociopathic youngster. Some of these schools have a ratio of one to one—one youngster to one adult—and, consequently, marvelous supervision. Of course, for board and therapy, the costs run around $700 per month for twenty-four-hour service. Some of these schools are phasing out their work with the socially maladjusted because they feel they can do more for the mentally retarded or for some other type of youngster than they can for the acting-out sort of adolescent.

As the city is encroaching on what originally was a rural environment, many of these young people need space for themselves and for others. Fewer and fewer schools are taking the acting-out youngster. Apparently there are only two schools left in California that will take the acting-out adolescent who is trying to find out "Who am I? What is this world all about?" As a result, these young people often come back to the public school because there is no other place for them to go. Sometimes these young people are on home-teaching programs. Sometimes they are put on medication by psychiatrists. Sometimes they are in special classes for educationally handicapped, which is a fancy name for emotionally disturbed kids. The public schools quite often get them because the private schools won't have them. The public school is the last refuge, and when the public school gives up, there just isn't much more that is left. The public schools, in some cases, do give up all too readily. Boards of education and the taxpayers have been willing to sustain programs that will help these youngsters. However, I would be foolish to sit up here and tell you that the schools are able to solve all the problems of all the children. One of the greatest disservices to the public schools has been silly titles such as: *Education for All American Youth.* That is misleading. Public schools don't educate *all* American youth or provide education for *all* youngsters. Schools can't educate the psychotic; they can't educate some of the terrifically mentally retarded youngsters that are below the TMR (trainable mentally retarded) level, and so on. I think the sooner we identify some of these youngsters and realize that the public schools can't do some of the things that are being expected of them, the more likely it is that we will put the school function into proper proportions. The public schools' basic job is education, not institutionalization.

Continuation school in California was initiated because youngsters at age 16 may actually go to work, with or without the permission of their parents. The way the labor law in California is written, the youngsters at the age of 16 may go to work on a full-time basis. Before the age of 16, he cannot do this. Consequently, at age 16, children can drop out of school and go to work. The only force that a parent has is that he can file with the juvenile court that the young person is out of his control. The youngster would then be placed in juvenile hall with the idea that he would go to school there. Parents are not willing to sign an application saying that the kid is out of their control and that they want him put in juvenile hall so he will go to school. Continuation school is set up so that those youngsters who are employed or employable will go to school part time.

The law, the first compensatory program in California, was set up in 1919. It was set up with the idea that youngsters who were employed should go to school part time. Actually, if you know anything about history, you know that World War I ended in 1918. In 1919, the boys came back from the war. They needed jobs, so the kids who had been filling the jobs, substituting for them, were told, "Thanks very much, boys, now go back to school." The adults passed laws about going back to school and about curfews: We can't control them, so let's make a law and make them go into the house.

How do you get kids to go back to school after they have once tasted money and jobs and that sort of thing? It hasn't worked. About two or three years ago, the California legislature reared back and made it mandatory that every district must have a continuation program and must see that every 16- and 17-year-old was in school part time—or else. The "or else" was 10 percent of the support from the state that the district would be penalized if a continuation program was not put into effect. Of course, it was not too hard to convince local boards of education that this was a program that had high merits. As a consequence, continuation schools were put into effect.

The continuation program is for kids who either have a job or want a job. Realistically, it also includes some other categories. It includes the dropout, the push-out—this is the kid who is *persona non grata* in school— and the fade-out, the kid who has more-or-less gotten to the point where he is doing nothing and has come to the realization that he is getting nowhere. An amiable separation is arranged so that he comes over to the continuation school on a part-time basis. He can then get individualized attention, a different type of curriculum, a different type of permissive attitude, and so on. I won't go into all of that, but the continuation program is quite radically different from the regular schools. We hope some of it rubs off on the regular schools one of these days, because they could learn a lot from the procedures of the continuation schools. They may be the ultimate answer to restoring perspective to disenchanted youth, too often classified as "maladjusted" because they rebel at lockstep education.

QUESTIONS AND ANSWERS

QUESTION: Are many of these socially maladjusted children suicidal?

ANSWER: According to the studies that have been done, the highest rate of suicide is among adolescents, teen-agers, because of the many pressures that are put upon them. A telephone service that enables a troubled teen-ager to talk to someone is available in many cities. Often, if they can unburden themselves, potential suicides begin to think that life may not be completely hopeless after all.

QUESTION: *In some schools it is still the policy for classroom teachers to send disruptive or difficult students to the office to be disciplined. Is not this punitive approach harmful to many of these children?*

ANSWER: Whether a child is sent to the office or not is a decision for the teacher to make. Control is always in the hands of the teacher. If a teacher's philosophy is different from that of the school, he would have to either reconcile this difference or go along with the policy, whatever it is. No one forces a teacher to send the youngster to the office. The youngster who is not doing his work may be a cause for concern from a psychological viewpoint—a concern because of his misbehavior, the fact that he is not accomplishing something or producing. It may be that this is a sign of serious mental problems, that it is a form of withdrawal. These are symptoms of the people who withdraw from society. This nonperformance might be one of the first indications that perhaps the child has a much more serious problem than the one he is acting out. The kid who calls you names or stands up and challenges you is acting out and getting rid of some of his feelings. In the case of the youngster who is not performing, it may not be the work that he is not accomplishing; it may be the very fact that twenty-nine other kids in the class are challenged enough or concerned enough or interested enough, or that they have the motivation or something. The problem is to discover why this youngster rejects this particular idea; and it may be voluntary or involuntary on his part. Personally, I would not think of sending him to the office for the vice-principal to run up and down his spine a few times in order to convince him to come back and apply himself. I would be more concerned with the reason behind the youngster's nonlearning. This may be a very deep problem. I would feel that the counselors and the psychologist should be concerned with this youngster and that we should try to see what could be done to assist the lad rather than to punish him.

QUESTION: *Who determines which children are seen by the school psychologist?*

ANSWER: Most central offices in school systems will not accept a referral for the psychologist from anybody without the permission of the principal, because the principal is the one who has to live with the parent who hotfoots it over there and starts asking questions. The principal is the one who coordinates the school, so consequently, if a teacher sees particular needs, it helps to have the principal at least look at the situation. Some referrals are for psychological services. It helps the psychologist if he knows what has already been done for the youngster. Has there been a parent conference? Has anyone sat down and talked with the kid? Has the teacher looked through the record? What remedial actions have been attempted? What does the teacher think the psychologist might do? What seem to be the particular needs? With this information and background, the psychologist—with the approval of the principal, because he needs to be in on this—will then sit down with the teacher to find out what the youngster's problems might involve.

SUMMARY

We have many youngsters with social-maladjustment problems. We can identify some of them as potential problems quite early in life. We have facilities to help work with children with these difficulties—teachers, counselors, psychologists, juvenile homes, girls' homes, boys' camps, youth authorities, and continuation schools—but so far the problems seem to be multiplying somewhat faster than the solutions can be mounted. Probably our best hope is still the patient work of a teacher who cares.

THE "MENTALLY RETARDED" CHILD

13

Thomas J. Murphy

Thomas J. Murphy has been director of special education for the Santa Barbara schools since 1960. From 1953 to 1960 he did the same work with a less prestigious title. Special education in Santa Barbara involves schooling for the mentally retarded, the physically handicapped, those who need speech therapy, and those who need home teaching; it formerly included programs for the gifted, who now do not have a special program.

Mr. Murphy obtained the B.A. from San Francisco State College, the M.A. from Stanford, and he has done post-master's-degree work at Stanford. Before coming to Santa Barbara, Mr. Murphy taught in San Francisco and was coordinator of special education in Hollister, California. He spent four years, from 1941–1945, in the U.S. Navy.

Mr. Murphy has been in steady demand as a college teacher, particularly during the summers. For many years he was on the summer staff of San Francisco State College when that institution was training most of the teachers in special education in California. He is an able man, and he has developed an outstanding program in special education.

I want to consider with you the field of the mentally retarded. When you talk about mental retardation you are talking about intelligence or lack of intelligence. We must first consider the question, "What is intelligence?" We could spend a long time defining this concept, but I find most comfortable the definition: "Intelligence is what intelligence tests measure."

This definition has been useful for many years. Theories of intelligence have been formulated to apply to intelligence testing. There are no operational theories of intelligence that have been constructed as independent entities; rather the theories are in terms of the application to the testing of intelligence.

DEFINITIONS OF INTELLIGENCE

There are three basic theories that have persisted over a long period of time. I will oversimplify them so you can see the basic elements within them.

Inherited ability

The first theory, the oldest one, is that you are born with a certain ability to learn or a level of intelligence. You have it or you don't. It was on this theory that most of our early intelligence tests were devised. The Binet scales were built on this premise. It was believed that you had a definite level of ability and that this level could be measured. If you had a low level, the deficiency was not correctable. It was believed in the early days of testing that if you tested at a certain level, assuming that the tester was not at fault, the test was not at fault, or the situation was not at fault, a true estimate of intellectual ability could be made. You would function at this level now and for all time. It was not long before professional people began to question this absolutist idea.

Binet devised his original scales in 1905 to determine the placement of youngsters in school and to identify those youngsters who were not going to be able to succeed in school. His tests were successful in helping school people make these assessments. However, as individuals began to use the various tests, many of which were modifications of Binet's early work and based on the same frame of reference, they found that factors other than genetically inherited ability were important. They began to qualify their findings and to think that perhaps intelligence is more complex than you are either born with it or you aren't.

Inherited ability influenced by outside forces

Evidence accumulated that if a child grew up in a situation in which he was deprived of certain experiences or had a meager and impoverished background, or if there were various kinds of disasters in his upbringing, or if there were other complications, then perhaps the test scores should have some qualifications relating to these factors. The application of the original theory became qualified in practice. The newer approach came to be that the individual is born with a level of ability but this level may be influenced by outside forces. This inheritance modified by outside forces was probably the second basic theory of intelligence.

Gestalt theory

The third general theory of intelligence—the one under which we are operating today—is the so-called gestalt theory, which is that intelligence is the sum total of all our experiences. We are born with ability that is modified by the stresses through which we have come in our learning experiences and other aspects of our environment. The whole complex of native ability and experience are interwoven so that you cannot separate one from the other. This concept of interaction is important when we are talking about mental retardation, because it brings us to the modern concept of mental retardation, which is quite different from the concept in vogue in the early 1950s.

DEFINITIONS OF MENTAL RETARDATION

Only a short time ago it was widely believed that if you made an extensive measurement of a youngster—i.e., completed a psychological differential diagnosis—you knew all about this youngster. If you came up with a diagnosis of mental retardation at that point, this diagnosis was irrefutable. In 1970 we are no longer so dogmatic. We are saying that mental retardation is an operational classification defining that a person is, at a given point in time, functioning at a certain level of performance. This new meaning for mental retardation has created some problems for special education personnel. It was comfortable to be able to categorize and say, "This is a mentally retarded youngster," and then be able to plan and deal with him accordingly. Now, we are not so sure. We have to look at the child from a completely different point of view.

The American Association on Mental Deficiency is a professional organization comprised of professional people from the fields of medicine, education, psychology, and the related fields that deal with mental deficiency. In 1959, the association developed the following concept:

> *In addition to subaverage intellectual functioning, mental retardation must be reflected by an impairment in one or more of the following aspects of adaptive behavior. (1) Maturation: The rate of maturation refers to the rate of sequential development of the self-help skills of infancy and early childhood, such as sitting, crawling, standing, walking, talking, habit training, and interaction with age peers. (2) Learning: Learning ability refers to the facility with which knowledge is acquired as a function of experience. Learning difficulties are most manifest in school situations. (3) Social adjustment: Social adjustment is particularly important as a qualifying condition at the adult level where it is assessed in terms of the ability of the individual to operate independently in society.*

If the individual has impairment in one or more of these aspects of adaptive behavior, together with subaverage performance on a measure of intellectual functioning, he may be classified as mentally retarded. Subaverage performance on a measure of intellectual functioning means performance that is more than one standard deviation below the mean of the age group of the person taking a standardized test. In other words, if a person taking an individual intelligence test falls one standard deviation below the mean of his age level on a test—plus the fact that he is subaverage on one of the areas of adaptive behavior—then he is considered to be mentally retarded at that time in his life and in that society. The definition is now functional and not absolute as it was only a short time ago.

It's interesting to go back to notes just ten years old, when mental retardation was defined as being almost absolute. This framework now is different. This point of departure is particularly significant when you start thinking about program development or meeting the needs of individuals who have been diagnosed as mentally retarded. The new definition leads to completely different instructional approaches from what would have been acceptable a few years ago.

CLASSIFICATION OF THE MENTALLY RETARDED

In today's society we are requiring more from individuals in terms of abstract learning. This area is where mental retardation shows up. We are talking about the person's ability to deal with the abstract. In school this is what is referred to as symbolic learning. We all have to do reading, writing, arithmetic, and similar tasks. The tests we use, such as the Wechsler tests and the Binet tests, generally measure this abstract learning. When we raised the minimum score to one standard deviation below the mean, we automatically increase the percent of the population that we are discussing. When we include the social aspects or other phases of adaptive behavior, we become a little more discriminating in terms of those who cannot function normally. A youngster with an IQ of 65 might be able to get along pretty well in a regular class. He could be especially well adjusted and mature so that he can fit in socially with the group, and he might be able to benefit on a marginal basis from some learning skills as taught in school. It is possible that he could deal with some abstract learning. Under these conditions this youngster would not be functioning as a mentally retarded pupil and should not be so classified.

When most of us think about mental retardation, and when most of us hear others talk about mental retardation, especially based on the information that comes out from national organizations seeking financial assistance, the information is usually about the severely mentally retarded, which is limited to a small percent of the population. These are basically the trainable mentally retarded or those even more seriously handicapped who need complete custodial care. In rough terms, these are individuals with intelligence quotients below 50. The propaganda that comes out from most of the national organizations, in terms of fund raising and things of that sort, is about this very small segment of the population, not the larger segment of the population, which can run above 5 percent, depending upon the criteria used. Most people identify mental retardation with severely retarded individuals, not with those who are moderately retarded and have educational problems that can be dealt with in school.

The factor of adaptive behavior in classification

One of the few complete surveys of mental retardation in the United States was done in Onondaga County, New York. The surveyors went into a community and tried to identify the retarded of preschool age, of school age, and of postschool age. They found a startling range shown in rates per thousands of mentally retarded by age groups. Under age 5 the rate was twelve per thousand; at age 5, twenty-two per thousand; at age 6, forty per thousand. In the age groups from 10 to 15 the surveyors found eighty per thousand; in the age group comprising 16- and 17-year-olds the

TABLE 13-1   NUMBER OF MENTALLY RETARDED BY AGE PER THOUSAND
POPULATION (SURVEY MADE IN ONONDAGA COUNTY, NEW YORK)

Age	Mentally retarded/thousand
Under 5	12
5	22
6	40
10–15	80
16–17	28
18 +	4

number dropped to twenty-eight per thousand; and at age 18 and over they found only four per thousand. This was a community survey. They went out into the community and tried to identify all those who were mentally retarded. They questioned people, asking them about "those youngsters under age 5 that you know to be mentally retarded; tell us about those that are 5 and tell us of those that are 6." They went to schools and obtained numbers of students for the school-age group. They went back to the older population, using all community resources in this survey. There have been many similar surveys done in various parts of Europe, but to my knowledge this has been the only one done in the United States.

This survey is an indication of the importance of the adaptive-behavior facet of classifying individuals as mentally retarded.

The children can function adequately in their environment before age 5 and over age 18, and in between, where their environment is chiefly school, they have trouble functioning. Mental retardation, as we think about it, is an artifact of the education process. The community really is not worried about it in postschoolers. Because of pediatric surveys, where children go to doctors, a number of the preschool children are seen as potentially likely to have problems. When they leave schools, they go into the community, they get a job, they earn money, and no one in the community knows that they are mentally retarded.

An interesting study was done in a work-experience project (Santa Barbara Work-Study Program, 1964). All the educable mentally retarded youngsters of high school age were placed on jobs in the community. The schools made the placements. Interviewers then went around and interviewed these employers, asking them various questions, including, "Do you consider this person mentally retarded?" Only an insignificant percentage, about 5 percent of the employers, knew that the students were mentally retarded. The school does not tell employers in the experience program when they are being sent a retarded youngster. As far as the community is concerned, once individuals are out of school, they usually are not identified as mentally retarded. They are able to fit into the population, and they are able to get along in our society if they are given certain help in school, so they will fit in and function. According to the definition they are not mentally retarded at that point. They were mentally retarded at age 10, but they are not mentally retarded at 18.

Effects of changing environments

Some students who have been classed as mentally retarded have been helped to function more normally as school programs have been changed. In general, as the program becomes more clearly defined in terms of expected behaviors, both the teacher and the student are able to know when they have reached the desired level of competence. In the work-experience program, the school work is closely tied to the job demands, and the success the pupil has on the job makes it easier for him to master needed arithmetic skills and reading skills, especially when the reading is related to the work he is enjoying. On the other hand, unskilled jobs that demanded very little competence in abstract thinking are disappearing and being replaced by work in service industries such as TV repairs. The new jobs are more demanding intelelctually and resemble school work more than did pick-and-shovel labor. It is possible that the percent of the population seen as mentally retarded in adulthood will increase as the effect of new job demands are felt through the economy.

PREVENTION OF MENTAL RETARDATION

Improved medical facilities are keeping alive marginal children who a few years ago died. Some of these children are mentally retarded, some are physically handicapped, and many of them have deficits in both mental and physical functioning. Some of the damage is an unexpected side effect of progress in medical research. Thalidomide was a chemical that reduced morning sickness in pregnant mothers, but it led to malformed babies. On the other hand, some of the causes of birth defects are more clearly understood than they were only a few years ago. The effect of rubella or German measles is a case in point. Probably the damage it causes has not changed, but now upsurges in mental retardation rates can be correlated with rubella epidemics. It might be expected that, because of improved medical science, there would be fewer brain damaged children at birth, therefore there would be fewer mentally retarded. However, it is actually the reverse because we have a higher survival rate at birth. If we analyze this situation, those who are surviving today are the ones who would not have survived before. They are usually the extreme cases who would be mentally retarded, physically handicapped, or physically deformed. The progress of preventive medicine has been much less effective than remedial medicine. Some discoveries have been highly publicized, and many people are looking forward to breakthroughs in medicine. So far, percentage improvement is really very small. One discovery that has received a great deal of publicity is the condition known as *phenylketonuria* (PKU). It is talked about with some awe, but when you look at the percentage of children involved in this disease, it is only one-half of 1 percent to 1 percent of the mental retardation population. Today, by diagnosing this problem at birth and by putting the child on a phenylalanine-free diet, most damage can be prevented. The inability of the body to absorb phenylalanine causes the mental retardation; it's a metabolic process. This is a striking medical advance, but the number of children involved is very small.

Another condition known as *galactosemia*, in which some children have a disastrous response to the galactose in milk, has been effectively controlled. If this defect is diagnosed early in life and proper treatment is given, children are saved who otherwise would have been mentally retarded; but again, only a small percent of the total mentally retarded population is involved.

The big breakthrough in understanding mental retardation has been the ability to identify the chromosome structure of the individuals. This knowledge makes possible genetic counseling that may prevent causes of mental retardation as counseling is heeded. So far, knowledge of prevention has not kept up with the knowledge of survival, resulting in a large increase in certain types of handicapping conditions. However, there are also bright spots. We have seen a decrease in certain handicapping conditions. We've seen a decrease, for example, in the incidence of cerebral palsy because of improved techniques of birth delivery and techniques for dealing with maternal Rh immunization. Since approximately 66 percent of the cerebral palsied were mentally defective, a drop in the cerebral palsy population leads to a drop in the mental retardation population. Two factors have been interacting; one improves the chance for better mental functioning, and the other increases the number of disabled. So far, the survival of malfunctioning has been more impressive than the elimination of causes of malfunctioning.

Chromosome-related deficits

The most sharply delineated chromosome-related deficit appears in the so-called Mongoloid child, now referred to as one suffering from *Down's syndrome*. The physical characteristics of many of these mentally retarded youngsters are quite obvious. Because of the peculiar shape of their eyes, which gives them a somewhat oriental appearance, a child suffering from this condition unfortunately has been referred to as a Mongoloid child. From analysis of the chromosomal structure, it is now known that many children who were thought to have other kinds of handicaps are really instances of Down's syndrome. There have been many theories about the causes of this affliction, ranging from metabolic malformation to the age of parents at conception. However, once it was learned how to do chromosomal research, part of the puzzle was resolved.

A system of classifying chromosomes called the Denver Classification System was worked out by a group of scientists who met in Denver in April of 1960. They finally all agreed to use the same system in order to eliminate some of the confusion resulting from everyone devising his private code. Research on chromosomes of children suffering from Down's syndrome indicates that there is a malformation in one of the twenty-two pairs of autosomes; one piece of it breaks off and connects to another chromosome. This malformation is always present in Mongoloid youngsters. When this finding was established, it was considered highly significant. The researchers expected to be able to analyze the chromosomal structures of parents and anticipated finding that one parent was a carrier. This hypothesis has not been fully substantiated. They found that they were not able to identify why a Mongoloid youngster suffers from a Down's syndrome. The reason for the chromosome breakage and attachment is still not fully understood.

In mental retardation there are various combinations of genetic malformations, rather than simple structures. Researchers are finding more and more genetic malformations that are associated with mental retardation. This area of research offers the greatest promise of supplying the key to prevention. When it is possible to identify how the genetic malformations are caused, it will be possible to do genetic counseling that probably will abolish or deter formation of such abnormalities as Down's syndrome and other less well-known patterns related to mental retardation.

SIGNIFICANCE OF IDENTIFICATION

Schooling can be varied for different children who have different prognosis for success. Those who are going to be able to fit into the community and lead a normal life require certain kinds of help from the school. The help may not be the same as that required by the more average children. Often the special help will be increasingly successful as it is given earlier in the child's school life. The training that we provide for these youngsters of certain ability is quite different from the training of the youngsters who are not going to be able to get along in the community. For lack of a better terminology, in education we have divided these children into two groups: the *educable mentally retarded* and the *trainable mentally retarded.*

Schools generally reserve the right to accept into school programs only those children who are able to profit from school experience. This limitation on who may attend is fairly universal throughout the United States today. The accepted fact is that almost all the mentally retarded within the trainable and educable group now come to school. This is relatively new. It's only as recent as 1956 that some half dozen states in the United States agreed to have the so-called trainable mentally retarded youngsters come to school. Acceptance of children in school when they are handicapped this severely is a new concept.

When the educable mentally retarded children go to school, what is the basis of the program that is developed for them? What should be school goals for these youngsters? In essence, we are making a prognosis at a very early age, usually around the time the child is starting school. We are trying to say that this youngster, when he gets to be about 18 years of age, is going to be able to go out into the community, is going to be able to earn a living, is going to get married, is going to raise a family, is going to pay taxes. In essence, he is going to be an independent person in our community on a marginal basis. When we say he's educable, we are saying he is going to be an independent member of our society; but he is going to need a lot of help along the way to get there.

The prognosis for the trainable mentally retarded is: This youngster is going to be able to fit into a community; he is going to get around the community. He is going to be able to take care of his own needs. He is going to take care of himself, but he is not going to be self-supporting unless there is some type of sheltered workshop, and he is probably going to need supervision all his life. For these individuals even to reach this level requires careful training over an extended period of time.

The third group is not going to be able to take care of their needs, they are not going to be able to get around in the community, and they are going to require custodial care or something similar. When we try to separate these three areas of retardation as to the prognosis for success, we realize that the majority of those people are going to be able to get along if we do the job of education properly. Only a very small percentage, about one-fourth of 1 percent, are going to be custodial cases.

The prognosis for post-high school life really sets up the goals for the school program. For the educable mentally retarded, the goal for our program is economic self-sufficiency and social adjustment. When we devise a program for the educable mentally retarded, this goal is the control that determines the curriculum. When a program for trainable mentally retarded is discussed, the goal is self-care, self-help, and social adjustment, with some training on marginal employment activities. Some people react emotionally to the difference in the words *education* and *training*. In terms of the retarded, a difference in goals and a difference in ways of reaching the goals should be apparent.

PREVALENCE OF MENTAL RETARDATION BY SEX

In all areas of any malfunctioning there is a much higher percentage of males than females. It has been traditional to think that the male is the sturdier of the sexes. This is not a true idea. We know, for instance, that the survival rate is higher for girls than for boys at birth. Women live longer in American society than do men, although this longevity was not true a century ago. The number of mentally retarded boys exceeds the number of mentally retarded girls by a ratio of approximately three to two. In part, this difference is probably genetic, but part of the difference comes from the superior adaptability of girls over boys in the school setting. The boys, more often than the girls, suffer from poor adaptive school behavior and are classified as mentally retarded because of their inability to function in school.

NATURE OF LEARNING
IN THE MENTALLY RETARDED

One fascinating area of study is the nature of the learning process and, particularly, why some children have great difficulty learning and others learn easily. There are four theories that I should like to review briefly, and then I should like to explore some implications of the effect of bisectioning the brain, as this operation throws light on learning in mentally retarded children.

Synaptic transmission

One of the principal theories has postulated that a most important aspect of learning is the process of bridging the synapse, or the gap, between an axon and a dendrite. The dendrite is the part of the neuron that receives impulses from other neurons, and the axon is the part of the neuron that transmits the energy away from the cell body. Between the axon and dendrite is a small space on the order of $1/1,000,000$ of an inch across. This space is called a *synapse*. There is considerable evidence that learning consists of building nets of neurons that are linked together as the synapses are bridged. One theory has this bridging accomplished by the secretion of acetylcholine across the gap, with the bridge being removed by cholinesterase after the message has been transmitted. At any rate, it would seem logical that if the gap were wider in some individuals than in others, bridging would be harder, learning would be harder, and in general individuals with wide synapses would be mentally retarded. On the other hand, individuals with unusually narrow synapses would have less difficulty forming bridges—it is easier to build a short bridge than a long one—and could be very bright individuals. So far, it has not been possible to measure the average width of the synapses and correlate these widths with any indexes of mental retardation or of brightness. The average size of the gap is so small that precise measurement has been impossible. The theory has the advantage of being logical and is attractive on that basis.

Increased dendrites or axons

Another theory that has the advantage of being logical but until recently has been difficult to explore empirically is that in bright people there are more dendrites and more axons per neuron than in the average person. On the other hand, in the mentally retarded the hypothesis was that the neurons had fewer dendrites and fewer axons. The effect of the increased number or the decreased number of axons and dendrites would be to make both simple and complex connections more or less difficult. The increased branching would bring the neuron into contact with many other neurons than would be possible with fewer branches. In addition, the increased number of branches would make additional contacts with a near neuron possible. In the latter case, the probability of transmission would be increased, and in the former case, unusual connections—possibly the basis of creativity—would be more likely. Researchers found evidence that perceptual experience in very young organisms increased the number of spikes on the axons and dendrites and that, if the experience were delayed beyond a rather short critical period, the spikes failed to develop. The spikes did not appear to be true axon or dendrite branches, but they seemed to have somewhat similar characteristics. In addition, it was not established that the organisms with the extra spikes were more intellectually able as adults, but the inference was clearly possible.

Growth of nodules

D. O. Hebb (1949) in Montreal was one of the first to postulate the growth of nodules as part of the learning process. He was of the opinion that the nodules were important in the secretion of acetylcholine in the bridging of the synapse and that as they functioned in this way they grew appreciably in size and decreased the size of the gap, or the synapse.

A group at Berkeley, headed by Edwin R. Lewis (1969), have been able to photograph synaptic knobs using an electron scanning microscope that magnifies twenty thousand times. These knobs seem to be involved in data transmission, although the exact function has not been established. The fact that there are knobs lends support to the theory that they have something to do with how easily things are learned.

Surface potentials

D. J. Albert (1966a), in a series of experiments with rats, found that learning could be expedited by passing a pulsating positive current over the surface of the brain. He also found that learning was broken up and destroyed by passing a pulsating negative current across the surface of the brain. Many of the mentally retarded, particularly the moderately retarded or the trainable mentally retarded, show learning characteristics that resemble the rats subjected to the pulsating negative current. The quiescent or. resting brain seems to have a pulsating negative-current state, which changes to positive as arousal and attention are generated. It is possible that the retarded child fails, for unknown reasons, to generate the necessary degree of positive potential, or current.

Learning and intellectual functioning are both highly complex. Probably the physiological foundation for mental retardation is a combination of many different separate strands. Studies going on in psychology, biochemistry, electrical engineering, stress reactions, and many other fields are helping untangle the nature of mental retardation. One difficulty in understanding the field is the impossibility of keeping up with all the research in all of the disciplines that are working in their own way on aspects of the problem.

Bilateral studies

Studies of the brain have indicated that learning is bilateral; the two hemispheres of the brain actually work together. They function together during the learning process. This conception is important in terms of relearning or retraining of individuals who have had serious brain damage. The work of the dominant hemisphere can be taken over after a period of retraining or reteaching them. They use the undamaged hemisphere to relearn motor-control activities that have been controlled by the damaged hemisphere. We have two hemispheres that work through a network of nerves that join them. Although we have a major or a dominant side and a recessive side that work independently, they work together. There have been many studies, which were started at the University of Chicago, in which the hemispheres are separated. The axons that form the corpus callosum and unite the hemispheres are cut. Most of this bisectioning has been done on monkeys and rats and other animals. They have been studying the learning of these animals after the operation. Recently they have used this operation on a few humans who had serious damage to one hemisphere, which was causing serious deterioration of the undamaged hemisphere. They have taught these individuals, who have had the brain split in half, to look in a mirror and copy a figure with one eye covered. Mirror copying is a new learning task for most people. When asked to copy something with their left hand using their left eye, these patients are able to do it. When they put the chalk in the right hand and are still using the left eye, they are unable to copy the figure. If the problem is reversed, the patient can copy the image seen by the right eye with the right hand, but not with the left.

D. J. Albert (1966b), who was mentioned earlier, used a process of anesthetizing one hemisphere of the brain at a time to study learning. This process has an advantage over the operation, since it is reversible. When both hemispheres are functioning, learning is stored in both hemispheres, but the connections through the corpus callosum and also through the optic chiasma are necessary for bilateral learning and storage to take place. If these are cut, the separate hemispheres act as though they are separate brains. Each side can be taught separately, without interference from learning on the other side. The left eye and left hand or foot function as an independent unit from the right eye and right hand or foot. This separation in learning is not possible when the optic chiasma and the corpus callosum are intact. In that case, what is learned through the left eye affects both hemispheres and is available to both sides of the body. In an experiment with cats, R. W. Sperry, at California Institute of Technology, trained a cat to discriminate between a door with a circle and one with a square; he put food behind the door with the circle. He had the cat learn with a patch over the right eye and then tested the cat with a patch over the left eye, which had been used for learning. The cat had no problem demonstrating the learning. The optic chiasma was cut, and then both the optic chiasma and the corpus callosum were cut. When both were cut, there was no transfer and each eye could be taught separately. In fact, the left eye could be taught the circle was food and the right eye could be taught that the square was food, and there was no interference in the learning.

In some brain damage cases there is interference or malfunctioning of learning between the separate parts of the brain. Some forms of mental retardation are caused by this type of malfunction.

THE MYTH OF THE MENTALLY RETARDED CHILD

There are variances with children in their ability to function. Adults are able to adapt to weaknesses by avoiding tasks that require a particular competence, but we set up certain procedures through which children must go. They are not allowed to pick and choose their tasks. We find there are variances in youngsters, and this is particularly apparent when they are in special education programs. I want to suggest that there is no such thing as a mentally retarded child and, further, that there are no such things as children with learning problems. There are no two mentally retarded children who are exactly alike, and there are no children who have learning problems that are exactly alike. It is a mistake to group children in a category if they are not the same. The same thing is true when we talk about children with perceptual learning difficulties. As we get them to go through different tasks so we can identify them, we find that there are no two children who have the same perceptual difficulties. There are no two children who have the same auditory perceptual difficulties. If we have a class of dysphasic youngsters, children with severe receptive-expressive communication disorders, we won't have one child in that program who is a classical aphasic youngster. In the same way, we do not have any children who fit the classical description of mental retardation.

Tests for mental retardation

Tests really play a very small part in the classification of individuals as mentally retarded. In California, there is a law that requires that a standardized individual intelligence be given. On the test, the individual must fall at least one standard deviation below the mean of the test. Many school systems use the Wechsler Intelligence Scale for Children (WISC) to provide both a performance scale and a verbal scale. Within this test there are subtests. These are individual pieces of the test that are of different importance when the results on the test are considered. One of the things that we watch for very carefully is the evidence of wide scatters in subtest results. The IQ score comes from averaging the different subscores of the test. You could theoretically have a youngster who is above normal on one subtest, at normal on three, and below normal on six. Depending on the amount that the subscores were below normal, the youngster might or might not be classified as mentally retarded if you depended solely on an IQ score, because the subscores would pull the mean total score down an indefinite amount. The significant part in the analysis, however, comes as you go back and look at the subscores and, for example, find three tests that fall within the average range. Is that youngster mentally retarded or not? On the basis of the total score you might want to say yes, but you must look at which three subtests are high. It makes a difference. Some of the subtests are concerned with most important areas; one is Comprehension, another is Information. These areas are important because weaknesses within these areas indicate probable problems in school. If a student is scoring up near the top on Information and Comprehension but is scoring low on the numerical concepts, he may have a learning problem rather than being classifiable as retarded. It may just be that he hasn't learned some significant skills.

The other thing that is important is a wide variance between performance and verbal ability. If a youngster tests near the normal range on performance and very low on verbal skills, it would be important to look carefully into his background. Does this youngster come from a bilingual home? Has he been culturally deprived? Has he had a lack of environmental stimulation? These are factors that might account for this discrepancy, and it would be imperative to check the cause of his difficulty before placing him in an MR (mentally retarded) class. The total score of the test itself is not the significant factor. It is what the youngster does on various aspects of the test that is important. After considering all these factors, we may decide that this youngster would be better off in a program for mentally retarded, because we know that in a regular class he would probably experience a great deal of failure.

The decision to make the placement is made by a certified school psychologist. There are no test scores at present in the state of California by which this decision is predetermined. The burden is thrown on the professional school psychologist to say either that this child is mentally retarded or that he is not mentally retarded. If the psychologist is not willing to say the child is mentally retarded, then the child cannot be accepted in the program. If the psychologist says he is mentally retarded, by law we have to accept him in the program. The psychologist has to take into consideration many things other than the results of one psychological evaluation. Teacher reports, health reports, case-study reports, and other background information are important ingredients that help the school psychologist make his decision. After he has made his evaluation and report, the parents must be consulted. Legally, the child can be placed in a mentally retarded class over the objection of the parents, but operationally a child is not so placed. In a sense, the school says to the parent, not in so many words, that we have tried to give you the benefit of our counsel and our information. If the child does not succeed, he is not succeeding by your choice, not ours. Legally, we could force the child to be placed in an MR class, and the parent would have no alternative. The law says that we have to provide for this child and that the parent cannot object to what the school provides.

SPECIAL CLASSES

California school districts with an average daily attendance (ADA) of over nine hundred must provide programs for the educable mentally retarded. In districts that have under nine hundred ADA, the county superintendent of schools has to offer a program. Usually this provision is made by contracting by the county superintendent with one of the larger districts. By law, every school district in California now has to provide a program, either of their own or through the county superintendent's office. The same rules apply to programs for the trainable mentally retarded, except that the cutting-off mark is eight thousand ADA. School districts with over eight thousand ADA have to provide their own program, while in school districts with under eight thousand, the county superintendent's office has to provide the service. The law makes it mandatory that programs for both the educable mentally retarded and the trainable mentally retarded be provided.

Teaching credential requirements for MR programs

In California, which is fairly typical, teachers for mentally retarded programs must have regular credentials plus special training. In California, fully credentialed teachers must have a minor in the education of the mentally retarded, which requires twenty-four units specifically designed for helping the teacher to understand these children and their problems. Some of these units may be acquired as part of the requirements for the bachelor's degree, but they are in addition to the requirements for a regular credential. California has had a special problem when it seeks teachers from other states for its mentally retarded programs. The regular credential requires an academic major. Many excellent teachers have an education major or a master's major in the mentally retarded. We couldn't get them to teach in California in the field because their preparation did not include an academic major. A new restricted credential has been authorized that allows teachers with this kind of preparation to teach in the state of California.

In the state of California there is a real shortage of teachers in this field. It is estimated that about one-third of all the programs will be manned by teachers with less than the required training, and approximately one-fourth of the required classes will not be opened because of a lack of teachers. There are graduate fellowships available in this field, many of which are substantial. There are also the NDEA (National Defense Education Act) teacher loan programs for training teachers. For every year a loan recipient teaches in the program, a percentage of the loan is forgiven.

CHARACTERISTICS OF THE MENTALLY RETARDED

Mentally retarded children are not a clear-cut group with obvious characteristics. The description that follows is in terms of degrees. No child has all of these characteristics. Most retarded youngsters have some of them. The more retarded the child, the more severe are the characteristics, and the more characteristics a child has, the more mentally retarded he is. It has been stressed that tests may only tap one characteristic, or they may tap none at all. The IQ is certainly not a valid indication of mental retardation. Personality is important, but it must be remembered that the mentally retarded have a full range of personality patterns. In other words there is no personality pattern for a mentally retarded that is different from that of a child who is not retarded. There is no such thing as kinds of mental retardation; the differentiation is in terms of degrees of disability.

Psychological traits

Some of the psychological characteristics of these youngsters are more important than others. The most significant one is that they have a short attention span. They are unable to attend for long periods of time. This is not only significant with the mentally retarded, for many other children who have learning problems are unable to attend for extended periods. The psychotic children at a mental health center have the same problem. The problem of the teacher trying to work with these kids is that they just sit down and then they want to be on the go again. To teach these children to attend requires work with them on one little concept at a time. This limitation is not only important with regard to individual mentally retarded children, but it is a characteristic that is important in terms of program development. Teachers working with these children must give information in short periods of time. One big problem for teachers working with retarded youngsters, slow-learning youngsters, or children who have learning problems is that the teachers don't get the concept of short dosages given over many periods of time; rather, they want to concentrate too much into one lesson. They lose the child's attention, and then they find they are having a discipline problem. They are trying to force the kids to attend well beyond what their attention span will allow them to attend.

An important characteristic is that these children have a short memory span. They tend to forget things rather quickly. We know in terms of good learning techniques that you give things in short quick dosage, give them often, and reinforce them. With retarded children, instead of trying to spread learning out in long periods of time, give them quick doses of things many times and eventually they will retain the learning.

A third characteristic is a weakness in the power of association. These children are not able to relate one thing to another. They have poor adaptive ability. This is very common, and the more retarded the child, the more obvious this trait. These children are afraid of the unknown, they are afraid of situations they get themselves into that they are unable to handle. They like the known and the familiar. They are secure in the areas in which they have had experience, in which they have some knowledge, and in which they have some information. In terms of teaching techniques, you build from the known to the unknown. You don't introduce new concepts cold. You don't introduce new areas without preparation. You start where the child is with some concept, and you go from that to something else, because otherwise you will find immediate resistance and inability to adjust to the new ideas. This characteristic relates closely to motivation. Mastery of the key to motivation with the retarded would result in solving most of the learning problems. Studies with programmed learning techniques have indicated success in motivation. After using programmed learning techniques, some concepts about the mentally retarded have not held up. They learn in programmed learning situations as well as do nonretarded. They learn as well, but they don't retain it and they can't apply it. They can learn the basic facts if the proper teaching techniques are used. Once the information we want learned is programmed, these youngsters can be taught on a sequential basis. They will learn. Our job will be to reinforce them as we go along and then to teach them how to apply the knowledge they have gained without spending so much time in trying to teach the facts. Most teaching programs with mentally retarded children are bogged down because of having to spend so much time trying to teach facts.

The *Encyclopedia Britannica* people, during the development of their programmed learning materials, went to the city of New York and paid school dropouts to come to school to try out their material. They had an interesting concept that if the students didn't learn it wasn't the students' fault, it was the materials' fault. Think about it. In most instances we, as teachers, don't operate on this basis. If a child doesn't learn, it's his fault, not our fault. It is not the way we prepared our teaching materials, not the way we presented our lesson, not the way we taught him, but it's his fault if he didn't learn it. The *Encyclopedia Britannica* researchers found that by using the reverse idea these youngsters were able to learn under the new conditions, when they had failed to learn for many years. In other words, if the youngster isn't moving along, then there is something wrong with the way we are teaching. We need to go back then and think about the way we are teaching and how to change it.

The next important characteristic is the ability to generalize, to deal with abstractions that have been discussed. This is a difficult task, even for highly capable children. It can be almost impossible for mentally retarded children unless the topic is approached with care. These children do learn to generalize as they are learning the syntax of the spoken language, but this learning is in immediately useful terms. The power to generalize can be fostered if the lessons are highly structured and utilitarian.

One of the characteristic strengths of MR children is in arithmetic. They do better with arithmetic than they do with other areas of abstract learning, because arithmetic in itself is not particularly abstract. It's very concrete during the early grade levels, but all of a sudden it gets abstract and the mentally retarded have serious trouble making the transition.

One area that presents a great deal of difficulty and one that requires careful work is dealing with time. Most people have no idea how compulsively we live by time. Everyone operates on a feeling for time without ever figuring time. Let me give you an example: When you get up in the morning, you go to a job at 8 A.M. You had set your alarm the night before at 6:30. Very few people consciously calculate that it is going to take a half hour to get up, get dressed, shower, and shave; another half hour to eat breakfast, etc.; and then a half hour to drive from here to here. You quickly summarize half here, half here, half here, and you come up with the time 6:30 to get up. In a less routinized situation, if you have to attend a meeting in a strange place, the thinking goes something like this: I have to be out there at four o'clock and, I'm thinking in my office, I have no idea where the room is; it will take me at least twenty minutes to find the building, twenty minutes to find the room, and another twenty minutes to drive. I don't add this all up and subtract from four o'clock. I put several pieces together and decide I had better leave by three, more or less. We figure time without elaborately calculating. The ability to make these calculations is terribly important. Inability to operate automatically is one of the reasons these students are late for work. It's often the reason they're late for school.

The schools need to start these children thinking about time from an early age, but not as this is done these days. At present, elementary teachers instruct cognitively: If the clock reads 3:40 and you left at 3:20, how long did it take you to get there? The student says, "Twenty minutes," but that's not figuring time. That is arithmetical computation, but it's not figuring out how long it's going to take him to get there. It has no personal involvement in spite of the use of the pronoun "you." How do you gauge yourself? This is the important part of the learning. It is the most interesting, most difficult, and one of the most important things we have to teach these youngsters. Time, the use of time, and the subjective measurement of time—I'm not talking about mathematical computation, but an ingrained feel for time—is terribly important. There are two implications: first, that at younger ages substantial basic experience with time is necessary; second, that systematic teaching needs to be done when the youngster is older than seems a rational age for teaching this concept.

With the retarded, you find a very narrow range of interest. They usually get bogged down with one particular kind of thing in which they become interested and do not wish to go into other areas. In part, this tendency is related to their need for the familiar and their fear of the unknown. Related to this deficiency is restricted observation. A teacher who takes these children out on field trips assumes that they are going to see what's going on around them. Actually, when children have a limited range of observation, you'll have to tell them what to look for. You'll have to tell them what to observe, how to observe it, and why they are going to see it. They need specific instruction about prominent or important features they need to see and the importance of these features to the whole composition. When they return to school, the teacher needs to review what they saw, because in spite of prior instruction, many will have passed by something and will not have observed it. This specific instruction is part of teaching to make them aware of the experiences around them. Just providing the experience itself doesn't teach. This need for instruction in observation is important with very young children too. You have to make them aware of what's going on around them in order to have them benefit from the observation or experience. Their memory of images and their logical memory—what comes first, what follows, etc.—is not very well established. On the other hand, their rote memory is, or may be, good. There is no relationship between intelligence and ability to memorize. The same thing is true of spelling. Many mentally retarded children are excellent spellers because this could be a familiar activity requiring only rote memory. There is no correlation between spelling and intelligence.

The most important area of deficiency in mentally retarded children, of course, is their limited ability to evaluate, analyze, and make critical judgments. These areas require prolonged emphasis on abstract thinking. This ability is the one in which these children are most likely to be deficient. Critical judgment—the ability to evaluate a situation, to understand it, and to act on the understanding—is very difficult for the retarded. These levels of thought require skills as substructures that are often lacking or have not been developed by the mentally retarded.

The list of characteristics from short attention span to lack of critical judgment are the psychological characteristics of the mentally retarded. Two other groups of characteristics are important. These are the social traits and the physical traits. In spite of all these traits that have been outlined, no one is retarded. There is no such thing as a retarded child being "lacking." We talk about characteristics from the negative point of view, unfortunately. So far the comparison with the average is the only way we have to describe characteristics of the mentally retarded. We talk about "lack of," or "weakness in," or "shortage of," when the emphasis should be on the strengths that are available. Even a youngster who is quite poor in critical judgment has a substantial ability compared to most animals. As schools are able to see these strengths rather than the missing strengths, they will be able to do a much more competent job of educating the retarded.

Social traits

Basically, the mentally retarded are limited in social adaptation. Social adaptation is one characteristic on which they are evaluated before being classified as mentally retarded. Many, although not all, of them really don't get along well. Generally, they are followers. They seek out friends and tend to follow them. They tend to follow those who will accept them, who will not ridicule or kid them, and unfortunately, this is where most of them get into trouble. Often they are used by individuals who recognize this tendency in them and want to use these followers in accomplishing the leaders' own goals. Most of the mentally retarded who get into trouble with the law don't do it on the basis of their own problems; they are used by others who recognize their willingness to be followers to gain a social place of any kind. Interestingly enough, the mentally retarded tend to be self-centered. They look out for themselves psychologically. If they are with someone who will accept them for what they are and will pay them off by giving them a place, they will follow. This tendency is a real problem. This is one of the reasons for the higher incidence, on a percentage basis, of mentally retarded in the penal institutions and in the youth-authority centers than in the general population. The play interests of the younger mentally retarded tend to be those of still younger children. For instance, youngsters of junior high school age would prefer to play with elementary grade youngsters. Their preoccupation with play rather than work lasts longer than is true of brighter children. Their competitive concepts come much later than is true for other groups of individuals.

Physical traits

Physically, the mentally retarded are usually shorter, weaker, and lighter than the general run of the population. This is contrary to our old stereotype of the big, strong, dumb football player. Usually the mentally retarded are shorter, weaker, slower, and not as well coordinated. They usually have poor eye-hand coordination. In a sample that includes both the trainable and the educable mentally retarded, the incidence of physical defects is about twice that found in a similar-sized sample of the general population. If the sample is limited to the educable group, the less severely handicapped, the number of physical defects is more nearly that to be expected in a sample of the general population.

Writers on the topic of the mentally retarded have confused readers by failing to clarify whether they were writing about the whole group of mentally retarded or only part of the group. Among the moderately mentally retarded, the trainable mentally retarded group, there is a higher incidence of physical difficulties and physical deformities than in the general population. When you get up into the educable group you don't find this separation. The same thing is true with speech. Among the trainable retarded you find that about 12 percent have severe speech defects, but in the educable groups about 6 percent have speech problems, which is the same distribution found in the normal population.

GOALS OF THE MENTALLY RETARDED

This discussion has been on the mentally retarded, but it really consists of making a prognosis about a special group of children. The important consideration is an estimate of where these children are going to be and how they are going to function. It is imperative to provide them with a program that will make them as nearly self-sufficient as adults as we can. Programs in schools are built around the following areas:

1. The area of academic fundamentals: The basic school tools—reading, writing, arithmetic—must be emphasized in programs for the educable mentally retarded, because these skills must be learned if the individuals are going to succeed in society. The school takes the youngsters

where they are, and they progress them as far as they can go. Emphasis on these areas last longer in school than they do for regular youngsters. In high school, normally there is very little teaching of reading. Emphasis is placed on the application of reading, but the actual teaching of reading skill is not part of the high school program for most youngsters. For the mentally retarded, however, teaching of reading skill and of math concepts, as well as application of these skills, is continued through the high school level because the intellectual development rate is slower. During secondary school, many of these children reach a mental age that enables them to profit from reading and arithmetic skill instruction. They need to continue to be taught after they have achieved, after they have gained the ability to learn. We used to quit teaching reading and math back at the junior high level. For many youngsters we ought to continue this instruction right on through secondary school. For the mentally retarded, particularly, a need exists for instruction all the way through the high school program. All citizens need to learn basic fundamentals, and if they cannot master them early, they should be taught when the ability to learn is gained.

2. The area of occupation and information: What the school is really trying to do is teach these youngsters to be able to go out and earn a living. This is emphasized all the way through school. This emphasis is present even in the primary grades, but it is done in simple ways. There is a concept of salable skills. These are skills that have to be mastered in order for a youngster to get a job. In many schools, the mentally retarded, as well as many other students, are placed by the school in jobs for part of the school day. They get paid and are supervised and they learn essential skills. The in-school work is related, on an individual basis, to the work the young person is doing. For instance, a boy working in a service station practices arithmetic by completing gas and oil tickets, making change, and doing other related tasks. A girl working in a piece-goods store practices calculating the materials needed to complete a dress from a particular pattern. The relation of the school work to activities really needed on the job provides a powerful motivating force to try for mastery of the necessary skills.

Through this program, we have learned what it is that should be taught these students all the way back to the beginning of school. There is a definite progression of things that need to be learned in order for the youngster to end school with a set of salable skills. These tasks are not as involved as you might think. They include the ability to tell time, to deal with money, to drive a car. Another interesting and important one is the ability to start and finish a job. That sounds simple, but it is one of the most complicated items on the list. Employers will fire individuals working in a service station more often because they have left the tools out on the driveway after they have changed a tire than if they didn't change the tire competently. This is a difficult concept for retarded individuals to master. A boy might change the tire, put the tire on the car, and do a beautiful job of it, but he is likely to get fired if he leaves the wrench out overnight to rust. The reasons people get fired are because they don't get to work on time or they don't get along on the job. If the school can teach these youngsters to get to work on time, to apply themselves and to finish the job, if it can teach them to manage themselves and money, then it has taught them to get along in life. The school doesn't have to teach them to change the tire. The old educational concept was that you taught them to change the tire, then they go out and get a job. This isn't so. The employer says, "You send him to us, teach him to get here on time, to ask questions about what he doesn't know so that he doesn't try something and ruin it, to clean up when he is finished, and to behave himself, and we will pay him and we will have a working employee."

How can these ideas be converted into classroom practice starting at an early age? One possible activity that could become a typical example, even though it is now very untypical, would involve a primary teacher with a class of mentally retarded. As part of the curriculum she will have an easel, and on this easel she wants the youngster to paint a picture for the esthetic creative experience. This is a very desirable activity. However, she will get out some milk cartons in which to mix the paint, put the milk cartons in a tray, and put the brushes and the colors in the milk cartons. All the youngster does is to take the paint out, paint the picture, put the brush back down, and hang the picture on the wall. The teacher has done all the preparation and the cleaning up for the youngster. If you help the child to develop a concept of work preparation from the beginning of school, he will learn that this is what he should do. *He* gets the paint out, *he* puts it in the bucket, *he* gets his brush out and mixes the paint. He does his painting. When he gets through *he* empties out his paint carton, washes the brush out, and puts the brush away. In terms of the future, he is going to be fired because he did not put the brush away, not because he did not paint the picture well, and he needs to learn at the earliest possible period in his life to begin and to finish a job.

Those who like the creative experience may argue and defend the present procedure, but I am trying to show the difference in what we teach. So often the teacher gets all of the materials prepared for the youngster to save time. She has them ready so that she can hand them out and the child can use his time on the middle of the operation, then she puts the things away. "It's recess time; you all leave; I'll clean up for the next lesson"—this kind of thing. The point is that if we build complete experiences for the youngsters all through elementary, junior high, and high school in beginning, doing, and *finishing* the job, then we prepare them for employment.

Proper use of the telephone is another skill that these youngsters need to learn. It is a salable skill. Driving a car is a salable skill. In some schools all of the youngsters are put behind the wheel. They are put into driver training and taught until they can get licenses.

There are other important areas of learning—things like cleanliness, self-care habits, persisting at things, social adjustments, leisure-time activities. All of these things need to be learned, and with mentally retarded children they need to be taught often in school. Self-care and personal care are all-important parts of the curriculum for the trainable mentally retarded, but they are also important to the educable mentally retarded.

In addition to the goal of making the educable mentally retarded self-supporting, there are a number of other parts of life in which these youngsters need help from the school in order for them to reach desirable levels of competence.

Most of these young people are going to marry and continue to live in the same community. The chances are that they are not going to move away. They will probably not marry other mentally retarded individuals. The patterns are quite stable with the educable mentally retarded; we can assume that a girl will have her first youngster two years after she leaves high school, that she will not be married to a mentally retarded individual, and that she will be living in the same community. An important part of the curriculum is systematic preparation for family, home living, and care of the home.

The curriculum for the trainable mentally retarded is more limited. What we are trying to do with these people is, first, to teach them self-care in their community and their home. We work on such things as dressing, undressing, shining shoes, brushing of teeth, combing of hair, keeping themselves clean. Second, we try to teach acceptance behavior in the knowledge that within our program we can control behavior much better than a mother can at home, because in a group situation they learn from each other. We use behavior-modification techniques and find the teaching much easier than the mother does, so we do a pretty good job in this area. The third part of the program is initiated when these youngsters get older. We teach them cooking, ironing, sewing; we try to teach them to garden, take care of their home, dust, vacuum, etc. The concept is that if they can be taught to care for themselves, then someone else does not have to care for them. This relieves some members of society—perhaps a number of people, depending upon the need for custodial care—of responsibility for caring for them.

SUMMARY

Let me summarize what I have been saying. Mental retardation is a term used to describe a varying complex of factors in the fields of maturation, learning ability, and social adjustment. All of the mentally retarded have varying strengths, even in the areas in which they are weakest. It is better to build on the strengths than to deplore the limitation imposed by lack of absolute strength, which no one has in any case.

Mental retardation becomes more-or-less apparent and more-or-less valid in different social situations. It's reported incidence is highest in the school setting, particularly during the ages from 10 to 15, when 8 percent of the population is so classified, although by adulthood less than one-half of 1 percent is so classified. In school, these youngsters are able to function more successfully as teaching is more highly structured, with well-defined goals; as the instruction is concentrated in short bursts with many repetitions; and as relations within the materials are clarified and made explicit.

Three levels of mentally retarded are identified: the educable mentally retarded; the trainable or moderately retarded; and the custodial cases, or severely retarded. The moderately and severely retarded, as compared to the population in general, have more physical defects, more speech defects; they are lighter, smaller, and less well coordinated. This is not true of the educable mentally retarded.

The custodial cases have to be cared for constantly. The trainable mentally retarded can learn to look after themselves physically and to survive in the community, although they cannot normally learn to support themselves economically. The educable mentally retarded do not function efficiently in school, although they can be taught to perform at a level that enables them to support themselves, to marry, and to carry on a relatively normal adult life.

School programs for the mentally retarded stress reading, computation, and other academic skills, and these skills are taught later than is desirable with more quickly developing children. Great emphasis is put on practical competence, including habits of beginning and finishing a job, of being on time, of getting along well with others, and of raising a family well. In many school systems, extensive work-experience programs help the mentally retarded to make a successful transition from school to the world of work. These programs are also useful to students who are not mentally retarded. The program for the trainable mentally retarded emphasizes personal care, simple tasks of housekeeping, gardening, and social adjustment. Study of ways to teach the mentally retarded can help change teaching methods for other children so that all can profit by learning that is more useful and more functional in the lives of all the children.

BIBLIOGRAPHY

ALBERT, D. J. The Effect of Polarizing Currents on the Consolidation of Learning. *Neuropsychologia*, 1966, 4, 65–77. (a)

ALBERT, D. J. The Effect of Spreading Depression on the Consolidation of Learning. *Neuropsychologia*, 1966, 4, 49–64. (b)

ALTUS, GRACE T. A WISC Profile for Retarded Readers. *Journal of Consulting Psychology*, November, 1956, 20, 155–156.

AMERICAN ASSOCIATION ON MENTAL DEFICIENCY. *A Manual on Terminology and Classification in Mental Retardation*. Monograph supplement to *American Journal of Mental Deficiency*, September, 1959.

AYRES, A. JEAN. The Development of Perceptual-Motor Abilities: A Theoretical Basis for Treatment of Dysfunction. Paper presented at the Conference of American Occupational Therapy Association, St. Louis, Missouri, October 1, 1963.

BARBE, W. B. *Barbe Reading Skills Checklist: Grades K–6.* Cuyahoga Falls, Ohio: Privately published, 1960.

BARNHILL, J. F., and WALES, E. DE W. *Principles and Practice of Modern Otology.* Philadelphia: Saunders, 1907.

BATEMAN, BARBARA D. *The Illinois Test of Psycholinguistic Abilities in Current Research.* Urbana: University of Illinois Press, 1965.

BEERY, K. E. Comprehensive Research, Evaluation and Assistance for Exceptional Children. *Exceptional Children*, 1968, 223–228. (a)

BEERY, K. E. *Remedialdiagnosis.* San Rafael, Calif.: Dimensions Publishing, 1968. (b)

BEREITER, C. and ENGELMANN, S. *Teaching Disadvantaged Children in the Preschool.* Englewood Cliffs, N.J.: Prentice-Hall, 1966.

BETTMAN, J. W., JR., STERN, E. L., WHITESELL, M. J., and GOFMAN, HELEN F. Cerebral Dominance in Developmental Dyslexia. *Archives of Ophthalmology*, Demember, 1967, 78, 722–729.

BLACK, M. Characteristics of the Culturally Disadvantaged Child. *The Reading Teacher*, 1968, 18, 467.

BLOOM, B. S. *Stability and Change in Human Characteristics.* New York: Wiley, 1964.

BOND, G. L., and TINKER, M. A. *Reading Difficulties: Their Diagnosis and Correction.* New York: Appleton-Century-Crofts, 1967.

BRUNER, J. *The Process of Education.* New York: Random House, Vintage Books, 1963.

BURKS, H. F., and BRUCE, P. Characteristics of Poor and Good Readers as Disclosed by the Wechsler Intelligence Scale for Children. *Journal of Educational Psychology*, December, 1955, **46**, 488–493.

CASPP AD HOC COMMITTEE ON SPECIAL EDUCATION. Position Paper on Supplementary (Special) Education, February, 1969. *CASPP Newsletter*, Spring, 1969, **16**(3), 10–12.

CAZDEN, C. B. Subculture Differences in Child Language: An Interdisciplinary Review. *Merrill-Palmer Quarterly of Behavior and Development*, July, 1966, **12**, 191–226.

CHALL, JEANNE. *Learning to Read*. New York: McGraw-Hill, 1967.

CICARELLI, V., and GRANGER, R. *The Impact of Headstart*. Vols. 1 and 2. *An Evaluation of the Effects of Headstart on Children's Cognitive and Affective Development*. Blandenburg, Md.: Westinghouse Learning Corporation, 1969.

CLAWSON, AILEEN. *The Bender Visual-Motor Gestalt Test*. Beverly Hills, Calif.: Western Psychological Services, 1962.

CLEMENTS, H. M., DUNCAN, J. A., and TAYLOR, W. M. Toward Effective Evaluation of the Culturally Deprived. *Personnel and Guidance Journal*, 1969, **47**, 891–896.

COHEN, ALICE. Relationship between Factors of Dominance and Reading Ability. In George D. Spache (Ed.), *Reading Disability and Perception*. Newark, Del.: International Reading Association, 1969.

COHEN, J. Factorial Structure of the WISC at Ages 7–6, 10–6, and 13–6. *Journal of Consulting Psychology*, 1959, **23**, 285–299.

COLLINS, BARBARA. Conflicts in Culture: Indian-Americans. *Curriculum Bulletin* (University of Oregon at Eugene), October, 1969, **25**, 9–10.

CRUICKSHANK, W. M., and JOHNSON, G. O. *Education of Exceptional Children and Youth*. Englewood Cliffs, N.J.: Prentice-Hall, 1958.

DE HIRSCH, KATRINA, JANSKY, JEANETTE J., and LANGFORD, W. S. *Predicting Reading Failure*. New York: Harper & Row, 1966.

DEUTSCH, M. The Disadvantaged Child and the Learning Process. In A. H. Passow (Ed.), *Education in Depressed Areas*. New York: Columbia University, Teachers College, 1965.

DiCARLO, L. M. *The Deaf*. Englewood Cliffs, N.J.: Prentice-Hall, 1964.

FARB, P. The American Indian: A Portrait in Limbo. *Saturday Review*, October, 1968.

FROSTIG, MARIANNE. *Developmental Test of Visual Perception*. Palo Alto, Calif.: Consulting Psychologists Press, 1961.

FROSTIG, MARIANNE. *Developmental Test of Visual Perception: Administration and Scoring Manual*. Palo Alto, Calif.: Consulting Psychologists Press, 1966.

GATES, A. I. *A Reading Vocabulary for the Primary Grades*. (Rev. ed.) New York: Columbia University, Teachers College, 1935.

GOODENOUGH, FLORENCE. *Measurement of Intelligence.* New York: World Book Co., 1926.

GRAY, B. B., and ENGLAND, G. *Stuttering and the Conditioning Therapies.* Monterey, Calif.: The Monterey Institute for Speech and Hearing, 1969.

HAMLIN, RUTH, MUKERJI, ROSE, and YONEMURA, MARGARET. *Schools for Young Disadvantaged Children.* New York: Teachers College Press, 1967.

HARLOW, H. F., HARLOW, M. K., DODSWORTH, R. O., and ARLING, G. L. Maternal Behavior of Rhesus Monkeys Deprived of Mothering and Peer Associations in Infancy. *Proceedings of the American Philosophical Society,* 1966, **110**(1), 58–66.

HEATH, R. G. Electrical Self-Stimulation of the Brain in Man. *The American Journal of Psychiatry,* 1963, **120**, 571–577.

HEATH, R. G., JOHN, S. B., and FONTANA, C. J. The Pleasure Response: Studies by Stereotanic Technics in Patients. In N. S. Kline and E. Laska (Eds.), *Computers and Electronic Devices in Psychiatry.* New York: Grune & Stratton, 1968.

HEBB, D. O. *The Organization of Behavior.* New York: Wiley, 1949.

HELD, R., and BAUER, J. A., JR. Visually Guided Reaching in Infant Monkeys after Restricted Rearing. *Science,* 1967, **155**, 718–720.

HEMENWAY, W. G., and BERGSTROM, LA VONNE. The Pathology of Acquired Viral Endolabyrinthitis. In F. McConnell and P. Ward (Eds.), *Deafness in Childhood.* Nashville, Tenn.: Vanderbilt, 1967.

HERNDON, J. *The Wayit Spozed to Be.* New York: Bantam Books, 1969.

ILG, FRANCES L., and AMES, LOUISE BATES. *School Readiness: Behavior Tests Used at the Gesell Institute.* New York: Harper & Row, 1965.

JANOFSKY, IRENE. Conflicts in Culture: Afro-Americans. *Curriculum Bulletin* (University of Oregon at Eugene), October, 1969, **25**, 7–9.

JENSEN, A. R. Learning Abilities in Mexican-American and Anglo-American Children. *California Journal of Educational Research,* 1961, **12**, 147–151.

JENSEN, A. R. Rote Learning in Retarded Adults and Normal Children. *American Journal of Mental Deficiencies,* 1965, **69**, 828–834.

JENSEN, A. R. How Much Can We Boost IQ and Scholastic Achievement? *Harvard Educational Review,* Winter, 1969, **39**(1).

JOHNSON, G. O. Special Education for Mentally Handicapped: A Paradox. *Exceptional Children,* 1962, **19**, 62–69.

KALLOS, G. L., GRABOW, E., and GUARINO, A. The WISC Profile of Disabled Readers. *Personnel and Guidance Journal,* February, 1961, **39**, 476–478.

KARVACEUS, W. C., and MILLER, W. B. *Delinquent Behavior: Culture and the Individual.* Washington, D.C.: National Education Association, 1959.

KATZ, PHYLLIS, and DEUTSCH, M. *Visual and Auditory Efficiency and Its Relationship to Reading in Children.* New York: New York Medical College, Department of Psychiatry, Institute for Developmental Studies, 1963.

KINSTLER, D. B. Covert and Overt Maternal Rejection in Stuttering. *Journal of Speech and Hearing Disorders,* May, 1961, 26(2), 145–155.

KIRK, S., and MC CARTHY, J. *The Illinois Test of Psycholinguistic Abilities.* Urbana: University of Illinois Press, 1961.

KOHL, H. R. *Teaching the Unteachable.* New York: A New York Review Book, 1967. (a)

KOHL, H. R. *36 Children.* New York: Signet, 1967. (b)

KOREIVA, BONNIE. Educational Implications for American-Indian Children. *Curriculum Bulletin* (University of Oregon at Eugene), October, 1969, 25, 19–20.

KUNZ, JEAN, and MOYER, JOAN E. A Comparison of Economically Disadvantaged and Economically Advantaged Kindergarten Children. *Journal of Educational Research,* 1969, 62, 392–395.

LARSON, R., and OLSON, J. L. A Method of Identifying Culturally Deprived Kindergarten Children. *Exceptional Children,* 1963, 30, 130–134.

LEMERT, E. M. Stuttering and Social Structure in Two Pacific Societies. *Journal of Speech and Hearing Disorders,* 1962, 27, 3–10.

LEWIS, E. R. Electron Microscope Used to Achieve First Photographic Mapping of Nerve Linkage. *University Bulletin: A Weekly Bulletin for the Staff of the University of California,* November 24, 1969, 18(15), 69–70.

LOBAN, W. *The Language of Elementary School Children.* Champaign, Ill.: National Council of Teachers of English, 1963.

MACHOVER, KAREN. *Personality Projection in the Drawing of the Human Figure: A Method of Personality Investigation.* Springfield, Ill.: Charles C Thomas, 1949.

MAWSON, S. R. *Diseases of the Ear.* (2nd ed.) Baltimore: Williams & Wilkins, 1967.

MEEKER, MARY. Differential Syndromes of Giftedness and Curriculum Planning: A Four-Year Follow-Up. *The Journal of Special Education,* Winter, 1968, 2(2), 185–196.

MISCHEL, W. Preference for Delayed Reinforcement: An Experimental Study of a Cultural Observation. *The Journal of Abnormal and Social Psychology,* 1958, 56, 57.

MONCUR, J. P. Parental Domination in Stuttering. *Journal of Speech and Hearing Disorders,* 1952, 17, 155–165.

MULLANIX, R. Conflicts in Culture: Mexican-Americans. *Curriculum Bulletin* (University of Oregon at Eugene), October, 1969, 25, 5–7.

MYKLEBUST, H. R. *Auditory Disorders in Children.* New York: Grune & Stratton, 1954.

NATIONAL INSTITUTE OF NEUROLOGICAL DISEASES AND BLINDNESS. *Hearing, Language, and Speech Disorders.* NINDB Research Profile No. 4. Public Health Service Publication No. 1156. Washington, D.C.: Department of Health, Education, and Welfare; Public Health Service, 1967.

NEVILLE, D. A Comparison of the WISC Patterns of Male Retarded and Non-retarded Readers. *Journal of Educational Research,* January, 1961, **54,** 195–197.

NORTH, A. F. Pediatric Care in Project Headstart. In J. Hellmuth (Ed.), *Disadvantaged Child, Volume II: Headstart and Early Intervention.* New York: Brunner-Mazel, 1968.

OLDS, J. *The Growth and Structure of Motives.* Chicago: Free Press, 1956.

OYER, H. J. *Auditory Communication for the Hard of Hearing.* Englewood Cliffs, N.J.: Prentice-Hall, 1966.

PEARL, A., and RIESSMAN, F. *New Careers for the Poor.* New York: Free Press, 1965.

PEARSON, G. H. A Survey of Learning Difficulties in Children. *Psychoanalytic Study of Child,* 1952, 7, 322–386.

PENFIELD, W., and ROBERTS, L. *Speech and Brain Mechanisms.* Princeton, N.J.: Princeton University Press, 1959.

PINES, MAYA. *Revolution in Learning: The Years from Birth to Six.* New York: Harper & Row, 1966.

PRESCOTT, D. A. *The Child in the Educative Process.* New York: McGraw-Hill, 1957.

RANKIN, R. J. Measurement of Cognitive Development. Paper presented at the NDEA (National Defense Education Act) Advanced Study Seminar on Improvement of Education for Disadvantaged Children, University of Oregon, July 3, 1968.

ROBECK, MILDRED C. Subtest Patterning of Problem Readers on WISC. *California Journal of Educational Research,* May, 1960, **11**(3).

ROBECK, MILDRED C. Children Who Show Undue Tension When Reading: A Group Diagnosis. In J. Allen Figurel (Ed.), *Challenge and Experiment in Reading: Proceedings of the International Reading Association Conference, 1962.* Vol. 7. New York: Scholastic Magazines, 1962.

ROBECK, MILDRED C. Effects of Prolonged Reading Disability: A Preliminary Study. *Perceptual and Motor Skills,* 1964, **19,** 7–12. (a)

ROBECK, MILDRED C. Intellectual Strengths and Weaknesses Shown by Reading Clinic Subjects on the WISC. *Journal of Developmental Reading,* Winter, 1964, 7(2). (b)

ROBECK, MILDRED C. Types of Reading Disability. In J. Allen Figurel (Ed.), *Reading and Inquiry: Proceedings of the International Reading Association Conference, 1965.* Vol. 10. Newark, Del.: International Reading Association, 1965.

ROBECK, MILDRED C. Acculturation and the Schools. *Curriculum Bulletin* (University of Oregon at Eugene), October, 1969, **25,** 307.

ROBECK, MILDRED C., and WILSON, J. A. R. *KELP Summary Test Booklet: Teacher's Edition.* New York: McGraw-Hill, 1967.

ROBECK, MILDRED C., and WILSON, J. A. R. *KELP Resource Guide*. New York: McGraw-Hill, 1969.

ROSE, FLORENCE C. The Occurrence of Short Auditory Memory Span among School Children Referred for Diagnosis of Reading Difficulties. *Journal of Educational Research*, February, 1958, **51**, 459–464.

SANTA BARBARA WORK-STUDY PROGRAM FOR THE EDUCABLE MENTALLY RETARDED. Unpublished study, Santa Barbara, Calif., 1964.

SCHEUER, J. H. Head Start. *Proceedings and Debates of 91st Congress, First Session*. House of Representatives. May 8, 1969, Vol. 115, No. 75. Washington, D.C.: Government Printing Office, 1969. E3787-8.

SCOTT, G. S. A Comparison of the Scores of Trained and Untrained Environmentally Deprived Male and Female Infants on the "Griffiths Mental Development Scale." Report at the Annual Meeting of AERA (American Educational Research Association), Los Angeles, Calif., February 6, 1969.

SEMPLE, R. Head Start Pupils Found No Better Off Than Others. *New York Times*, April 14, 1969.

SHIDA, S., SUGANO, T., and OKAMOTO, M. Some Observations of the Ototoxic Effect of Kanamycin. *International Audiology*, 1967, **6**, 359–364.

SNIDECOR, J. C., and others. *Speech Rehabilitation of the Laryngectomized*. (2nd ed.) Springfield Ill.: Charles C Thomas, 1968.

SPACHE, G. D. A Satirical Epilogue. In George D. Spache (Ed.), *Reading Disability and Perception*. Newark, Del.: International Reading Association, 1969.

SPERRY, R. W. Cerebral Organization and Behavior. *Science*, 1961, **133**, 1749–1757.

TERMAN, L. M., and MERRILL, MAUD A. *Stanford Binet Intelligence Scale*. Boston: Houghton Mifflin, 1960.

THOMPSON, ALICE. A Crisis Report and Some Opinions. *CEC State Federation Journal*, November, 1968, **18**(1).

TRAVIS, L. E. *Handbook of Speech Pathology and Audiology*. New York: Appleton-Century-Crofts, 1971.

VALETT, R. E. The Evaluation and Programming of Basic Learning Abilities. *Journal of School Psychology*, Summer, 1968, **6**(4).

VALETT, R. E. *Programming Learning Disabilities*. Palo Alto, Calif.: Fearon, 1969.

VERNON, M. Current Etiological Factors in Deafness. *American Annals of the Deaf*, 1968, **113**, 106–115.

WEBSTER, S. W. *The Disadvantaged Learner*. San Francisco: Chandler, 1966.

WECHSLER, D. I. *WISC Manual: Wechsler Intelligence Scale for Children*. New York: The Psychological Corporation, 1949.

WECHSLER, D. I. *WPPSI Manual: Wechsler Preschool and Primary Scale of Intelligence*. New York: The Psychological Corporation, 1967.

WILSON, J. A. R., and ROBECK, MILDRED C. *The Kindergarten Evaluation of*

Learning Potential (KELP): A Curricular Approach to Evaluation. New York: McGraw-Hill, 1967.

WILSON, J. A. R., ROBECK, MILDRED C., and MICHAEL, W. B. *Psychological Foundations of Learning and Teaching*. New York: McGraw-Hill, 1969.

INDEX

Convulsion, 131
Corpus callosum, 124, 314, 315
Coup de glotte, 70
Courtship, 268, 290
Creativeness, 12
Creative self-directed learning, 4
Creative self-direction, 22, 23, 29, 32
Creativity, 313
Crossed-eyes, 47
Cruickshank, W. M., 246, 332
Cultural disadvantage, 7, 202
Culturally deprived, 317
Culturally disadvantaged, 200, 227
Curfews, 297
Custodial care, 328

Decoding, 165, 166, 171–173
Defense mechanism, 281, 282
Defiance, 283, 285
Dehirsch, Katrina, 332
Delacato, C. H., 54, 126
Delinquent, 286, 294
Dendrite, 312, 313
Denver Classification System, 309
Dependence, 265
Dependent, 242, 294
Depression, 267
Deprivation, 266
Deutsch, M., 183, 203, 332
Developing Vocal Skills, 61
Development, 249
Developmental sequence, 250
Devereux Ranch Schools, 229
Deviant, 287
Devil, 274
Devine, A., 69
Dexedrine, 122
Diabetes, 45, 59
Diagnosis, 250, 253, 286, 303
Diagnosogenic, 86
Diagnostic profile, 164
Diagnostic-teaching models, 248, 254
Dialect, 155, 156
DiCarlo, L. M., 104, 332
Dihydrostreptomycin, 105
Dilantin, 121–123
Disabled readers, 158, 167

Disadvantaged, 190, 226
  culturally, 200, 227
Disaster, 303
Discipline, 283, 319
Disease, 278
Disregard for consequences, 286
Dissocial, 284
DNA, 128, 129
Doctor of Optometry degree, 42
Dodsworth, R. O., 240, 333
Dogmatic, 303
Dominance:
  cerebral, 53
  confused, 175
  mixed, 53, 126, 139, 140
Domination, 89
Down's syndrome (mongoloid), 309
Draw-a-figure test, 149
Draw-a-horse, 212
Draw-a-man test, 212
Dreyfus, 122, 123
Driving, 327
Dropout, 297
Drug addiction, 275
Dull normals, 52
Duncan, J. A., 212, 332
Durflinger, G. W., 160
Dysarthic, 87
Dyslectic, 54, 127
Dyslexia, 53, 127, 139, 140
Dysphasia, 6, 111, 316
Dysphasic, 80, 81, 114, 259
Dysphemia, 94
Dystonias, 112

Ear:
  auditory meatus, 99
  cochlear duct, 99
  drum, 99
  eustachian tube, 99
  pinna, 98
  tympanic membrane, 99
Eclampsia, 110
Educable mentally retarded (EMR),
  256, 258, 310, 311, 318, 324,
  327, 328
Education, compensatory, 244, 259

Grabow, E., 160, 333
Grand mal epilepsy, 114, 116, 118, 121, 129, 131
Granger, R., 196, 332
Graphemes, 182
Gray, B. B., 94, 333
Grievance, 293
Guareno, A., 160, 333
Guilford, J. P., 253
Gutteral voice, 76

Hanley, T. D., 61
Harlow, H., 240, 333
Harlow, M. K., 240, 333
Headstart program, 2, 150, 192, 196, 197, 202, 203, 218, 220
Heath, R. G., 15, 25, 333
Hearing, Language, and Speech Disorders, 98
Hearing loss, 208
Hebb, D. O., 313, 333
Hedley, Carolyn N., 135
Hedley, W. E., 135
Held, R., 183, 333
Heminway, W. G., 104, 333
Hemispheres of brain, 314, 315
Hermits, 265
Herndon, J., 226, 333
Hewett, F. M., 253
Hierarchic sequence, 251
Hierarchy, 249
High School Equivalency Programs (HEP), 198, 199
Hippie movement, 283
Holmes, J., 169
Home:
    borstal, 9
    foster, 295
    girls' 294, 299
    juvenile, 299
Home teaching, 296, 301
How to Cure Ear Aches, 102
Huntington's chorea, 120
Husband, 268
Huxley, A., 57
Hyperactive child, 106, 112, 121, 122
Hypoxia, 110

Iatrogenic, 104
Identification, 281
Ilg, Frances L., 333
Ilg-Ames Developmental Scale, 186
Illegitimate children, 206
Illinois Test of Psycholinguistic Ability, 142, 149
Impairment, 304
Incentives, 31
Ineffectualness, 284
Information, 316, 325
Information processing level, 249
Inherited ability, 302
Intellectual potential, 181, 185
Intelligence, 248, 273, 302
Intelligence test scores, 137, 139
Intensity, 75
International Society of Audiology, 97
Introverts, 44
IQ, 305, 319
Irresponsibility, 284
i/t/a, 152

Jails, 9
James, W., 180
Janofsky, Irene, 206, 333
Jansky, Jeanette J., 332
Jealousy, 268–270
JEFF (Joint Effort for Foster Families), 295
Jensen, A. R., 165, 197, 212, 213, 333
Job Corps Training Program, 200
John, S. B., 15, 333
Johnson, G. O., 246, 247, 332, 333
Johnson, W., 83, 86
Joint Effort for Foster Families (JEFF), 295
Journal of School Psychology, 252
Judgment, 323
Juvenile delinquent, 287
Juvenile hall, 9, 291, 292, 294, 295, 297
Juvenile home, 299

Kallos, G. L., 160, 333
Kanamycin, 105
Karvaceus, W. C., 286, 333

Motivation, 34, 165, 244, 248, 266, 298, 320
Moyer, Joan E., 203, 334
Mullanix, R., 205, 334
Mumps, 104
Murder, 273
Murphy, T. J., 301
Myklebust, H. R., 106, 334
Myclonic attack, 115
Myringotomy, 101

Narcotics, 292
Nasopharyngeal opening, 99
Nasopharynx, 81, 99
National Defense Education Act (NDEA), 318
NDEA (National Defense Education Act), 318
Nearsighted child, 44
Nearsightedness, 43, 50, 57–59
Need, 264, 265, 283, 291
    biological, 264, 265
    biosocial, 264, 265
Neonate, 33
Neurological integration, 185
Neurologically handicapped, 235
Neurologist, 87, 110, 119, 121, 126, 132, 138
Neurology, 116, 133
Neuron, 12
Neurophysiology, 245
Neuropsychiatry, 133
Neuroses, 279
Neurotic, 232
Neuroticism, 232
Neville, D., 160, 334
New England Primer, 138
Nodules, 71
Normals, dull, 52
North, A. F., 202, 335

Object relations, 249
Observation, 322
Obturator, 80
Occupation, 325
OEO, 196, 198, 200
Okamoto, M., 105, 336

Olds, J., 14, 335
Olson, J. L., 191, 334
Onondaga County, 305, 306
Ophthalmologist, 5, 42, 48, 50, 132, 141
Ophthalmology, 41, 42
Optic chiasma, 315
Optician, 42
Optimist, 267
Optometrist, 42, 49, 50, 54, 55, 141
Organ of Corti, 103
Oropharynx, 81
Orthodontistry, 63
Orthoptics, 56
Orthoscope, 56
Otitis media, 100
Ototoxic, 104
Otoxin, 105
Overweight, 281
Oyer, H. S., 107, 250, 335

Pachucos, 204
Palate, cleft, 80, 84, 98
Palm Springs, 295
Paranoia, 15
Paraprofessionals, 180
Parents, 271
Parkinsonian procedure, 112
Passive-aggressive technique, 237, 242
Passow, A. H., 183, 203, 332
Patriarch, 271
Patriarchal family, 205
Peace Corps, 276
Pearl, A., 203, 204, 335
Pearson, C. H., 249, 335
Pectoral voice, 76
Pediatrician, 49, 56, 115, 132, 133, 197
Peers, 266, 287, 304
    rejection by, 285
Peer associations, 275
Peer-group associations, 275
Penal institution, 323
Penfield, W., 14, 335
Penitentiary, 9
Perceptual and motor skills, 157
Perceptual learning difficulties, 316

	DATE DUE		
NOV 5 1980			
FEB 1 2 1982			
MAR 11 1988			
JUL 8 1989			
JUL 2 0 1989			
DEC 0 1 1992			
MAR -5 2004			